THE CHURCH OF ENGLAND
AND THE FIRST WORLD WAR

Alan Wilkinson

THE CHURCH OF ENGLAND AND THE FIRST WORLD WAR

LONDON
SPCK

First published 1978
SPCK
Holy Trinity Church
Marylebone Road
London NW1 4DU

Printed and bound in Great Britain at
The Camelot Press Ltd, Southampton

ISBN 0 281 03616 0

TO
SARAH, JOHN, AND CONRAD
Shalom!

Contents

Illustrations

Thanks are due to the British Library, *The Illustrated London News*,
and the Imperial War Museum for permission to reproduce the above
pictures from their collections.

Preface

Among those who have helped with the making of this book, I am particularly grateful to the following: Dr S. C. Aston, Bursar of St Catharine's College, Cambridge; the late Bishop F. R. Barry; Canon G. V. Bennett, Dean of Divinity, New College, Oxford; Mr E. G. W. Bill, Librarian of Lambeth Palace Library; the Revd Dr Paul Bradshaw; the Revd John Byrom; Miss Jane Carmichael, of the Imperial War Museum; Professor Owen Chadwick; Lt-Col G. C. E. Crew, Curator of the Museum of the Royal Army Chaplains' Department; the Revd Dr Bryan Halson and other colleagues; Canon Eric James; Dr Brian Lake; the Librarian and Brethren of the Community of the Resurrection, Mirfield; the Very Revd Peter Moore, Dean of St Albans; the Revd Ashby Owens, Vicar of St Mary's, Alsager; Miss J. M. Petersen and Mr David Craig, of S.P.C.K.; Dr John Rae; the Revd Charles Ralph, Rector of Theberton; the Revd C. Rawlinson, Chaplain of the Royal Military Academy, Sandhurst; Professor H. E. Root; the Revd R. A. Smith; Mrs Ann Treen; the Revd J. M. Turner; the Revd Dr A. R. Vidler; the Revd C. G. Wilson, Chairman of the Anglican Pacifist Fellowship; Canon A. R. Winnett; John Wyatt, formerly Principal of Culham College.

The late Canon Philip Cecil of Peterborough Cathedral very kindly wrote for me a short memoir of his father, the Revd Henry Cecil, which I have used in Chapter 2.

I am indebted to Dr Donald Read, Professor of Modern English History in the University of Kent, a friend of long standing, for a valuable discussion about content and presentation.

It has been a great pleasure to work with Miss Lesley Riddle of S.P.C.K. and Mr Herbert Rees in the preparation of the manuscript for publication.

I owe much to my parents for providing a home in which the issues of war and peace were regularly discussed. From them I learnt to be critical of conventional patriotism.

My wife, Fenella, has typed the final manuscript and provided indispensable help by patiently checking it. But above all she has given me that companionship on the way which has made it possible for me to write this book.

March 1977

A.B.W.

Acknowledgements

Thanks are due to the following for permission to quote from copyright sources:

The Father Superior, The Community of the Resurrection, Mirfield: *CR-Quarterly Review of the Community of the Resurrection* (1914–19)

Constable Publishers: *Papers from Picardy* by Tom Pym and Geoffrey Gordon

Curtis Brown Ltd, on behalf of J. G. Lockhart: *Cosmo Gordon Lang* by J. G. Lockhart

David & Charles Ltd: *People at War 1914–18*, edited by Michael Moynihan

J. M. Dent & Sons Ltd and Dr John Laffin: *Letters from the Front 1914–18*, edited by John Laffin

Faber & Faber Ltd: 'Little Gidding' in *Four Quartets* by T. S. Eliot (by permission also of Harcourt Brace Jovanovich Inc.); and *Complete Memoirs of George Sherston* by Siegfried Sassoon, © 1967 Siegfried Lorraine Sassoon (by permission also of the US publishers Giniger/Stackpole)

Mrs Nicolete Gray and the Society of Authors, on behalf of the Laurence Binyon Estate: 'The Fallen' by Laurence Binyon

William Heinemann Ltd: *Charles Gore* by G. L. Prestige

HMSO: *With a machine gun to Cambrai* by George Coppard

Hodder & Stoughton Ltd: *Period of My Life* by F. R. Barry; *Handley Carr Glyn Moule* by John B. Harford and Frederick C. MacDonald; *Memories and Meanings* by W. R. Matthews; *Woodbine Willie* by William Purcell; *Rhymes* by G. A. Studdert Kennedy

Hutchinson Publishing Group (for Skeffingtons): *For All We Have and Are* by Basil Bourchier

Longman Group Ltd: *The Letters of Oswin Creighton*, edited by Louise Creighton; *The War and the Kingdom of God*, edited by G. K. A. Bell

MacGibbon & Kee Ltd and Granada Publishing Ltd: *Disenchantment* by C. E. Montague

Macmillan, London and Basingstoke: *The Faith and the War*, edited by P. J. Foakes-Jackson; *The Church in the Furnace*, edited by F. B. Macnutt; 'Flower of Youth' in *Collected Poems* by Katharine Tynan; and *The Army and Religion*

Methuen and Co. Ltd: *The War and the Soul* by R. J. Campbell

John Murray (Publishers) Ltd: 'Envoi' in *Picardy and Other Poems* by Edward de Stein

The Owen Estate and Chatto & Windus Ltd: *Collected Poems* by Wilfred Owen, edited by C. Day Lewis. Copyright © Chatto & Windus Ltd, 1946, 1963. Reprinted by permission also of New Directions Publishing Corporation, New York

Oxford University Press: *Randall Davidson: Archbishop of Canterbury* by G. K. A. Bell; *Retrospect of an Unimportant Life* by H. H. Henson; *The Collected Letters of Wilfred Owen*, edited by Harold Owen and John Bell; 'The Ballad of Purchase-Money' by Wilfred Owen, quoted in *Wilfred Owen* by Jon Stallworthy

George Sassoon Esq. and Viking Press Inc: *Selected Poems* by Siegfried Sassoon

Vernon Scannell Esq: 'The Great War' in *A Sense of Danger* by Vernon Scannell

SCM Press Ltd: *Neville Stuart Talbot* by F. H. Brabant; and *B. K. Cunningham* by John R. H. Moorman

The Society for Promoting Christian Knowledge: *Mervyn Haigh* by F. R. Barry; '*Quit You Like Men*' by Randall T. Davidson; and *Reports of the Archbishops' Committee of Inquiry* (1919)

The *Spectator*: 'Christ in Flanders' by 'L.W.' (Lucy Whitmell) in the *Spectator*, 11 September 1915

A. P. Watt & Son, on behalf of the Kipling Estate: 'Justice' by Rudyard Kipling. The lines by Kipling on p. 304 are quoted by permission of the National Trust.

Introduction

It is surprising that no full-length study of the Church of England in relation to the First World War has yet appeared in England. Roger Lloyd devoted a valuable chapter to the topic in *The Church of England 1900–1965* (1966), but the material he drew upon was limited, and his conclusions were, in my opinion, over-sanguine. Professor Albert Marrin's *The Last Crusade: The Church of England in the First World War* was published in the United States in 1974. I am indebted to this pioneer work, and particularly for directing my attention to sources of information. Inevitably both Professor Marrin and I have traversed some of the same ground, though naturally our assessments and selection of material sometimes differ. On the one hand, for example, Professor Marrin devoted more space than I have to the state of the Church of England before the war and to English attitudes to German thought and philosophy. On the other hand, some themes which he treated only cursorily, such as the National Mission of Repentance and Hope, the pastoral and theological implications of widespread bereavement, and the impact of the war on ecumenism, I have treated at much greater length. His book concludes with the end of the war. I have continued the story up to the mid-1920s and therefore cover such topics as the development of remembrance rituals and the role of the Church in post-war reconstruction. The literary writings of the period which figure at certain points in this book find no place in Professor Marrin's study. I read Dr Stuart Mews's unpublished Cambridge Ph.D. thesis, 'Religion and English Society in the First World War' (1973) with great interest after I had completed my own manuscript. At some points he drew upon unpublished sources which I have not used, which gave extra detail to certain events of the period. He also paid much more attention than I have to the views of the non-Anglican Churches. Naturally, as one would expect in a thesis, his treatment is more intensive and less extensive than mine. But, rightly or wrongly, I did not feel that I ought to modify my own approach in the light of his researches.

In these ecumenical times it may be surprising to concentrate upon the role of the Church of England, though I have made some reference to both Free Church and Roman Catholic attitudes. To focus on the Church of England provides a necessary boundary to the vast amount of material available. Moreover, at the beginning of this century the Church of England was still the national Church to a degree which was not true in the second war, and is even less true today. The reactions of the Free Churches ran along similar lines to those of the Church of England, though with differing emphases. There were, for example, proportionately more Free Church than Anglican conscientious objectors. The English Roman Catholic Church also gave its support to the war, but it was a much smaller and more private body than either the Church of England or the Free Churches. Whereas Anglicans and Free Churchmen wrote frequently to the newspapers, Roman Catholic participation in public political debate about the war was rare.

The references to the Churches in most of the secular histories about this period are often brief and sometimes snide.[1] Does this reflect an unwillingness on the part of such historians to engage deeply with institutions and beliefs which they find uncongenial? Or does their treatment imply that the Churches were in fact marginal to English life – a necessary corrective to the tendency of church historians to overestimate the influence of the Churches in their desire to hearten the faithful?[2] Ecclesiastical biographies of the period often give the impression that church leaders had close friendships with, and a good deal of influence upon, certain political and military leaders. Yet when one turns to the biographies of these secular leaders, frequently not even a passing reference is found to the ecclesiastics concerned. Perhaps church leaders were, and are, too ready to confuse secular deference to their office with the exercise of decisive influence.

I have tried to present church history as interacting with contemporary society, though to do so at all adequately would have meant a much longer book and have required a more competent author. We should, I believe, cease to speak of 'church history' as such, and rather speak of 'the Church in history'. God speaks to the Church through the world, as well as to the world through the Church. God's Word emerges through a ceaseless dialectical interaction between Church and world. In this period, that Word emerged more authentically from the prose and poetry of Siegfried Sassoon and Wilfred Owen than it did from, say, the sermons of Bishop Winnington-Ingram. It is often pointed out that poets like Sassoon and Owen did not necessarily represent the feelings of ordinary soldiers. Nevertheless, as Fr Martin Jarrett-Kerr C.R. has written,

> In any age the artist is one who advances through the night with sensitive antennae. He is the first to feel the long coils of bramble in the forest, the trip-wire or the hidden pit covered with brush-wood. He is the seismograph, recording the shock of the distant earthquake, which will be on its way to us next.[3]

I have taken samples of Anglican opinion from a number of church periodicals. The *Guardian* (founded in 1846) gave extensive weekly coverage to church news, and regularly printed sermons verbatim or in lengthy summary. The *Church Times* (founded in 1863), more definitely Anglo-Catholic, had a larger circulation than all other Anglican weeklies put together. The weekly *Challenge* (founded in May 1914) represented a liberal Anglican viewpoint. William Temple was editor from 1915 to 1918, and Tissington Tatlow of S.C.M. was for a time chairman of the editorial board. *Commonwealth* (founded by Henry Scott Holland in 1895) was the monthly organ of the Christian Social Union. In 1901, A. C. Headlam became editor of the *Church Quarterly Review* and gave it a new lease of life as the main intellectual periodical of the Church of England. *The Modern Churchman* was founded in 1911 and edited by H. D. A. Major as the forum for the Churchmen's Union (after 1928 The Modern Churchmen's Union). To measure how far, say, episcopal utterances were regularly reported in the popular press would require another study. But it is clear that on occasion they were widely known. The fact that the support of church leaders was desired by politicians at certain junctures suggests that they were thought to possess political influence. That politicians who were consulted by Archbishop Davidson sometimes counselled him to avoid or to make utterances indicates that his words were credited with having an appreciable effect on public opinion.

Some find it hard to forgive people and institutions, not least the Church and its leaders, that fail to live up to idealized images of them. To the Christian, the Church is both more glorious and more scandalous than to those who see it only from outside. At the end of an Open Lecture given under the auspices of the Cambridge Faculty of Divinity in 1968, Michael Howard asked that we should recognize that the 'moral' statesman plays a 'tragic' role, deserves our compassion and needs our prayers.[4] If this is true of statesmen, it is also true of the Church. When we look at the Church in the first war we have the right and the duty to be critical. But in doing so, we have no superiority of achievement to parade, despite our more sophisticated theological and ethical systems, despite our international organizations, political and ecclesiastical. We, with little idealism or optimism left either to inspire or delude us, are kept alive by a balance of terror. Margaret Thrall, surveying the attitudes of the bishops of the Church of England to nuclear weapons in the period after the second war, concluded: 'the official contribution of the Church of England has been minimal or non-existent during the first two and a half decades of the nuclear era.'[5] Leslie Paul has written finely about the need to face the fact that the Church is a compromised institution:

> It is compromised. Such is the situation of the Church of England, one which it shares with every other great Church. It is tempting to say, this has nothing to do with Christ, let it end, and let us start again. But starting again has its problems, particularly if it means the same old cycle, and it has been tried. It is unhistoric too. There are other things to be said. The struggle of the Churches for incorruptibility in the midst of corruption adds profoundly to our religious understanding of the tragedy and hope of man's situation, and what it means in the absence of hope to be the recipient of grace. What the Churches tried to be, and what they became, and what they sought to undo, has added a rich strain to our culture and every culture is a form of man's understanding of himself and his potentiality. We have to hold on to that understanding through the institutions which enshrine it, and remember that the Church is a sinning Church.[6]

What was the general state of the Church of England at this time? In the latter part of the nineteenth century all the Churches in this country felt that the tide was flowing in their favour, though most were acutely aware of their failure to attract the majority of the working class. It has been recently pointed out that 'the phase of Anglican growth spanning the Victorian and Edwardian years represents the one prolonged period after the Restoration in which the Church of England succeeded in improving its quantitative position within English society'.[7] The Student Volunteer Union (the missionary wing of the S.C.M.) in 1896 adopted its watchword: 'The Evangelisation of the World in this Generation' – significantly it was dropped in 1918. In the period immediately before the first war some foreboding voices were heard. In a remarkable sermon to the 1906 Church Congress, Bishop Charles Gore described a sense of impotence in the Church (with which the twentieth-century Church has become all too familiar):

> We have won victories; but they have proved barren. We stand far stronger on the merely intellectual or apologetic ground than we stood thirty years ago. We have vindicated the liberty of Biblical criticism. . . . We have practically won the battle of the liberty of Catholic ceremonial. What is much more important, we have had great revivals of spiritual life, and if only there were more driving-power behind our organizations, we should be on the way to get rid of many old-standing abuses. The idea of the Church, free and self-governing . . . is awake and alive again. We understand, again, our great Mission in the evangelization of the world. Above all, we have laboured very hard for the poor, and amongst them. And yet; and yet – it all hangs fire. . . . Such a feeling is in the mind of very many of us as we take stock of the powerlessness of the Church, in spite of even splendid exceptions in this or that parish, to produce any broad, corporate effect, to make any effective spiritual appeal by its own proper influence, in the great democracy of England today.

Gore's answer was that of the Christian Socialist (his text was Mark 10.23–6). The Church of England was not in touch with the vast mass of the labouring people. The bishops' incomes linked them with the wealthy. The clergy sought their friends among the gentry and professional people. So clerical opinions and prejudices reflected those of the upper and middle classes, not those of the wage-earners. Episcopal incomes should be reduced. More clergy should be drawn from the working class, and be encouraged to maintain the tastes and sympathies of their background. The working class must be represented at all church meetings.[8] Gore's solutions, though admirable, were oversimplified.

C. F. G. Masterman presented a more complex analysis. In close touch with Gore and the Christian Social Union, and consulted by Temple on social questions, Masterman lived for a period in a tenement flat in Camberwell, studying social conditions. He became a Liberal M.P. in 1906 and a member of the Government two years later. In 1909 he published *The Condition of England*. Religions, he wrote, can revive, but

> present belief in religion, as a conception of life dependent upon supernatural sanctions or as a revelation of a purpose and meaning

beyond the actual business of the day, is slowly but steadily fading from the modern city race. Tolerance, kindliness, sympathy, civilization continually improve. Affirmation of any responsibility, beyond that to self and to humanity, continually declines. Life therefore gradually ceases to be influenced or coloured by any atmosphere of 'other worldliness'.

Yet the Churches are extremely active and their social work is widely appreciated. 'Their definite dogmatic teachings seem to count for little at all. They labour on steadily amid a huge indifference.' People are no longer impelled by fear towards religion, for life is more orderly and secure.

The tide is ebbing within and without the Churches. The drift is towards a non-dogmatic affirmation of general kindliness and good fellowship, with an emphasis rather on the service of men than the fulfilment of the will of God. . . . It is the passing of a whole civilisation away from the faith in which it was founded and out of which it has been fashioned.

In this analysis he anticipated many of the discoveries of the more perceptive chaplains during the Great War. During and immediately after the war, important elements within the Church of England tried hard to reform its life, restate its doctrines and draw nearer to the working class. But Masterman in 1909 was sceptical about the similar hopes which Christian social radicals then held that their programme of reform would bring back the working class to the Churches. He believed that the creation of the towns was a more potent cause of the drift away from organized religion than either intellectual difficulties or the class character of the Churches.[9]

Accurate and comprehensive statistics of church attendance for this period are not available, but such as they are, they confirm the forebodings of Gore, Masterman and other observers. Censuses of 1886 and 1902/3 showed a marked decline in London churchgoing in proportion to the population between those dates, particularly in the Church of England.[10] The proportion varied considerably from area to area, usually according to its class composition. After surveying various statistics from different parts of the country Owen Chadwick concludes:

Until the last fifteen years of the century, the churches succeeded marvellously in their endeavours to keep pace with the rising population. After 1886, though the leaders of most churches had just as powerful a feeling of advance, the figures show that the churches failed markedly to keep pace with the rise in people; and more, that in towns where the population was still rising, the number of attendants at church began to decline.[11]

On the other hand, in 1888 about three out of four children attended Sunday Schools in England and Wales, a remarkable proportion when it is remembered that parents of the higher social groups did not particularly favour attendance.[12] In 1906, the Wesleyan Sunday Schools alone included over a million children. During the next half-century, numbers in the Sunday Schools of all denominations were to fall drastically.[13] As the chaplains discovered, the religion of the average private soldier had been formed in the Sunday and day schools, not by adult worship in church. The war revealed the extent of the alienation of the majority of the English male population from the life and practice of the Churches – it revealed it, it deepened it, but it certainly did not create it.

Randall Davidson (1848–1930) had been Archbishop of Canterbury for eleven years when war broke out. Church and nation were fortunate to have as Primate one whose concern for the Church was set in the wider context of his concern for the Kingdom. His was a lay rather than a priestly mind. During his primacy (1903–28) he knew each of the seven prime ministers personally, and four intimately. His cautious temperament made him unwilling to act precipitately. During the war, when easy emotions ran high, and some churchmen succumbed to them, Davidson's emotional reserve, his undramatic, sober realism, and his feeling for the international dimension of Christianity, preserved him from indulging in a narrow patriotism. As Dean of Windsor he had been prepared to stand his ground with Queen Victoria. During the war he was ready on occasion to take unpopular attitudes. But a cautious temperament has its drawbacks in a period of change and crisis. Sometimes he was too ready to take advice from politicians, too reserved to make those imaginative gestures that are needed from those in positions of leadership. A pragmatist rather than a theologian, out of touch with the world of the universities, he was not the one to realize how searching were the theological and ethical questions being wrung out of men's hearts by the experience of war, and how much the Church needed to change. Davidson was incredulous at Canon Peter Green's refusal of the see of Lincoln in 1920 on the ground that the size of episcopal residences and incomes was scandalous to ordinary people. Cosmo Gordon Lang (1864–1945) was a much more complex personality. Though both as Archbishop of York (1908–28) and as Archbishop of Canterbury (1928–42) he was capable of acting with independence on political questions, national and international, and put his weight behind the ecumenical movement, he was too patrician to be in touch with the lives of ordinary people – it was said that after becoming Archbishop of York he never entered a shop. During the war E. S. Talbot (Bishop of Winchester 1911–24), Charles Gore (Bishop of Oxford 1911–19) and A. F. Winnington-Ingram (Bishop of London 1901–39) were at the height of their powers and influence. The older generation of such Protestant evangelical leaders as H. C. G. Moule (Bishop of Durham 1901–20), E. A. Knox (Bishop of Manchester 1903–21), and F. J. Chavasse (Bishop of Liverpool 1900–23) was being replaced by a new generation of liberal evangelicals committed to ecumenism and a social application of the Gospel, typified in the episcopate by Theodore Woods (Bishop of Peterborough 1916–24, of Winchester 1924–32). The new generation of bishops which was to dominate the post-war leadership of the Church of England was emerging: William Temple (Bishop of Manchester 1921–9, Archbishop of York 1929–42, Archbishop of Canterbury 1942–4), Hensley Henson (Bishop of Hereford 1918–20, of Durham 1920–39), Cyril Garbett (Bishop of Southwark 1919–32, of Winchester 1932–42, Archbishop of York 1942–55), Geoffrey Fisher (Bishop of Chester 1932–9, of London 1939–45, Archbishop of Canterbury 1945–61), George Bell (Bishop of Chichester 1929–57), and F. R. Barry (Bishop of Southwell 1941–63). Their experiences between 1914 and 1918 equipped them to provide seasoned leadership in the second war.

Of the party groups, the Anglo-Catholics and Liberal Modernists were nearing their peak of influence and coherence as the first war ended. But Evangelicalism was gravely weakened by a series of disputes between its conservative and liberal wings. In 1910, Cambridge conservative Evangelicals withdrew from S.C.M. Later, conservative Evangelicals formed their own national student society, the Inter-Varsity Fellowship. In 1922 a conservative group broke away from the Church Missionary Society to form the Bible Churchmen's Missionary Society. The Group Brotherhood of liberal Evangelicals, formed in 1906, published in 1923 a volume of essays, *Liberal Evangelicalism*. In 1923 the rather private Group Brotherhood became the much more public Anglican Evangelical Group Movement. After the war the liberal Evangelicals began to demonstrate a quality of scholarship which the older generation of Evangelicals had lacked. How did these three groups of churchmen, Catholic, Liberal, and Evangelical, react to the war? The relation between theological belief and political stance is notoriously complex. Charles Gore, Scott Holland, Fr Paul Bull C.R., A. F. Winnington-Ingram, and Basil Bourchier were all Catholic churchmen, yet they took differing attitudes to the war. H. D. A. Major, Charles Raven, Dean Inge and Hensley Henson were all Liberal churchmen, yet they also differed in their approach to the war. On the other hand the opinions of conservative Evangelicals like Chavasse, Moule, Taylor Smith and Knox were more cohesive. Nevertheless, those Anglicans (like Gore, Scott Holland, Peter Green and Bell) whose primary allegiance was to the Catholic Church, transcending nationality, felt the scandal of war between Christian nations more acutely than those whose primary allegiance was to the Church of England as the national Church.

In seeking to determine a Christian attitude to the war the Churches were able to draw upon a long experience, although the Great War was in some ways different from any previous one. St Ambrose and St Augustine in the fourth and fifth centuries had laid the foundations of Christian thinking about the Just War, which had been developed in the thirteenth century by St Thomas Aquinas and by Vitoria and Suárez in the sixteenth and seventeenth centuries. Article XXXVII of the Church of England stated: 'It is lawful for Christian men, at the commandment of the Magistrate, to wear weapons, and serve in the wars.' The official Latin version rendered the final phrase as 'et justa bella administrare'. Traditionally, Anglicans have resorted to such passages as Matthew 22.21 ('Render therefore unto Caesar . . .') and Romans 13.1–7 ('the powers that be are ordained of God') to expound their theology of the State. In the later nineteenth century, Christians noted with satisfaction the embodiment of principles of the Just War in international conventions established by the Law of Geneva and the Law of The Hague.

The Crimean and Boer Wars drew varying reactions from the Churches. The Crimean War (1854–6) was the last English war to have begun with the proclamation of a General Fast; during the war military disasters prompted the holding of another General Fast.[14] Two main views of the spiritual significance of the war were proclaimed by the clergy: the war was a solemn duty laid upon the nation by God; it was a divine punishment for a variety of national sins. Though sermons mostly proclaimed that the war was just, a defence of international order, they also emphasized the evil and sufferings of war. In evangelical circles, it was widely believed that England had replaced the Jews as God's chosen people and instrument. The failures or successes of the war were frequently explained in terms of divine punishments or rewards. As the war proceeded, and it became more difficult to present it as a crusade, clergy turned to expound it as human folly which God could use for his purposes, for example in order to rouse England from selfishness and complacency – sentiments which found eloquent expression in Part III of Tennyson's *Maud* (1855), and were often echoed during the Great War. Christian reactions to the Crimean War showed a deep belief in the direct and identifiable providence of God. This was also evidenced in the reactions to other disasters of the period. In 1866 there was an outbreak of cattle plague in Warminster. The people observed Days of Humiliation. It was a chastisement from God, wrote the vicar, 'a loud call to us to mend our lives, and to walk more closely with our God'.[15] (Some countrymen rejected such Christian interpretations of the cattle plague and resorted to magic instead.)[16] The Christian tradition of interpreting specific events as revelations of divine providence received a fatal battering during the two world wars, and the Churches are now notably reluctant to venture in this field. Christian opinion about the Boer War (1899–1902) was sharply divided, though the majority in the Churches supported the war.[17] Many Christian socialists, led by Gore and Scott Holland, publicly attacked the war as an expression of British imperialist arrogance, regarded its military reverses as a divine chastisement of this spirit, and denounced the concentration camps. Peace Night sickened and frightened Scott Holland. In Hereford, rowdies tried to attack the palace of the Bishop of Hereford (John Percival). He and Canon E. L. Hicks of Manchester (later Bishop of Lincoln) had also been forthright critics of the war. In 1901, over 5,000 Nonconformist ministers signed a manifesto against the war. However, B. F. Westcott (Bishop of Durham 1890–1901), President of the Christian Social Union, supported the war. He believed that imperialism embodied the principles of brotherhood and service. Fr Bull of Mirfield, who had been a chaplain in South Africa, wrote *God and our Soldiers* (1904) in the style of a romantic adventure story 'to claim for our army that respect which is due to it, and to show what God has shown to me, the strong virtues which burn so brightly in our soldiers' lives'.[18] A Christian socialist, he regarded war as a product of the competitive economics of capitalism; imperialism, like socialism, extended man's visions beyond nationality.

During the Boer War, in a speech to the Church Congress of 1900, H. E. J. Bevan, Professor of Divinity at Gresham College (later Archdeacon of Middlesex) produced an apologia for war. Its themes were echoed in many sermons and speeches during the Great War. He cited the classic Victorian sources: J. B. Mozley's sermon 'War' (1871), Ruskin's *Crown of Wild Olive* (1866) and *Maud*. He declared:

History lends but scant support to the theory that a great nation is necessarily demoralised by war such as this. Rather does it arouse a slumbering patriotism, and call citizens from the luxurious enjoyments of peace, and from petty and selfish interests, to sacrifices and self-denial for a common cause. It awakens in many a lively consciousness of the perishableness and insecurity of human affairs, destroys the artificial barriers between class and class, and teaches multitudes to pray.

War, he considered, did not on the whole brutalize the soldier but elicited 'nobler and gentler qualities just in proportion as his courage and endurance have been more or less severely tested'.[19] In 1899, Winnington-Ingram, then Bishop of Stepney, preached a sermon which included this description of the role of the Church in time of war: '. . . there are worse things than war. . . . We remember that when the commanders of a ship are steering round a difficult corner the crew and the passengers ought not to choose that time to shout advice in their ears . . . we hold that in silently praying for their guidance we best do our duty.' In the Great War also he always assumed that the military and political leaders of the nation could and should be trusted. In 1901 when he preached his first sermon as Chaplain to the London Rifle Brigade he chose Joshua as his subject. The title 'The Happy Warrior' was taken from Wordsworth's poem so often cited during the Boer and Great Wars.[20]

Perhaps the most powerful (and ambiguous) contribution which the Churches made to the nation during the Great War was in the realm of imagery. Horatio Bottomley, editor of *John Bull*, regularly laced his articles and speeches with biblical imagery and religious sentiments. When he calculated that an audience would pay well he inserted a set piece of oratory about 'the patient figure of the Prince of Peace pointing the Star of Bethlehem which leads us on to God'.[21] Donald Hankey, officer and churchman, went over the top shouting to his men: 'If wounded, Blighty – if killed, the Resurrection.'[22] The public schools had taught their pupils patriotism, self-sacrifice, athleticism, spartan habits and discipline in the name of 'The Manliness of Christ' (the title of a book by Thomas Hughes published in 1876).[23] At a popular level, the imagery of the Christian life as one of warfare was universally diffused through well-known hymns and memories of baptismal promises. The Salvation Army consistently used the metaphors of war. Its publication was called *The War Cry*. Preachers of all traditions reached all too readily for texts like Ephesians 6.12 ('For we wrestle not against flesh and blood, but against . . . the rulers of the darkness of this world'). The comradeship of the trenches was described in language from the Gospels. The potent biblical imagery of sacrifice was widely used to describe the slaughter. Some drew with eagerness and damaging naïvety upon the more pathological imagery of apocalyptic. Biblical apocalyptic writings depict a world catastrophe in which evil political forces mass themselves in cosmic combat against God who finally and totally defeats them. The saints, thus vindicated, begin their reign, and history is over. The language of apocalyptic was particularly dangerous for Christians to use during the war because of its sadistic undertones, because of the bestial imagery used to describe the opposing powers, because it encouraged a view of the war as a straight conflict between good and evil, Christ and Anti-Christ, God and the powers of darkness, and because it offered an eschatological escape from wrestling with the moral ambiguities of contemporary human history.

1

The Coming of War

'Then suddenly, like a chasm in a smooth road, the war came', wrote Virginia Woolf.[1] But in fact the Edwardian era was a period of considerable upheaval and unrest: the Boer War of 1899–1902; the intense controversies about the social services introduced by the Liberals from 1906; the trade union unrest of 1911–12; suffragette demonstrations; the bitter debates about education between Government, Church of England and Free Churchmen; the 1911 Parliament Act; the renewed conflicts in Ireland which seemed to threaten civil war in 1914; the acceptance of a new type of commitment, however vague, towards France and Russia which was an important factor in the British participation in the war when it came. Back-bench Members of Parliament knew little more of the conduct of British foreign policy than the ordinary Edwardian citizen. Sir Edward Grey, the Foreign Secretary, had agreed to secret military conversations with France in 1906, but most members even of the Cabinet were ignorant of them until 1912. So many warnings of an impending catastrophe had been given by newspapers, novels, and plays that when it actually happened it seemed unexpected. In the first half of July 1914 the British government was still not expecting war; its main concern was the Irish crisis. On 24 July it held its first discussion on foreign affairs for a month. But on 4 August Britain declared war.[2]

For the first time for a century, a war had broken out which involved the whole nation. Many greeted it with relief and excitement. A crowd of 30,000 sang 'God save the King' outside Buckingham Palace; others smashed the windows of the German embassy. Though there was much talk of it all being over by Christmas, Kitchener's appeal on 7 August offered a service of 'three years, or until the war is concluded'. By 15 September, half a million men had volunteered. The length and the character of the war were largely unforeseen.

To the vast majority of Christians the outbreak of war was at first as unbelievable and unexpected as it was to almost everyone else. Hensley Henson, Dean of Durham, wrote:

There had been warnings and protests in plenty, yet when the stroke actually fell, it seemed to have the benumbing shock of an almost unimaginable disaster. The nation, conscious of its own devotion to peace, still smarting under the losses and humiliations of the South African War, and largely leavened with the perilous sophistries of pacifism, was reluctant to admit the possibility of war between nations so closely linked by ties of interest, culture, and tradition.[3]

The Principal of the Church of England training college at Culham wrote to his students: 'that the clash of arms should so suddenly and violently break in upon our harmony and comradeship never once entered into my calculations'.[4] But then on 9 July 1914, Lloyd George, Chancellor of the Exchequer, had remarked to a group of bankers at the Guildhall: 'In the matter of external affairs the sky has never been more perfectly blue.' On 23 July he had told Parliament that British relations with Germany were 'very much better than they were a few years ago'.[5] The *Church Family Newspaper* on 31 July 1914 stated its conviction that the Kaiser was using his great influence for peace.[6] In 1913, the Assembly of the Free Church of Scotland had passed a resolution supporting all efforts for international understanding especially between Britain and the 'great Protestant nation of Germany'. Rising to their feet, the delegates applauded an address of congratulation to the House of Hohenzollern on the recent marriage of the Kaiser's daughter.[7] In 1912 the leaders of the Student Christian Movement had been startled by the possibility of war with Germany, and had exchanged messages with the German student movement, but the danger passed. 'The war took us by surprise', wrote Tissington Tatlow, S.C.M. General Secretary; 'few of us had thought about the question of Christianity and war.' At the summer conference at Swanwick, which began on 23 July 1914, war seemed 'utterly remote'.[8] The August number of *Commonwealth*, the organ of the Christian Social Union founded by Scott Holland, contained no mention of the Sarajevo murders or of the approaching crisis. It did, however, include an announcement that the International Congress of Social Christianity would be held at Basle in September when papers would be read on 'Christianity and Universal Peace'. (The English Committee for the Conference included Percy Dearmer as Chairman, and the Bishops of Birmingham, Chelmsford, Lichfield, Lincoln, Winchester, and William Temple.) On 26 August, Scott Holland wrote in a letter, 'War is Hell':

My one comfort now is to remember that I never insisted on War as inevitable, never shouted Armaments, never saw the Kaiser as the one unspeakable devil. It is just this which I denounce in the Germans. By talking like this, they have made the war inevitable. Our folk who did it are open to the same damning charge.

On 6 September, he was using to Neville Talbot language similar to that which he had criticized: 'every day reveals the black blind horror of Prussianism. It is the very devil. It has to be fought: and killed. It is the last word in iniquity. I could not have believed that man could be so diabolical.' A few days later he wrote to Frank Thorne:

> The paradox of Christianity and War falls *within* Christ Himself. He is dumb before his shearers: yet a sharp sword goes out of His mouth. He yields: yet he judges. . . . War is right when it is fought on behalf of Peace. . . .

In November he wrote to Neville Talbot: 'We are eschatologists. God *must* win.'[9] It is significant that Scott Holland, the Regius Professor at Oxford, contributor to *Lux Mundi*, a leading member of the Christian Social Union, should have been surprised that man could be diabolical.

Fr J. N. Figgis, priest of the Community of the Resurrection, and a noted historian and preacher, was more prescient. He had written in the preface to his prophetic lectures, *Civilisation at the Cross Roads* (1912): 'Something is crumbling all around us.' In the second lecture he declared: '"There is death in the pot" of modern civilisation, and it is not like to heal itself.'[10] An ordinand at Mirfield remembers Figgis saying to him in 1913: 'You can hear something cracking every day.'[11] About the same time he said in a sermon: 'We can almost hear the thunders of the avalanche of war – war on a scale unknown. Hardly does the world even look stable any longer.'[12] Temple Gairdner from Cairo in mid-July 1914 addressed forty or fifty laymen in business, politics and diplomacy, in Eastbourne. One of them recalled:

> He began by describing the trend of European philosophy during the last half-century, showing how Nietzsche's teaching had been woven in to make for Germany a new *Weltpolitik*. He talked also about the insurgent nationalities of Europe and especially of Ireland, and indeed he foretold the whole tremendous crash that was to come not much more than a fortnight afterwards. I shall never forget the impression it made on us, and our heavy hearts at the end.[13]

W. R. Inge, Dean of St Paul's, was deeply depressed: 'I never thought to have lived to see such a return to barbarism. Civilisation is in danger of dissolution. Neither religion nor philosophy gives me any comfort.'[14] A former curate of Canon Peter Green's remembers sitting up with friends in Salford to hear the clock strike twelve and enjoying the 'suppressed excitement of the moment, and with little if any realization of all that it portended. The Rector went to bed as usual. He knew what it meant more than most people.'[15] Peter Green wrote in his 'Artifex' column in the *Manchester Guardian* on 6 August: 'What has struck me most has been . . . the almost complete lack of appreciation, on the part of most people with whom I have spoken, of what war implies today.' Bishop E. S. Talbot of Winchester had foreseen some disaster, but nevertheless the war was a great shock. 'In one hour the judgement has come.' The crisis was shaking every stone in the national house. He was grateful for the new sense of unity, sacrifice and service in the nation, and was convinced that the cause was righteous, but he urged penitence for the English share of responsibility for the war. He asked people to pray for greater things than victory and peace alone, and to remember to love their enemies.[16] For Bishop Gore of Oxford, who had taken a sombre view of the movements of history, and had denounced the nationalistic spirit of vengefulness at the time of the Boer War, the coming of war broke upon him with 'a horror of great darkness'. 'Truly war is not a Christian weapon. It "cometh of the evil one"', he said, and hated it with all his heart. But he was convinced that British participation was right. It was as a judgement of God and it had to be endured to the bitter end. 'I feel as if we must be greatly chastised before we can be strengthened.'[17] Archbishop Lang of York reacted somewhat similarly: 'I hate War. I detest it. It is the bankruptcy of Christian principle', he said in York Minster on 9 August. But he believed the war to be 'righteous' and that 'we were bound in honour to enter it'. Both he and the Bishop of London in Pastoral Letters warned against hatred and stressed that the quarrel was not with the German people but with their rulers.[18] But, argued correspondents in the church weekly *Guardian* on 3 September, if the cause was morally right, surely was it not the duty of the clergy to enlist as well?

Fr P. N. Waggett, of the Society of St John the Evangelist, and a Chaplain from September 1914, wrote a powerful message in the September issue of the *Cowley Evangelist*:

Since we last read the *Evangelist* a great change has come over all our lives. In the interval we were forced to face the dread of war, and a little later we faced the dread of peace which would have been purchased by the desertion of duty, and the fatal acknowledgement that might is right . . . we recognise a great day of God, a time of reckoning with the Eternal Justice, a time of testing and inevitable transition. For the Day of God, when it comes and passes, leaves nothing as it was before. . . . Already in our mood and feeling we have died the saving death. In mood and hope and feeling all littleness has passed away. It is burned in the furnace of affliction. It is evaporated in the *greatness* of the event. Where now are selfishness, and pretence, and animosity, and luxury, and sloth? Surely they are gone for ever. Where are they? They are hiding still at the bottom of the heart. . . . What is abandoned there must be abandoned in reality. . . . If each prays for this death and resurrection, if the Church with one heart thus prays, then the nation, now softened and ennobled by affliction, will not, when the great floods pass, climb again to the old shores of worldly care and pleasure. . . .[19]

The hope that out of the trials of war a more godly Church and a more just nation might arise was to become the theme of many sermons and speeches during the war.

The Archbishop of Canterbury, Randall Davidson, a shrewd but cautious statesman, always in close touch with government circles, had been lulled into thinking that war between England and Germany was inconceivable, partly as a result of his contacts with German Christian leaders, though he was aware of the tensions. Dr Dryander, chief court chaplain to the Kaiser, had written on 17 July 1914 to inquire whether the Anglican Church would be likely to accept an invitation to take part in the celebrations to mark the 400th year of the Reformation in 1917. In his reply of 1 August, Davidson pointed out that because the Church of England had a relationship with 'the historic doctrine and system of the Western Church' as well as with the principles of the Reformation, there would be a 'very grave difficulty' in a public identification of the Church of England with a commemoration of Martin Luther. He had opened his letter by saying that he was sure that Dr Dryander was joining with English people in praying that 'the possibility of international conflict may be removed far from us. War between two great Christian nations of kindred race and sympathies is, or ought to be, unthinkable in the twentieth century of the Gospel of the Prince of Peace.' The Archbishop was watching the situation with grave anxiety. On 30 July, J. Allen Baker, a Quaker M.P., called on the Archbishop on his way to the founding conference of what became known as the 'World Alliance for Promoting International Friendship through the Churches'. He wanted the Archbishop to sign a memorial to Asquith, the Prime Minister, in favour of non-intervention. The Archbishop refused on grounds which were very characteristic of his approach to complex political questions:

> I objected to much of its phraseology and also said that I could not possibly sign it without an assurance that it was on lines which the Government would find helpful and not harmful.

On 31 July he saw Asquith, who convinced him that Britain's influence on events depended upon keeping Europe in suspense. Asquith begged him to use his influence to prevent demonstrations or memorials in favour of non-intervention which could lead the European powers into thinking that Britain would be merely a spectator.[20] On 2 August Davidson preached in Westminster Abbey. He contrasted the present situation with the hopes for international brotherhood which had developed in the last half-century, and which had found expression in the growth of support for a system of international arbitration:

> What is happening is fearful beyond all words, both in actual fact and in the thought of what it may come to be. . . . This thing which is now astir in Europe is not the work of God but the work of the devil.[21]

H. G. Wells's novel *Mr. Britling Sees It Through* (1916) depicted vividly the careless enjoyment of the pre-war leisured classes, and the dawning horror that the more sensitive began to feel as the reality of war was revealed. Mr Britling (to some extent a portrait of Wells himself) mused: ' "On the very brink of war – on the brink of Armageddon", he whispered at last. "Do they understand? Do any of us understand?" '[22] But for many in the nation the war came as a relief, cutting away all the complexity of national disputes, creating at last a clearly defined enemy, even a necessary turn in the evolutionary cycle. A letter of Wilfred Owen's to his mother on 28 August 1914 echoed the neo-Darwinians of the period who argued that civilization was produced only through conflict. Owen shows a studied but revealing ambivalence, even élitism; he was still a civilian:

> While it is true that the guns will effect a little useful weeding, I am furious with chagrin to think that the Minds which were to have excelled the civilization of ten thousand years, are being annihilated –

and bodies, the product of aeons of Natural Selection, melted down to pay for political statues.[23]

R. J. Campbell, Minister of the City Temple, worked for a few months for the Y.M.C.A. at the beginning of the war. He recorded how he met a young officer who considered that the political causes of the war were less important than the fact that 'human beings like fighting'. He believed that this was part of 'the struggle for existence', and that war was necessary when life became colourless in order to release heroic virtues. Though Campbell was uncomfortable with this view, he confessed:

> . . . as humanity has been constituted up to the present, war has been the means, more than any other agency, of bringing out on the grand scale that truth of sacrifice without which flesh can never be made to serve the ends of the spirit and the kingdom of the soul be won. This could be realised without war if only the race as a whole could be lifted up to the requisite level. It often has been realised without war in individual cases, but never for long on the wider basis of communal life. Please God, it will one day be universally realised without war. . . .[24]

Note that here Campbell, while rejecting the cruder aspects of neo-Darwinianism, accepts some elements from the tradition, but expresses them in language derived from St Paul and Romantic writers like Ruskin.[25] One also detects the way in which war could appeal to a Christian socialist like Campbell because it united the community in one grand co-operative enterprise. Though there was a section of English opinion, both within and outside the Churches, which believed that conflict and struggle were the appointed means of progress, this view was often severely criticized, when war came, as the essence of 'Prussianism' – that might is right, and that the weakest must go to the wall. Dr Chalmers Mitchell, who published *Evolution and the War*[26] in 1915, was one of several writers who repudiated the widespread belief that Darwinianism justified war. Like T. H. Huxley in his lecture 'Evolution and Ethics' (1893), he emphasized that man could influence evolution in a moral direction. If the theory of evolution posed problems for faith, it also enabled those who believed in progress to justify pain and suffering as the necessary price to be paid for it. So Archdeacon Basil Wilberforce, Chaplain to the Speaker, and a veteran Modernist,[27] said in a sermon in 1915:

God is travailing in pain in His creation . . . the law of progress is the law of evolution. The law of evolution necessitates, both on the physical and the moral plane, the fiery ordeal of war with the opposite of good, which is the only means of transition into higher, nobler life, and Infinite Immanent Mind must share every pang that ever racks any individual soul or any part of animated nature.[28]

Julian Grenfell, brought up in a social group whose men found the regular killing of animals a ritual release of aggressive energies, 'adored' the war when it came. He wrote to his mother in October 1914:

It is all the most *wonderful* fun; better fun than one could ever imagine. I hope it goes on a nice long time; but pigsticking will be the only tolerable pursuit after this or one will die of sheer ennui. . . . I *adore* war. It is like a big picnic. . . .

He listed the Germans he had killed in his game book together with the 105 partridges he had killed at home. 'The fighting excitement revitalises everything. . . . One loves one's fellow man so much more when one is bent on killing him.' To those brought up on Greek drama, Keats, and Shelley, it was glorious to die young, especially in battle. 'He whom the gods favour dies young' – the lines of Plautus were often quoted. Many of the messages of sympathy received by Julian's mother after his death in 1915 spoke of the wonderful privilege of motherhood to be able to give sons to the death in war.[29] When, in April 1915, Michael MacDonagh called on another mother to express his condolences, she told him that she had no grief, only pride that her son should have died for his country.[30] On 4 April, Easter Day, 1915, Dean Inge preached to a large congregation in St Paul's Cathedral. He preached on Isaiah 26.19: 'Thy dead men shall live. . . . Awake and sing, ye that dwell in the dust.' He spoke of the thousands of parents, widows, and orphans who were thinking of 'hastily made graves in a foreign land'. When peace dawned, were the dead to be excluded from it? He then read Rupert Brooke's 'The Soldier' ('If I should die, think only this of me: . . .') by 'a young writer who would . . . take rank with our great poets'. He commented: 'The enthusiasm of a pure and elevated patriotism, free from hate, bitterness, and fear, had never found a nobler expression. And yet it fell somewhat short of Isaiah's vision, and still more of the Christian hope.'[31] Edward Marsh wrote at once to Brooke to tell him that he had become famous overnight.[32] On 23 April Brooke died of septicaemia in a hospital ship in the Aegean.

By contrast, for the working-class recruit, enlistment offered not only a way of serving his country but also an alternative to a humdrum job or unemployment. George Coppard describes how he was stirred by the military bands and the tramping feet of the Territorials. He enlisted at the age of sixteen years, seven months, by declaring that he was nineteen.[33]

The question of war and peace had been discussed by Lambeth Conferences in 1897 and 1908[34] and by several Church Congresses. Christians had often followed the lines laid down by the Lambeth Conferences in urging arbitration and other peaceful methods of settling disputes.[35] The Church of England Peace League formed in 1910, though never a large body (it had only about 100 members in 1913), numbered among its members Bishop Gore, Bishop Percival of Hereford, Bishop Hicks of Lincoln, William Temple, Hastings Rashdall, and George Lansbury. Of the main Christian groups, only the Quakers maintained a corporate witness to peace, though in fact 33 per cent of Quakers of military age enlisted. The first British National Peace Congress in 1904 included many Quaker and secular participants, but very few other Christians. Asquith was one of several speakers at a Christian Conference for Peace in 1908 who criticized the Churches for their lack of support.

Ecumenically, contacts between European Christians were very limited, and were only just beginning before the war. J. Allen Baker, a participant in the second Hague Conference of 1907, in consultation with a German delegate, conceived the idea of exchange visits of German and British churchmen to follow up the visit of the Kaiser to Britain in 1907 and exchange visits between newspaper editors and civic leaders. Accordingly, a German delegation of about 130 Roman Catholic and Protestant churchmen visited Britain in 1908. A writer in the souvenir volume declared:

> Two nations closely allied by common blood and spiritual history have yet in recent years failed to understand each other aright. . . . What was needed was that some ray of Divine light should pierce through the misunderstandings, and reveal to men the ties that bound them to each other.[36]

In the sermons and speeches, as Dr John Clifford, the Free Church leader, commented, Germans and British tried to 'outrival' each other in their proclamations of 'mutual indebtedness'.[37] In General

Superintendent Faber's opinion they were 'one race – connected by blood and by language'.[38] Bishop Winnington-Ingram, in a speech laced with German phrases, spoke of his love for Germans, and the kindly feelings of Germans towards England. The two delegations passed a resolution which recognized 'how greatly the world's peace depends upon the amicable relations between our two countries' and appealed to all classes to promote friendship and goodwill. 'Our nations are closely allied by the stock from which both peoples spring, by the kinship of our Sovereigns, by our history, our long friendship, our mutual indebtedness in Art, Literature, and Science, and above all by our common Christianity.'[39] Fulsome tributes were paid to the Kaiser. The Archbishop of Canterbury wrote of the 'eloquent expressions of the great Sovereign of the German Empire in favour of peace'.[40] Allen Baker said that it was largely due to 'the peace-loving character of the German Emperor' that Germany had not been engaged in a great war in the last quarter of the nineteenth century.[41] Archdeacon Basil Wilberforce in a sermon linked the visit to the evolutionary theology popular among liberal churchmen like himself:

> I believe in my soul that the direction in which the immanent Spirit of God, the spirit of evolution which is in all, above all, and through all, is mainly working in the present day is towards unity: friendship, brotherhood, mutual understanding, international amenities are in the air, . . . is there a single department of human energy in which we have not learnt much from you? Your nation – ruled by a sovereign unique in European history for the loftiness of his ideals, the variety of his accomplishments, the earnestness of his religion, the intensity of his patriotism . . .[42]

In 1909 a similarly-sized interdenominational British delegation, including Anglican diocesan bishops, visited Germany. Once again the souvenir volume was prefixed with photographs of the two sovereigns whose healths were proposed with cheers on a number of occasions. The delegates were warmly received at Potsdam by the Kaiser. The speeches and sermons again celebrated Anglo-German brotherhood founded on a common culture and faith. Professor Harnack and Dean Armitage Robinson particularly stressed the mutual indebtedness of German and English theology. The Chaplain-General, Bishop Taylor Smith, declared: 'English and Germans are brothers, both for time and eternity.'[43] At the end of the visit the two groups sang together 'Now thank we all our God'. As the boat prepared to sail the British delegates sang 'Should auld acquaintance be forgot' from the bridge of the steamer. A Baptist summed up the general impression of the British delegates: 'We return home absolutely convinced that the great majority of the German people honestly and earnestly desires peace.'[44] But to judge from the extensive contents of the two souvenir volumes, the visits took place in an atmosphere of such euphoria and hyperbole that the hard political, military, and economic realities of Anglo-German relations were simply ignored. As one German remarked, 'We see in the air, not airships, with spies, soldiers, bombs, but we see the angels of God. . . .'[45] The two groups resolved to establish permanent means of communication between the Christians of the two nations. 'The Associated Councils of Churches in the British and German Empires for Fostering Friendly Relations between the Two Peoples', formed in 1910, was launched in Britain at a meeting in the Queen's Hall, London, in February 1911. The Archbishop of Canterbury presided, and leading German Christians present included Professor Harnack, who spoke. The first annual meeting in March 1912 was told that already 7,000 people in Britain and the colonies had joined the movement. At the annual meeting in May 1914, Davidson felt optimistic enough to believe that the two Councils in Germany and England had practically secured the mutual friendship for which they stood.

In 1914, as a result of a Swiss initiative, what was called after 1915 'The World Alliance for Promoting International Friendship through the Churches' was created at a conference in Constance. But, meeting on 2 August, the delegates (depleted in number by closure of frontiers and troop movements) had to disperse quickly before war broke out. They passed, however, four resolutions urging united Christian action for peace and proposing means by which the work of the Alliance could be furthered. National committees of the World Alliance were formed even in the belligerent countries, including Germany and England, and managed to achieve a limited amount of work, though in Germany its literature appeared with blanks due to censorship. It is clear that some within the Churches were beginning to realize the international implications of Christianity; but too little was done too late and with insufficient support from the official leadership of the Churches; and what was accomplished did not impinge on the Church at the local level.

When war actually came, most neutralists changed their minds. Bishop Hicks of Lincoln and Bishop Percival of Hereford had been deeply involved in various peace movements in the pre-war period.

They joined the Neutrality Committee which had been quickly formed, and which included Gilbert Murray and Ramsay MacDonald among its leaders. But both bishops after a brief wrestle with their consciences gave their support to the war. Liberal and radical journals which had advocated non-intervention soon transferred their allegiance. Gilbert Murray in late July 1914 had signed a declaration (supporting some Cambridge Fellows and the Bishops of Hereford and Lincoln) in favour of neutrality which was published on 3 August. But after the invasion of Belgium and having studied the various documents from the respective governments, Murray concluded sorrowfully: 'the Power whose good faith I had always championed . . . in part meant murder from the beginning.'[46] A private organization (but with the Prime Minister as Honorary President), 'The Central Committee for National Patriotic Organizations', secured the writing of pamphlets supporting the war. Contributors included six members of the Oxford Faculty of Modern History. Those leaders of the nation who had been educated at either Oxford or Cambridge – and they included nearly all the bishops – naturally treated such opinions with considerable respect. Even Wilfred Owen wrote a patriotic jingle:

> O meet it is and passing sweet
> To live in peace with others,
> But sweeter still and far more sweet
> To die in war for brothers.[47]

John Percival was Bishop of Hereford from 1895 to 1917; before that he had been successively the first Headmaster of Clifton, President of Trinity College, Oxford, and Headmaster of Rugby. He was a man of independent thought and action. On occasion he made himself unpopular in the diocese – by his fierce criticism of the Boer War and the protectionists, by his appointment of the noted Modernists Streeter and Rashdall to canonries, and by his invitation to Free Churchmen to receive Communion in the Cathedral at the time of the Coronation in June 1911. (Kingsley Martin's father was a Congregationalist minister in Hereford and took part. 'In thanking the Cathedral authorities for taking this step towards Christian unity, Father astounded his hosts by suggesting that they should pay a return visit to a chapel service. They thought him mad.')[48] In 1904 he attended a Peace Congress in Boston, U.S.A. He strongly attacked 'Christian nations' for 'squandering their wealth and their manhood on armies and navies':

We have to learn to feel that the jingo spirit which swaggers in its pride and delights in warfare and aggression is in the main a survival of those brutal instincts that should be eliminated from every civilised and Christian life.

Christians were put to shame, he said, by those outside the Christian allegiance who were spending their lives in the cause of peace. Greed and militarism had spread like an epidemic. Whereas American poets had celebrated peace, Kipling 'is the exponent of strife and violence, we might even say of brutality'. A 'High Court of the Nations' was needed to substitute law for force.[49] He had long had the cause of peace at heart, addressing the Church Congress in 1896 on the subject, preaching at The Hague in 1899 while the Hague Conference was sitting, presiding over the annual meeting of the International Arbitration and Peace Association in 1900, the National Peace Congress at Bristol in 1905, and the annual meeting of the Christian Conference on Peace in London in 1908. However, he was never a pacifist; he had indeed urged the use of force on behalf of Armenia and Macedonia because he believed in the use of arms to help oppressed peoples. (He had for many years advocated Welsh disestablishment.)

In late July 1914 he watched the international scene with growing alarm. He joined in a committee of protest 'against the mischievous utterances of our jingo Press'. On 1 August he urged priests to hold prayers in church, and to call meetings of parishioners to send to the Prime Minister resolutions urging neutrality and efforts for peace. In a letter of 2 August he suggested that the Mayor of Hereford should be asked to call a meeting for the same purpose. But when Germany invaded Belgium he changed his view completely, instinctively supporting the small nation. In a letter in *The Times* of 12 August he sought to clarify his position. He said that he had believed assurances from the Prime Minister and Sir Edward Grey that England was free from all treaty obligations, and had therefore been at liberty to remain neutral; now he realized that 'there had been commitments by way of understandings which, though entered into without authority of Parliament, made it difficult for us as a nation to stand aside with honour'.

Under these circumstances I am brought to the conclusion that, in obedience to our treaty obligations, and in support of Belgium's just claim, our country had no choice but to take up the sword if honourable dealing was to have any chance of surviving in international affairs. . . .

The war, he hoped, would surely bring us nearer the day when the people would rise up and sweep military governments away.[50] (This is the voice of the traditional English Christian gentleman, who keeps his word, tries to care for the weak and to do his duty, and speaks in chivalric language about 'taking up the sword'. He had not only established Clifton as a school in which games were regarded as an important part of education; he had also inaugurated a separate House in which Jews could corporately follow their own observances.)

In September he kept his 80th birthday; the following month his son was killed in the war. Persuaded of the justice of the nation's cause he gave it his support, believing, as he said in 1915, that 'along with our Allies we are the predestined instruments to save the Christian civilisation of Europe from being overcome by a brutal and ruthless military paganism'; therefore the war must be fought 'till the victory is won and the law of Christ is firmly established as the paramount authority in all national and international affairs'.[51]

Edward Lee Hicks (Bishop of Lincoln 1910–19) had long felt that the maintenance of peace was one of the most urgent needs of the period. When residentiary Canon of Manchester and Rector of St Philip's, Salford, he had preached a controversial and much criticized sermon against the Boer War, later published by the Manchester Transvaal Peace Committee. He was labelled pro-Boer. From 1910 he was President of the Church of England Peace League. This aimed to combat the 'war-spirit' by arbitration and international friendship; he remained President until his death in 1919. Canon W. L. Grane, in a sermon for the League in April 1913, had imagined Christ saying to the Church:

> How can you say you love Me if you twist my teaching? How is it you believe the opposite of what I taught? Even the Press and Pulpits of your Church now proclaim that they who take the sword shall *flourish* by the sword.[52]

In May 1914, Canon J. H. B. Masterman (Bishop of Plymouth 1922–33 and brother to the Liberal politician C. F. G. Masterman) in a sermon published by the League pointed out that the Church of England had never spoken with a united voice for peace. But there was strong reason to hope that if the need arose, at least some contemporary church leaders would 'dare to withstand the sudden madness that drowns the voice of reason and turns a sober people into a wild beast howling for blood'.[53]

In 1913, Bishop Hicks hesitated about blessing regimental colours. War to him, wrote his biographer, was 'the sport of a corrupt gang of financiers, armament-makers and imperial filibusters, made popular through an equally corrupt Press'. Hicks rejoiced that Norman Angell was a Lincolnshire man. (Angell in *The Great Illusion*, 1910, had argued that a major war would be as economically disastrous for victor as for vanquished; this book, popular among pacifists and neutralists, was also widely read throughout the world, and translated into many languages.) On 2 August 1914, Hicks preached in Cleethorpes, pleading for British neutrality. When war came he felt his hopes shattered and his lifetime's ideals brought to nothing. But events dispelled his doubts. On 6 August he wrote to his daughter: 'England did not want this war: I hate it. But it seems as if the Kaiser and his friends were bent on it.'[54] In *The Church and the War* (1915) Hicks restated his beliefs. Prussian militarism must be overthrown; a 'balance of power' policy was not the way to preserve peace; the independence and neutrality of small states must be protected; there must be no more secret treaties – foreign policy must be democratized; the manufacture of arms should be nationalized.

By contrast with both Bishops Percival and Hicks, Handley Moule, the veteran evangelical Bishop of Durham, sent a letter to every parish two days before the English declaration of war to say that it was our 'plain duty' to defend Belgium, even though such a policy would mean declaring war on Germany.[55]

In 1908 Ben Tillett told a Labour demonstration for peace that the 'churches were strong enough to prevent war if they chose, but they were supported by capitalists, war-mongers, scare-mongers and people of that kind'.[56] But Hyndman and Blatchford warned of the military power of Germany, which they did not believe the German socialists could control. In 1909 Blatchford wrote a series of articles for the *Daily Mail* recommending national service and preparation for war as the only hope of preserving peace. The 1907 International Socialist Conference passed a resolution calling on the working classes to prevent war by appropriate action, and to intervene to bring it to an end if it started. Keir Hardie nevertheless failed in attempts in 1910, 1912, and in late July 1914, to gain a pledge of an international strike of the working classes in the event of war. Immediately before war broke out, both German and French socialists indicated their readiness to support their respective governments. The ideal of international socialism collapsed before the more powerful forces of nationalism.[57] In 1916 Lord French was able to pay a warm tribute to Ben Tillett's tireless work for the war effort,[58] for when war arrived all the working classes of the various countries obediently (with a few exceptions) supported their respective governments. The Kaiser was delighted when German socialists voted for war. 'I see no parties any more, only Germans', he said.

Individuals like Ramsay MacDonald and Keir Hardie continued their opposition but the 'rape of little Belgium' swept aside dissent; the trade unions were almost unanimously in favour of fighting. Though English socialists were, like Christians, in theory internationalist, they also longed for their country to be united in a common cause. They hoped that the war would promote state intervention and a breaking down of social barriers. Members of the Church Socialist League (founded in 1906) were divided. George Lansbury, an Anglican, and some others continued to oppose the war. Lansbury and Dick Sheppard asked for men and women to stand sacrificially between the opposing armies. Conrad Noel, socialist Vicar of Thaxted, and his friends supported the war as a way of helping small nations against Prussianism.[59] Some Christians expressed their horror at the spectacle of Christian nations in conflict, remembering the exchange visits of churchmen between England and Germany. Keir Hardie, a socialist of Christian inspiration, was shattered by the failure of international socialism to live up to its ideals:

> Ten million Socialist and Labour voters in Europe, without a trace or vestige of power to prevent war! ... Our demonstrations and speeches and resolutions are all alike futile. We have no means of hitting the warmongers. We simply do not count.[60]

After a stroke and a mental breakdown, he died in September 1915. His constituency elected in his place a fervent Labour supporter of the war.

George Bell (Bishop of Chichester 1929–57) was asked by the Archbishop of Canterbury to be one of his chaplains just before war broke out. He arrived for consultations at Lambeth on the night war was declared. Next day he assisted the Dean of Wells and others in drawing up official forms of service and prayers for wartime. Some complained that the prayers did not contain direct petitions for victory. To a protesting peer Davidson replied:

> . . . if there was one request which poured in more strenuously upon me than others from all quarters when we were compiling these prayers, it was that we should abstain from identifying ourselves with the Divine Will to such an extent as to claim that God is simply on our side, and that this is a matter of course.

A senior fellow of Trinity College, Oxford, suggested a prayer 'something like this':

> 'Strike the fear of God (at last) into the heart of the Kaiser (or our Enemy) so that he depart and go back whence he came: strike the fear of God into his hosts so that what is left of them may make haste to return with him' (even as Sennacherib, King of Assyria, and his remnant arose early in the morning and made haste to go back and dwell in Nineveh).[61]

The *Guardian* praised the restrained language of the official prayers.[62] But Canon Peter Green wrote of their 'almost incredible absence of power, relevance and dignity'.[63]

Very soon, some were looking back at the days of peace with distaste. Neville Talbot, one of the sons of Bishop Talbot, wrote from an O.T.C. camp on the last Sunday of peace: 'I feel that a great deal of our long peace has been a false peace, oblivious of God and His Righteousness. My thoughts turn towards a chaplaincy to the troops.'[64] Lloyd George had exploited this theme in a speech in September 1914; his sentiments were often echoed by churchmen in the years that followed. Indeed the speech used many of the 'props' of popular pulpit rhetoric. The images have just enough biblical echoes[65] to give them a sonorous and hallowed authority, but they remain vague enough to prevent any precise and embarrassing identification of their contexts:

> We have been living in a sheltered valley for generations. We have been too comfortable and too indulgent – many, perhaps, too selfish – and the stern hand of Fate has scourged us to an elevation where we can see the everlasting things that matter for a nation – the high peaks we had forgotten, of Honour, Duty, Patriotism, and, clad in glittering white, the great pinnacle of Sacrifice, pointing like a rugged finger to Heaven. We shall descend into the valleys again; but as long

as the men and women of this generation last, they will carry in their hearts the image of those great mountain peaks whose foundations are not shaken, though Europe rock and sway in the convulsions of a great war.[66]

Both Lloyd George in the state, and, as we shall see, A. F. Winnington-Ingram, Bishop of London, in the church, had the ambiguous gift of being able to articulate what most Englishmen wanted to hear. E. A. Burroughs, Fellow of Hertford (Bishop of Ripon 1926–34) praised this speech in a celebrated letter to *The Times* of 4 March 1915.[67]

So, many gave thanks for the new sense of national unity, self-sacrifice and purpose as Labour leaders, Ulstermen, and suffragettes dropped their antagonisms in the face of the common enemy. (Members of the Labour Party were to hold office for the first time in the coalition of 1915.) Whereas a respected minority, both inside and outside the Churches, had opposed the Boer War, few voiced any opposition to the Great War once it had broken out. H. G. Woods, Master of the Temple, was able to say early in the war: 'God be thanked, there has been no division of Christian opinion among us as to the righteousness of our cause.'[68] In the autumn of 1914, Welsh Baptists were annoyed by Anglican claims that most of the recruits were coming from the established Church. The Baptists refuted such claims, and pointed proudly to the numbers of Nonconformists who were enlisting. Yet until August 1914 Baptists had been opposed alike to militarism and the social establishment.[69] Roman Catholics were equally eager to demonstrate their patriotism.[70] A Free Church commentator ascribed the remarkable 'revolution' in Nonconformist attitudes which before the war had been so internationalist and pro-German, to the 'sense of horror and fear at the moral madness of Germany'.[71] The invasion of Belgium had particularly shocked and united Christian opinion in England. It seemed a flagrant violation of the principles of international law, the gradual building up of which Christians had been at pains to support as the best hope for future peace and international order. The Bible with its story of the small state of Israel always at the mercy of conquering world powers; the stories of Christ's care for the downtrodden and weak; the stories of the early Christian communities persecuted by the might of the Roman Empire; the public school ideal which encouraged the well-off to go to the aid of the less fortunate: all seemed to support the moral necessity of Britain's intervention on behalf of Belgium. Furthermore, Christian socialists had often celebrated the Magnificat as the revelation of God's purpose for social and political relationships: 'He hath put down the mighty from their seat: and hath exalted the humble and meek.'[72] Preachers compared the invasion of Belgium with Ahab's seizure of Naboth's vineyard (1 Kings 21).[73] Free Churchmen's self-understanding was inextricably bound up with their own bitter experience of oppression by the power of the social and religious establishment. So they too were especially ready to identify with the cause of Belgium.[74] The English Christians who were so ready to spring to the defence of Belgium only rarely recalled with penitence examples from British imperial history when Britain too had used its power to conquer small defenceless nations.

2

The Church and the War Effort

Unlike France and Germany, Britain until January 1916 relied on the voluntary system to maintain the armed services. 'A voluntary system seems to entail that the finest spirits are the first victims.'[1] But at the beginning of the war conscription was regarded by many as un-English. To propose it seemed like a lack of faith in the patriotism of the people. If sacrifice was compulsory, where would be its moral glory? Labour leaders feared that military conscription would be followed by industrial conscription. Asquith believed that there was such formidable opposition to conscription that he could not ask for it until the voluntary system had been shown to be insufficient. The Derby Scheme of October 1915 was a half-way house. It involved a personal canvass of all men between eighteen and forty who were invited to attest their willingness to serve. Tribunals were created to hear appeals for exemption on personal or occupational grounds. These tribunals were later to have an important and controversial role in relation to conscientious objection. But a significant proportion of those eligible declined to attest. So the first of a series of conscription measures was introduced in January 1916, to be followed quickly by a Bill for universal conscription in May. Conscription created a new sense of corporate purpose, opened more and more spheres of employment to women, and gave one in three of the adult male population an experience of the armed services, and in many cases a participation in the horrors of the trenches.

In October 1914 Lord Kitchener made it clear that he had no wish for recruiting campaigns from the pulpits; nor had Archbishop Davidson. In November 1915 the Archbishop refused Lord Derby's request that clergy should be asked to appeal for recruits from their pulpits.[2] However, bishops and clergy did appeal for recruits in several ways. Davidson wrote in his Pastoral Letter of December 1914:

The well-being, nay the very life, of our Empire may depend upon the response which is given to the call for men, and I think I can say deliberately that no household or home will be acting worthily if, in timidity or self-love, it keeps back any of those who can loyally bear a man's part in the great enterprise on the part of the land we love.

But he also reminded Christians that they had a loyalty to the city of God, 'an even greater cause' than patriotism.[3] *The Times* issued a special *Recruiting Supplement* on 3 November 1915, in an attempt to make the Derby Scheme a success. The Archbishop of Canterbury in his message said that no one was exempt from offering some form of service to the nation, but strongly defended the non-combatant status of the clergy. The Archbishop of York was more forthright: 'The country calls for the service of its sons. I envy the man who is able to meet the call; I pity the man who at such a time makes the great refusal.' Others who sent exhortations included the Bishops of London and Birmingham, the Archbishop of Armagh, Cardinal Bourne, the Reverend F. B. Meyer (on behalf of the Free Churches), General Booth of the Salvation Army, the Chief Rabbi, Arthur Henderson, Horatio Bottomley, Ben Tillett, the Vice-Chancellors of Manchester, Sheffield, Leeds and Birmingham Universities, the Poet Laureate (Robert Bridges), Thomas Hardy and H. G. Wells.

During the war, many diocesan bishops deepened their already close relationships with regiments which had strong and often ancient local roots. A year before the war, Bishop Chavasse of Liverpool at the age of nearly 67 spent a week-end with his battalion on the moors in camp; this included a route march and an overnight bivouac.[4] Bishop Moule's biographers wrote of his 'manly, sportsmanlike interest' in the progress of the war. Moule sent a letter on folded card 'With the Bishop of Durham's Greeting and Godspeed' in November 1914 to the Durham Light Infantry. In June 1915, he spoke emotionally about the 'holiness of patriotism' and declared that it was a fallacy to assert that Christ had abolished nationality. It was no more a sin to bar the gates against Germany than to lock the house doors to keep the children safe from burglars. In 1919 he sent a battalion of the Durham Light Infantry in Archangel a St George's Day message which was included in battalion orders:

We owe a huge debt of admiration and gratitude to you, as you stand between us and the awful ruin, red with blood and fire, and worse, which we should suffer but for our glorious men. . . . God bless you all and bring you back to us after your fight with the Arctic cold and those Bolshevist forces who represent ideas and aims so awfully destructive of all that makes life fit for living.

The C.O. replied expressing his gratitude for the message and added that copies had been distributed and that the men treasured them greatly.[5]

Though Hensley Henson was usually very reluctant to support movements and causes, he supported both world wars with undisguised, but not uncritical, enthusiasm. He dedicated the third volume of his *Retrospect* (1950) to Winston Churchill in language of exultant admiration. He felt deeply that the Church of England was called to be the Church of the nation, however convinced he became, after the rejection of the 1928 Prayer Book in Parliament, that disestablishment was now the only honourable (if disagreeable) course. He may have felt a particular need to prove his patriotism, because socially he sometimes felt rather an outsider. He was conscious of not coming from an aristocratic background and of not having been to a public school.[6] His patriotism and friendliness to Nonconformists, as well as his intellectual and preaching gifts, commended him to Lloyd George. After much doctrinal controversy created by his alleged modernism, Henson was consecrated as Bishop of Hereford in 1918. He had too great an intellect and knowledge of history, too much distrust of easy emotion and the power of the demagogue, to become a narrow nationalist, but when war came, he threw himself into the recruiting campaign with ardour and enthusiasm. Lord Durham as Lord Lieutenant and Henson as Dean of Durham went together through the county 'as representatives respectively of the State and of the Church'. Henson describes the crowded meeting in the Town Hall in Durham:

> The Mayor presided. It was symptomatic of the new sense of fellowship which the crisis had created that both old John Wilson, the labour leader, and his political opponent, Hills, the Tory member for the City, attended, and made excellent speeches. I followed with a ten-minute appeal which aroused much enthusiasm. At the close of the meeting more than 200 names were handed in.

The argument that seemed most effective was the 'genuinely altruistic' one: the German invasion and treatment of Belgium 'stirred a flame of moral indignation' among the miners, who were determined to become 'chivalrous' rescuers. Though he realized that some felt that it was wrong for him as a clergyman to assist in recruiting, he was quite unrepentant. He believed that no loyal citizen, especially one like himself in a prominent position, could stand aside when the nation was in peril. 'I felt so strongly the moral obligation to resist Germany in her career of cynical and violent aggression, that I welcomed the opportunity of vindicating for the National Church a full measure of responsibility for the National decision.' When conscription was introduced later, he regretted that the clergy were not included. He disliked any suggestion of two moralities, one for clergy, the other for laymen. In any case, how could he appeal for others to enlist when he was exempt? Many chaplains, he believed, shared his view and agreed that the exemption of the clergy lessened their influence with the troops.[7] The Archdeacon of Westminster, Basil Wilberforce, began a sermon on the First Sunday in Advent 1914 by declaring bluntly: 'I have tried to make it clear that recruiting appeals from the pulpit are intended to stimulate hearers to become eager amateur recruiting sergeants.' In another sermon he said: 'Women of England, do your duty! Send your men *today* to join our glorious Army.'[8]

No leading churchman was more successful at recruiting than A. F. Winnington-Ingram (Bishop of London 1901–39). Untroubled by doubts, ambiguities or much self-knowledge, equipped as a popular preacher by his experience as a missioner, made familiar with the thought-forms of ordinary people by his experiences in the East End as Head of Oxford House, Bethnal Green, and Bishop of Stepney, much in demand as a speaker to men in universities and parishes, he could always be relied upon for enthusiastic, if sometimes naïve and sentimental, patriotism. He had been Senior Chaplain of the London Territorial Rifle Brigade since 1901. At the beginning of the war he was in camp with them, and stayed for two months. General Fry appealed to him before the first Sunday of the war: 'Put a little ginger into your sermon, as some of these men have not volunteered as yet for foreign service.' After the sermon the whole brigade volunteered for foreign service, as did all the men of another brigade, to whom he spoke from a wagon covered with the Union Jack when he visited them next day at the invitation of General Smith-Dorrien. When he asked them 'We would all rather die, wouldn't we, than have England a German province', there was 'a low growl of assent'. Later he published the sermon as a pamphlet, *A Call to Arms*, 'Addressed on August 31st from a waggon to 5,000 Territorials at Bulswater Camp'.[9] The frontispiece showed the bishop in the military uniform of a chaplain. In the sermon he asked the men to think what the Germans had done to Belgian

women and children, though he added inconsequentially: 'I do not want
to say an ill word of another nation.' Oxford could be ruined like
Louvain. Quoting *Henry V* to them, he told them that the men of
Agincourt, Crécy, Inkerman, Alma and Waterloo were with them.
Though God was not a 'tribal' deity, our duty to our country was 'part
of our duty to God'. They must be ready to go overseas. Had not Christ
said 'If ye love Me keep My commandments'? Love was to be shown by
obedience. Altogether 10,000 men volunteered as a result, and the
Bishop received the thanks of Lord Kitchener. The Bishop again
received his thanks when the London branch of the Church Lads'
Brigade, under his presidency, recruited 1,000 men.[10] In the preface to a
volume of his sermons, *The Church in Time of War* (1915), he wrote:

> ... the Church encouraged every young man under its influence to
> volunteer at once as a duty to God as well as to the country. The
> exodus from all the Church choirs, the Church Lads' Brigades, the
> Church Scouts, and the ranks of the servers, had been enormous.

(The Church of England played a leading part in the Scouting
movement which was founded in 1908 with its motto 'Be Prepared' and
its atmosphere of energetic and conservative patriotism. In July 1915
the Archbishop of Canterbury sent a personal message to all Scouts
who were then soldiers.)[11] In a sermon on Trafalgar Day 1915,
Winnington-Ingram declared that after the atrocity stories, the sinking
of the *Lusitania* and now the execution of Nurse Cavell, recruits would
flow in: 'there will be no need now of compulsion.'[12]

The fact that many of the leading clergy were drawn from the same
social groups as many of the leading politicians and military leaders,
meant that close personal relationships already existed between Church
and State. Bishop Talbot's brother-in-law was General Sir Neville
Lyttelton. Lord Bryce was a close friend of Davidson and of the
Talbots. Winnington-Ingram claimed personal friendship with General
French and Admiral Jellicoe. When Fr Waggett, S.S.J.E. wanted to
volunteer as a chaplain at the beginning of the war, he discovered that
General Congreve was in command of the Guards Division camped
almost opposite his house in Cambridge. General Congreve was the
brother of Fr Congreve who, like Fr Waggett, belonged to the Cowley
Fathers. A. C. Headlam (Bishop of Gloucester 1923–45), Professor at
King's College, London, wrote regular reviews of the military and
political situation for the *Church Quarterly Review* which he edited. His
brother James served in the Propaganda and Information Departments,

and a cousin was a Major-General. Both helped him with their advice.

Of the 1,274 ordinands in the Anglican theological colleges, some withdrew almost immediately to enlist at the beginning of the war. The number of ordinations fell drastically. By Christmas 1914 over 30 per cent of the ordinands at the College at Mirfield and its hostel at Leeds had enlisted. Some university and college tutors urged their classes to volunteer. Soon after the outbreak of war the bishops had agreed that after Trinity 1915 they would not normally accept for ordination any men who were fit for military service.[13]

The ordinand in college was faced with a difficult choice. He could continue the course and reply to the charges of cowardice and lack of patriotism by declaring that the nation had a desperate need of the pastoral ministrations of its priests. He could go forward to ordination and offer his services as a chaplain. He could withdraw and become a combatant or non-combatant in the forces. He could declare himself a pacifist. In such a situation, the Principals of the theological colleges agreed that no uniform policy was feasible. B. K. Cunningham (Warden of the Bishop's Hostel, Farnham, and after the war Principal of Westcott House, Cambridge) wrote about those who volunteered:

> To speak of them, however, as being 'loss' is surely to have an altogether false idea of the value of numbers; if only a small percentage survive and be, in consequence of their experience, deeper and fuller and broader men, the Church will not be the 'loser' . . .[14]

Fr Bernard Horner, C.R., Principal of the College at Mirfield, while realizing the need for combatants and chaplains, pointed out, in *CR* for Christmas 1914, that the Church faced an urgent task at home in meeting the pastoral challenges of war and in preparing for the problems of the nation after the war was over.

W. R. Matthews (Dean of St Paul's 1934–67) was Vicar of Christ Church, Crouch End, London. He came from a middle-class family and had been educated at a grammar school and at King's College, London. When he was appointed Dean of St Paul's, the senior Canon protested that his London degrees did not qualify him for the post. Matthews took a very different line from his bishop about recruitment:

> A spiritual and moral problem demanded some action from the moment when I took over the responsibilities of vicar: the question, 'Ought I to volunteer and fight?' was haunting, and torturing, many young men. In my opinion, conscription ought to have been enacted

from the day war was declared . . . I hope and believe that I never urged a man to join the forces in war, though I certainly tried to clear up the thoughts of some men so that they might make their own decisions. There were pulpit orators in those days who spoke like recruiting officers and stoked the fires of hate. At least one used my pulpit for his diatribe; I shuddered and I hope I made it clear to my people that I did not say 'Amen'.

Matthews was not, however, a pacifist; he believed that the Church had become inextricably involved with civilization, and that no one had the right to accept the protection of the state unless he was prepared to uphold it against an enemy. The precepts of the Sermon on the Mount referred to the Kingdom of God, for which Christians must work until a society can be realized in which the Sermon will be 'the obviously reasonable law'.[15] Henson 'rejoiced' when conscription was introduced, because the voluntary system was unfair; as did Tissington Tatlow of the S.C.M.[16] In the *Church Quarterly* for January 1915, Headlam pressed the case for conscription; individuality and freedom had to be sacrificed for the sake of the national effort. Bishop Michael Furse of Pretoria (Bishop of St Albans 1920–44) visited the front in 1915. His brother was G.S.O.1 to the General commanding the Second Army Corps in Flanders. Pressure was put on him by his brother and others to emphasize to the authorities at home the desperate need for conscription and an adequate supply of munitions. He saw Davidson, addressed a meeting of the bishops, wrote to *The Times* and interviewed leading politicians including Lloyd George.[17] He appealed to Lloyd George to visit the big industrial centres to speak on these two needs. A few days later in June, Lloyd George spoke strongly in Manchester and other industrial cities about these matters. In July 1915 the National Registration Act was passed, by which a national register was compiled of all persons between fifteen and sixty-five.[18] William Temple, Rector of St James's, Piccadilly, preached a sermon on 30 May 1915 appealing for united action by the country now that a national government had been formed.

I am sure the Bishop of Pretoria is right; we ought all to be under orders. If it were possible, I wish the whole wealth of the country might be taken over by the Government, and every one of us given a soldier's wages and a soldier's rations, and a soldier's discipline.

He called for total prohibition and asked the government, employers, and workers to ban strikes.[19] But Basil Bourchier, the militant Vicar of St Jude's, Hampstead, said of conscription: 'I deplore the fact that England should have fallen so low as to require it.'[20]

From the beginning of the war, the question as to whether the clergy should be combatants was a live and emotional issue. If some clergy were so keen to advocate conscription, why should the clergy be exempt? Frank Richards, a private soldier, described the clergy on both sides as 'a funny crowd: they prayed for victory and thundered from the pulpits for the enemy to be smitten hip and thigh, but did not believe in doing any of the smiting themselves'.[21]

In September 1914, Archbishop Davidson wrote to the diocesan bishops that he had been receiving inquiries from both clergy and laity, as to whether clergy should volunteer as combatants. He was quite clear that such service was 'incompatible' with ordination, and that the whole history of the Church supported this view. On the other hand, non-combatant service, with the R.A.M.C., for example, was perfectly congruous. The passing of the National Registration Act in July 1915 increased the pressure on the Church. In August 1915 the two Archbishops decided that the clergy should be encouraged to offer special skills to the community, that they should particularly care for members of the forces and their dependents, should encourage thrift, and might offer as chaplains or as non-combatants; but combatant service was 'unsuitable'. Some clergy and bishops reacted restively to the latter restriction. Lord Derby pointed out to Davidson that even the Church's supporters 'feel that the Church is being very much weakened by this exceptional treatment'. The Archbishop replied that clergy were being unfairly regarded as 'shirkers'. When the first Conscription Bill came up for debate in January 1916, the exemption of the clergy again aroused criticism. The Archbishop spoke in the Lords' debate, and did not simply base his argument on Church tradition and Canon Law. He emphasized that spiritual assets, which the clergy had a special responsibility to safeguard, were vital for both the right conduct of the war and a true peace.[22] But the Archbishop did not convince many of his critics in church or state, at home or at the front. Ben Tillett, a Congregationalist, asked at the annual meeting of the T.U.C. in September 1916, 'Why should these men who are so fond of talking about heaven be so afraid to go through its gates?'[23] Parish priests in industrial areas were accosted by small boys who, thumb to nose, shouted 'Kitchener wants *you*'.[24]

After protests by the Archbishop of York and the Bishops of Bangor and Pretoria about the lack of munitions, a few clergy began to work for armament firms in 1916. Early in 1917, plans were drawn up for additional national service for clergy by Neville Chamberlain and the Archbishop of York.[25] A Clergy National Service Committee was created, and by May 1917 it was able to announce that nearly 4,000 clergy had offered for special service, while another 2,000 were rendering general service. Some worked as car mechanics, stokers on merchant ships, miners, postmen, engineers and tax collectors. In Birmingham sixty-five clergy acted as special constables. One priest worked as a research chemist at a poison gas factory. In the York diocese, claimed Lang, practically every able-bodied priest was engaged in some form of national service in addition to normal duties – in agriculture, munition factories, in government and other offices, in hospitals, and so on. Some clergy joined local defence units. Professor A. C. Headlam drilled enthusiastically as Private Headlam under the direction of his gardener. The theologian, Hastings Rashdall (Dean of Carlisle 1917–24), joined the volunteer corps at Oxford and regularly turned out for early morning drill. In 1917 he worked as a historian for the Admiralty Intelligence Department.[26] Those clergy who came from upper-class families had learnt to be good shots in field sports. As public schoolboys they drilled and used weapons in the Cadet Corps. At Oxford and Cambridge the Training Corps continued their military education.

In March and April 1918 the Germans launched an all-out offensive. Haig issued his famous order beginning 'With our backs to the wall...'. On 9 April the Government introduced a new military service Bill which raised the age to fifty and in some cases to fifty-five. It also abolished the exemption of the clergy. Recognizing what he called 'a new emergency', Davidson agreed to clergy conscription. But six days later, the Government withdrew the clause because it feared the consequences if it attempted to conscript Roman Catholic clergy in Ireland. Davidson declared in the Lords: 'let no man say hereafter that the clergy of the Church of England have asked for exemption at this hour ... the very contrary is the case.' A few days later, a meeting of diocesan bishops agreed to allow clergy to volunteer. But after all the previous appeals for various forms of national service, few eligible clergy were left. For example, in May 1918, the Bishop of Bristol reported that out of 310 clergy, 71 were already chaplains, 4 were combatants, and 4 worked for the Church Army. Of the 124 of military age, only 41 were immediately available.[27]

Randall Davidson in opposing the idea of clergy combatants for almost the whole period of the war reflected the opinion of nearly all Anglican leaders. Gore tried to dissuade his clergy and ordinands from enlisting as combatants. In 1918, he was greatly relieved when the Government withdrew its clause about clergy conscription. He had said in 1914 that the nation needed to be reminded that there was a loyalty to the Kingdom of God which was higher than loyalty to the national cause, a vital 'counterpoise to the emotions of war'.[28] Bishop Talbot recognized that for a number of clergy it meant a real sacrifice to face criticism rather than to enlist. 'Those that minister about holy things and hold their Lord's commission must not have blood upon their hands, however justly shed.' This was a true Christian instinct and tradition, he believed.[29] Darwell Stone, Principal of Pusey House, Oxford, said that the French clergy would not be allowed to fight by their superiors if they had not been compelled to by the state.[30] Ronald Knox, son of the Bishop of Manchester, wrote to a friend that a priest 'ought never to have known that blood lust which I suppose everybody more or less gets in battle'.[31] B. K. Cunningham gave this opinion:

> While it is no more wrong for a doctor than for any other man to take life in defence of his country, there is surely something particularly incongruous about it. . . . So in the case of the priest, it is not more wrong for him than for others to kill, but the special work for which he was set apart was to call men to live in fellowship with God, and to help them to do it, and there is something particularly incongruous in his hurling men unprepared into the presence of their Maker; moreover, as in the case of a doctor, his commission extends to men as men, and not as members of any one nation.[32]

Temple argued that by allowing laymen to fight, the Church met the legitimate claims of nationality. By discouraging clergy from being combatants, it maintained its catholic and international witness.[33] Bishop Moule had always believed that clergy should not be combatants except in 'extreme necessity'. But in 1918 with the Government's Man-Power Act he felt that the necessity had arrived, and wrote to all his eligible clergy accordingly.[34]

Attacks upon the clergy for being cowardly and unpatriotic were wounding. Clergy are always liable to be thrown on to the defensive when accused of not being 'real men', and in days when 'masculinity' was more stereotyped than it is today, such accusations were less easily rebutted. It can be argued that the exemption of the clergy was a fatal mistake – that just as the Church would have had a deeper understanding of the world beyond the home if its ordained leadership had daily experienced ordinary jobs, so if the clergy had shared the sufferings of the trenches, this would have bridged a gulf in the post-war world. On the other hand, if it is argued that the monastic life is a vital witness to the total demands of God upon all Christians, and that pacifists similarly are a necessary leaven in church and society, then the exemption of the clergy was a reminder of a higher ideal and loyalty beyond that of the nation and its cause. This latter position was, however, harder to maintain when, as happened in the first world war, some of the clergy indulged in a vicarious and compensatory bellicosity much fiercer than that exhibited by those at the front.

In France most of the clergy conscripted served as combatants. Of the 32,699 mobilized, 4,618 were killed, and large numbers were decorated or commended for bravery. The courage of the combatant clergy did much to moderate anti-clericalism. A truce was declared during the war between most anti-clericals and the Church, a 'Union Sacrée'. Teilhard de Chardin worked as a stretcher-bearer and was twice decorated. A wounded soldier recalls Teilhard imperturbably coming towards him under terrible fire. 'I thought I had seen the appearance of a messenger from God.' When asked why he seemed so calm in battle, Teilhard replied: 'If I'm killed I shall just change my state, that's all.'[35] His *Writings in Time of War* (Eng. tr. 1968) related his war experiences to his cosmic theology. Whatever the value to Church and nation rendered by the combatant French clergy, it is clear their service did little to ameliorate that alienation of the French working class from Church and clergy so painfully experienced by the French worker-priests who accompanied the conscripted working men to Germany during the second world war.[36]

A few Anglican clergy did enlist as combatants or non-combatants. Robert Callaway was working as a mission priest in South Africa with his brother Godfrey, a Cowley Father, when war broke out; he returned to England to join the army as a chaplain. But he was dissatisfied with his role and became a combatant officer. In September 1916, a few days before he was killed on the Somme at the age of 44, he described to his wife a lecture which the brigade had heard. The language of the letter reveals the paradoxes of his position which he felt keenly, though unsentimentally – note the irony implied in the use of the word 'conversion':

> . . . to me the interest of the lecture lay not so much in the lecture itself as in what the lecture stood for – the entire conversion of our whole attitude of mind as a nation. For it was instruction as to how best to *kill* (with the bayonet), and every possible device that had been found by experience useful to enable a man to kill as many Germans as possible was taught. As one writes it down it sounds the most hideous brutality and yet yesterday I don't suppose there was an officer or man present who did not agree that if the war is to be won we must fight to kill. Personally I still shudder at the idea of sticking six inches of cold steel into another man's body or having his steel stuck into my body, but I shudder merely with the natural instinct of repulsion, which is common to at least all educated people. I don't shudder because I think it any more wrong of me as a priest. I have never for a single moment regretted becoming a combatant. In one way I can say with St. Paul, 'I glory in the things which concern my own infirmities.' I am proud of just those very things which other people think must be such a bore for me, e.g., coming down in rank [as a chaplain he had been a captain], being under the orders of boys of eighteen, having to trudge along on foot, etc., and for that reason I rejoiced when I gave up the Lewis Gun job, though everybody thought me a fool to do so.[37]

In 1916, one of the several Mirfield Fathers who were chaplains, Fr Fitzgerald, wrote to his brethren of the Community of the Resurrection that he had met a combatant priest who both led men into battle and said Mass for them in the trenches. 'I wish I knew if he is right to go on like this, as it seems to me so incongruous.' Two years later, in the early part of 1918, a member of his own Community enlisted as a private in the Artillery with the permission of the Bishop of Wakefield. The private was Fr Hubert Northcott, later in life well known as a spiritual director, retreat conductor and writer on prayer. Extracts from Fr Northcott's letters were reprinted in the Community Chronicle, *CR*. In the first letter he described what it felt like to be 'a new boy' again: 'it must be good for one occasionally to feel such a complete fool'. He explained that he had enlisted to share fully the lot of ordinary soldiers:

> The Christian soldier has to be a Christian under almost impossible conditions: at least he has to revise his whole moral outlook. . . . I

have felt for myself that strange sense of being in a new world where old standards no longer apply.

Everyone was left to his own conscience, but as most men had not learnt to think morally for themselves, there was moral drift.

> Going to church brings back other atmospheres, and one longs to be at the altar again oneself. I feel in my wrong place. On the other hand, I do feel more and more that my present position gives me the opportunity of a very valuable experience. It seems to me worth while that one of us, especially an unimportant one, should be having it, if only the whole Community can in some way share it, though it means that one has to forgo his own functions for the time.

Though he could only rarely attend church and was deprived of saying Mass, he still felt very much a priest:

> I find one can't lay aside one's priesthood by donning khaki – I mean, I find it a fact as well as a theory. One can't get away from the sense of responsibility for those with whom one is brought into contact. Always there is the feeling of Our Lord trying to reach them, and to reach them through oneself – and one seems to fail Him every time. . . . Perhaps opportunities will come. At present I have done nothing. I've chiefly been trying to find my own feet. Nor do I see how I'm to begin. However, I'm learning to love the lads here, and that is one essential for any effective work.

He dreaded being treated as 'a camouflaged chaplain' and therefore submerged himself in army life in a type of incarnation. 'Under canvas one's last remnants of privacy seem to be stripped away.' In France he travelled in cattle trucks. He slept crammed twelve in a tent and competed with all the others to wash at the one tap. He described emptying the swill tubs and scrubbing the floor at a Salvation Army hut in France: 'Do you realise the irony of the situation – a priest of the C. of E. sorting out the Salvation Army's swill-tubs . . . I said Terce as I did it as a kind of Te Deum.' He constantly asked himself, Where were the churchmen and the servers who had enlisted? He knew the answer: usually 'camouflaged under a mask of indifference':

> I no longer wonder why men are not particularly moved by matters of religion. You know what it feels like to be a convalescent after an illness. Every faculty seems dormant save the physical, and they are clamouring insistently for satisfaction.

His contacts with the Church were limited. 'Only once in the last month have we seen a chaplain and had a Mass', he wrote in September 1918. On one occasion he was going to Holy Communion, but he was prevented by being told to have his hair cut! When he was on cookhouse fatigues for two days a chaplain called; Fr Northcott had shaken hands with him before he remembered that his hands were coated with jam and grease. 'Of course, after our own discipline, [i.e. in his own Community] Army discipline is a comparatively easy thing.' He had not only to learn to use the bayonet, but also 'the spirit of the bayonet – a fearsome, devilish thing, but the only way, I suppose, to make an effective combatant'. After a time in France he was assigned the job of stretcher-bearer and wrote of a new attack: 'I am tremendously happy at the thought of being right in it.' After the end of the war, his Colonel asked him to assist the official chaplain until demobilization.[38]

Clergy at home helped the war effort in other ways too – for example, by exhorting people to give generously to War Loans. Such appeals fitted naturally into the Christian tradition of self-denial and thrift. On becoming Prime Minister in December 1916, Lloyd George called for 'a National Lent'.[39] Once again Winnington-Ingram surpassed all other church leaders. He offered to place the entire machinery of the diocese of London at the Government's disposal for the second War Loan campaign of 1915. He distributed half a million copies of 'A Message from the Bishop of London to the People of London'. Every Londoner must tell himself, 'I cannot "have a good time" at home when the lads at the front go through what they truly call "a hell".' In 1917 he played a leading part in the organization of a huge War Loan demonstration in Trafalgar Square with sermons, patriotic speeches, 'O God, our help in ages past' to massed brass band accompaniment, and the Lord's Prayer. Early that year he had initiated legislation permitting certain city churches to be closed on Sundays in order to release clergy to be chaplains, or to offer themselves for other forms of national service. Archbishop Lang closed up much of Bishopthorpe, his episcopal residence, during the war, cut his living expenses by half and put the remainder in War Loans. Between June 1915 and February 1917 six Anglican groups, including the Ecclesiastical Commissioners and Queen Anne's Bounty, invested over £4,500,000 in government securities.[40]

Some bishops travelled to the United States to tell the American people about the British war effort. In forty days in 1918, Archbishop Lang visited sixteen cities, delivered eighty-one addresses, met the

President and other leading politicians, was asked to open the Senate with prayer, and then paid a short visit to Canada.[41] Bishop Gore visited the States in September 1918 on behalf of the Ministry of Information at the request of the Church Peace Union. He commented with characteristic wryness, 'It is rather odd & I sd. think useless. But it will be rather a lark.' Some of his friends were as amused as he was that he was being sent by a Government which he had criticized so freely. He spoke about war aims, the League of Nations, Faith and Order, labour relations and the Armenian Relief Fund.[42]

Although support for the war was virtually unanimous, a small current of opposition continued. Most neutralists and waverers were soon won over by the 'rape of Belgium', the burning of the library at Louvain, the shelling of East Coast towns, the Bryce Report on German atrocities, the Zeppelin raids and the execution of Edith Cavell. As conscription became increasingly likely, opposition to compulsory service became more vocal. The No-Conscription Fellowship had been formed in November 1914. Among its leading members was Bertrand Russell, who was fined, deprived of his Trinity College lectureship at Cambridge in 1916, and eventually in 1918 was imprisoned for his activities. E. W. Barnes (Bishop of Birmingham 1924–53) was Tutor of Trinity 1908–15 and a convinced and vocal pacifist. Barnes was one of the strongest objectors to the steps taken by the College Council against Russell. The College failed to renew Barnes's Fellowship and so deprived him of the chance of becoming a Life Fellow, no doubt in part because of his pacifism. He became Master of the Temple, and ironically was nominated to a canonry at Westminster Abbey by Lloyd George in 1918.[43] The Union of Democratic Control was founded in September 1914 by a group of Liberals and Socialists. Its aims were to secure democratic control of foreign policy and to oppose conscription and censorship. Most I.L.P. members were opposed to the war but the majority of the working class supported the war, as did most Labour M.P.s. The Fellowship of Reconciliation, founded at the beginning of 1915, was a specifically Christian pacifist group. George Lansbury (Anglican), W. E. Orchard (Presbyterian) and Maude Royden (Anglican) were among its members. By the end of the war the movement had spread to other countries and the international F.O.R. was created in 1919.

The first Conscription Act of January 1916 created the term 'conscientious objection'. It directed that the tribunals created under the

Derby Scheme should now hear appeals made on grounds of conscience. There were three main types of objectors: those who accepted non-combatant service; those who accepted alternative service under civilian authority; and those who were 'absolutists' and refused to undertake any form of service as a condition of exemption. Asquith and his Cabinet had not expected the confrontation which developed. Gilbert Murray, who did much to publicize cases of injustice, wrote in April 1916:

> Some of the conscientious objectors are obstinate mules but the military authorities are like rampant griffins and I think that there is a good deal of unnecessary friction and suffering.[44]

There were about 16,500 objectors of military age, including about 3,300 who accepted non-combatant service, and about 1,500 absolutists. The total was about .33 per cent of the men who volunteered or were conscripted. Though Quakers were the only religious group well known already to the tribunals as pacifists, Christadelphians, Jehovah's Witnesses and Plymouth Brethren also objected to military service. Among the Free Churches, Methodists predominated. There was only a handful of Roman Catholic objectors. It was calculated in 1918 by a Quaker source that only about seven per cent of the objectors were Anglicans, lower than the number of twelve per cent who were atheists. But accurate figures about the religious affiliations of objectors are impossible to obtain.[45] Roughly 1,100 men objected on specifically Socialist grounds. Winnington-Ingram, who often described the war as 'The Nailed Hand against the Mailed Fist',[46] was regarded by many tribunals as the authentic voice of the Church of England. Article XXXVII could be quoted against Anglicans. (Edmund Blunden prefaced his memoirs, *Undertones of War* (1928), with the words of this Article.) Of course Anglicans were much less liable than Nonconformists to rebel against the state. But military metaphors were common in the phraseology of all Christian traditions. Some originated from the Bible, some from the Prayer Book (the Baptism service exhorts the newly baptized 'manfully to fight under his banner against sin, the world and the devil, and to continue Christ's faithful soldier and servant unto his life's end'); some from popular hymns like 'Soldiers of Christ, arise', 'Fight the good fight', and 'Onward, Christian soldiers'. Winnington-Ingram entitled a 1910 collection of his sermons *Into the Fighting-Line*; its preface drew heavily on military metaphors:

A Bishop is rightly expected today to be always in the Fighting-Line: . . . he must be in the thick of the fight, leading the mission work of his diocese, sending out troops to the front, and leading the attack on the strongly entrenched forces of evil at home. . . . Only 'in the Fighting-Line' shall we heal our divisions, and close up our ranks. . . .[47]

The terms for conscientious objectors in Britain were more generous than in many countries, but there was much public hostility to the objectors, especially the absolutists, and some were badly treated. Some tribunals at first did not understand the regulations – they held that they had no power to grant absolute exemptions on conscientious grounds, and continued to take this line even after the regulations were clarified in May 1916. Initially Asquith had given the impression that objectors would be exempt from combatant duties alone. Nearly 6,000 men either refused to accept the tribunal's decision or failed to apply for exemption. If they failed to join the forces they were arrested as deserters. In June 1916, thirty-four were taken to France and sentenced to death. Haig had been ordered to commute such death sentences. In May the Cabinet decided to transfer objectors who had been court-martialled to civilian hands, but neither decision was at first made public to avoid encouraging objectors. Though the majority of tribunals tried to be fair, they had been originally created to hear appeals made on grounds of personal and economic hardship. Public opinion was often contemptuous of objectors, and fierce about any suggestion that they were being treated leniently. Some objectors were of poor education, and found it hard to answer members of tribunals, who were more accustomed to asking questions than the objectors were to giving replies. Tribunals found it almost impossible to understand the motives of the absolutists.

The objectors, however, had supporters among a group of M.P.s who pressed for the investigation of any cases of unjust treatment. In 1917, Mrs Margaret Hobhouse published *I Appeal unto Caesar* to plead the case of the objectors, of which her son, Stephen, was one. Over 14,000 copies were sold. Politically and socially she was well-connected. Her husband had been an M.P. from 1885 to 1906, and was also an Ecclesiastical Commissioner. One of Mrs Hobhouse's sisters was Beatrice Webb; another was Lady Parmoor, the mother of Sir Stafford Cripps. Stephen's proxy godparents were Beatrice Webb and Lord Milner (Minister of War 1918–19). Stephen became a Tolstoyan pacifist in 1902 and later forsook the Church of England and became a Quaker. During the war he was imprisoned as an absolutist.[48] The Earl of Selborne, Lord Parmoor and Lord Hugh Cecil,[49] all leading Anglican laymen, wrote commendatory prefaces to Mrs Hobhouse's book. Gilbert Murray wrote the Introduction, to explain the position of absolutists, and to demand an end to their 'persecution'. He said that in 1916 the Government and other authorities had been prompt in investigating any cases of alleged ill-treatment, 'and sincerely anxious to prevent wrong being done'. He also believed that cruelty in barracks was the exception.[50]

The new policy of handing over recalcitrant objectors to the Home Office for work of national importance soon, however, ran into difficulties. Such work was not easy to find or define. Some refused to work alongside objectors. Dartmoor was turned into a C.O. work camp in 1917. A defiant minority created problems by acts of disobedience. Being confined in a military detention barracks, or in a prison like Dartmoor, or working in the camp at Dyce near Aberdeen, were severe experiences, particularly for those unaccustomed to manual work. Some died and several suffered physically and mentally. But some had courted ill-health by various forms of non-co-operation. The scheme for employing objectors on national work ceased in April 1919. The non-combatants often suffered from ridicule. The Non-Combatant Corps was nicknamed the 'No Courage Corps'. Members were discriminated against by being refused the pay increase of January 1919, were denied any final gratuity, and were demobilized more slowly than combatants. The last members of the N.C.C. were not released until January 1920. All prisoners were released by August 1919. But when objectors tried to obtain employment they found that their personal history was a barrier. They lost their vote until 1926 unless they could satisfy a tribunal that they had done work of national importance.

In July 1916 Lloyd George said of the absolutists:

> I do not think they deserve the slightest consideration. With regard to those who object to the shedding of blood it is the traditional policy of this country to respect that view, and we do not propose to depart from it: but in the other case I shall only consider the best means of making the lot of that class a very hard one.[51]

In October 1917 the Bishop of Exeter (Lord William Cecil) recommended that the political objector should be placed in the area of England most likely to be bombed, but that the religious objector should be released.[52] The *Guardian* supported his proposal and commented: 'We have no sympathy whatever with people who call in their consciences to help them in their refusal to defend their country.'[53] When the King heard that objectors were being imprisoned at Dartmoor, he protested to the Home Secretary.[54] In November, a memorial calling for the end of repeated sentences on absolutists, and for the release of Stephen Hobhouse, was organized by his mother. The signatories were predominantly clerical – eighteen diocesan bishops, eight suffragan bishops, seven deans and two hundred other clergy. Hobhouse and Clifford Allen in December were the first of over 300 who were released on medical grounds in the next eighteen months.

Though no leading Anglican ecclesiastic was a pacifist, several major figures in the Church of England expressed their concern at the harsh treatment of objectors, and used their influence to secure amelioration of their conditions. Archbishop Davidson spoke in the Lords' debate initiated by Lord Parmoor in May 1917 – though Gilbert Murray protested that the debate was 'scantily reported' and some speeches including the Archbishop's were 'practically suppressed'.[55] The Archbishop said:

> . . . nobody can doubt that there are at this moment men undergoing terms of imprisonment whose character is high, whose motives are unimpeachable, however extraordinary and illogical we may deem them to be; and you are not going to shake them by the adding of month after month or year after year of penal infliction upon them.[56]

Though Davidson found it impossible to understand the absolutists, he spent a great deal of time on individual cases as the hundreds of letters on this subject in the Davidson papers make clear. He had a discussion with Dr Alfred Salter, a Quaker and a Socialist, on this question at the end of 1916. As a result he wrote to the President of the Local Government Board pleading the case of a young man, who, according to Dr Salter, had been refused exemption, arrested, forced to wear khaki and then faced with a court martial. He told the Minister that, after many interviews with the Government, he had hoped that 'these hopelessly unreasonable people' were now no longer placed under military rule which was 'as irrational as it is cruel'. But the Minister was highly unsympathetic, declaring that if the whole matter were raised again, 'much more drastic treatment' would be demanded by public opinion, and that it was not in the interest of C.O.s to 'disturb the present practice'. In May 1917 Davidson wrote to Lord Milner asking him to exercise more common sense and flexibility in their treatment. Davidson expressed the bewilderment of the man of common sense whose deep instincts were law-abiding, in a letter to a correspondent in April 1917:

> We have certainly managed to *muddle* the question of the conscientious objector. But he does make our helping of him nearly impossible. When a man (one of those these letters mention) won't help to make bandages for the sick, or food for the hungry, or relief packets for the destitute, and then refuses to let the doctor examine him even superficially, and yet claims the rights and properties of a *citizen*, for whom the State is responsible, he puts despair into the hearts of those who want to help him, and have spent day after day trying to do it.

A year after the war was over, he wrote to the Chancellor of the Exchequer protesting against the refusal to reinstate conscientious objectors as permanent civil servants on their return to civil employment.[57]

On three occasions Bishop Gore spoke in the House of Lords against the misguided treatment of C.O.s, which was causing great embitterment, though he found many of them 'among the most aggravating human beings with whom I have ever had to deal'. But Gore had a natural sympathy with at least some types of rebellion. The Chief Constable in one area had prohibited the sale of his book *The Sermon on the Mount* (1896) as being likely to undermine the national interest.[58] William Temple protested against popular attitudes to objectors. He believed that from the beginning the Government had 'messed' the question. He wrote in 1916 that the 'contemptuous approach' of the worst tribunals 'remains a reproach to our civilization'.[59] One of the few leading Christians who really understood the absolutist case, though not a pacifist, was Professor A. S. Peake, the Primitive Methodist scholar. His articles, published in 1917 as 'Who is offended and I burn not?', were collected under the title *Prisoners of Hope* in 1918. To those who argued that Christians had no right to citizenship without respecting its obligations, Peake recalled Jeremiah and the early Christian martyrs, who were convinced that love of country could involve strong protests against its policies. Stephen Hobhouse wrote to Peake to tell him that he had described and understood the position of the absolutists more successfully than even their closest sympathizers could have done.[60]

Though only about 5 per cent of the membership of S.C.M. was pacifist, in 1916 the movement was accused of encouraging shirkers and employing pacifists. Some of the strongest support for the right of pacifists to work for and be members of S.C.M. came from its members in the forces. Tissington Tatlow considered that the movement had shown a more balanced attitude towards pacifists than had the Churches.[61]

Victor Gollancz and D. C. Somervell, who were on the staff of Repton, proposed to Geoffrey Fisher, the Headmaster (Archbishop of Canterbury 1945–61) that they should start a Civics class to give boys some idea of the political background of the war and the problems to be faced in the future. Fisher agreed. The classes began in January 1917 and Fisher gave them his support. But, in the words of Fisher's biographer, 'enthusiastic idealism began to outrun discretion'. Fisher took the opportunity of the German offensive of March 1918 to gather the school together to tell them that at such a moment of crisis division in the school was unthinkable. Fisher, who had become alarmed at the turmoil and ferment being created, suspended the classes. He sacked Gollancz, and Somervell withdrew from the school rather than agree to keep silence on political matters. As Gollancz later confessed, he and Somervell, in reaction to the prevailing Toryism of the school and the increasing opposition to their views, had become partisan campaigners for the radical cause.[62]

One of the most interesting and significant protesters was Siegfried Sassoon, an officer from an Anglican and establishment background. After a bad war wound he was invalided back to England, met pacifists including Bertrand Russell, and issued a statement in July 1917:

> I believe that this War, upon which I entered as a war of defence and liberation, has now become a war of aggression and conquest. . . . I have seen and endured the sufferings of the troops, and I can no longer be a party to prolong these sufferings for ends which I believe to be evil and unjust.

Questions were asked in the House, but his protest was smothered by his friend Robert Graves, who felt bitter towards the pacifists who had encouraged Sassoon in his protest. Graves gave the Army an opportunity to hush it all up by giving exaggerated evidence about Sassoon's mental condition. But Sassoon grew to distrust the pacifists and to dislike many of the features of civilian life, and felt an increasing desire to share again the sufferings of his troops, and so returned to the fighting. In a hospital for the shell-shocked he met Wilfred Owen whom he encouraged to express his feelings in poetry.[63] One of Sassoon's poems was entitled 'They':

> The Bishop tells us: 'When the boys come back
> 'They will not be the same; for they'll have fought
> 'In a just cause: they lead the last attack
> 'On Anti-Christ; their comrades' blood has bought
> 'New right to breed an honourable race,
> 'They have challenged Death and dared him face to face.'
>
> 'We're none of us the same!' the boys reply.
> 'For George lost both his legs; and Bill's stone blind;
> 'Poor Jim's shot through the lungs and like to die;
> 'And Bert's gone syphilitic: you'll not find
> 'A chap who's served that hasn't found *some* change.'
> And the Bishop said: 'The ways of God are strange!'

Charles Carrington, who served in both world wars, considered that many soldiers respected 'true pacifists'. Philip, his ordinand brother at Cambridge (later Archbishop of Quebec), was a pacifist. Through him he met other pacifists including a priest who travelled around defending pacifists when they came into conflict with the law.[64] In 1916, R. J. Campbell, by then an Anglican priest, wrote that, though he was not a pacifist, those who like the Quakers were engaged in the dangerous work of mine-sweeping were 'entitled to full respect'.[65]

There were few pacifists among the parochial clergy of the Church of England, but at least in the two cases I have discovered the diocesan bishops concerned acted with magnanimity.

The Reverend Henry Cecil (1882–1954) was born in Bethnal Green, worked as a Billingsgate porter's boy, and then for a cocoa and chocolate manufacturer. Continuing his education at Stepney Working Men's College, he came across many Labour leaders including MacDonald, Henderson, Snowden, and Lansbury. So began his lifelong commitment to Socialism, Education and Pacifism. He was prepared for ordination at King's College, London. After a curacy in Edmonton, in 1913 he joined the staff of Sheffield Parish Church, soon to become the Cathedral with the creation of the diocese in 1914. After the outbreak of war, the spacious stone-flagged churchyard, ideal for out-door meetings, became the scene for regular recruiting campaigns for the armed services, with the active co-operation of the Vicar, and in due course, of the first Bishop and Provost. Henry Cecil found all this deeply repugnant. He therefore began a one-man campaign to counter every such meeting with a rival meeting denouncing the war and church support for it. His only supporters were local pacifists and socialists. He was bitterly opposed by members of the Cathedral congregation, and more than once badly mauled by hostile crowds. But he persisted right through the war. When Bishop Burrows appointed him to his first living, St Philip's, Sheffield, in 1917, he continued his pacifist campaign in this steel-making parish and won over many of his parishioners. The bishop was petitioned to unfrock him, to suspend him, or to remove him from his post. But though the bishop strongly disagreed with him, he always supported his right to express his pacifism. (At first Cecil was opposed with equal conviction to the second war; but as he realized the truth about Hitler and his treatment of the Jews, he abandoned with deep reluctance the pacifism of a lifetime.)[66]

In 1918 a vicar (unnamed) in the diocese of Durham responded to his Bishop's letter in connection with the Man-Power Act by declaring himself to be a pacifist. Bishop Moule (an enthusiastic supporter of the war and a keen patriot) replied to convey his 'deep regret over a view which I can by no means share'. He urged him not to make a parade of his views, but counselled him to make a 'brief and guarded statement' of his views in the parish magazine, suggesting that he might perhaps be sent a copy of the statement before its publication. The bishop disagreed with the parish letter when he saw it; Christ's precepts, he believed, 'primarily affect the individual, and not the organized community, whose organized multiplicity brings in quite new conditions'. But he generously wrote: 'It should win you nothing but respect for your courage of conviction and balance of expression.' In his June magazine the vicar stated bluntly that the 'old way' of 'an eye for an eye' could not be harmonized with the new commandment 'Love your enemies'; 'I cannot square the way of war with the way of Christ.' The bishop on another occasion explained his understanding of the text 'Love your enemies': 'There is no strict analogy between . . . a community . . . and a person.' The state is morally right to take action against another state 'if it violates or threatens its own members in their lawful interests'.[67]

Anglican opinion was almost unanimous in rejecting pacifism. A. C. Headlam wrote, in the *Church Quarterly* for October 1916, that one of the main causes of the war had been the 'well-intentioned but wrong-headed action of pacifists'.[68] Neville Figgis believed that objectors should have liberty to express their consciences, but severe measures were necessary to test the reality of their convictions. In September 1914 he argued that to regard death and suffering as the worst calamities was a form of materialism. Christianity does not seek to abolish force but to consecrate and use it aright. War, like divorce, is part of a sinful world, inevitable because of 'the hardness of our hearts'.[69] Fr Paul Bull, a chaplain in both the Boer and Great Wars, and a fellow-member of the Community of the Resurrection, in 1917 published *Peace and War*. He hoped that these addresses might help 'to justify the honourable profession of our Royal Navy and Army against the false teaching of Pacifism'. He glorified the self-sacrifice of the soldiers as congruent with the Catholic faith which has at its centre the sacrifice of the Mass. War, he believed, was created not by soldiers but by a competitive society and the 'economics of individualism'. Pacifists are enemies to true Peace:

> They invent a religion of their own which is made by omitting from the Gospel all that is painful in it, such as the teaching on Judgment and Hell, which might jar on the high-strung nerves of a luxurious age.[70]

Hastings Rashdall agreed that objectors had the moral right to dissent, but that it was the duty of the state to try to stop the spread of 'such anti-social conduct'.[71]

Writers in *Commonwealth* on a number of occasions denounced what one called, in the November 1917 issue, 'this barbarous state of things'. In May 1916 the question was considered at some length in an article, probably by Scott Holland. The objector, he said, is often charged with neglecting the duty to the national and social conscience:

> But he ought to counter it, not by the personal claim to individual value over against the claim of the state, but by appealing to the higher community, the transcendent fellowship, of which he is a member. The earthly State is *not* the ultimate and absolute category of his conscience. To say so is to be guilty of the very 'Prussianism' which we abhor. The individual personality has that in it by which it looks beyond all the divisions of peoples and nations, and breathes the air of the higher patriotism in loyalty to the Kingdom of Heaven. Therefore, by virtue of the supreme citizenship, it refuses to be absolutely bound within the limits of the lower citizenship of earth. . . . And one cardinal obligation laid upon him by his common

membership of the body is to respect other people's consciences as they have respected his. . . . In claiming to be more than national, he must make it perfectly clear how valid and imperative and holy is the claim of nationality upon him in all that it may rightly ask of him.[72]

That is a particularly fine and perceptive assessment of the pacifist position by one who did not share this view. But, as we have seen, there were many other leaders in the Church of England who were prepared to defend the right to conscientious objection, even though they did not agree with pacifism.

3

The Church's Ministry at Home

Herbert Butterfield wrote movingly in *Christianity and History* (1949) about the ordinary, day-to-day life of the Church, which is almost invariably ignored by the average secular historian:

> The ordinary historian, when he comes, shall we say, to the year 1800 does not think to point out to his readers that in this year, still, as in so many previous years, thousands and thousands of priests and ministers were preaching the Gospel week in and week out, constantly reminding the farmer and the shopkeeper of charity and humility, persuading them to think for a moment about the great issues of life, and inducing them to confess their sins. Yet this was a phenomenon calculated greatly to alter the quality of life and the very texture of human history; and it has been the standing work of the Church throughout the ages – even under the worst of popes here was a light that never went out.[1]

In a study like this it is all too easy simply to concentrate upon the statements of Archbishops, Bishops, and other leaders, and to forget the ordinary priests and people who also compose the Church and by doing so also affect the life of the nation. In trying to imagine the ordinary churchman (or citizen) of the first war period, it is important to remember how much more insular he inevitably was in every way than the ordinary churchman (or citizen) of our own time. Today it is common practice to enclose the diocesan newsletter in the parish magazine to bring a wider viewpoint. In the period of the first war this was unusual. Therefore the average churchman was unlikely to be regularly aware of what Archbishops or Bishops were saying, unless he was one of the minority who read a serious newspaper. If aware at all of the world-wide Church, he would be conscious only of the missionary society supported by his parish. He was not ecumenically-minded towards the other Christian traditions of his own parish, nation or world. He had almost certainly never travelled abroad, and had probably never been further than his own local big town or seaside resort. There was no television or radio to enlarge his horizons or his sympathies.

Therefore in considering the ministry of the Church at home during the first war, it is worth first of all recounting the life of a small parish as revealed in the monthly parish magazine of Alsager in Cheshire. Alsager lies between Crewe and Stoke-on-Trent; its population in 1901 was 2,597. The two Anglican churches were run as one parish under a vicar and a curate. The picture that emerges from the magazines is both heartening and depressing. It is heartening, in so far as we see the Church trying to keep a community in good shape under stress, organizing many good works of charity and compassion, aware of its responsibilities to Christians in India as well as to the troops, praying, celebrating the sacraments and reading the Scriptures faithfully, and putting much effort into the National Mission. It is depressing, in that only once did any note of dissent about the war appear through the magazine. And the exception is significant: a donated war memorial picture seemed to unite the sacrifice of soldiers with the sacrifice of Christ in a manner which offended the vicar's theology. (We shall discuss this particular incident further in Chapter 8.) In Martin Luther King's phraseology, the Church was, broadly speaking, a thermometer reflecting the temperature of surrounding society, rather than a thermostat trying to alter it.[2]

Reading the issues of the magazine immediately prior to the war, one receives the impression that the war came from nowhere. Everything was going on normally with the usual round of events; then suddenly the issue for September 1914 was full of war news. The vicar was gratified that Alsager had so readily contributed men to the front, and money to the National Relief Fund. Daily services of intercession (which lasted throughout the war) were immediately established and well attended. The vicar exhorted the people to pray and expect privation, to be cheerful and steadfast. The war is on a hitherto unknown scale, he said, and 'it must be many months before the last shot is fired'. What is happening is 'hastening the coming of the Lord'. The Alsager Red Cross Working Party held its preliminary meeting six days after the outbreak of war. Already, yards of tape, calico, shirting, red flannel and cotton, pounds of wool for socks and mufflers had been purchased. Next month the vicar announced that the Parish Mission due in January would be postponed. The missioner was becoming an Army Chaplain, and would not be available unless the war was over by the end of November. The appeal for the Belgian Relief Fund had been a success. By the end of September the working party had sent to the headquarters of the Red Cross: 56 bandages, 24 pillow-cases, 56 nightshirts, 7 pairs of bedsocks, 48 mufflers, 2 pairs of cuffs, 35 day shirts, 24 pairs of socks, 30 bedjackets, 24 hot-water bottle covers and 2 pairs of sheets.

In December 1914 we read that a muffled peal was rung for Field-Marshal Earl Roberts and that the Dead March had been played after morning service. The vicar wrote that the war was bringing out the good characteristics of people which in peacetime often lie below the surface, but also the 'callousness and selfishness of others . . . shown up by the continued round of pleasure-seeking and utter indifference to the needs of our country at this time'.

In the new year, the vicar celebrated the 'old alliance between Church and State which is still happily here' – symbolized by the hanging of the Union Jack in the two churches, and by the singing of the National Anthem at Sunday services. We could not have withstood the German armies, he wrote, 'unless the God of battles had been with us'. The Church of England Men's Society listened to a *Daily Mail* war lecture on 'How British pluck won through in France', illustrated by slides. Patriotic songs opened the meeting. The Alsager branch of the Northern Children's Union 'At Home' included a tobacco stall run for men at the front; there was also 'a roaring trade in patriotic buttonholes'. A play entitled 'The War of the Fairies' depicted soldiers of different nationalities, including the 'truculent Kaiser' and 'our treasured Tommy Atkins'. A 'stirring rendering' of 'Your King and Country wants you' was also given. The Fire Brigade, Ambulance Corps and Boy Scouts were among a large congregation for National Intercession Sunday on 3 January 1915. The February magazine included a letter from a chaplain expressing gratitude for pipes, mittens, socks, scarves, and gloves.

In June 1915, the news was given that the curate had joined the R.A.M.C. as a private. In August he gave a realistic account of army life – little food; 120 sleeping in a barn with rats; much bad language; the one or two who tried to pray were ridiculed. By September 1915 the first casualties were recorded; letters giving the details of their brave deaths were quoted. In October the former curate was now writing from Gallipoli; the men were living in the open in dug-outs; stretcher squads went to the dressing station near the firing line to bring back the wounded to the field hospital.

In December 1915 the vicar began to prepare the parish for the

National Mission. The first Sunday of 1916 was a 'Day of Humiliation and Prayer'. The council and other civic groups attended. The Congregationalist Minister read one of the lessons. The collection was given to the Serbian Relief Fund. The main feature of the magazine for January 1916 was a long article on 'War Work for Women'. Every available woman and girl should respond to the country's need. At Easter the statement of accounts included £6 for Aircraft Insurance. That summer a framed list of men on active service was placed in the porch. Month by month the plans for the National Mission were unfolded. The vicar clearly expected the parish to take it very seriously. Intercessions for it were regularly offered, every house circulated, groups formed to study the Mission handbook and courses of addresses delivered. A procession was made through the village with addresses and prayers at suitable points along the route. When the Bishop's Messenger came, sixty resolution cards were taken by the congregation.

In February 1917, a strong appeal was launched for War Savings. The two Sunday schools, the Church of England Men's Society, the Girls' Friendly Society, and the Girl's Club started Savings Associations. An appeal was also made for the work of the G.F.S. among young girls working in munitions factories. A contribution was sent to the St Dunstan's Home for Blind Soldiers. The Food Controller's restrictions were printed in black type in the magazine. Easter services that year were held according to the new summer time. The vicar repeated his conviction that the coming of the Lord would now not be long delayed. In accordance with the King's command, on four successive Sundays the royal proclamation about food economy was read in church. The C.E.M.S. continued to study the National Mission outlines. In August the awards of war decorations to Alsager men were detailed. An Appeal was made for more men to join the Home Defence Corps. By November, the dead from Alsager totalled twenty-five. They were specially remembered at an All Saints' Day Communion and at the annual memorial service at All Saints'-tide. Also in November, the special Missionary week was hampered by lack of literature owing to the shortage of paper. Food restrictions prevented any refreshments being served at the annual Parish Tea.

The magazines for 1918 appeared on very thin brownish paper. The new scale of food rations was announced, and it was suggested that the scale should be cut out and hung up in the dining room — 'a most practical way to win the war'. The deliverance of Jerusalem from the Turks 'seems to point to the dawn of a new era in the world's history', wrote the vicar. On Sunday 6 January, the King's call for a special Day of Prayer and Thanksgiving was answered by extra celebrations of Communion, a civic service and open-air services round the village: 'At each place the King's Proclamation will be read, followed by two or three prayers and the names of the men serving with the colours, whose homes are in the vicinity, and a special invitation will be given to attend the Services in the Church.' In the same issue, the vicar wrote: 'Everyone read with a thrill of pride and pleasure Sir Douglas Haig's account of the splendid attack made by our troops on Tuesday, Nov. 20th', in which tanks played an important part; an Alsager man was killed in the battle. (This presumably was at Cambrai; church bells were rung in London, the only time during the war, to celebrate the victory.)

Meanwhile the C.E.M.S. were looking ahead with a discussion on 'Trade with Germany after the war'. The collapse of Russia caused the vicar to urge more prayer and greater attendance at the daily intercessions. The war took men to far-off places which they had previously only heard about in Sunday School.[3] One wrote to say that he had just marched through Hebron, Bethlehem and Jerusalem. When he received his Easter Communion in Jerusalem, the padre gave him a special commemorative card. The former curate, who had served with the R.A.M.C., was now a chaplain to 'the newly constituted Royal Air Force'. The present curate had started to help the national effort by working three days a week on a farm and therefore would do less parish visiting. In June 1918 the vicar wrote: 'The clergy were very sorry that it was eventually decided to leave them out of the recent Man-Power Bill.' The vicar of the next parish was going to be a chaplain, and as the Alsager clergy would have to be responsible for that parish as well, services would be curtailed. It was hoped that the seat-holders at Christ Church would be 'only too pleased' to accommodate their neighbours from St Mary's where all seats were free. That summer wounded soldiers from a near-by hospital were entertained. An Aeroplane Week was held; the area was asked to raise £10,000 for war purposes; one aeroplane was to bear the name 'Alsager'. By the autumn of 1918, lighting and fuel restrictions were causing alterations to services; though many parishes had given up evening services, they continued in Alsager. The parish was 'rejoicing' at the 'splendid victories that are now being granted to us'.

In Alsager, the Armistice was greeted with 'profound thankfulness to the All-Wise and All-Loving Father, Who has heard our prayers and given us the victory'. 'Let us say nothing and do nothing', wrote the vicar, 'to mar what has been won for us by our glorious dead and by those who have faced death so long.' On Armistice Day, the bells rang out, the school children cheered, the streets were crowded, the flags were waved, the church was full for a service of thanksgiving. The war was over. But the 1919 magazine began with further news of deaths as a result of the war. Former prisoners of war were to be guests at the Annual Parish Tea. By March the vicar was lamenting a decline of religious observance after the celebrations. The C.E.M.S. had its horizons widened by hearing about a gunner's experiences in India, Mesopotamia, and South Africa. It also discussed Church Endowments. In the May magazine the plans for the first Parochial Church Council were announced. The War Working Party ended its work. In four and a half years they had made 5,443 articles for the fighting men. Choir trips and Sunday School trips were resumed. A memorial window was placed in the church with pictures of St George in armour and St Alban in Roman dress, both with drawn swords. In July a Peace Thanksgiving Service was held in which Nonconformist ministers took part. But in the August 1919 magazine the vicar was distressed at the state of the nation:

> The spirit of patriotism and comradeship which was so manifest during the dark days of the war seems to have given place to a spirit of reckless selfishness and disinclination for work. . . . Trade is being driven out of the country very rapidly and there are other nations eager to supplant us in the markets of the world. The only thing that can save us is work. . . . The Germans have already realised that work is the only remedy for the disasters they have brought upon themselves by the war, and they are now settling to work with a will, many being content to take lower wages than in pre-war days. . . . It will be deplorable if we lose by our folly and selfishness what our sailors and soldiers and airmen have fought and died to save. So let us 'be strong and work', trusting in the same God Who has been our refuge all through the war.

When the war memorial was erected in Alsager in 1920, 41 names out of a population of 2,693 were placed on it. The inscription was taken from Revelation 12.11: 'They loved not their lives unto the death'.

How did leading Anglicans define the ministry of the Church of England to a nation at war? In 1894, Mandell Creighton (Bishop of London 1897–1901) had said in his Primary Charge to the

Peterborough Diocese that the Church 'must always be the guardian, the educator and the exponent of the national conscience'.[4] In 1915 Winnington-Ingram, his successor in London, wrote that the Church

> exists to inspire the nation to take a noble and high-minded line of policy, to fill the sailors and soldiers with fortitude and courage, and give them in abundance the spiritual and sacramental help they need; to set an example itself of self-sacrificing service; to visit the sick and wounded; to comfort the mourners; and to lead day and night the intercessions of the people.[5]

This is admirable in many ways, but we note that he did not envisage any prophetic or dissenting role for the Church. Hensley Henson, as we should expect, was a good deal clearer about what the Church should avoid than about what it could actually accomplish:

> . . . war confronts the responsible leaders of the Christian Churches with a situation of extraordinary complexity and danger. They cannot ignore the abnormal responsiveness to spiritual appeals. They cannot escape the formidable risk of compromising with superstition when they seek to strengthen religion.[6]

Gore was too keenly aware of the dangers of patriotism and the fundamental tragedy of war to indulge in easy jingoism. He was too oppressed by the failures of the Church of England to try to use the war to bolster up the established regime. 'You youngish ones', he wrote to a naval chaplain, 'must start off the Church of England again. We old ones have made a mess of it. The only thing fit for us would be to send us to the trenches to be food for Black Marias.'[7] By contrast, Winnington-Ingram told the boys at Marlborough that the Church was 'the oldest fighting regiment in Europe'. In his Pastoral Letter of July 1915, he asked the clergy to redouble their prayers and provide more celebrations of Holy Communion. The soul of the nation must be appealed to for a spirit of unselfish service. St James's Day should be set aside for prayer, but in the afternoon or evening street processions with short addresses might be held. Invitations could be sent to other religious communities and heads of public bodies. The 'unrivalled organisation' of the Church could be used – to help the poor to fill in registration forms, and to explain the Registration Bill; to persuade women to take on men's jobs and relatives to allow loved ones to go to places of danger. 'In all these ways the Church must justify its claim to be the National Church.' Half a million copies of his special message to the people of London were distributed. In it he quoted the boy who wrote to his mother before he was killed, 'I have come out, mother, that you and the sisters may not be treated as the Belgian women have been.' Pray, repent, serve, save, the bishop exhorted his people; there must be no waste, and people should invest in War Loans. He quoted St Paul: 'I die daily'. He gave this challenge: 'Is the message of CHRIST from the Cross to be the standard of mankind, or the modern German teaching that might is right?'[8] Sassoon's George Sherston arrived at Charing Cross on a stretcher after travelling with 'a cargo of men in whose minds the horrors they had escaped from were still vitalized and violent'. At the station, as he was carried through the crowds, a woman handed him a bunch of flowers 'and a leaflet by the Bishop of London who earnestly advised me to lead a clean life and attend Holy Communion'.[9]

In dealing with questions such as reprisals, hatred for Germany, the use of poison gas and the treatment of conscientious objectors, Archbishop Davidson was prepared to take an unpopular line: 'we mean to come out with clean hands' he said in 1917.[10] He was in constant contact with politicians. In August 1918 he summarized his political activities during the preceding three months:

> I have been in pretty close touch with prominent actors and thinkers who have been handling English affairs and policy. Abundant talks with men like Curzon, Bryce, Crewe, sometimes Asquith, occasionally Arthur Balfour, and occasionally Lloyd George. Also with men of a different group or grade, Sanderson, Newton, Kenyon of the British Museum, the Speaker, the Lord Chancellor, and military men like Maurice, occasionally Robertson, and the War Office administrators, and so on. Besides this, I have been in close and constant touch with Stamfordham, who has kept me abreast of many things, and prevented my ever being quite out of touch with any important things which were happening, or under debate. I have also had my ears open in the House of Lords, where I have attended with great regularity, and in the House of Commons when important things were under debate.[11]

This activity was in line with his considered definition of the role of the bishops in national life which he had expressed in his Charge to the Clergy of the diocese of Winchester in 1899:

> Bishops, in short, are entrusted, as I believe, with a place in the

Legislature not only for what are technically called Ecclesiastical questions, but for whatever things directly concern the moral life and the social well-being of the English people.[12]

He had no doubt that the British were fighting 'on behalf of what is just, righteous, and true'. But his pastoral concerns were not only expressed through political channels. His sensitive heart responded to a wide range of human need. After each raid on towns in the Canterbury diocese in 1917, he visited everyone who had been wounded and large numbers of the bereaved in their own homes. Throughout the war, he repeatedly pressed the Government to negotiate an *en bloc* exchange of prisoners of war and in October 1918 spoke of the widespread indignation at the slowness of the Government to respond. Being so immersed in the many problems raised by the war, he could not understand why questions of liturgical reform seemed to occupy the forefront of the minds of certain churchmen.[13]

Nearly all the bishops at this period had been educated at the leading public schools and at Oxford or Cambridge. Many were connected by birth or marriage with the landed gentry or the peerage.[14] Most of the parish clergy came from different educational and social backgrounds from their parishioners. At the beginning of the century the Society of the Sacred Mission and the Community of the Resurrection had established courses of theological training for ordinands, many of whom, because of their lack of money and education, might not otherwise have been ordained at all. Before the war, ordinands without private means had to rely on charities or sporadic and ill-organized diocesan help. Fr Bull told the Chapter at Mirfield: 'We have invented a class priesthood with a money qualification.' Gore, then Superior, agreed and described the system as 'a new form of simony'.[15] In 1902, therefore, the College of the Resurrection was established. It was not until after the war, in accordance with decisions made in 1909, that at least a year's residence in a theological college was required from all graduate ordinands.[16] Before 1914 some graduates, particularly those from Oxford and Cambridge, were ordained without any theological college training, and others spent only a term or so in a college.[17] Several of the theological colleges were situated in close proximity to, and had close relationships with, the ancient cathedrals, and ordinands at a formative stage were apt to envisage the ministry in the context of a small town rather than in the context of the far more secularized industrial cities. Mirfield broke with these conventions. Its college looked not over a cathedral close, but over the mill chimneys of the Calder Valley, near Huddersfield. Nevertheless, to give working-class ordinands a theological college training was inevitably to predispose them to become more middle-class in outlook.

The war brought clergy into a closer relationship with the people, both through the work of chaplains at the front, and through the sharing of privations, bereavement and a common cause, though clergy were sometimes sneered at for not being combatants. As we have seen, some of the clergy joined the home defence forces, and others did part-time work in secular occupations. Mrs Paget, wife of the Bishop of Stepney, queued for food up to three hours at a time. She felt that in this way she could share the experiences and difficulties of her neighbours.[18] But there was a gulf between those at home and those at the front, and both sides felt this. Peter Green wrote in the *Manchester Guardian* for 1 June 1916:

> Often as I sit opposite some lad back from the trenches, a mere boy in years yet a man in the horrors he has seen and endured and in the responsibilities he has shouldered, I ask myself two questions – namely 'Why is so much that is all important to me of such small importance to him?' And again 'What right have I to pass judgment on a man's destiny, and on the real values of things, before this lad whose experience is not of books but of life?'

Bishop Talbot had three sons at the front, one as a combatant and two as chaplains; he was chairman of the commission which produced *The Army and Religion* in 1919; but he also felt a gulf between himself and the troops. He had been brought up in what now seemed the secure days of Victoria. He wrote to Neville: 'you have been through the Fire; which was just what we had not.'[19] When the Revd Arthur Hopkinson asked Talbot, who was his bishop, for permission to leave his parish to serve as a naval chaplain, Talbot replied by giving him an extra parish to look after; he told Hopkinson that his job for the duration was 'patient continuance in well-doing', a view which Archbishop Lang and B. K. Cunningham and others stressed to those who felt restless as parish priests.[20]

In a Charge to his clergy Bishop Talbot in 1916 told them that, for the Church, the slogan 'Business as usual' was an inadequate response to the war situation.[21] Certainly, the Church of England tried hard, both nationally and locally, to minister pastorally to the nation. There were occasions of special effort – one was the National Mission (which will be surveyed at the end of this chapter); another was the organization of National Days of Prayer. Special prayers for the war were issued on 4 August 1914. Special days of prayer were held regularly throughout the war. But when the Evangelical Alliance pressed for a Day of Prayer to be held by royal proclamation in 1917, Lloyd George and Bonar Law were nervous lest such a proclamation would be misunderstood by allies and enemies alike. For these special occasions of prayer the Victorian term 'Day of Humiliation' was not used; Davidson had been opposed to its use in the South African War.[22] In addition, special local days of prayer were held in many parishes and cathedrals. Many churches had services in the late evening; in the East End as many as a hundred people might attend. In its back streets small shrines decorated with flowers sprang up spontaneously. On them the names of those from the street who had joined up were recorded. Intercessions were constantly made at the shrines. During the raids on London, East End churches were often used as shelters, and people would bring their belongings and pets. A priest in Haggerston described a typical scene:

It was a wonderful and pathetic sight to see our people grouped round the altar, taking part in simple devotions in the Presence of the Blessed Sacrament, and this has been going on for a week (Sept. 1917), so you can understand how tired we all are. A serious raid was on from 11 p.m. till 3.15 a.m. this morning and we were in church with our people. The noise outside was terrific, but Father Walters at the organ kept us singing hymn after hymn. Then at last, with children fast asleep and weary mothers with their little ones in their arms, and fathers of families keeping cheerful to hearten others, we made thanksgiving to God for the protection again vouchsafed to us. As there were many present who would miss their Communion in the morning after their long vigil, I decided to say Mass at once and there were thirty communicants. I got to bed 4 a.m. and said Mass again at 8 a.m.

When a bomb killed between twenty and thirty children at a school in Poplar, the Bishops of London and Stepney took the funeral.[23]

Soon after the war began, Conrad Noel placed a group of Allied flags in one aisle at the church at Thaxted grouped round a picture of St George slaying the dragon; kneelers and votive candle stands completed the wartime shrine. During 1916 he added the Red Flag, symbol of world socialism and internationalism. The old Irish flag was replaced with the Sinn Fein emblem.[24] During the war Dick Sheppard began the practice of keeping St Martin-in-the-Fields open day and night for all sorts of people to drop in. The crypt was used as an air raid shelter.[25] At the end of the war the parishioners of St Philip's Salford – most of them poor – clubbed together to give their Rector, Peter Green, a presentation to express their love and gratitude to him for his care of them over the war years. The Salford Royal Hospital also made a presentation, to express gratitude for all his work in the hospital.[26] At the beginning of the war he devoted two of his weekly articles in the *Manchester Guardian* to the pastoral opportunities provided by the war. (He was in much demand as a lecturer in pastoralia and wrote several books on the subject.) The parish priest should call at every home when he hears that a member of the family is joining up, pray with the family and give the service man a blessing. The priest should warn him about the dangers of drunkenness and vice, and should write to him at least once a month while he is away. Parents should be regularly visited. Passages from the letters of service-men should be read out at services of intercession. These should be held daily, led by priest or laity and be as informal and *ex tempore* as possible. Churches should be kept open for prayer. Duplicated sheets with suggestions for prayer should be provided. A daily Communion was of great intercessory value. He understood the desire of younger priests to enlist, but he believed that the priest had a vital role: 'Our work may not be heroic. But I think it is worth doing.'[27]

Ronald Knox published a penny book of meditations *An Hour at the Front* early in the war. It sold over 70,000 copies. There were twelve sections of two pages each, each section headed by a clock face marking the passage of five minutes:

> Pray for Victory for the arms of the country . . . remember in the sight of God the justice of our cause . . . the untried whose hearts fail them at the moment of battle . . . that Churches may be spared, that Church worship may be unhindered . . . Picture to yourself that, even now as you pray, there are probably numbers of souls enduring the terrible agony of parting from their bodies and few of them able to face the next world with sure confidence . . . Think of the poor souls in Purgatory . . .

These meditations were the fruit of a retreat he spent during the Long Vacation of 1914 when he spent six hours a day at prayer. When he returned to Oxford in October to his work as Chaplain of Trinity, the empty quadrangles made him sick at heart.[28]

In 1915–16 the S.P.C.K. published a series of 'War-Time Tracts for the Workers'. Various writers, including Bishops Gore and Paget, Albert Mansbridge and Canons Peter Green, Cyril Garbett and J. H. B. Masterman, tried to answer a variety of questions in the brief space allowed. On the whole the Tracts were written in notably temperate language; indeed two (Nos. 4 and 15) quoted the famous words of Edith Cavell on patriotism. Cyril Garbett (No. 2) argued that 'the Christian citizen is guiltless if he uses the sword in the cause of his country', when the war is just. The soldier, like the executioner, can kill without hating.[29] Peter Green in 'Wasted Lives?' (No. 4) declared that the selfish man is the unhappy man, but if he has responded to the call of duty he has 'learned life's lesson. His is no wasted life.' Howard Masterman in 'The Life Beyond Death' (No. 7) wrote of his conviction that life beyond death makes present sacrifice fruitful. 'Take away the belief in a future life and you take away all adequate motive for high and noble action.' Men who have died in battle have faced death prepared, because they have shown 'patience and cheerfulness and courage'. But there are lessons to be learned beyond the grave. 'We should hardly dare to say of any man that he had become so evil in will that he can never be saved.' We should pray for the dead as they pray for us. Other Tracts dealt with the alienation of the working classes from the Church, the necessity of church reform to give laity a share in government, the nature of prayer and the duty to forgive our enemies while hating their evil deeds. Some attacked the sins of the nation (drink, gambling, impurity, pleasure-seeking, 'profit-making callousness', the competitive spirit in commercial and industrial life) and celebrated the restrictions on alcohol in England, France and Russia. The Church must be concerned not only with the cultivation of souls, but also with social justice. Many of the Tracts appealed for more people to support the principles of Christ through active membership of the church – e.g. No. 8, 'The King Needs You', by Howard Masterman.

But as the war went on, criticism of the Church mounted. The casualty lists grew, with little or nothing to show for them. It was inevitable that the public at home and the soldiers at the front, in their weariness and anger, should seek out familiar and broad targets to attack. In February 1918 Archbishop Davidson talked with Asquith about the question:

I asked him, did he think that the Church, using that word in its widest sense, was fairly chargeable with having failed to find and use its opportunities during the war. He replied that, on the whole, he did think so, though it was difficult to speak positively, and he admitted that everyone is apt to criticise everyone else at such a time. I asked him to put his finger, if he could, on any special lack of duty on our part, or to name any time during the war when it had been specific and definite. He could not do so, and I pressed him as to whether the dissatisfaction in the matter, which undoubtedly exists, is not the rather fretful criticism of other people which is the outcome of general dissatisfaction with the condition of things. It would be different if he could name anything specific, but he certainly could not.

He also asked Asquith whether the Church could do more at the moment for the cause of peace and goodwill. Asquith considered that the Archbishop in his public utterances had done what he could in contrast to Bishop Winnington-Ingram 'who preached . . . sheer jingoism of the shallowest kind. He thought his utterances deplorable.' Davidson told Asquith that, like Lord Lansdowne, he thought that 'peace by sheer victory' was unobtainable, and asked him to tell him frankly if he had any suggestions to make as to a way in which he could help. But Asquith had no suggestion to offer.[30]

The National Mission of Repentance and Hope in the autumn of 1916 was an attempt by the Church of England to respond to the spiritual needs of the nation in wartime; an attempt to discharge its sense of vocation to act as the Christian conscience of the nation. It was also intended as a powerful reply to those (including Horatio Bottomley) who argued that the Church of England was not rising to the needs of the hour. Peter Green gave strong voice to this conviction in the *Manchester Guardian* as early as 20 August 1914. His Catholic churchmanship, socialist sympathies and experience of slum parishes had made him critical of the religious establishment. The war deepened his conviction that all the churches had much less influence on English society than they supposed. On 14 and 21 January 1915 he wrote on 'The Total Failure of the Church'. It was not enough, he said, to assure the nation that its cause was righteous. It was no good concentrating on the few weeks before the war while neglecting the previous forty years. It was a time for searching of hearts and beating of breasts, but so often churchmen seemed only too eager to believe evil of Germany. He returned to these themes on many occasions, and called upon Nation and Church to repent, particularly in a series of articles from 6 January to 16 March 1916. The churches' present failures were but a continuation of pre-war days. They had taught neither the meaning of non-resistance, nor Christ's call to evangelical poverty. They had failed to understand the aspirations of the workers, failed to enlist the support of the intellectuals and upper classes, failed to give adequate training and nourishment to regular churchgoers, failed to create a genuinely popular style of worship. 'Men look to her [sc. the Church] and see not a nation on its knees seeking its God, but a corporation on its defence taking care of its endowments', he wrote on 17 February. That a successor of the apostles should live in a palace was a scandal, and implied that a bishop by his style of life belonged to the upper classes. Nothing would impress the nation more than a great surrender by the Church of England of its wealth and privilege. He called for a surrender of spiritual privilege as well: Free Churchmen should be able to receive Communion and preach in the Church of England – a very unusual proposal for a Catholic churchman of that period to make.

In retrospect, the remarkable thing is not the comparative lack of success of the National Mission (though it is difficult to know what the best hopes of its organizers really were) but that it should have been mounted at all. Today, sixty years later, the Church of England still does not find it easy to act as a corporate body; that it should have attempted to do so in a period when rivalries of churchmanship and clerical, parochial and diocesan individualism were much greater than today is creditable, though of course the war effort had tended to unite the church in a common cause. Much hard work went into both the Mission itself and into the five follow-up committees. William Temple, then Rector of St. James's Piccadilly, was at the heart of the Mission, as he was the main leader of the 'Life and Liberty Movement' which followed and in some ways grew out of it.

At the beginning of the war, it was widely asserted that a religious revival was under way. The churches were full, it was said, because at last people were faced with basic and ultimate realities, and had turned from selfishness and squabbles to respond sacrificially to a great moral cause. Theodore Woods, Vicar of Bradford (he became Bishop of Peterborough in 1916) wrote in October 1914:

I believe the Church is about to have the chance of her life. . . . The churches are crowded with worshippers, and people seem to be up against the realities in a way which three months ago would have seemed impossible.[31]

But soon it became apparent that a religious revival was not occurring.[32] In 1915 the Archbishop of Canterbury invited twelve priests of different schools of thought to report to him on 'The Spiritual Call to the Nation and the Church – what is being done by the War and what should be done'. The group included four who later became bishops (William Temple, W. H. Frere, E. A. Burroughs and G. C. Joyce), Bishop Gore and Canon Peter Green, an experienced parish missioner. Despite the pessimism of Gore and Peter Green, in October 1915 the group recommended 'a National Mission led by the Archbishops . . . through all the cities and towns and villages of the land'. It aimed to remove misconceptions about the Gospel, to call the people to repentance, both corporate and personal, and so to claim that in the Living Christ 'lies the one sure hope'. Under the enthusiastic chairmanship of Winnington-Ingram, and with William Temple as one of the secretaries, the Council set about organizing the Mission, though each diocese was asked to formulate its own precise plans.[33]

The Free Churches were kept informed of the plans for the Mission, and sent their good wishes, but could not see their way to conducting a parallel operation. An official outline of the message of the Mission was provided for the missioners, though its use was optional. It began with a passage from Deuteronomy 30: 'See, I have set before thee this day life and good, and death and evil; . . . therefore choose life'; God has a purpose for the nation, but the nation has ignored God. This has resulted in corruption and disorder:

> Our great social cleavages and industrial strifes show that something is fundamentally wrong in our national life. . . . We have a righteous cause in the great war; but the civil war which seemed imminent in Ireland in the summer of 1914, and the great industrial war, for which preparation was then being made, were evidence of something radically wrong among ourselves.

The nation must therefore repent and return to God to work for the Kingdom through Jesus Christ in the fellowship of the Church. Temple believed that there had been too much individualistic Christianity in the past. We needed now to return to the Old Testament belief that God deals with nations as nations. There had been signs of repentance in the national life already, for many had turned from selfishness to sacrifice. But this repentance had been ethical rather than religious; it must be rooted in religion if it was to last when the crisis was over.[34]

E. A. Burroughs's long book, *The Valley of Decision* (1916), is a good example of the type of thinking which produced the National Mission, and of the widespread desire to use the catastrophe of war to shock both Church and nation into a new way of life. In the first two months of the war, wrote Burroughs, 'we seemed to be emancipated into a higher, purer air'.[35] But the mood soon cooled. Strikes, selfishness in capital and labour, drunkenness, brothels, desecration of Sunday, gambling, the failure of churches and politicians to rise to the occasion, the lack of any real revival of religion at home or among the troops: all indicated the tragic fact that the nation was failing to realize how decisive was the hour. The British, with their policy of 'muddling through', had not grasped the need for a powerful philosophy of life with which to combat the well-organized and articulate philosophies of Germany: for this was 'a philosopher's war'.[36] Going to war was itself the beginning of a surrender to God, but Church and nation lacked complete commitment to unselfishness and sacrifice. 'The baptismal promise is a soldier's oath.'[37] 'Christianity, in fact, thus viewed as the completest system for subordinating the principle of self to "the Spirit of the Whole", is, humanly speaking, a *sine qua non* for anything like full national recovery.'[38] Burroughs entitled his final chapter 'For Their Sakes'.

Davidson himself summoned all the clergy of his diocese to Canterbury Cathedral in January 1916 for their corporate preparation for the Mission, which was due to begin in October. Afterwards the Vicar of Ramsgate described the deep impression which the Archbishop's addresses had made:

> It was all very deliberate, very simple, very grave. He managed to convey to us straight away on the first evening his own sense of the almost overpowering opportunity of such a moment.[39]

Bishop Gore, throwing aside his doubts, gave a strong lead in his own diocese of Oxford, and through it to the whole Church. Over 600 priests, virtually all the parochial clergy, attended one of the five retreats he arranged for them. His Diocesan Council, like that of many other dioceses, was prodded into asking why the Church of England was not more effective as a spiritual and moral force.[40] In the Manchester diocese, Bishop Knox called his clergy to a day conference in

September; nearly 1,000 of the 1,025 priests attended. After Holy Communion, the Bishop addressed them on the divine judgement brought by the war – is it to be a 'day of hardening in unbelief, or the beginning of a new life'?, he asked them. He stressed the missionary task of the Church; among the hymns was 'There were ninety and nine' to Sankey's tune. As in other dioceses, outline sermons were produced – one of the contributors was Peter Green – and the Pilgrimage of Prayer was organized with little bands of women going from village to village, their necessities in knapsacks.[41] In the Durham diocese, another Evangelical, Bishop Moule, had a personal interview with each Messenger before sending them out on their missions at a great service in the cathedral. His summary of the achievements of the Mission was expressed almost exclusively in terms of the deepening of individual spirituality.[42] Theodore Woods, Bishop of Peterborough, told his diocese: 'Our supreme hope is that the National Mission may issue in a reformed Britain. But this can only come from re-formed Dioceses, re-formed parishes, and of course ultimately from re-formed individuals.' When the Mission was over, he continued the Diocesan Mission Council to promote the evangelistic work of the diocese, and to deepen the spiritual life through retreats and conferences. Another result of the Mission was his decision in 1917 to spend two or three weeks each year walking round the village parishes in his purple cassock, staff in hand, talking to all he met, visiting homes, churches and schools, a practice which he continued when he became Bishop of Winchester in 1924. It appealed strongly to the public imagination. Cyril Garbett followed his example, first in the rural areas of Southwark, then as Bishop of Winchester, and later as Archbishop of York.[43]

Far removed from the solemn gathering called by the Archbishop in Canterbury Cathedral, its monuments protected by sandbags, were the activities of Geoffrey Studdert Kennedy who was asked to cover the whole army in France on behalf of the Mission. For ten days he preached three times a day to audiences ranging from 500 to 1,500. Horatio Bottomley of *John Bull* (popularly known as 'Tommy's Bible') had ridiculed the Church for calling the fighting men to repentance: they were 'saints and heroes' not sinners. Studdert Kennedy told the troops, 'I see *John Bull* says you're all saints; well, all I can say is, "eyes right" and look at your neighbour.' Frederick Macnutt met Kennedy at Boulogne to talk over the Mission and, discovering that Kennedy wrote verse, he suggested that he should write a poem for the men. The result was 'A Sermon in a Billet', the first of the dialect poems:

Our Padre says I'm a sinner, and John Bull says I'm a saint,
And both of 'em's sure to be liars, for I'm neither of 'em, I aint' . . .[44]

(The dialect poems were in the style evolved by Kipling in his 'Barrack-Room Ballads'.) Another chaplain, Fr Keble Talbot C.R., also went round speaking to the troops on behalf of the Mission. He tried, he wrote to his brethren at Mirfield

> to challenge men, in the light of war's apocalypse at once of true and of false values, to recognise the Kingship of our Lord, to ask whether there was any rival, and if not to make devotedness to His Kingdom the core of their religion. . . . I tried to meet the prophet of thousands, Bottomley, in his denunciation of repentance.[45]

Douglas Downes (later Brother Douglas of the Society of St Francis) was Chaplain of a convalescent camp near Cairo. Three hundred men, glad to get away from barracks, went to the opening meeting to hear the missioner, E. A. Burroughs. Bishop Gwynne, deputy Chaplain-General with special responsibility for the troops in France, threw himself into the organization of the National Museum on the western front with characteristic enthusiasm, stimulated by messages of support from the Archbishop of Canterbury, generals and many commanding officers.[46] The Bishop wrote the introduction to an account of the Mission at the front which bore the significant title *Religion and Morale* (1917).

John Bull had accused Winnington-Ingram of obsession with the sins of drink and lust. The Bishop asked Horatio Bottomley to come to tea. His charm prevailed and Bottomley offered him free space in his magazine for three weeks to write about the Mission, and offered to pay £500 to a charity. The Mission Council, however, did not approve of the idea of an article beginning 'Dear Brother', and confessing the sins of the Church, in a publication edited by a man of already dubious reputation. With some reason Winnington-Ingram regretted this lost opportunity (though he was less fitted for this task than he believed): 'I wanted to reach the ordinary man in the street, whereas I am afraid the Mission only reached, in the main, those who were already Church people.' Field-Marshal Robertson produced the odd slogan which appeared on posters all round London: 'Some put their trust in horses, and some in chariots, but I am old-fashioned enough to put my trust in the Lord God'. Winnington-Ingram visited every diocese in the country. The message which he took to them was that this was a war to end war; that the comradeship of the trenches would continue after the war; that as duke and ploughman had died together, so all classes would understand each other better now; that there would be a new church after the war, better adapted to the needs of the people; that there would be a new world when the war was over.[47] The title of the Mission created confusion in the minds of many; it was not only Bottomley who failed to understand the call for 'repentance'. Winnington-Ingram took up this theme in one of his addresses. Certainly, he said, the war arose from the sin of Europe as a whole but 'the special guilt attaches to Germany, and not to us or our allies'. It would have been 'sinful' for Britain to have avoided fighting. He suggested some national sins to be penitent about: national disunity revealed by strife in industry and conflict between the sexes before the war; the neglect of prayer and Sunday worship; the size of the national drink bill; ten per cent of the population was infected by contagious diseases – we are, he said, a 'nation of lust'; only £1m. was spent annually on foreign missions, compared with £5m. a day on the war. The Church needed to repent for its lack of training in sacramental religion – on one battleship only twenty men were regular communicants; the Church was out of touch with organized labour; it lacked brotherhood; some parishes were slothful and dull. But with characteristic inability to let himself feel depressed, he added: 'everybody is becoming more and more conscious that every man is born to be a Christian'.[48] Archbishop Lang tried to explain the title of the Mission to Convocation:

> We have called it a National Mission of Repentance and Hope; Repentance because we are called to bid men and women everywhere to repent of the sins which have stained our civilisation and brought upon it the manifest judgment of God; and Hope because, during the closing period of this terrific ordeal in the midst of increasing strain and sacrifice and sorrow, our people will need the strength of Hope, and in those difficult days that are coming, when the old order will have gone and the duty will be laid upon the nation of seeking a new order in a new world, we must present before the minds of the nation the one hope, Christ, His Mind, His Spirit, for the rebuilding of a new world.

When it was over, he recognized that many of the hopes of the Mission had been disappointed, but he felt a great effort and an important witness had been made.[49] William Temple, touring the country on behalf of the Mission, also defended the title ('repentance and hope are practically the same thing'); he contrasted the capacity for heroism which the war had evoked with the failure of the Church to evoke a like sacrificial allegiance.[50]

But of course those with an evangelical background tended to emphasize the need for individual repentance, while those who had been influenced by the Christian Social movement laid more stress on what Scott Holland called 'corporate sin'.[51] One Missioner wrote in *Commonwealth* that no one seemed to know whether the aim of the Mission was to convert the individual or to christianize the social order.[52] But the usual approach was to stress both. Bishop Kempthorne of Lichfield (Chairman of the Mission Consultative Committee) wrote in the *Church Quarterly* that the nation had much to repent of: drunkenness, gambling, impurity, but above all, covetousness and the 'shameful contrast between blatant luxury and sordid poverty . . . squalid destitution which depresses and degrades'.[53] However, few seemed to say anything about the ways in which British foreign and economic policy might have contributed to the war itself. Sometimes the Mission became a matter of what Scott Holland called 'placarding our clerical failings on every high hill'.[54] In a leader the *Church Times* declared that 'the masses must be won by the Mass'.[55]

At the time, Henson and Peter Green were keen critics. Peter Green was doubtful about the Mission, because as an experienced parish missioner he believed that it was impossible for the whole Church to be ripe and prepared for a simultaneous effort. But when the Mission arrived, he put every ounce of energy into its work in his own Salford parish. Henson stood sardonically aside from the Mission, though he placed Durham Cathedral at the disposal of the Missioners. He wrote in his journal for October 1916:

> If religious revival is to take place, I suspect that it will come from outside the Church, not from inside. The much-trumpeted 'National Mission' appears to become more utterly conventional every day. Those who are running about the country, exhorting little companies of puzzled women, have no vision of any larger teaching than that which has passed on their lips for years, and is now admittedly powerless. A dervish-like fervour cannot be maintained, and is not really illuminating or morally helpful.

In retrospect, he was particularly critical of Winnington-Ingram:

> It implies no inability to appreciate the attractive personality and admirable evangelistic zeal of the late Bishop of London (Dr.

Ingram) to maintain that he was peculiarly unfitted, both by temperament and by habit, to direct a mission which was designed to break with convention, . . . The National Mission was in my belief a failure. . . . I cannot observe or discover any lasting improvement in the religious situation. The churches are still confronted with the perturbing problem of popular indifference.

He considered that the Church of England was too divided to make a successful national appeal; that the Christian message needed a degree of re-statement too little realized by either churchmen or missioners who were accustomed to traditional methods, and that the nation was too distracted by the war to be able to listen.[56] In February 1917 he wrote:

The 'National Mission' seemed to me to be a grave practical blunder, for the time was inopportune, and there were none of the conditions of a success. Its only permanent consequences to the Church will be the raising into sudden and wholly unmerited importance a number of foolish persons, ardent, bigoted, and ill-informed, who would not otherwise have gained a hearing, or been given any authority. The problem demanding solution at the hands of the Archbishops is *how to end the Mission without loss of dignity*. In order to save their faces they are lending themselves to a whole series of 'continuation' movements, crude and ill-considered, which in normal times they would never have sanctioned.[57]

From the other end of the ecclesiastical and political spectrum, Conrad Noel dubbed it the 'Mission of Funk and Despair'. He believed that there was no sign that the Church of England wanted the sort of Catholic socialist society for which he agitated. Thaxted contracted out of the National Mission and held its own parish mission to proclaim true socialist Christianity.[58] But Percy Widdrington of the Church Socialist League (from which Noel had just resigned) became the missioner for the Worcester diocese. He believed that Christian Socialists should support the Mission because at last the Church of England was calling for corporate, and not merely individual, repentance. It was, he believed, a great opportunity for Christian Socialists to come out of their isolation into which they had been driven by their opposition to church authorities.[59]

By the end of 1917, certain uncomfortable truths became clear to the Council: throughout the country few really outside the Churches had attended the special services, though more outsiders had attended the public (and often open-air) meetings. In many places spiritual life had been quickened, parochial isolation broken down, priests given a new stimulus, and a desire for church reform and its greater involvement in social questions strengthened. But as Iremonger wrote, 'there were no signs of a renewed desire on the part of the people of England to identify themselves and their ideals with the fellowship and the worship of the National Church.'[60] The revival of church attendance in the first few months of the war had been short-lived. In Lent 1918, the Archbishop of Canterbury, in his Foreword to the Reports of the five Committees of Inquiry, was more sanguine: 'The call told: not, of course, universally, but very widely. We found that people were ready to face familiar facts afresh; that a new spirit was breathing upon dry bones: that we must, and could, be up and doing.' Certainly the National Mission failed to make much appreciable difference to church attendence. But it did force the leadership of the Church to consider not only the Church's mission to the nation in wartime, but also the structure and role of the Church in the post-war period. Its two most obvious fruits were the 'Life and Liberty Movement' (to be considered in Chapter 11), and the five Reports which we shall now survey.

Lord Parmoor, the Archbishop of Canterbury's Vicar-General, wrote in October 1914: 'Each day the weakening influence of Christianity becomes clearer', and went on to say that the Churches instead of preaching the Gospel of peace were encouraging an opportunist war spirit because it was popular, and so were losing their real power.[61] During the war, many (particularly the idealistically-minded) both inside and outside the Churches, criticized them for their failure to prevent war or to have a greater impact on, and a greater following in, the nation. As the Church of England was regarded as the Church of the nation (in various senses of that term) its broad back received most of the criticism. The Church was criticized because it was too pacifist, or not pacifist enough; because Christians had failed in their discipleship. It was said that because German Christianity had been corrupted by Lutheran erastianism and theological liberalism, it too had failed and become the tool of Prussianism. The Church had insufficiently applied Christianity to social questions, so the working classes were alienated from it. The catholic unity of the Church had been broken by the Reformation. Religious education had failed: the majority of the English population knew little about the Christian faith, and what they knew was often incomplete, muddled and lacking in churchmanship. The Churches squabbled among themselves, and the Church of England itself was disunited. The Prayer Book needed revision and the Church of England was hampered by lack of self-government. Various groups declared that the Christian religion had been misrepresented by either Evangelicals, or Liberals, or Anglo-Catholics. The clergy were out of touch with the 'ordinary man'. The Church failed to live by the Sermon on the Mount. These were but some of the many criticisms which were heard both inside and outside the churches. A catastrophe releases a lot of free-flowing anger, and that anger seeks someone to blame just as a person suddenly bereaved may turn angrily on the doctor to blame him for the death. It is surely to the credit of the Church of England that it tried to express, however imperfectly, at the height of the war, its own sense that it needed to repent for the past and to work hopefully for the future, and that it sought to move the nation to do the same.

To follow up the National Mission, five Committees were created by the Archbishops, each with an impressive membership, to examine five areas of the life of the Church and nation, and to produce reports for discussion and action. These reports were published in 1919 in one volume under the title of *Reports of the Archbishops' Committees of Inquiry*. The title page was headed: 'The Kingdom of God is at hand; repent ye and believe the Gospel.' The Archbishop of Canterbury wrote an identical Foreword to each Report which included these words:

> The roadway to right knowledge and effective action is now open. It is a roadway which is offered not to those only who approach it as churchmen and churchwomen, but to the English people as a whole. It is the most important stage of the National Mission. . . . We want critics as well as advocates. Let there be quiet reading of all that they contain. Let there be meetings large and small. Let there be sermons and addresses and study circles, that we may perceive and know what things we ought to do, and that together, as the needs of our day demand, we may 'go forward'.

Certainly all five committees were very ready to express their keen awareness of the Church's failures and inadequacies. The First Report on 'The Teaching Office of the Church' began by examining 'The Alleged Failure': 'It is widely stated that the Church fails in the task of giving its message.'[62] The Second Report on 'The Worship of the Church' opened with these words: 'The Committee is confronted at the outset of its work with the grave fact that the instinct for worship has seriously diminished in the people as a whole.'[63] The Third Report on 'The Evangelistic Work of the Church' stated:

> Though the Church is ready to confess that many of the obstacles which hinder its evangelistic work are of its own making, yet that is but half the truth. It is evident that organised Christianity is faced with real and new difficulties which are largely inherent in the conditions of our time.[64]

The Fourth Report on 'The Administrative Reform of the Church' declared on its first page: 'We believe that the spiritual efficiency of the Church is in many ways greatly hampered by anomalies in the existing administrative system'.[65] The Fifth Report on 'Christianity and Industrial Problems', while it recalled with thankfulness all that the Church had done in this area in the past, also confessed: 'We are conscious of the lamentable failure in the Church's recent witness.'[66] All five committees were conscious of the way in which the war had (in the words of the Third Report) 'brought us a startling and vivid revelation of need and opportunity'.[67]

The First Committee on 'The Teaching Office of the Church' was chaired by Bishop Chase of Ely and included E. W. Barnes, A. C. Bouquet, C. F. Garbett, A. C. Headlam, Scott Holland, Bishop Gore, and William Temple. The Church is charged, said the Report, with various types of failure: (i) intellectual – the Christian message as delivered 'is out of touch with the thoughts and ideas of the time';[68] (ii) practical – though 70 per cent of the Army are described as 'C. of E.', only a very small proportion really know the faith and use the sacraments; (iii) the Church lacks brotherhood and fellowship; (iv) the clergy are out of touch with ordinary people because of 'their professional habit of mind', and also out of touch with 'the normal intellectual life of the time'.[69] Though it had become 'a habit to say hard things of the Church',[70] yet its critics are often unable to offer alternatives; indeed their criticisms often unconsciously proceed from standards and beliefs which they have learnt from the Church itself. Nevertheless, there is much truth in the charges. What are the causes of failure? They arise partly from the tendencies of the age which have separated sacred and secular and left religion as but one department among many. They also arise from the failure to keep clergy and laity in touch with the considerable amount of good theology available. The quality and payment of clergy are often inadequate. The Church has now a weaker position in the older universities, and theology is little represented in the newer universities. The theological colleges have been hampered by inadequate resources, by the shortness of courses and by a narrowness of outlook, though despite these problems they have done much good work. After ordination, study is often neglected. For lack of a proper pension scheme, the clergy are encouraged to remain in parish work until too advanced an age. The Church should co-operate with other bodies to establish theological training in the new universities. The theological colleges should be centrally supervised and approved and be as closely connected with universities as possible. Candidates should have a wide education especially in modern science, and have an experience of lay work before ordination. Ordination courses should be longer and should include the study of educational method, of moral and social questions and of comparative religion. Candidates from poor backgrounds should receive financial help. Clergy should be encouraged to study throughout their ministry.

But the laity are also failing to spread the faith – the clergy often neglect to teach them and to give them responsibility. Divisions weaken witness; church people should participate in interdenominational movements. The methods of the Workers' Educational Association should be used to teach theology to laity. The laity, among whom the majority of the committee wished women to be included, should be used much more in the teaching of the faith. More specialist teachers of religion should be trained and the quality of Sunday School teachers improved. The Catechism urgently needs revision, and Confirmation instruction should be improved, and should continue after Confirmation. When the men return from the war 'we must be able to show them a true "earnest" of that renewal of our spiritual inheritance which they will then do their part to bring to perfection'.[71] Reports of several sub-committees occupy another sixty pages, and cover such topics as preaching, ordination training, the training of teachers, the freer use of churches for tableaux, lantern lectures and retreats, religion and art, and public school religion. Less of the Old, and more of the New Testament, should be taught to children: 'The first eleven chapters of Genesis are not fitted for them. Nor are the plagues, though the deliverance from Egypt is.'[72] Nearly sixty years later, many of the issues raised and the recommendations made in this First Report are still familiar topics for debate and attempted action.

The Second Committee on 'The Worship of the Church' was smaller than the First, but its members were also distinguished, with Walford

Davies, Fr Frere C.R. (Bishop of Truro 1923–35), F. A. Iremonger, F. B. Macnutt, Bishop Paget of Stepney, Neville Talbot, Francis Underhill among its signatories. It believed that worship, both public and private, had declined in recent years. The laity should be encouraged to take a more active part in worship, and they should be consulted about its conduct. The growth of industrialism had created over-large parishes. The pressures of the competitive system creates a 'temper alien from the very nature of the Church's worship'.[73] Prayer Book and lectionary urgently needed reform. The Communion should be restored to its central place in the Church's worship. The training of the clergy in worship should be improved. The laity should be taught simple methods of prayer. A majority of the Committee agreed with the widespread desire for more adequate provision of prayers for the dead. Musical standards should be improved, and parish music should normally be congregational. 'The disappearance of local orchestras, especially in the villages, is to be regretted.'[74] Three members of the Committee who were chaplains (H. K. Southwell, F. B. Macnutt and Neville Talbot) made an additional statement. Their experience at the front had quickened their desire for Prayer Book revision (though some chaplains and men were averse to change):

> . . . a refusal to reform has meant, and will mean, the alienation from the Christian religion of the important minority of men of all classes who are in some real degree mentally and spiritually alive. We would press for bold and wide experiment. It is, we believe, the opinion of a very great majority of chaplains at the Front that such experiment is needed. As a body of men we shall be unable to go back merely to the old pre-war grooves.[75]

The pastoral needs of the troops had forced chaplains to make changes in the liturgy. Though the majority of men neglect Holy Communion,

> at the same time it has vindicated its power and it wins its way, and we think almost all chaplains will return home anxious to make this service the main, corporate, family, congregational act of worship and fellowship.[76]

The chaplains had discovered that soldiers had usually no training in prayer:

> Contact with all and sundry of British manhood has revealed the crying need of a simple form of devotion, known from childhood, and

the common and familiar possession of all. This would indeed be a Godsend to the Church. At present the masses are entirely unprovided with really popular devotions. They have no primary liturgical structure engrained in their minds.[77]

Neville Talbot added this vivid comment on the Prayer Book: 'It assumes so much as "going without being said". The effect is to let people into worship at an upper storey and not on the ground floor.'[78] He believed that Communion should be celebrated at a convenient hour, and in the evening for those who cannot come at other times. But two members of the Committee were unhappy at this latter suggestion as contrary to Catholic tradition.

The Third Committee on 'The Evangelistic Work of the Church' met under the chairmanship of Bishop Burge of Southwark. The National Mission had shown the unpreparedness of the Church, and the paltriness of the demands made by the Church upon its members. Though the Church is regarded by 'thousands as the hereditary enemy of the ideals of the working classes',[79] both in the Army and at home there is much 'inarticulate religion'.[80] If in the early days of the war people were easier to reach, many have now grown hardened, sceptical, and embittered because 'God does not stop the war'. Habits of prayer, worship, and Sunday observance have declined. Industrial society is again blamed: 'the conditions under which hundreds of thousands of our fellow-countrymen and women live and work make fullness of life, in the moral and spiritual as well as in the more material sense, practically impossible.'[81] Many discover in trade unions, the Labour Movement and other causes an inspiring objective which they do not find in the Church. The strongest impulse is not to seek salvation through repentance and faith, but to offer for service: 'It is remarkable that among men at the front the call to service is being found to have more arresting power than the old evangelistic appeal.'[82] Because 'the divine indwelling in the soul of man' is more widely recognized, the need is to proclaim the Holy Spirit as 'the spring of all human progress'.[83] The attraction of Jesus is as 'heroic Leader' rather than as Saviour.[84] 'The translation of our creed into action by social service rendered from Christian motives is a true *praeparatio evangelica*.'[85] But when it came to practical suggestions, the Committee, apart from proposing the creation of diocesan evangelistic councils and stressing the value of women evangelists, fell back on well-tried methods – parish missions, visiting, open-air services, retreats, refresher courses for clergy, gatherings for silent prayer, and the like. Of greater interest is a special memorandum from the S.C.M. This began by describing the difficulties created in its work by misleading religious teaching:

> Some of the most serious prejudices which stand in the way of students becoming Christians are the result of their contact with the Churches. . . . Crude ideas about God, unchristian theories of inspiration, confused views about the Person of Christ, seem to be the result of such religious training as they have had. . . . There is a suspicion that there is a good deal of intellectual dishonesty in the pulpit, and that the clergy are concerned by every means in their power to press a particular point of view, and if anyone wants to study the pros and cons for this point of view the clergy are apt to be resentful and to press the authority of the Church. . . . Students as a class share with the workers the view that the Church is more interested in the rights of property than in the rights of human personality. . . . They cannot understand why the services of the Church of England are not made more relative to the needs of actual life. . . .[86]

This memorandum had also something to say about students' attitudes towards the Church in the light of the war:

> The effect of the war has been to make students more patriotic. . . . They are specially responsive to any appeal to work for social betterment. The desire for the redemption of society is very strong. . . . They are very conscious of the sin of war, and are completely and utterly out of sympathy with clergy and ministers who make no reference to the sin of war unless it be to lay the entire burden of sin upon Germany. The majority of our members who have gone to fight have gone feeling that England chose the least of two evils in 1914 in deciding to enter the war, but that the fact that she had only a choice of evils was due not merely to German wickedness, but to her own sinfulness in the past. In thinking thus, they were not thinking of things like Sunday observance and the drink traffic, but rather of the ideals of what was most worth aiming at which are cherished by the majority of Englishmen, ideals which make our nation the servant more of Mammon than God. It has seemed to the student class that the Church has had nothing distinctive to say to a world at war. It has done little more than support the State. The result has been a marked weakening of

allegiance to the Church since the outbreak of war, and in some quarters a strong desire to see the Church find new leaders.[87]

The Fourth Report on 'Administrative Reform of the Church' was prepared by a Committee which included William Temple, Lord Hugh Cecil, and Tissington Tatlow. It made a large number of recommendations, a few of which were to find legislative expression in the Enabling Act of 1919 and subsequent reforms. Others, for example the proposal that clergy should be appointed for an initial term of ten years, were not carried out, but were reiterated by the Paul Report of 1964, and still await action. Some of its proposals reflected the new egalitarianism which was widespread in the younger leadership in the Church – it disliked terms such as 'Palace' and 'Castle' for episcopal residences,[88] it spoke of the disparity of incomes among the clergy as a 'scandal', and it believed that it had been 'a serious loss' that women were unrepresented in the councils of the Church.[89] It did not give close attention to relations between Church and State because these had recently been dealt with by the Report of the Archbishops' Committee on the subject (1916), but it concluded its report by stressing with 'all possible emphasis, *that the Church should at the earliest possible moment recover freedom of legislation through its own representative assemblies*'.[90]

The Fifth Committee, on 'Christianity and Industrial Problems', was chaired by Bishop Talbot of Winchester (a veteran of the Christian Social Union) and included G. K. A. Bell, George Lansbury (who had written a pamphlet for the Mission), Bishop Kempthorne, Albert Mansbridge, Bishop Gore, Bishop Woods, and R. H. Tawney. The Chairman recognized that much of its Report would be unwelcome to churchmen. As one would expect from a Report drafted by Bell (with Tawney and Talbot) the task of social witness was described ecumenically:

> . . . we say deliberately that in the region of moral or social questions we desire all Christians to begin at once to act together as if they were one body, in one visible fellowship.[91]

Though the Church's work in the past for social betterment was recalled with thankfulness, it had none the less failed by concentrating on 'ambulance work' while neglecting to attack the 'forces of wrong'.[92] A future age will probably look back at 'some features of our industrial system' with something of the same feelings with which we look back upon the nineteen centuries which it has taken to apply Christian principles to the institution of slavery.[93] There is no aspect of life which falls outside Christian teaching. Christian ethics are social as well as individual. The war has 'undoubtedly had a tremendous effect in awakening the social conscience of Christians'.[94] The industrial system itself is 'gravely defective':

> It is defective not merely in the sense that industrial relations are embittered by faults of temper and lack of generosity on the part of the employer, of the employed, and of the general public alike, but because the system itself makes it exceedingly difficult to carry into practice the principles of Christianity. . . . The solution of the industrial problem involves, in short, not merely the improvement of individuals, but a fundamental change in the spirit of the industrial system itself.[95]

Wage-earners are placed in a position of subordination and treated as 'hands'. The system produces 'excessive inequalities of wealth'. Christians must ask whether this is compatible with Christianity. The livelihood of many workers is 'precarious and uncertain'. There is 'mutual antagonism and suspicion' between employer and employed.[96] The system should be inspired by co-operation for public service, not competition for private gain. The nation must secure for workers a 'living wage' and reasonable hours of work to allow adequate leisure. Christians must direct their attention to the evil of unemployment, for example, by condemning 'casualisation', by urging that industrial change should take place with full consultation with workers, and that in times of unemployment authorities should promote public works. Provisions for unemployment insurance should be extended. Children and young people should not be regarded primarily as wage-earners; the school-leaving age should be raised to 15 and ultimately to 16. The participation of workers in the running of industry should displace 'industrial autocracy' (though there was some division of opinion on this point).[97] The new positive attitudes towards the employment of women created by the war should be fostered. Excessive profits should be checked. Local authorities should have more power to undertake the provision of more goods and services. Bad housing should be tackled. The clergy should be drawn from all classes of society and their training should include economics and social science. A larger proportion of the national income should be devoted to education, to the provision of nursery schools, the reduction of the size of classes, the promotion of further education and the allotting of grants for adult education. An Appendix by Cyril Garbett underlined the need, already asserted by the Committee, for more working-class clergy: 'We have really a class ministry', said Garbett, which therefore cannot feel as the working classes do about trade disputes and unemployment.[98] The Committee stated: 'no boy who has a vocation for the ministry should be prevented by poverty from entering it'.[99] Such candidates might start their training in adult education while continuing their daily work to avoid severing them from their background, as residential education tends to do. The quality of the Report, the contents of the six-page bibliography, and the wide-ranging membership of the Committee, indicate that this Report was a piece of well-informed, prophetic thinking about society which deserves fuller mention in both the secular and the church histories of this period.

In various ways these five Reports contributed to the post-war reconstruction undertaken and advocated by the Church of England. The Second Report helped forward Prayer Book revision which culminated in the proposals of 1927 and 1928, and helped in general to foster more imaginative and freer styles of worship in parish churches and cathedrals. The Fourth Committee stimulated the movement towards that degree of self-government for the Church of England which was granted in the Enabling Act of 1919. It was the Fifth Report which gave rise to most discussion. Naturally, Christian Socialist opinion was on the whole favourable to it, but Henson among the conservative critics called it 'this dangerous pamphlet'.[100] The Lambeth Conference Committee of 1920, however, which dealt with this subject, found itself in general agreement with its approach. The Report of the Fifth Committee became the charter of the Industrial Christian Fellowship, which was created in 1919. From 1924 Bishop Kempthorne (who had been a member of the Fifth Committee) was the Chairman of I.C.F. John Oliver in *The Church and Social Order* (1968) described the Report as 'one of the finest and most important expressions of Christian opinion on social and industrial affairs ever produced by the Church of England'.[101] The Report was one of several indications of the extent to which the ideals of the Christian Social Union had successfully permeated the leadership of the Church of England. Sixteen out of the fifty-three new bishops between 1889 and 1913 were C.S.U. supporters.[102]

However radical the sympathies displayed by some features of these five Reports – though it had become almost orthodox to attack the competitiveness of industrial society and to bewail the failure of previous generations of Christians to be more socially-minded[103] – theologically speaking, the Reports were conservative. All the Committees assumed that they knew what Christianity was, but that for various reasons the Church was proclaiming it inadequately. There is a sad and striking absence of any real wrestling with the theological and ethical problems raised by the war itself. It is astonishing that nowhere in the Reports is there any discussion of the ethics of peace and war. The Third Report, on Evangelism, is a failure because it neglected to discuss the theological significance of 'inarticulate religion' at any depth. It failed to grasp the significance of the incognito Christ discovered by chaplains and men, and memorably described by Owen, Sassoon, and other poets. Above all, it failed to discuss the meaning of salvation, and whether the secular has a necessary and God-given role; the assumption was that the secular was to be assimilated by the Church, not wrestled with dialectically. I have in mind here a sentence written by Leonard Hodgson:

> The reason why a particular revelation is given to one man and not to another is that the interplay of their differing minds is for the mutual benefit of both, and it is this mutual benefit that of His love for both God wills with impartial justice to bestow upon them.[104]

I think too of Simone Weil who wrote:

> I have never once had, even for a moment, the feeling that God wants me to be in the Church. . . . So many things are outside it, so many things that I love and do not want to give up, so many things that God loves, otherwise they would not be in existence.[105]

This is strangely reminiscent of a passage in D. H. Lawrence's *The Rainbow* (1915). Will Brangwen visits his 'beloved' Lincoln Cathedral with his wife, but after the visit realized its limitations as a total statement about life:

> Outside the cathedral were many flying spirits that could never be sifted through the jewelled gloom. He listened to the thrushes in the gardens and heard a note which the cathedrals did not include: something free and careless and joyous. . . . There was life outside the church. There was much that the church did not include. . . . He thought of the ruins of the Grecian worship, and it seemed, a temple

was never perfectly a temple, till it was ruined and mixed up with the winds and the sky and the herbs.[106]

The Committee did not ask, for example, what it meant for God to choose and use Cyrus, what it meant that God should 'surname' him though he did not know God.[107] The only 'Cyrus' for the Committee was the Labour Movement, and it had become commonplace to point out its Christian inspiration and to lament that it often enlisted an enthusiasm which the Church did not. The Committee talked as if the conversion of the whole nation was not only desirable, but possible; it refused to face the fact that this was not going to happen. If it could have faced that fact, then it could have tried to work out more deeply the theological significance of 'inarticulate religion', and the relationship (to use Tillich's terms) between the 'manifest' and the 'latent' church.[108] Is Christ the possession of the Church? If so, then evangelism is the drawing of men out of darkness to cross the drawbridge into the safety and light of the ecclesiastical fortress. But what of the Christ who is Lord of the Church, Lord of history, the Logos? What of the relationship of Kingdom to Church? E. R. Wickham suggests an image of the Church, not as a monolithic rock, nor as an ark, but as 'a deep current itself running in the seas'.[109] To mention Tillich or Wickham may seem anachronistic, but the pastoral realities which caused them to write as they did were exactly the same ones which were evident at home and at the front in the first war. As we shall see when we come to look at the ministry of the Church at the front, these pastoral realities were frequently remarked upon. But their true significance could not be grasped without a re-thinking of evangelism, salvation and the meaning of the secular. Evidently that was too frightening a task for the Committee even to suggest.

Meanwhile as these Reports were published, the men were returning home after the war, carrying with them unique and often incommunicable experiences. As Sassoon's George Sherston put it:

We were the survivors; few among us would ever tell the truth to our friends and relations in England. We were carrying something in our heads which belonged to us alone, and to those we had left behind us in the battle.[110]

4

Moral Issues in Wartime

At the beginning of August 1914, Dean Inge wrote in his Diary: 'how unprepared we and everybody else were for the terrible news. . . . Our people were thinking of three things – their summer holiday, the danger of civil war in Ireland, and the abominable outrages of the suffragettes. . . .'[1] The Royal Commission on Divorce and Matrimonial Causes (1909–12) recommended that women should be allowed equality with men with respect to grounds for divorce. The novels of Arnold Bennett and H. G. Wells and the plays of Bernard Shaw were questioning traditional views about marriage and the role of women. In 1897 the National Union of Women's Suffrage Societies had been created. In 1903, the Women's Social and Political Union was founded by Mrs Emmeline Pankhurst, and in 1905 it turned to militant action to gain attention. When war came the suffragettes patriotically ceased their militant actions. The eventual imposition of conscription lowered most of the remaining barriers to the full-scale employment of women. In July 1915 Mrs Pankhurst organized a demonstration in London of 30,000 women to claim their 'right to serve'. It was financed by the Government. Churchill and Lloyd George reviewed the procession. The war itself was sometimes described in sexual imagery. To Mrs Pankhurst and her eldest daughter, Christabel, Germany was 'militaristic, tyrannical and male', whereas France and Belgium were 'innocent, threatened, invaded, and female'.[2] Sexual outrage ('the rape of Belgium') was a frequent analogy for German aggression, quickly stirring up moral indignation both among those who thought of women in Victorian terms, and those who espoused women's rights. The contribution of women to the war effort[3] convinced waverers and opponents of the case for women's suffrage. In 1918, women over thirty were given the vote. The influence of the war and the women's movement was also to be seen in the later relaxation of the divorce laws.

The Church of England showed some sympathy for the women's movement. The Church League for Women's Suffrage was formed in

1912; its membership of over 5,000 included Bishop Maud of Kensington, Bishop Hicks of Lincoln and Scott Holland.[4] S.C.M. promoted discussion of the place of women in universities and colleges, urged greater representation of women in the work of the Church and pointed to the equality of the sexes in the work of its own movement.[5] Archbishop Davidson, a supporter of votes for women, was predictably critical of the violent language and actions of the suffragettes. On 22 May 1914, Miss Annie Kenney tried to sit-in at Lambeth Palace until the Bill was passed. Davidson listened to her case, but told her that militant methods were injuring the cause in which he himself believed. This was also his message to delegations and correspondents.[6] Bishop Talbot of Winchester was also a supporter of women's suffrage, and had been the main driving force behind the founding of Lady Margaret Hall, Oxford, in 1878. Bishop Percival of Hereford, when Headmaster of Clifton, had taken a lead, with his wife, in the promotion of secondary and university education for girls and women in Bristol. In 1879, when President of Trinity College, Oxford, he became the first chairman of the Council of Somerville College. But by many suffragettes the Church was regarded as one of the main bulwarks of the subordination of women. Churches were among the buildings burnt down by militants, and church services were interrupted by protesters. A bomb damaged the Coronation Chair in Westminster Abbey.

There were protests from both Anglo-Catholic and Evangelical wings of the Church of England when the Central Council of the National Mission proposed that the bishops should give definite instructions as to the best ways of using women as speakers in church and elsewhere. Athelstan Riley, a leading lay member of the English Church Union, protested to Archbishop Davidson in July 1916 that the use of women for ministry during the Mission was the beginning of a movement to ordain women to the priesthood.[7] But Bishop Gore, one of the most respected Anglo-Catholic bishops, established in the diocese of Oxford an organization of Women Messengers on a permanent basis after the Mission was over. Miss Maude Royden, a prominent speaker, a writer on the Women's Movement, and a member of the National Mission Council, became a member of the Life and Liberty Council, formed under Temple's leadership in 1917. When the Council wished to meet at Cuddesdon Theological College in October 1917, the Principal (J. B. Seaton, later Bishop of Wakefield), a member of the Council, declined to allow Miss Royden to sleep under the college roof, because, though an Anglican, she had been officiating recently at the City

Temple. Though Seaton made a concession allowing her to attend sessions provided she slept in Oxford, she felt she had to resign, much to the indignation of many of the members of the Council. Temple understood Seaton's difficulties as Principal of a college in the Catholic tradition and strongly sympathized with Miss Royden, but did not wish to break up this crucial meeting.[8] Nevertheless, Miss Royden continued her work with many movements in the Church – she was a member of the Fellowship of Reconciliation, she was closely associated with Charles Raven in the organization of C.O.P.E.C. after the war, and she was much in demand as a preacher and speaker, especially with S.C.M.

Percy Dearmer (a friend of Maude Royden's) wrote an article in the *Guardian* on 20 July 1916 advocating the greater use of women in the Church's ministry, A week later Darwell Stone replied. He considered Dearmer's interpretation of St Paul 'perverse'. Stone believed that St Paul's teaching was based on 'permanent principles', and had rightly become 'a foundation for the general method of the Church'. Therefore, a priest who accepts a woman as a server at Mass 'is liable to severe censure'; according to Roman Catholic canon law, a woman may make the responses if a male server cannot be present, but 'she is forbidden to be near the Altar for this purpose or to assist the priest by handing the Elements to him'. Stone claimed to be in sympathy with many features of the Women's Movement, but concluded:

> And what a tragedy it is that, when we should all be united for the work of the National Mission, there is a project for prompting such ministrations of women as would make it necessary for those women and men who pay regard to Holy Scripture and the tradition of the Church to stay away from and discountenance the services in which these take place![9]

All five Reports following the National Mission proposed, however, that women should participate far more in the work, worship, and government of the Church of England. The Fifth Report, in a section on 'The Industrial Employment of Women', proposed not only 'equal pay for equal work' for women, but also 'equal freedom in the choice of their occupation, equal justice and consideration, and an equal voice in controlling the conditions of employment'.[10] Temple and others fought for, and won, the right of women to be members of the Church Assembly as well as of the other organs of government established by the Enabling Act of 1919, right down to parish level – an indication of the changed status of women brought about by suffragette agitation, by the war, and by pressures from certain quarters of the Church of England.[11]

A famous poster of the first world war depicted two women (the lady of the house and her maid) watching with pride and anxiety the soldiers marching away; the caption read 'Women of Britain Say Go'. Winnington-Ingram told 2,000 women at Church House in October 1914 that they must say to their men: 'Go, with my love and blessing.'[12] The Mothers' Union published a pamphlet in 1914 entitled 'To British Women, How They Can Help Recruiting'. A British poster depicted a German nurse pouring water on the floor in front of a British soldier tortured with thirst, while she and German soldiers laugh sadistically. The slogan proclaimed 'There is no woman in Britain who would do it. There is no woman in Britain who will forget it.' Some preachers endorsed and encouraged the propaganda image of German soldiers as promiscuous and lecherous, and with naïve eagerness told stories of the rape and mutilation of women by the enemy. The Master of St Catharine's College, Cambridge, the Reverend C. H. W. Johns, in a sermon in 1914 described what he believed would follow a German invasion:

> Half the children born next year in a town occupied by German troops would have a German soldier for a father. That is what it means when the poor Belgians tell with utter anguish and shame of the order to leave every door open at night to the German soldier. Can any woman be indifferent to her prospects as not to shudder when she reads the papers? Let every woman resolve to have nothing to do with a man who can enlist and fight for the protection of his home and will not.[13]

As part of a Quiet Day for the clergy (of all occasions!), Winnington-Ingram repeated a story told him by a young officer:

> 'There is a young girl naked in my trench. She has been wronged by a German soldier. I have given her my shirt and all I can. I saw another poor girl last night having her breasts cut off by a Uhlan officer. I dropped him at seven hundred yards. She is in my trench now, but I am afraid she will die.' What a contrast does the conduct of this German present to the splendid chivalry of our young knights! We are proud that not a single accusation has been made against one of our soldiers of having disgraced himself with regard to the women in the country through which he has passed.

In another sermon he asked how 350,000 people could watch football matches each week so long as the wrongs of 'poor girls' in France went unredressed.[14] Basil Bourchier told a story of German soldiers cutting off the breasts from wooden statues of the Virgin Mary.[15]

Though British soldiers were portrayed as stainless knights in some quarters at home, there are many descriptions of the queues of British soldiers waiting their turn in the French brothels. They waited not only because they wanted a little sexual pleasure before they died, but also because their world was completely devoid of any kind of female comfort: a totally unpredictable world where one man might be killed on his first day, and another survive for years; an increasingly futile world in which thousands might die to gain a few yards of mud, only to lose it a few days later. Tom Pym, a chaplain, assessed the situation with realism: 'gonorrhoea is a minor discomfort compared to wounds or death cheerfully faced in battle, and is much more pleasurably obtained.'[16] A soldier wrote to his girl-friend:

> I should like to think that there are women in the world who will be very compassionate to us when war is ended. The Frenchwomen are like that already. In their hospitals they call a wounded man 'Mon petit', and take him in their arms and hold his head against their breasts. . . . What we crave most of all is rest and the mercifulness of a woman who cares.[17]

Another said that 'the most glorious moment in all his experience was when he woke to consciousness in a base hospital, and saw the face and smile of a woman and heard her voice and the rustle of her skirt'.[18] An American Chaplain prepared brochures of prayers and hymns for soldiers, but he discovered that nearly all of them had been sent home to their mothers to reassure them that they had not been brutalized by war.[19] When Robert Graves returned to England on sick leave, he found it difficult to adjust himself 'to the experience of woman love'.[20] Charles Raven, who was a chaplain in the war, believed that the most humanizing influence in the war had been the presence of women in the hospitals, clubs and canteens, leavening an all-male society. This and other experiences made him into a leading advocate of the admission of women to every area of life, including the priesthood.[21]

Various images of womanhood and motherhood were used for propaganda purposes. The execution of Edith Cavell, a vicar's daughter, in October 1915 came at the end of a series of events which had inflamed anti-German feeling. In January, Zeppelin raids began; in

April, poison gas was used by the Germans for the first time; in May, the *Lusitania* was sunk and the Bryce Commission reported on German atrocities. Forgetting her last statement, 'Patriotism is not enough', British propaganda used Edith Cavell's death in the cause of the war effort. A postcard was printed showing a spike-helmeted German looking with satisfaction at the dead body of a sylph-like girl radiant in heavenly light. The caption reads: '*Miss Edith Cavell Murdered, Remember!*' When her body was re-interred at Norwich Cathedral in 1919, Bishop Pollock in his address described her as 'an innocent, unselfish, devout and pretty girl',[22] though in fact she was 50 when she died. Elizabeth Wordsworth (the former Principal of Lady Margaret Hall) wrote in the *Church Quarterly* in January 1915 on the subject of 'Women and the War'. She painted a romantic picture of St George and the Dragon, with the men in khaki like knight errants. But she had a more realistic picture of her own sex. There were many lonely bereaved women needing pastoral care. Women should help in teaching, restaurants, banks and offer themselves for pastoral work in the parishes and as nurses in hospitals. (The Archbishops formed a committee which in 1918 sent out over fifty workers to look after the welfare of women employed in the munition factories.) Women were portrayed as not only saying 'Go' to their men, but also 'Stay over there until the enemy is beaten'. A sentimental postcard 'To one I love so far away from me' included a verse beginning:

> Would I have my lover back again?
> Yes, when the fight is o'er,
> When the duty's done and honour's won –
> But never a day before.

Then there was 'A Mother's Answer to "A Common Soldier"' in *The Morning Post*, citing Jeremiah to dreadful effect (forgetting how he was hated by the conventional patriots of his day):

To the man who pathetically calls himself a 'common soldier', may I say that we women, who demand to be heard, will tolerate no such cry as 'Peace! Peace!' when there is no peace. The corn that will wave over the land watered by the blood of our brave lads shall testify to the future that their blood was not spilt in vain. . . . Send the Pacifists to us and we shall very soon show them, and show the world, that in our homes there shall be no 'sitting at home warm and cosy in the winter, cool and "comfy" in the summer'. There is only one temperature for the women of the British race, and that is white heat. . . . We women pass on the human ammunition of 'only sons' to fill up the gaps, so that when the 'common soldier' looks back before going 'over the top' he may see the women of the British race at his heels, reliable, dependent, uncomplaining.

Queen Mary described the letter as 'beautiful'. Seventy-five thousand copies were sold in less than a week.[23] Mrs E. K. Paget, wife of the Bishop of Stepney, struck a very different note: 'Sorrow remains common to all. There is neither German nor Russian, Belgian, Austrian, Servian, French nor English. . . . Motherhood, womanhood, has reached her Calvary. Then let the words on our lips be words of forgiveness and love.'[24]

Sassoon wrote a bitter poem on the theme of womanhood in wartime, 'The Glory of Women':

> You love us when we're heroes, home on leave,
> Or wounded in a mentionable place.
> You worship decorations; you believe
> That chivalry redeems the war's disgrace.
> You make us shells. You listen with delight,
> By tales of dirt and danger fondly thrilled.
> You crown our distant ardours while we fight,
> And mourn our laurelled memories when we're killed.
> You can't believe that British troops 'retire'
> When hell's last horror breaks them, and they run,
> Trampling the terrible corpses – blind with blood.
>   O German mother dreaming by the fire,
>   While you are knitting socks to send your son,
>   His face is trodden deeper in the mud.

Some of the moral problems and dilemmas raised by the war were new, some were old problems in a new or freshly urgent form. Both individually and corporately Christians were ethically ill-prepared to meet the subtlety and complexity of many wartime moral problems. The world of day and Sunday school religion, the only sources of religious education for the majority of the population, was no preparation for the world of the trenches. Fr John Groser, a chaplain, found that some troops believed that it was against the Ten Commandments to fight on Sundays.[25] A twenty-year-old soldier wrote in a letter home in 1917:

> . . . the moral situation is damnable – we can only beat Germany by assuming her mentality, by recognising the State as the supreme God whose behests as to military efficiency must be obeyed, whether or no they run counter to Christianity and morality. We call their use of gas inhuman, but we have to adopt it ourselves. . . .

He described how they had had to smoke out German soldiers but then were forced to bayonet them because they had no spare men to take prisoners:

> As for the morals of war, they are horrible . . . I doubt whether it will have helped us to find God. Among the millions actually fighting it seems only to have increased the drunkenness and vice. . . .[26]

Others preferred to stress the war as eliciting from men unexpected resources of courage, self-sacrifice and stamina; some wrote about this in the language of naïve patriotism, some in the full realization of the moral irony and paradox that this implied. Scott Holland pointed out that Christianity goes beyond nationality and can never identify itself absolutely with any national cause: 'it is as an organ and medium of international fellowship that CHRIST establishes and sanctifies Nationality.' We fight for that international fellowship by fighting for Belgium and for the rule of law between nations: 'It was war: or dishonour.' But he continued:

> How swiftly our conscience deteriorates under the stress of battle! . . . The natural conscience is dislocated. I read quite calmly, and with gentle satisfaction, the assurances of the Press that the losses of the enemy were most gratifying. This is the war-temper. Such a temper is an outrage against man, a sin against GOD. It is under the curse of CHRIST.

War, however, is bound to be 'crude': 'It cannot keep the fine distinctions between right and wrong.' But we must 'allow no war-passion to becloud our conscience, or brutalise our instinct'. We must still love those whom we fight, and 'desire nothing more than to be reconciled and at peace with them, in the blessed bonds of brotherhood'.[27]

One of the most difficult of moral dilemmas in the first war, as in the second, was that of reprisals. In 1916, some were urging through the press a declared policy of air-reprisals on Germany in retaliation for

Zeppelin raids on London. Joynson-Hicks, for example, argued: 'If our airmen dropped bombs upon the open towns of Germany, and insisted upon an eye for an eye, and a tooth for a tooth, the Zeppelin raids would soon cease.' Others like the King[28] and Lord Bryce took a different view, but the agitation was considerable. In February 1916, Archbishop Davidson raised the question in Convocation and proposed this motion (drawing on the long Christian tradition of teaching about the 'Just War'),[29] which was passed unanimously:

> That this House, while fully recognising that it does not lie within its province to express any opinion on matters purely military, desires to record its conviction that the principles of morality forbid a policy of reprisal which has, as a deliberate object, the killing and wounding of non-combatants, and believes that the adoption of such a mode of retaliation, even for barbarous outrages, would permanently lower the standard of honourable conduct between nation and nation.

The Archbishop felt it was the duty of the Church to give guidance about the ethical issues; he was deeply concerned lest there should be a gradual debasement of the moral currency: 'let us take care that at an early stage of the wrong doing we stand across the path and warn people that there are ethical as well as military considerations which attach to action such as is now being suggested . . .' His words (and the debate) were bitterly resented at the time.[30] That he felt acutely the complexity of the moral questions of war, and the great difficulty in providing Christian leadership in its context, is evident from an entry in his Diary for May 1916 when he was in France. Kept awake by all he had seen and by the firing of the artillery, he mused:

> One felt more and more the fearsomeness of all this going on between Christian peoples, and the helplessness of religious leadership to intervene, and *per contra* the gain and opportunity which is coming to the manhood of England and of France, and our obligation to use it.[31]

It should be noted that here, as elsewhere, he thought of Germany as a 'Christian nation' and did not fall into the popular identification of Germany as anti-Christ or as a complete mass of barbarians.

In the spring of 1917 there was a renewed agitation for reprisals. In February three British liners were torpedoed. Bombs were dropped on Kent. After two British hospital ships had been torpedoed in March, a large squadron of British and French planes bombed Freiburg in retaliation. In May, the Archbishop questioned the Government in the House of Lords as to whether a policy of reprisals had now been adopted. He spoke of the way in which innocent people in his own diocese had suffered from bombing, but he asserted:

> I do know that the Christian judgement of England – and I do not shrink from using that term in its fullest sense – is that when we come out of this war (scarred and wounded, yes; bereft of some of our best and noblest and most hopeful, yes) we mean to come out with clean hands and with the right to feel sure that in the coming years, whatever record leaps to light, we never shall be ashamed.

The previous day the Upper House of Canterbury Convocation had reaffirmed the resolution of February 1916, and the Archbishop was also able to cite the opposition of the Free Church Council to reprisals. But again the Archbishop was subjected to considerable and often bitter criticism. Many failed to understand the principle he was enunciating. He took his stand on the traditional limitations of the Just War, as he explained in a letter published in *The Times* in June:

> The question of our moral duty in the matter is admittedly a difficult one, and it has a margin line which may easily be blurred. . . . The key of the situation lies in the intention of the act – not an uncertain hope of ultimate consequence, but its immediate practical intention. Of course in one sense 'reprisal' is of the essence of war. But what kind of reprisal? We bombard a fortified town. This must often involve risk to innocent non-combatants. But that is not its object. Its object is to harm the enemy's combatant forces. The incidental harming of non-combatants is lamentable, and it will, so far as military conditions permit, be avoided. But it is sometimes inevitable. Quite different from this is an attack the direct object of which is to harm or kill non-combatants, either for reasons of vengeance, or in order to promote terror, or in the hope of deterring the enemy from perpetrating outrages. That is the kind of 'reprisal' in which some people wish us in England to indulge. . . . I am urged, for example, to see to it that we insist upon 'reprisals, swift, bloody and unrelenting. Let gutters run with German blood. Let us smash to pulp German old men, women and children', and so on. Do those who described the terrible sight of little London children lying dead really want to see little German children lying slaughtered in like manner by us?

If Britain were to adopt such a policy, he said, the German would always 'out-distance us in ruthlessness'. If we were to act in such a manner, then history would place all nations on the same moral level. Moreover, in any future war, 'it would doubtless begin by outrages of this sort as the perpetration of them could no longer be regarded as outside the pale'. He told Hall Caine in July that he had been appalled by the number of letters which had poured in to him 'breathing blood and slaughter, not against combatants but against the people of Germany if only they can be got at, with a special wish for the destruction of women and children'.[33]

Bishop Gore also protested strongly when the British bombed German towns in 1917 as reprisals for German raids: 'If we allow ourselves to be led by the Germans, the descent is easy and the end certain degradation.'[34] In the summer of 1917, at the burial of child victims of an air raid, Winnington-Ingram spoke out strongly against the agitation for reprisals, which may seem surprising in view of his often bellicose utterances. But he did teach that the conduct of the war should be just. So at the funeral he said he did not believe that the mourners would want sixteen German children killed to avenge the dead British children. On the other hand he added: 'What all demanded was strong deterrent naval and military action . . . on the places from which these raiders came, and that the strongest punishment should be given to the perpetrators and designers of these raids.'[35]

Archbishop Davidson's stand against reprisals did not carry more than a minority of churchmen with him, despite the support he received from his fellow-bishops in Convocation, and the approval of a writer in *Commonwealth* for September 1917.[36] More typical of much popular sentiment inside and outside the Church were two articles written by H. D. A. Major, the noted liberal theologian, in *The Modern Churchman*, of which he was Editor, in 1917. In the first, he supported reprisals 'if they can be undertaken effectively';[37] in the second article he asserted:

> The Christian sentimentalist is one who will not face the facts of life. . . . The strongest moral argument against reprisals is that some are punished by them who are not actually guilty. . . . If the innocent cannot be separated from the guilty, ought the guilty therefore to be spared and allowed to continue unpunished their evil ways? It is not for the good of humanity that the guilty should be spared even though the innocent should suffer with them. . . . If the only way to protect adequately an English babe is to kill a German babe, then it is

the duty of our authorities, however repugnant, to do it. More particularly is this so, when we reflect that the innocent German babe will in all probability grow up to be a killer of babes himself, or at least an enthusiastic advocate of that horrible policy of frightfulness of which the killing of babes is one of the features. Whereas the English babe whose life is saved by this means will, we may reasonably anticipate, grow up to be a protector of babes, and a detestor of those who would slay them.[38]

If the moral difference between the two nations was as absolute as Major suggested, then it was a short step to regarding the enemy as anti-Christ, so non-human that the moral limitations imposed by the Just War no longer applied, a view which is always reasserted as part of the national reaction to any barbarity.

Before the war, public houses in London were allowed to open from 5 a.m. to 12.30 a.m. on weekdays; in other areas the hours were only slightly shorter. But with the coming of war opening hours were somewhat curtailed. The temperance movement, particularly in the Free Churches, was still a powerful influence, and ten days after war began, the Archbishop of Canterbury began receiving stories of widespread drunkenness among the troops as a result of excessive treating of the soldiers. He wrote to the Home Secretary asking for earlier closing; in October he also saw and wrote to Lord Kitchener, who had just issued an appeal to stop the practice of treating. In February and March 1915 Lloyd George attacked the damage that alcohol was doing: 'We are fighting Germany, Austria and Drink, and, as far as I can see, the greatest of these deadly foes is Drink.'[39] Lloyd George asked various leaders, including the Archbishop, to give a lead in favour of total abstinence. On 30 March the King announced that he was giving up alcohol for the duration of the war and issued orders against its consumption in the royal household. On 6 April the Archbishop issued a statement, signed by himself, the Archbishop of York, Cardinal Bourne, and the President of the Free Church Council, asking the nation to follow the royal example. Peter Green constantly campaigned for much stricter licensing hours. The Central Control Board, created that summer, gradually extended its powers throughout most of the country, forbidding treating, in certain areas (including Carlisle) taking over licensed premises to be owned by the state, and stage by stage prohibiting the sale of alcohol before midday and in the afternoon. Taxation on alcohol was increased and its strength reduced. In 1914 average weekly convictions for drunkenness were 3,388 in England and Wales; by the end of 1918 they had fallen to 449. Temperance and total abstinence was also encouraged by the provision of dry canteens under the auspices of the Church Army, the Y.M.C.A., the Y.W.C.A., and the Salvation Army.[40]

But some Anglican opinion was uneasy at this capitulation to puritanism, however necessary it seemed for the war effort. Lord Halifax was dismayed when he found only lemonade to drink at Bishopthorpe; at Lambeth there were only four bottles of water on the table at dinner.[41] Bishop Gore's loyalty to the royal example and desire for a more sacrificial spirit in the nation overcame his own dislike of abstinence, and he requested his diocese to follow the King. Though he kept the pledge meticulously, he refused to be drawn into the ranks of the teetotallers. At a meeting called to promote the pledge he told his audience: 'All my life I have been accustomed to a liberal supply of generous wine. My doctor told me that to give it up suddenly at my age might prove dangerous.' When he added slowly: 'I have never experienced the least inconvenience from not taking wine', the teetotallers cheered loudly. Gore went on: 'Many of my teetotal friends assured me that I should experience greatly improved health, and marked clearness of mind.' Again he added impressively: 'I have never experienced the slightest benefit from not taking wine.' The audience at first responded with a horrified pause, then roared with laughter.[42] In January 1916, *The Times* published a long letter from Henson on the subject. He surveyed the 'continual stream' of exhortation 'argumentative, impassioned, sarcastic, pathetic, threatening', all designed to persuade the public to adopt Total Abstinence. But 'Total Abstinence is no part of morality, and certainly has no support either in the teaching of Christ, or in the practice of the Christian Church'. Why, Henson asked, had the appeal failed? First, because English people have a 'rooted distrust' of abstainers as politicians. Second, because 'an immense revolution in popular habits' should not be attempted in the midst of 'a desperate conflict'. Third, while the need for a reduction in consumption and drunkenness is supported, why single out one particular expenditure for 'public obloquy'?

> To offer total abstinence as a cure for national drunkenness is as reasonable as to offer celibacy as a cure for national impurity. . . .
> Instead of these impetuous and demonstrably futile attempts to make

English people total abstainers, I would plead for a considered and reasonable effort to encourage and assist moderate drinking, the habit of that genuine temperance which is both a natural virtue and a Christian tradition.

Naturally Henson received many angry letters![43] It was not commendable to the dissenting and evangelical traditions to deal with the problems of sex and drink with a consciously cultivated neo-Augustan wit, as Henson did here; and in choosing that style, he knew how to outrage his earnest opponents. Gore, Halifax and Henson all reveal a certain Anglican distaste for becoming committed to an ethic which was so closely identified with the politics and culture of dissent.

Those churchmen who were always ready to denounce drunkenness, lust and strikes were able to increase the emotional level of their denunciations by branding these things as unpatriotic. A. C. Headlam wrote a blanket condemnation of workers for excessive holidays and selfish strikes in the *Church Quarterly* for July 1916.[44] The evangelical Bishop Chavasse of Liverpool linked several themes together in a sermon preached in April 1915 before the Lord Mayor and Corporation of London:

Looking nearer home, we saw the hideous selfishness which sought to squeeze a more abundant gain out of the very lives and life-blood of its own people, and, side by side with it, the shameless callousness of men ready to rise and drink themselves drunk, while their own kith and kin were facing death, wounds, and hardships in the trenches; seeming almost to despise the very blood that was being shed by the defenders of their own homes, the honour of their women, the love of their little children, and preferring rather to strike for the addition of a penny per hour, or even less, to their daily wage.[45]

But Peter Green protested against such wholesale denunciations of the working class, which (he pointed out) had produced the common soldier whose praises were on the lips of all: 'there is a working class attitude towards life, as noble and as valuable as the public school spirit.'[46]

Inevitably the war made sexual relationships more casual: by 1918, the illegitimacy rate had increased 30 per cent compared with before the war. Early in the war the question was raised as to whether common-law wives or unmarried mothers of serving men should receive the same separation allowances as wives. The Archbishops and Bishops considered the matter in October 1914, and the Archbishop interviewed Asquith and other politicians as well as social workers on the question. He gave evidence to a government committee in March 1915, and pleaded that while the same allowances should be paid, 'there must be the utmost care taken not to break down the distinction between the married and the not married'. He claimed that the scheme adopted owed much to the efforts he had made: allowances would be paid to dependents, other than wives, only after consideration had been given to their cases by a local Pensions committee, and on the condition that the dependent must be receiving a proportion of the soldier's pay agreed voluntarily by himself.[47] A writer in the *Church Quarterly* considered that it would show false sentimentality and be an attack on marriage to treat both types of dependent alike. Instead of being able to go to the Post Office for her allowance, the woman who cohabited with a soldier should receive her money through 'some agency which could combine moral influence with pecuniary help'.[48] Frances Stevenson, Lloyd George's secretary and mistress, wrote in her diary for 23 October 1914 about the Archbishop's representations to the Cabinet: 'It appears that the Archbishop does not wish them or their children to starve, but he does not wish them to be treated as deserving of relief, – which is a piece of blatant hypocrisy.' Lloyd George (who 'had fought hard for these unmarried women') had seen two Free Church Ministers (J. H. Shakespeare and R. J. Campbell) and told them that it was not right to take the lives of men for their country, and afterwards to say 'that you do not approve of their morals'.[49]

The war brought considerable changes in sexual morals and an increase in marital problems. By the end of the war contraceptives were much more freely available. Between 1910 and 1920 there was nearly a threefold increase in divorces. During the war Tom Pym forecast a wave of promiscuity when peace returned: 'Pent-up forces will be loosed; money for a time will be abundant and women will be complacent.'[50] After the war, Archbishop Davidson found that the number of requests made to him to help with marriage problems had greatly increased. 'Tubby' Clayton was much distressed in the post-war period by the number of requests made to him by members of Toc H to be remarried in church after divorce. He consistently refused to officiate at such marriages, and declined to allow/All Hallows to be used by other priests for this purpose. He was grudging in his permission to allow the so-called 'innocent' party to communicate; the 'guilty' party to a divorce 'is definitely excommunicate', he ruled.[51] During the war, Mrs

Matthews (wife of W. R. Matthews), as a result of her friendship with some of the women doctors at the Royal Free Hospital, realized the need for sexual education for women. She organized a meeting for women on the subject, with a woman doctor and a representative of the Mothers' Union as speakers and with the wife of the Bishop of Willesden in the chair. 'For the time and place, this was a pioneering achievement', her husband commented.[52]

Archbishop Davidson kept a close watch throughout the war on the problem of sexual morality in the Forces. Early in 1918 public opinion was stirred by reports that the military authorities took a rather nonchalant view of licensed brothels and venereal disease. Bishop Brent, the unofficial Chaplain-General to the American forces, was pressing hard for joint action between the American and British authorities. The Archbishop consulted with Bishop Gwynne, Deputy Chaplain-General, and with Lord Derby, Secretary of State for War. When the Archbishop asked for a direct report to be prepared by Bishop Gwynne to reflect the views of Chaplains, the military authorities were indignant that they were being by-passed. Equally the Archbishop was annoyed at the attempt by the authorities to interfere with direct communication between himself and Bishop Gwynne. He put down a motion in the Lords. One effect of the fully representative conference called by the Government as a result of pressure from the Church, was an amendment to the official circular on early treatment so that it now emphasized that 'continence and self-control' were the only real safeguards against venereal disease. 'It is a miserable subject', the Archbishop, who had attended the conference, reflected, 'and one which inflames people almost beyond any other.'[53] A private soldier, George Coppard, described a brothel at Béthune:

There were well over a hundred and fifty men waiting for opening time, singing *Mademoiselle from Armentières* and other lusty songs. Right on the dot of 6 pm a red lamp over the doorway of the brothel was switched on. A roar went up from the troops, accompanied by a forward lunge towards the entrance. At that period in my youth I certainly had no idea that the carnal desires of men went to such lengths. . . . It was said that Red Lamps were frequently inspected by RAMC doctors, and the women medically examined. But many Tommies made random contacts with women in the back streets and got VD for their pains. These were the most unfortunate of men. Fifty years ago the disease was regarded as a dreadful and shameful contagion. Military authority subscribed to this view and dealt harshly with a Tommy VD case. He was clapped in a kind of prison hospital as an outcast, down at the base. Hard labour was his portion, with a court-martial hanging over his head. . . . The stigma was such that very few front-line Tommies, in spite of the misery and danger they had to endure, would have swapped places with a VD man at a base hospital.[54]

Another moral issue was that of Sunday work. Early in 1917 a late frost deepened anxiety about the nation's food supply. The Chancellor of the Exchequer, Bonar Law, went to see the Archbishop of Canterbury to sound out his attitude to Sunday sowing. The President of the Free Church Council (J. H. Shakespeare) had already told the Chancellor that many Nonconformists would be opposed to it. In March it was arranged that a letter from the Archbishop should appear in the press. He stated that, while mindful of the 'God-given boon' of the English Sunday, he had 'no hesitation in saying that, in the need which these weeks present, men and women may with a clear conscience do field work on Sundays', though conscience must be respected. (Cardinal Bourne on behalf of the Roman Catholic Church issued a similar ruling.) But some Evangelicals and Nonconformists were extremely unhappy. Dr R. F. Horton, an eminent Nonconformist minister, wrote to *The Times* in April arguing that it was easier to dispense people from their obligations than to restore them once the emergency was over. The Bishop of his own area had advised churchmen to fulfil their religious duties before going into the fields; Horton pointed out that this would involve attending Holy Communion and hearing the Ten Commandments. The Archbishop replied that Christ had taught the disciples to use the Sabbath for 'acts of beneficent service' and that Christ's teaching and example took precedence over the directions from Mount Sinai. In a further letter to Dr Horton in October, the Archbishop gave a picture of the way in which his endeavours to give a lead on moral issues made him the object of abusive attacks:

I am regarded apparently as the representative mouthpiece of those who object to reprisals . . . and I am in consequence the recipient of a continuous shower of protests, denunciations, and often virulent abuse, from every part of England, especially from London. I am said to be the cause of the Air Raids, to be in league with the Germans, and to be responsible for the death of those who have suffered, and so on. Devout prayers are expressed that I (and

occasionally my wife, to whom they sometimes write) may be the
next person to be blown to pieces. It is all coupled, strangely enough,
with my action in approving a certain amount of agricultural work
on Sundays as an emergency measure. . . . I think therefore that I
have said my say and, so to speak, nailed my colours both
adequately and with sufficient publicity.[55]

When the ruling about Sunday work was published, in some cases
church services were held on allotments; some country priests worked
in the fields on Sundays themselves. The Bishop of Exeter granted
permission for potatoes to be grown in consecrated ground.

The fact that the Government had to approach the Archbishop of
Canterbury to sanction Sunday work in this way is an indication that
the Church of England was still considered to have a binding and
loosing function over the majority of the population at this period. Even
during the second war, Hugh Dalton, President of the Board of Trade,
found it necessary to elicit a public statement from the Archbishops of
Canterbury and York that women need not wear hats in church. (The
Government wished to discourage the wearing of hats in order to save
scarce materials.)[56] It is a measure of the decline in the authority of the
Church of England, the changed relationship of Church and society, and
the slackened hold of evangelical morality in England, that such
requests would be inconceivable today. No doubt most soldiers thought
it was farcical and tragic that there should be such a prolonged furore
about a minor ethical issue. Sassoon's George Sherston, invalided
home, and becoming bitterly critical about the morality of continuing
the war, reacted mordantly to the Archbishop's ruling:

Remembering the intense bombardment in front of Arras on Easter
Sunday, I wondered whether the Archbishop had given the sanction
of the Gospel for that little bit of Sabbath field-work. Unconscious
that he was, presumably, pained by the War and its barbarities, I
glared morosely in the direction of Lambeth Palace and muttered,
'Silly old fossil!'[57]

5

The Church at the Front

In 1916, Henri Barbusse, a French novelist, published *Le Feu* based on his own trench diaries. Translated into English as *Under Fire* and published in 1917, it soon became a classic. It influenced both Siegfried Sassoon and Wilfred Owen who read it in the same hospital. In *Under Fire* a badly burned and partly delirious pilot tried to describe what he had seen, flying low the previous Sunday morning. He had been puzzled by two almost identical crowds of soldiers on either side of the line. He flew lower to investigate:

> Then I understood. It was Sunday, and there were two religious services being held under my eyes – the altar, the padre, and all the crowd of chaps. The more I went down the more I could see that the two things were alike – so exactly alike that it looked silly. One of the services – whichever you like – was a reflection of the other. . . . I went down lower. . . . Then I could hear. I heard one murmur, one only. I could only gather a single prayer that came up to me *en bloc*, the sound of a single chant that passed by me on its way to heaven. . . . I got some shrapnel just at the moment when, very low down, I made out the two voices from the earth that made up the one – 'Gott mit uns!' and 'God is with us!' – and I flew away. . . . What must the good God think about it all?[1]

This picture catches both the necessity and the absurdity of the Church's ministry in the fighting line, and the way in which Christianity is always trying to impel men to recognize some kind of transcendence – here symbolized by the experience of seeing life from a plane in the sky. Whereas some soldiers mused and wrote about the way the sun or moon, sky or birds transcended national divisions at the front, Isaac Rosenberg in 'Break of Day in the Trenches' wrote about a rat (the rats fed on German and English corpses, indifferent to nationality):

> Droll rat, they would shoot you if they knew
> Your cosmopolitan sympathies

(And God knows what antipathies).
Now you have touched this English hand
You will do the same to a German –
Soon, no doubt, if it be your pleasure
To cross the sleeping green between.

The wartime ministry of the Church of England in general and the wartime ministry of Anglican chaplains in particular – both have had a bad press. Our first task in this chapter is to look at some of the accounts given, and some of the accusations made, by serving soldiers as they encountered the Church in the course of army life.

Robert Graves's dismissive picture of the work of Anglican chaplains in *Goodbye to All That* (first published 1929) has been frequently quoted as the standard verdict. Graves wrote that though initially many commanding officers had a respect for 'the cloth', it soon disappeared; ordinary soldiers were in his opinion scornful of Anglican chaplains. He believed that if they had shown 'one-tenth the courage, endurance, and other human qualities' of the regimental doctors, a religious revival might have occurred. Under orders, the Anglican chaplains avoided the fighting, and stayed behind the front, whereas the Roman Catholic chaplains visited areas of danger to give unction to the dying. He considered that 'Anglican chaplains were remarkably out of touch with their troops' and he instanced the chaplain who preached a sermon on the commutation of tithes on the eve of a big battle in Mesopotamia.[2] Though even casual references to Anglican clergy in his memoirs were always derisive, he was always ready to go out of his way to praise Roman Catholics – no doubt in part a reaction against his background: his grandfather was Bishop of Limerick and he had several other relations in Orders. Yet when he returned to France he took the Bible with him as well as Shakespeare, read it, quoted from it, and phrases from it echoed round his mind in times of danger; when Augustine Birrell asserted that the Apocrypha was never read in church services, Graves took pleasure in correcting him. Graves's criticisms of Anglican chaplains are often retailed by historians at their face value. The readers' pencil marks of approval in library copies at the side of passages critical of the Church of England show that Graves knew how to select an ever-popular target. It is worth recalling that he had deliberately set out to write a book which would be popular, and that he acknowledged that he wrote to some extent tongue-in-cheek – a satire rather than a sober autobiography.[3] Nevertheless, the type of criticism he makes, as we shall see, was made by others as well.

Guy Chapman's *A Passionate Prodigality* (first published in 1933), was highly praised. He served in both wars and became in later life Professor of Modern History at Leeds. He, like Graves, wrote from a literary and professional background. As a boy he regularly attended St Mary Abbots, Kensington.[4] He drew a sharp contrast between the Roman Catholic and Anglican chaplains:

> These Catholic priests impressed one. Leeson [the R.C. padre] never dropped a word of religion in my hearing, but one felt a serenity and certitude streaming from him such as was not possessed by our bluff Anglicans. Already there was growing a dislike of these latter. They had nothing to offer but the consolation the next man could give you, and a less fortifying one. The Church of Rome sent a man into action mentally and spiritually cleaned. The Church of England could only offer you a cigarette. The Church of Rome, experienced in propaganda, sent its priests into the line. The Church of England forbade theirs forward of Brigade Headquarters, and though many, realizing the fatal blunder of such an order, came just the same, the publication of that injunction had its effect.[5]

Earlier he had told the story admiringly of the way in which Fr Leeson had crawled under the wire into no-man's-land to give absolution to three members of his flock. No doubt in his mind the Church of England was identified with the same cult of amateurishness which so shocked and depressed him about the Army itself when he first joined up on the eve of 1915.

Sassoon's George Sherston (a self-portrait) was brought up in a Christian and Anglican environment. The Church of England was a familiar, even loved, feature of the pre-war landscape. But the Church was pushed into the background by his war experiences and became almost invariably a target for sardonic remarks, or, on occasion, a trigger for nostalgia. In the first days in camp after the outbreak of war, he heard the bells of Canterbury Cathedral refusing 'to recognize the existence of a war'.[6] On leave from France he was glad to avoid the 'painful' experience of calling at the Rectory of which he had fond pre-war memories. When the Rector in a letter had quoted 'What I do thou knowest not now; but thou shalt know hereafter' (John 13.7) as a basis for Faith in wartime, it touched him but left him unconvinced.[7] He often used the Church calendar to date occurrences, but the incongruity between the Church's seasons and his present experience was so evident that the Church and Christianity were made to seem even more remote. His close friend Dick had just been killed: 'I remembered that it was Easter Sunday. Standing in that dismal ditch, I could find no consolation in the thought that Christ was risen.'[8] He noted that his tours of duty in the trenches occupied the last thirty days of Lent:

> This essential season in the Church calendar was not, as far as I remember, remarked upon by anyone in my company, although the name of Christ was often on our lips. . . . These innocuous blasphemings of the holy name were a peculiar feature of the War, in which the principles of Christianity were either obliterated or falsified for the convenience of all who were engaged in it. Up in the trenches every man bore his own burden; the Sabbath was not made for man; and if any man laid down his life for his friends it was no part of his military duties.[9] To kill an enemy was an effective action; to bring in one of our own wounded was praiseworthy, but unrelated to our war-aims. The Brigade chaplain did not exhort us to love our enemies. He was content to lead off with the hymn 'How sweet the name of Jesus sounds'! I mention this war-time dilemma of the Churches because my own mind was in rather a muddle at that time.[10]

(Again, the pencil lines in the library copy indicate how gratifying the modern reader finds such sentiments.)

A friend reading a letter from his wife exclaimed that he wished he were a cathedral organist, and together they reminisced with pleasant nostalgia about cathedral closes, and pictured themselves sauntering back to one of 'those snug old houses', anthem books under their arms after Evensong.[11] In the *Memoirs* we discover Sassoon's familiarity with the Church's year, the Authorized Version and the services of the Church, but the remoteness of the Christian world can only promote sarcasm or nostalgia; chaplains are not credited with any capacity to build a bridge between Christianity and the present realities of the war. When visiting Rouen Cathedral, Sherston thought he could 'escape from the War' in its atmosphere. But he heard the priest telling the congregation, or so he inferred, 'to love one another and be like little children'. Sherston's own sardonic reflections on such a sermon prevented him from engaging with the message, though he was moved by the solemnity of the cathedral.[12] In the trenches he kept seeing a pair of hands ('nationality unknown') protruding from the soaked ground:

'Each time I passed that place the protest of those fingers became more expressive of an appeal to God in defiance of those who made the War.'[13] After being wounded, he reached the dressing station, and he listened to an Anglican chaplain 'who was painfully aware that he could do nothing except stand about and feel sympathetic. The consolations of the Church of England weren't much in demand . . .'.[14] When he rebelled against the war, and was interviewed by a baffled Medical Board, he did not claim any particular religious grounds for his objection, and it was decided that he was suffering from shell-shock. Later, he went back to active service because he felt more comradeship with his troops than with the civilians he met, who had either been broken or enriched by the war. Sassoon entitled this final section of his *Memoirs* 'Sherston's Progress' and prefixed it with an ironic quotation from Bunyan: 'I told him that I was a Pilgrim going to the celestial City.' Back in France he attended a church parade addressed by a bishop in uniform ('a fact which speaks for itself'), who told them that they were like the early Christians being thrown to the lions, and that Christ was not 'the effete figure in stained-glass windows but the Warrior Son of God'. He concluded with a recitation of two verses from the American hymn 'God goes marching on'. 'Except, perhaps, for the early Christian comparison, the troops rather liked it', commented Sherston.[15]

Wilfred Owen had at one time considered becoming an Anglican priest. His experiences from 1911 to 1913 as lay assistant to the vicar of Dunsden deepened his social awareness and compassion as he visited the poor of the parish, but it also destroyed the evangelical faith which he had inherited from his mother.[16] There are few biblical and Christian references in his juvenilia, but the majority of his war poems show him testing biblical and Christian images and doctrines to see whether they will bear the weight of the increasing revulsion he felt against the slaughter.[17] Like Sassoon, Owen initially reacted to the war with the conventional patriotism which dominated the minds of those at home. He grew (partly under the influence of Sassoon whom he met in hospital in 1917) increasingly contemptuous of simple-minded, idealistic pictures of heroic soldiers; he expressed this contempt most savagely in his poem 'Dulce et Decorum est'. Visiting a hospital at Bordeaux in September 1914, while still a civilian, he wrote to his brother Harold (illustrating his letter with drawings):

One poor devil had his shin-bone crushed by a gun-carriage-wheel, and the doctor had to twist it about and push it like a piston to get out the pus. . . . I deliberately tell you all this to educate you to the actualities of the war.[18]

In 1914, the literary Dean of Norwich (H. C. Beeching) wrote an Introduction to a collection of patriotic verse for children compiled by Charles S. Evans and entitled *Our Glorious Heritage*. The Dean wrote that war gave the poet the opportunity to celebrate patriotism, love of freedom and heroic exploits. There was 'no more honourable service' than that of the poet in wartime. Owen was killed on 4 November 1918 – the telegram reached his parents an hour after the Armistice had been signed. Among his papers was found a draft Preface for a volume of poems:

> This book is not about heroes. English poetry is not yet fit to speak of them. Nor is it about deeds, or lands, nor anything about glory, honour, might, majesty, dominion, or power,[19] except War. Above all I am not concerned with Poetry. My subject is War, and the pity of War. The Poetry is in the pity. Yet these elegies are to this generation in no sense consolatory. They may be to the next. All a poet can do today is warn. That is why true Poets must be truthful.

In May 1917, four and a half months after going to France, he wrote to his mother:

> I am more and more Christian as I walk the unchristian ways of Christendom. Already I have comprehended a light which never will filter into the dogma of any national church: namely that one of Christ's essential commands was: Passivity at any price! Suffer dishonour and disgrace; but never resort to arms. Be bullied, be outraged, be killed; but do not kill. It may be a chimerical and an ignominious principle, but there it is. It can only be ignored: and I think pulpit professionals are ignoring it very skilfully and successfully indeed.

He criticized evangelists who did not have 'the courage' to become conscientious objectors, but reflected: 'And am I not myself a conscientious objector with a very seared conscience?' Christ transcends nationality:

> Christ is literally in no man's land. There men often hear His voice: Greater love hath no man than this, that a man lay down his life – for a friend. Is it spoken in English only and French? I do not believe so.

Thus you see how pure Christianity will not fit in with pure patriotism. . . . Christians have deliberately *cut* some of the main teaching of their code.[20]

In August 1917 he was in hospital with shell-shock. He wrote to his mother that the Archbishop of Canterbury should be sent a New Testament with the text ('at which he winks his eyes'):

'Ye have heard that it *hath* been said: An eye for an eye, and a tooth for a tooth: But I say that ye resist not evil, but whosoever shall smite thee on thy right cheek, turn to him the other also.' And if his reply be 'Most unsuitable for the present distressing moment, my dear lady! But I trust that in God's good time . . . etc.' – *then there is only one possible conclusion*, that there are no more Christians at the present moment than there were at the end of the first century. While I wear my star and eat my rations, I continue to take care of my Other Cheek; and, thinking of the eyes I have seen made sightless, and the bleeding lad's cheeks I have wiped, I say: Vengeance is mine, I, Owen will repay.[21]

Though he protested strongly against the Church's failure to proclaim the difficult and unpalatable parts of Christianity, he was honest enough to recognize that he was a divided being himself; he also had 'a very seared conscience'. He wrestled with the sayings of Jesus, but he did not withdraw from the war or become a pacifist, though no doubt his breakdown was in part caused by his inner conflicts about the war. But only as a combatant did he feel that he could effectively articulate the sufferings of his men.[22] On Easter Day 1918 he wrote to his mother: 'God so hated the world that He gave several millions of English-begotten sons, that whosoever believeth in them should not perish, but have a comfortable life,'[23] – a bitter parody of a favourite evangelical text and also one of the 'Comfortable Words' (hence his use of 'comfortable') in the Prayer Book Communion. In October 1918 he told his mother: 'Shells made by women in Birmingham are at this moment burying little children alive not very far from here.'[24] Yet he was glad to be recommended for the M.C.,[25] and he could write about going over the top in excited, semi-sexual language: 'There was an extraordinary exultation in the act of slowly walking forward, showing ourselves openly.'[26] Paradoxically, he found himself through his work as a soldier close to Christ in his passion, though his calculated humour betrays his sensitivity to the irony (see also his poem 'Soldier's Dream'):

For 14 hours yesterday I was at work – teaching Christ to lift his cross by numbers, and how to adjust his crown; and not to imagine he thirst until after the last halt; I attended his Supper to see that there were no complaints; and inspected his feet to see that they should be worthy of the nails. I see to it that he is dumb and stands to attention before his accusers. With a piece of silver I buy him every day, and with maps I make him familiar with the topography of Golgotha.[27]

In a pre-war poem 'Maundy Thursday' he told how he had refused to kiss the 'very dead' Christ on the crucifix, and instead had kissed the 'warm live hand' of the server which held it. But his war experiences brought the 'dead' Christ to life, and he discovered the crucified figure alive and present through the sufferings of the war. His pictures of God and Christ have depth and irony (there are some resemblances between his pictures and those of Studdert Kennedy). Through his experiences of the war, his understanding of God and of Christ became more ironic and more profound, richer and wider in scope than anything he could have received from his evangelical upbringing. He wrote to his mother about the religion of his family:

If I do not read hymns, and if Harold marks no Bible, or Colin sees no life-guide in his prayer-book, it is no bad sign. I have heard the cadences of harps not audible to Sankey, but which were strung by God; and played by mysteries to Him, and I was permitted to hear them. There is a point where prayer is indistinguishable from blasphemy. There is also a point where blasphemy is indistinguishable from prayer.

And he quotes an early draft of his poem 'The Last Laugh'.[28] Yet if he had moved a long way from being lay assistant to the vicar of Dunsden, the biblical stories and the language of the Authorized Version which had nourished him then now provided him with not only a store of imagery enabling him to communicate with readers (who at that date still knew their Bibles), but also with doctrinal boundaries against which he could push: both Bible and doctrine provided that element of 'constriction' which is necessary to great art. As a result we now have such poems as 'At a Calvary near the Ancre', 'Exposure', 'Anthem for Doomed Youth', 'Soldier's Dream', 'Strange Meeting', and 'The Parable of the Old Man and the Young':

> Then Abram bound the youth with belts and straps,
> And builded parapets and trenches there,

And stretchèd forth the knife to slay his son.
When lo! an angel called him out of heaven,
Saying, Lay not thy hand upon the lad,
Neither do anything to him. Behold,
A ram, caught in the thicket by its horns;
Offer the Ram of Pride instead of him.
But the old man would not so, but slew his son,
And half the seed of Europe, one by one.

('Parable of the Old Man and the Young')

Like Jeremiah or Isaiah's Servant he chose to bear and was constrained to express the sufferings of others:

For leaning out last midnight on my sill
I heard the sighs of men, that have no skill
To speak of their distress, no, nor the will!
A voice I know. And this time I must go.

('The Calls')

So he was able to say:

I, too, saw God through mud

('Apologia pro Poemate Meo')

C. E. Montague enlisted in his late forties. He served in the army during the whole war. He was on the staff of the *Manchester Guardian* for thirty-five years. His reflections on the war with the representative title *Disenchantment* were published in 1922, written in the belles-lettres style. His attitude to the Church was critical and rather lofty. In his chapter, 'The Sheep that were not Fed', he gave voice to his conviction that the Church had had a great opportunity among the soldiers, but was incapable of seizing it. A soldier might be six months in France before a religious service came his way. Though there were some heroes and saints among the chaplains like T. B. Hardy, the typical chaplain of all denominations so often overdid 'his jolly implied disclaimers of any compromising connection with kingdoms not of this world. For one thing, he was, for the taste of people versed in carnage, a shade too fussily bloodthirsty.' He was a 'good sort' and was a constant source of tobacco, good at talking shop about the war, always ready to do a good turn, but 'had the parsons really nothing to say of their own about the noisome mess in which the good old world seemed to be floundering?'.[29] The average soldier had folded up whatever religion he had with his civilian clothes. He felt that Christ's teaching, however much respected, was irrelevant to the war. From the beginning of the Church, both clergy and laity had ignored the difficult sayings of Jesus, though from time to time a St Francis or a Tolstoy had taken them seriously. During the war there were many embers of religious experience about, only waiting for the sensitive interpreter to fan them into a flame – many soldiers had moments of religious awareness: a 'queer little rent in the veil of common experience'. The soldiers lingered around 'the uncrossed threshold of religion'. 'They were prepared and expectant.' But instead of finding someone to 'refine the gold out of all that rich alluvial drift', the typical chaplain came on the scene:

> As soon as his genial bulk hove in sight, and his cheery robustious chaff began blowing about, the shy and uncouth muse of our savage theology unfolded her wings and flew away. Once more the talk was all footer and rations and scragging the Kaiser, and how 'the Hun' would walk a bit lame after the last knock he had got. Very nice, too, in its way. And yet there had been a kind of savour about the themes that had now shambled back in confusion, before the clerical onset, into their twilight lairs in the souls of individual laymen. . . . When you are given an infant earth to fashion out of a whirling ball of flaming metals and gases, then good humour, some taste for adventure, distinction at cricket, a jolly way with the men, and an imperfect digestion of thirty-nine partly masticated articles may not carry you far. . . . So, in his own way, the army chaplain, too, became a tributary brook feeding the general reservoir of disappointment and mistrust . . .[30]

Major John Baynes, author of a recent study of the Second Scottish Rifles at the battle of Neuve Chapelle (1915), agrees with the generally received picture. Few officers, he believes, looked at the chaplains critically because many chaplains came from the same social group as themselves. Many officers were sons of clergy or had clerical relations. Chaplains were regarded by officers as part of the normal social system. While Roman Catholic chaplains were on average of high quality, and ready to expose themselves to danger, other chaplains were 'rather inadequate'. The type of soldier who felt that being married would be a distraction from wholehearted devotion to the regiment, had a natural sympathy with the celibacy of the Roman Catholic clergy. Few of the people he consulted had any strong recollections of the activities of chaplains. One captain had a vivid memory of a Christmas

Communion in a barn in 1914, but apart from that could not remember ever having seen a chaplain in France 'certainly nowhere near the front'. There were of course exceptions. One soldier firing at a group of German soldiers was astonished to see a chaplain at his side digging to make a head cover for him; a few minutes later the chaplain was killed. What a religious revival would have been possible, Baynes considers, if the chaplains had shared the dangers of the trenches![31]

Donald Hankey wrote a series of articles for the *Spectator* and the *Westminster Gazette* which were published as *A Student in Arms* in April 1916; in October he was killed on the Somme. His articles and book were widely read; by December 1916 the book had reached its seventh edition. Harry Blackburne, then Senior Chaplain to the First Army, wrote: 'I think *A Student in Arms* by Donald Hankey, is excellent; and I am trying to get all chaplains to read it.'[32] Hankey was a junior officer and a keen churchman. One of his brothers, Colonel Sir Maurice Hankey, was Secretary of the War Cabinet. Two main themes emerge from the book – the breaking down of social and class barriers in the New Army; and the need for the churches and theology to be humble and open enough to be able to comprehend (in all senses) the deep experiences of the men at war.

He called 'the new citizen Army' an 'Experiment in Democracy' and used St Paul's words, 'diversities of gifts, but the same Spirit' to describe the way in which each man found his own level. He deeply hoped that the experience of shared danger, when 'one sees men as God sees them, apart from externals such as manner and intonation', would after the war do away with class strife.[33] He underestimated both the strength and power of the English class divisions, and the degree to which they would in some ways be reinforced by the war. Every night at Victoria station when soldiers joined the leave trains for France, five out of the six trains were badly lit and crowded – those for regimental officers and men. The sixth was brightly lit, it had two dining cars and all the coaches were first class. Attendants saw the Staff officers to their places and then took orders for drinks. Major-General Herbert Essame, who describe the scene, commented: 'The irony of this nightly demonstration at Victoria Station of the great gap between the leaders and the led, this blatant display of privilege was to rankle in the minds of the soldiers in the front line and to survive in the national memory for the next half century.'[34]

Chapter VII of Hankey's book, 'The Religion of the Inarticulate', was often quoted by chaplains and others.[35] It tried to grasp the issue which pervaded the report *The Army and Religion*, the rhymes of Studdert Kennedy and the perplexed thinking of many chaplains. The Church, wrote Hankey, has great opportunities. But chaplains find men inaccessible, however hard they try to reach them. In pre-war days, clubs were opened in poorer areas by the upper classes, but they failed to bridge the gap. The war provides another chance of doing so. But neither philosophizing nor prayer come easily in the barrack room. We have to learn the fundamental lesson that the working man is inarticulate, and that to understand him we must look not to words, but to actions and the objects of his admiration. (Fifty years later Canon Eric James asked Bishop Ian Ramsey at the Parish and People Conference in 1967 how he would teach a miner to pray. Ramsey replied that he would try to find out a man's enthusiasm, for his children or his car: 'Enthusiasm is so often the gateway to adoration!' he said.)[36] Men believe in unselfishness, generosity, charity and humility, but hardly ever connected these with Christianity. Christianity in their minds is associated with believing that Jonah was swallowed by the whale and with not swearing, drinking or smoking. Chaplains confuse inarticulateness with lack of religion.

> I am certain that if the chaplain wants to be understood and to win their sympathy he must begin by showing them that Christianity is the explanation and the justification and the triumph of all that they do now really believe in. He must start by making their religion articulate in a way which they will recognise. . . . In doing this perhaps he will find a stronger faith than his own. It is certainly arguable that we educated Christians are in our way almost as inarticulate as the uneducated whom we always want to instruct. . . . If the working man's religion is often wholly inarticulate, the real religion of the educated man is often quite wrongly articulated.[37]

In Chapter XIV, 'A Mobilization of the Church', he argued that the clergy do not understand the ordinary man:

> The sin against which they preach is sin as defined in the Theological College, a sort of pale, lifeless shadow of the real thing. The virtue which they extol is equally a ghost of the real, generous, vital love of good which is the only thing that is of any use in the everyday working life of actual men.[38]

Many ordinands have become combatants, younger clergy have joined the R.A.M.C. or even become combatants, but that is not enough. The majority of younger clergy and all ordinands should be set free for army service. Then at the end of the war, having shared the life of ordinary men in barrack room and trench, they would understand their weaknesses and their language: 'With such men as clergy a new era might dawn for the Church in this land, and the Kingdom of God be brought very nigh.'[39] (He was once an ordinand himself.)

In Chapter XV he tried to relate his belief in the community of the Church with his experience of comradeship in the forces. He recalls going to Communion with only two other communicants (both women) present. But when he shut his eyes, he saw a whole host of people there, men who had hardly ever been to church, let alone to Communion. Such men, his comrades, are surely members of the Church whether they realize it or not. He will never be satisfied, he writes, until the Church of England is 'the Church of all good men and women in England, and until all the good thoughts and deeds in England are laid at the feet of the Lord of All Good Life, through the medium of His body the Church'.[40] The natural world, so often flourishing in the midst of destruction, this belongs to the Church as well. Surely the fellowship of heaven must be wide enough to include men like his 'Beloved Captain' (note the echo of the Fourth Gospel), killed trying to rescue his men in a torpedoed trench:

> But he lives. Somehow he lives. And we who knew him do not forget. We feel his eyes on us. We still work for that wonderful smile of his. . . . I think that those who went West have seen him. When they got to the other side I think they were met. Some One said 'Well done, good and faithful servant.' And as they knelt before that gracious pierced Figure, I reckon they saw near by the captain's smile. Anyway, in that faith let me die, if death should come my way; and so, I think shall I die content.[41]

George Coppard came from a very different background from Donald Hankey. He left school at thirteen and worked in various jobs before enlisting as a private in 1914. He recalls how on Good Friday 1916, being a former choirboy, his thoughts turned to the meaning of the day and the three-hour services he had attended in the past:

> All that was over and seemed meaningless. My identity disc and pay-book said my religion was 'C of E'. To me and most Tommies this meant compulsion to attend church parade on Sundays if the company happened to be well out of the fighting zone.

He had a 'glimpse' of a chaplain now and then, but never anywhere near the trenches. He had heard a talk by Studdert Kennedy who told the men how he had been in the front line when a 'strafe' started. A sergeant saw him and said, 'Who are you?'. 'I'm the Church', replied Kennedy. 'Then what the bloody hell are you doing here?' The only person Coppard could remember who had benefited from his religion was a Jew who had been given a week's leave in England to attend Passover much to the resentment of the other soldiers.[42] Another volume of reminiscences by a private soldier, Frank Richards, *Old Soldiers Never Die*, was even more scathing about chaplains, ordinands and clergy.[43] At the end of *Under Fire* Barbusse, writing in a French context, classed the 'parsons' as among the 'enemies' of the common people together with financiers, speculators, the opponents of progress and those who are dazzled by military glory.[44]

At first, many troops arrived at the front with naïvety and simple patriotism. 'We believed all they said, all the propaganda', an East Anglian private recalls. 'We were fighting for England. You had only to say "England" to stop any argument.' He had joined the army in March 1914 to get away from being 'worked mercilessly' for low wages by a farmer who would not pay his workers when it rained. When he went to the Dardanelles, they landed at night and waited on the beach till dawn came. They saw a large marquee:

> It didn't make me think of the military but of the village fetes. Other people must have thought like this because I remember how we all rushed up to it, like boys getting into a circus, and then found it all laced up. We unlaced it and rushed in. It was full of corpses. Dead Englishmen, lines and lines of them, and with their eyes wide open. We all stopped talking. I'd never seen a dead man before and here I was looking at two or three hundred of them. It was our first fear. Nobody had mentioned this. I was very shocked. I thought of Suffolk and it seemed a happy place for the first time.[45]

But experience and time brought an inevitable hardening. Another soldier wrote:

> I spoke of the hardening of experience. Here's an instance. All the innumerable stories of stay-at-home writers about the genius of place — I've just come from where fifty thousand bodies lie, bones and barbed wire everywhere, skeletons bleached if one takes a walk over

the frightfully contested and blown up hill. – Boots and bones protruding from one's dug-out walls, and yet – one is merry there.[46]

But usually soldiers did not describe their more horrible experiences in letters to avoid worrying those at home. 'With the wounded, cheeriness has almost become almost a convention', commented one chaplain.[47] When on leave, the experiences the soldier had undergone were often too difficult or distressing to try to describe. In any case, after a time terrible experiences became too normal to shock any more. The films which the public saw (the first British propaganda film was shown in December 1915) left out the worst horrors of the fighting. Henson wrote to *The Times* (1 September 1916) to protest against the showing of a film depicting the battle of the Somme. 'I beg leave respectfully to enter a protest against an entertainment which wounds the heart and violates the very sanctities of bereavement.' So the gap between the front and those at home widened into a gulf. In 1917, Charles Raven went from being Dean of Emmanuel College, Cambridge, and teaching at Tonbridge into the midst of the war as a chaplain. When he returned to London from the front he found the contrast a very bitter one: the contrast, for example, between the war profiteer knighted for his work and the deserter at the front waiting to be shot for a failure of nerve. On leave from a conflict which he felt was not so much a conflict between nations as between 'unchained and apocalyptic forces', he was sickened to meet in Cambridge an Anglican Professor of Theology 'gibbering with blood-lust' and a Free Churchman obsessed with the problems of venereal disease.[48] R. H. Tawney, churchman and economist, enlisted as a private, refusing a commission, and rose to the rank of sergeant in the Manchester Regiment. On 1 July 1916 he was seriously wounded in the battle of the Somme. In October he published an article in the *Nation* 'Some Reflections of a Soldier'. He said that though it was nice to be home again, he felt like a visitor among strangers whose modes of thought he neither altogether understood nor approved. When soldiers at the front read about, for example, Lloyd George's 'latest rhapsody about "cheerful Tommies with the glint of battle in their eyes"', they discounted such statements as unrepresentative. But after being in England for some months Tawney had come to the conclusion that the papers accurately reflected what people thought at home. The fighting soldiers and the public at home had drifted apart.[49] Tawney had been seriously wounded in the Somme attack of 1 July 1916; recovering in hospital he was visited by his friend and mentor Bishop Gore. Gore told the matron that she had one of the most valuable lives in England under her care. After Gore had gone, she rebuked Tawney: 'Why ever didn't you tell us you were a gentleman?'[50] Kingsley Martin remembers visiting him regularly after the war, when Tawney was on the staff of the London School of Economics, and found him always wearing 'an ancient, dirty, and torn sergeant's tunic' from the war[51] – an indication not only of Tawney's frugality, but also of the way in which ex-soldiers found it hard to let go of their wartime experiences.

We have surveyed a good deal of evidence about attitudes to chaplains; we have remarked on the gulf which opened between civilian and army life. What of the chaplains themselves?

Chaplains appeared on the payroll of the English army as early as the reign of Edward I. The Chaplains' Department as such dates from 1796. During the nineteenth century some Roman Catholic, Nonconformist and Jewish chaplains began to be appointed in addition to the Church of England clergy. At the outbreak of war in 1914, there were 117 chaplains, of whom 89 were Anglicans. By the Armistice the total number had risen to 3,475, of whom 1,985 were Anglicans. The total number of Anglican clergy commissioned as chaplains during the war was 3,030. Of the 172 who were killed or died as a result of the war, 88 were Anglicans. Four chaplains were awarded the Victoria Cross. Many others were decorated or commended for bravery.[52] When the British Expeditionary Force of about 100,000 men went to France in August 1914, about 65 chaplains went with them, of whom about 20 were attached to headquarters staff. One chaplain was attached to each General Hospital or Field Ambulance, and a maximum of four to each brigade.[53]

It was tragic that the Chaplain-General from 1901 to 1925 was Bishop John Taylor Smith, a pietistic Evangelical with no university theological training. Going as a missionary to West Africa in 1891, he became Bishop of Sierra Leone in 1897. A fervent believer in the Empire, in 1896 he accompanied an expeditionary force against the Ashantis as chaplain. (In the company was Prince Henry of Battenberg who caught a fever and died. Taylor Smith preached a memorial sermon before the Queen and so became a friend of the Royal Family.) Taylor Smith described the Sunday service held at Kumasi during the campaign:

On the Sunday morning, from a pulpit of biscuit boxes covered with the Union Jack, I conducted Divine Service. I shall never forget the heartiness of the men's voices in joining in the service, nor in the singing of the hymn 'Onward, Christian Soldiers', and also 'God save the Queen'. The text of the sermon was, 'Thy Kingdom Come'. The Ashantis looked on in wonder and astonishment.[54]

(The total absence of irony in this account is characteristic.) He was a believer in what he called 'aggressive' evangelism, and he was invariably determined to turn every possible occasion to evangelistic ends, even asking the barber on board ship about his soul while he was being shaved. He always carried a shilling in his pocket: 'This shilling is for the first man or woman who catches me out of temper', he would explain. As one would expect, he seems to have had no doubts or questioning about the war when it came: 'the greatest spiritual war that we have ever been called upon to take part in', he called it.[55]

Interviewing candidates for chaplaincies, he often asked the question, 'If you had five minutes, and five minutes only, to spend with a man about to die, what would you say to him?'[56] He ensured that soldiers were supplied with a copy of one of the Gospels, the Book of Proverbs and a prayer written by himself. Did he choose the Book of Proverbs partly because of its stern warnings about the dangers of associating with loose women? Two million copies of his message entitled 'Strategic Retreats' warning men against lust were distributed to the troops just after the retreat from Mons. In 1911 he became Vice-President, and in 1924 President, of the Alliance of Honour, an association for the promotion of sexual purity; he frequently spoke on this subject, both publicly and privately.

He had the evangelical gift of using vivid, if sometimes naïve, illustrations, as for example when, visiting a hospital in France, he saw an inverted bowl. He pointed out to the men that, turned upside down, it was full of darkness, but, turned the right way up (converted), it became full of light. But he had neither the theological insight, nor (in the true sense of the word) the sophistication that was needed to be a spiritual guide to chaplains or men. His religious faith tripped too easily off the tongue to make much contact with men facing deep and agonizing perplexities. He was too a-political, and his view of faith was too atomistic, to appreciate that the conversion of individuals to a pietistic religion was an inadequate answer to the issues raised by the war both for faith and for society.

At first, appointment and deployment of the Church of England chaplains was ill-organized. Before the war Bishop Taylor Smith had carefully worked out a scheme so that chaplains would have a clear place in the army establishment in wartime. But the Army Council had not accepted his suggestions, so the organization of the Chaplains' Department was hopelessly inadequate. Although, for example, 75 per cent of the soldiers registered as 'Church of England', the chaplains in France were at first under the command of a Northern Irish Presbyterian, long past the age of retirement.[57] Archbishop Davidson in a memorandum of December 1914 complained that the appointment of chaplains was chaotic. By 1 September 1914, 900 more volunteers than could be used had offered their services.[58] The pronounced evangelical attitudes of Bishop Taylor Smith added to the problems. In October 1914, Lord Halifax, President of the English Church Union, protested to Lord Kitchener that Anglo-Catholic chaplains were being discriminated against. Halifax wrote to Bishop Taylor Smith that soldiers ought to have an opportunity of attending Holy Communion every Sunday, and that there must be 'hundreds and thousands of men who would wish to make their confessions and receive Holy Communion before going into action'. In response to the charge of discrimination, Taylor Smith contended that he did appoint Anglo-Catholics, adding however, 'An Extremist is out of place in the Army'. The *Church Times* supported Halifax's campaign.[59] Davidson was also under pressure from the Bishop of London and other Bishops to make some change. An Anglo-Catholic friend of Ronald Knox's, who applied, was said to have been asked by the Chaplain-General what he would do for a dying man. The priest replied, 'Hear his confession and give him absolution.' He was turned down. The proper answer should have been, so the story goes, 'Give him a cigarette and take any last message he may have for his family'.[60] But no doubt the story is a highly-coloured piece of Anglo-Catholic naughtiness: Bishop Taylor Smith was a non-smoker and too keen to save souls to make a remark like that. When Anglo-Catholic chaplains were appointed more readily, one of the Knox brothers termed it the 'Uriah the Hittite policy',[61]

The question of the discrimination against Anglo-Catholics as chaplains was not the only issue. There were also widespread criticisms in church circles that religious ministrations in the army were badly organized.[62] The chaplains and men in France needed episcopal oversight on the spot, as the Bishops of London and Pretoria, *Challenge*, and the *Guardian* all urged.[63] Bishop Taylor Smith was necessarily preoccupied with administration in London. So Bishop Gwynne was appointed Deputy Chaplain-General in July 1915 with special responsibility for chaplains and troops in France. He broadened recruitment and made the organization more efficient. (His brother was H. A. Gwynne, editor of the Tory *Morning Post*.) Ironically, when Bishop Gwynne had first applied to become a chaplain, Bishop Taylor Smith (an old friend) had waved him away and told him that at fifty he was far too old to go to France. Only after several visits to the War Office was he accepted, though he had acted as chaplain to troops in the Sudan since 1900.[64] In 1934, Dean Inge noted in his Diary the opinion of Lord Plumer that of all men Bishop Gwynne did most to win the war.[65] Gwynne had been Bishop of Khartoum before the war; when the war was over, he refused high office in England to return to Egypt where he spent the rest of his life. F. R. Barry was a chaplain under Gwynne and his words are representative of the opinions of many others:

> ... many of us, I think, would have gone under or have suffered shipwreck of their faith had it not been for the pastoral care and guidance of the great and saintly Bishop Gwynne, Father in God to a whole generation of young men. . . . I have used the word 'saintly' deliberately. For he made it easier to believe in God. . . . He was a commanding figure in that period. . . .[66]

Gwynne got on well with Sir Douglas Haig, who was a devout Presbyterian. Soon after Haig took over the command of the Expeditionary Force in 1915, Gwynne was summoned to his headquarters. Haig told him that he regarded his job as one of the most important under his command. 'A good chaplain is as valuable as a good general. . . . We are fighting for Christ and the freedom of mankind', Haig declared. A few days later Haig attended a Christmas Day service at which Bishop Gwynne preached. Haig was so impressed that he had the sermon printed and circulated among the troops.[67] Lord Halifax paid tribute to the tolerance and fairness of Bishop Gwynne. But Lord Halifax and Fr Bull continued to campaign against Bishop Taylor Smith for what Fr Bull called the 'gross scandal of inefficiency' of his department. Halifax declared that if Taylor Smith would not undertake reforms he should be replaced. Halifax and Bull were deeply concerned about the inadequate number of chaplains, the lack of sacramental ministrations and the Chaplain-General's efforts to forbid vestments and sacramental confession. Bishop Gwynne, however, gave support to Catholic-minded chaplains under his care in France, and the English Church Union felt its protests were having an effect.[68]

Bishop Gwynne's pastoral care of the chaplains improved the religious situation in France. At home, steps were taken to strengthen and broaden Bishop Taylor Smith's staff in London, and an Advisory Committee was created under Lord Salisbury, but the inefficiency of the Chaplain-General's office continued. In 1917, when the supply of chaplains was not meeting the figures required, Bishop Gwynne proposed that clergy should be conscripted like doctors for service as chaplains as required. The Archbishop of Canterbury did not agree with this suggestion, but created an organization to ensure a steady flow of chaplains from the home Church.[69] In July 1918, the Archbishop wrote to Bishop Woods of Peterborough to suggest that several of the younger suffragans might go out as chaplains for six-month periods. In reply Woods offered his own services, but the Archbishop felt that diocesan bishops could not be released.[70]

Guy Rogers (later Rector of Birmingham) believed that chaplains in France were so attached to Bishop Gwynne that they were never quite fair to Bishop Taylor Smith. After hearing stories about what it was like to be interviewed by him, he was agreeably surprised. But no doubt Rogers, with his Irish evangelical and Keswick Convention background, would be more immediately acceptable to Taylor Smith than most candidates.[71] Harold Woolley, a Territorial Officer awarded the V.C. in 1915, was ordained in 1920 and served in the second war as a chaplain; his comments on Taylor Smith were more critical: 'He was an extreme low churchman and not, I think, very well-read. Perhaps most of the Regular Chaplains were of his type – many of them Protestant Irishmen. This tendency continued for some time, and imagination and initiative were liable to be smothered.'[72]

For about the first couple of years of the war, chaplains were thrust into service with no real preparation apart from interviews at the Chaplains' Department. By 1916 an initiation course was established at Woolwich.[73] In 1915, F. R. Barry was commissioned straight from an Oxford chaplaincy. He had been a priest for no more than a few months and was only twenty-five years old. He was put on board ship bound for Egypt. 'I had very little idea what to do; no one had given me any kind of briefing.' Having lived a sheltered life, he was 'scared stiff'; but once in Egypt he established a canteen in a tent and began to make relationships and find his feet.[74] In August 1914 Walter Carey applied for a naval chaplaincy one day, and received a telegram the next day ordering him to report to a ship for duty twenty-four hours later.[75] In September 1914, Fr Waggett, having intimated that he wished to serve as a chaplain, without any warning heard that he would be leaving for France in two days' time. Riding round on his horse in France, he found a hospital with no chaplain and asked permission to stay and work there.[76] Studdert Kennedy was appointed chaplain on 21 December 1915. Four days later he was conducting a Christmas service for 400 men in the pouring rain in a French village square.[77] Barry recalls his arrival in France after being transferred from Egypt. His division went straight to the Somme. 'I had never seen a dead man before, much less bloody bits and pieces of men, and as near as nothing I turned and ran.'[78]

In the mobilization plans no provision had been made for either transporting, accommodating, paying or even feeding the chaplains.[79] Again Barry provides a vivid picture of the early bewildering days:

> When the padres first went out with the B.E.F., the army had little idea what to do with them. In battle, they were left behind at the base and were not allowed to go up to the fighting front. What on earth, it was asked, could they do up there? A colonel would say, 'No work for you today, padre', meaning by that, no corpses for burial. The chaplains' job was to take church parades, on such rare occasions as these were practicable, to run entertainments, to help in censoring letters, and in general to act as welfare officers, thereby helping to keep up morale. But was that what they had been ordained to do?

But in 1916, when he arrived in France himself, all this was changed.

> The chaplains were allowed to move freely everywhere and when the units 'went up' we went with them. Several were awarded V.C.s, and a substantial number were killed in action. (I lost two at Gouzeaucourt.) We would give Holy Communion in the dugouts, minister to the wounded and dying, share, so far as we might, in what the troops endured. But we did not share the worst thing of all that those kind and often sensitive men had to suffer: we did not have to kill other human beings. We did what we could to serve them in Christ's name – and surely the distribution of cigarettes was a relevant form of the cup of cold water – and they understood that this was why we were doing it. They did not regard us as just welfare officers. In some dim way they discovered that they needed what the ministry of the Church sought to offer.[80]

But controversy continued (and still continues)[81] as to the best location for chaplains in time of war. In September 1914, Fr Bull (drawing on his experience as a chaplain in the Boer War) advised chaplains to ride into battle with the guns, to cheer the troops and to share their dangers.[82] At first chaplains were discouraged from visiting the front line, and many chaplains were severely reprimanded for doing so. It was felt that they would be in the way; stretcher-bearers had enough to do, it was argued by army authorities, without having to attend to wounded or dead chaplains. To see a chaplain carried away would have a bad effect on the morale of the troops. Commanding officers believed that the chaplain should be stationed at the dressing station where he would be able to attend to the wounded passing through. But in 1915, as a result of pressure from some of the chaplains themselves, an army order was issued which encouraged chaplains to move freely about. Some chaplains (including Bishop Gwynne) and the *Guardian* had been strongly pressing for a change.[83] Neville Talbot had been regularly going up to the front line trenches ever since his arrival in France in August 1914. On 20 October 1914 he wrote to his Senior Chaplain:

> May I say as strongly as I can, that experience has shown me, what I believed to be true before, that there is much scope and work to be done with a unit as a whole and with fighting troops. One can get to know them, see them in the trenches, help them about daily prayers, have services for them when they are in billets . . . and be available for help in other ways. . . .

He wrote to his mother: 'I want to get a general change. It is just a sort of stupid convention that the Padre is next door to an undertaker.' His representations to the authorities created a good deal of commotion, and clearly his pressure was chiefly responsible for the change in the order.[84] When Davidson visited France in May 1916, Haig spoke warmly of the work of chaplains, and strongly stressed the value of the 'changed administrative order' which now encouraged chaplains to go up to the trenches.[85] But the charge that chaplains were cowards who skulked as far from danger as possible, still widely believed and repeated, is also answered by the number of casualties they suffered, and the number of decorations for bravery which they were awarded. The accounts given by some of the chaplains of their own work have also to be taken into account. But we must remember when reading these accounts that inevitably their own activities loomed larger in their own eyes than they did in the eyes of the soldiers themselves. We have already noted that to the ordinary soldier they seemed rarely to be around. Harold Woolley, chaplain in the second war, recalls how as a first war Territorial Officer it was more than a month after landing in France in November 1914 before he saw a chaplain.[86] Today the hard-worked vicar of a large parish may feel that he is to be seen everywhere, and may not be able to comprehend that to the vast majority of his parishioners his work is unknown. Randall Davidson on his visit to France in May 1916 recorded how he had pressed Haig hard for criticisms of the chaplains, 'but I could not elicit anything except laudation'.[87] In 1919, the King, 'in view of the splendid work' done by chaplains during the war, approved the addition of the word 'Royal' to the Army Chaplains' Department.[88] Nevertheless, it is quite clear that throughout the war the chaplains laboured under the stigma created by the stupid administrative order forbidding them near the front, and though this was disregarded by some, and soon changed, the stigma persisted, and indeed still persists. For the first period of the war, they had to take up their very difficult task quite unprepared. Clearly, too, the administration and deployment of chaplains was pretty chaotic especially at the beginning of the war. The discrimination exercised by Bishop Taylor Smith seems to have had unfortunate results in producing, at least initially, a more than average number of chaplains who had narrow sympathies. But Bishop Gwynne was a liberal Evangelical with a large pastoral heart open to chaplains of all traditions.

Class also played a part in the reactions of the ordinary soldier to chaplains. Whereas many ordinary soldiers came from working-class backgrounds, and knew what hardship and privation were, the clergy of the Church of England were almost entirely from a professional background, and most had no experience of an ordinary job before ordination. The Church of England was regarded by many ordinary people as part of that establishment which was blamed, particularly as the war went on, for what seemed increasingly to be the apparent futility and mismanagement of the war. Working-class memories are long. No doubt some soldiers from East Anglia thought of the Church of England as the institution which had maintained a gaol at Ely under the civil jurisdiction of the Bishop from 1109 until 1836, a temporal power hated by Fenmen. Some would have heard tell how in 1816 the Bishop had entered his cathedral preceded by his butler carrying the sword of state, for a service before the trial of some seventy-five men who had rioted at Littleport and Ely because of rural distress. Five were hanged, nine transported, and ten gaoled. Afterwards, a group swore over the coffins that they would tell their children, generation after generation, what 'the Bishop and the gentry had done to those Fenmen who'd only done when they were drunk what the college lads had done many a time in Cambridge without anything being done about it'. That story was still being told when the soldiers went from the Fens to fight in the first war.[89] Some from London would recall the often repeated story how during the dock strike of 1889 Bishop Frederick Temple had gone on holiday, leaving Cardinal Manning to work out the final compromise. Ben Tillett, the dockers' leader, was contemptuous about the Bishop of London's attitude. In June 1905 a group of 440 unemployed men set out to march to London from Leicester singing 'Lead, kindly Light' led by the Rev. F. L. Donaldson, a leading member of the Christian Social Union. When they arrived in London, Archbishop Davidson refused to see them. When the correspondence between the Archbishop and Donaldson was published, Davidson's refusal caused considerable criticism. Keir Hardie was particularly scathing in an 'open letter' to the clergy which he published in the *Labour Leader*:

> The Archbishop of Canterbury . . . said he had to devote 17 hours a day to his work and had no time left in which to form opinions on how to solve the unemployed question. The religion which demands 17 hours a day for organisation and leaves no time for a single thought about starving and despairing men, women and children has no message for this age.[90]

To the ordinary soldier the chaplain seemed socially a class apart, both by background and rank. When Dick Sheppard invited some soldiers to Communion, they told him that they thought it was a service for officers.[91] The chaplain was also apart, because while he supported the war, sometimes in a bellicose fashion, he did not fight himself. On to the chaplain was projected the charge that if only the Church had really been obeying Christ, there would have been no war at all. Many hoped that the Church would have a wider vision than the politicians, and would transcend nationalism, and they were angry and depressed when it sometimes seemed that the Church in each country was only concerned to give religious sanctions for that country's particular cause.

It is understandable also why Roman Catholic chaplains seemed to some to be superior to the Anglican chaplains.[92] For one thing, Roman Catholicism was to most soldiers quite novel, while the Church of England was all too familiar. But there were deeper reasons for the widespread admiration of the Roman Catholic chaplains. High churchmen like the Talbot brothers admired the professionalism of the Roman Catholic system, which they felt was far more adapted for pastoral work in crisis situations. Though the Church of England had accepted rituals for Baptism, Confirmation, Marriage, Communion, and Burial, there was no authorized form for sacramental confession and absolution (apart from a little-known provision in the Prayer Book), no adequate ritual for the commendation of the dying and no official form of unction. In any case the average Anglican soldier had not been taught to think sacramentally. Particularly in emergencies when little time is available, sacramental rituals have an objectivity and 'professionalism' that can be more effective than improvised prayer and counsel. In the front line, Roman Catholic priests had the tangible ministry of the viaticum and unction to offer, while only a small minority of Anglican chaplains carried the reserved sacrament about with them or administered unction to the dying. The War Office allowed a higher ratio of Roman Catholic chaplains to men than for other denominations, because Roman Catholic soldiers expected a regular sacramental ministry.[93] The *Guardian* pressed for what it regarded as a more equitable proportion of Anglican chaplains.[94] Bishop E. S. Talbot deplored the failure of the Church of England to make Holy Communion 'a natural and beloved part of the life of soldiers',[95] and Anglican chaplains like Harry Blackburne lamented the fact that soldiers seemed shy about Communion because they felt they had to be particularly good to come. But Anglicans rarely reflected that while 'going to Communion' sounded like a display of individual and hardly masculine pietism, for a Roman Catholic soldier to talk about 'going to Mass' sounded to his fellows more like an act of objective and therefore acceptable obedience – 'something Catholics had to do'. Also the Church of England had no method of popular prayer as simple and objective as the rosary or traditional Catholic litanies. Moreover, the Roman Catholic priest was able to rely on his role as a priest in a way which was not possible for the Anglican chaplain. The latter arrived trailing behind him the image of the stage parson, who was upper-class, naïve, shockable, only really at home with women, and who never did any proper work: a well-meaning but ineffective and rather comic figure like the local clergyman Sassoon recalled who would tell soldiers about to go to France to trust in their Saviour, concluding, 'And now God go with you. I will go with you as far as the station.'[96] In situations that are totally new and bewildering, rituals can supply boundaries and signposts, so reducing the sense of chaotic novelty; through the familiar rituals a sense of solidarity is established with both 'normal' life beyond the emergency, and with previous generations. Rituals can 'contain' feelings too overwhelming or perplexing to be otherwise expressed. The calm exercise by a priest of his role can give a parent-like as well as a professional reassurance of order, love, and meaning in an otherwise chaotic and unbearable existence. But the academic training of the Anglican clergy in the pre-war period had been given priority over priestly training. So as priests they were often uncertain of their role, in every sense of the word, in a situation in which all the familiar supports of their parochial surroundings were removed.

In addition, the Roman Catholic chaplains almost wholly came from a working-class background, unlike the Anglican clergy, but like the majority of the soldiers. Cardinal Heenan told (with that inverted pride which sometimes characterizes those outside the establishment) how he was at seminary with ex-Lance-Corporal Masterson, later Archbishop of Birmingham, and ex-Sergeant Griffin, later Archbishop of Westminster.[97] How many Anglican Archbishops could or would point to fellow Archbishops or Bishops as having served in the ranks? The reviewer in *New Blackfriars* was scathing about Heenan's remark and commented:

we have suffered from the social origins of our bishops. . . . We have indeed had the worst of both worlds – all the constriction of Dissent without its vigorous instinct for popular consultation; all the prelacy of the Established Church without its national and cultural heritage.[98]

But it is precisely the Church of England's pride in its 'national and cultural heritage' which has prevented it from evolving a genuinely working-class priesthood or churchmanship. So, both Anglican chaplains and soldiers arrived at the front with virtually no commonly accepted sacramental shorthand with which to communicate, either with God or with each other.

Geoffrey Gordon was one of the chaplains who wrote about these themes.[99] Whereas the soldier, he wrote, is sent under clear orders, for example to hold a trench, until relieved, in times of emergency, the chaplain has no superior or orders:

Each moment he must choose for himself between conflicting claims, resisting alike the temptation to do conspicuous things simply because they are conspicuous, and the other temptation to stay too far behind when his friends and companions are in the place of danger.

At home the curate may be nicknamed 'Mister Gawd' by the children; at a base camp in France they may call him 'Monsieur Cinéma'. Does the soldier, Gordon asked, think of the chaplain as 'Mister God' or 'Monsieur Cinéma'? If he stands exclusively for spiritual things, his contacts will be limited. If he tries to get to know the battalion as a whole he throws himself into a number of minor activities, running canteens and cinemas, and providing comforts. The Roman Catholic chaplains, he said, had decided to work on a 'frankly sectarian' basis, dealt simply with their flocks, shunned canteens, and tried to minister almost exclusively on a spiritual level. Most Anglican chaplains had chosen the wider type of ministry: 'not only have I run canteens, but at advanced dressing stations I have been content for hours together to busy myself with blankets and hot soup for their needs, happy if just once or twice in a night I could put in a word of more articulate religion.' Over against those, inside and outside the Church, who see Christianity as 'something outside and beyond ordinary life', we preach, he wrote, 'the all-inclusiveness of Christianity'. Because today the Church of England is 'humbled and penitent', it cannot speak with the authority people would recognize: 'We cannot stand detached and cry aloud that if only the world would come to us all would be well.' On the other hand 'we have now a unique opportunity of sharing with men a hundred intimate occupations of daily life, in a far closer and more natural way than was possible in peace time', and by doing so learning a 'truer sympathy which may fit us better in the coming days to supply their deeper needs'.[100] Gordon expressed the dilemma acutely and sensitively. There is no evidence that critics like Graves, Sassoon, and Montague had ever begun to consider the kind of ministry which it was open to an Anglican chaplain to exercise, and the problems he faced in exercising it.

6

Some Chaplains

In this chapter we shall look more closely at some of the chaplains, their outlook and experiences. Inevitably, one has to select, and in any case the number of those about whom information is available is small compared with the number of chaplains who served.

When Geoffrey Studdert Kennedy died in 1929 a packet of Woodbines were placed on his coffin. He wrote a poem about his nickname which was given to him by those who had shared what he called the 'glorious madness of God' in the war, a nickname which he prized but also felt as an accusation:

> For the men to whom I owed God's Peace
> I put off with a cigarette.

> ('Woodbine Willie')

He experienced in every fibre of his being all the ludicrous and agonizing paradoxes of war, yet he was curiously unquestioning about being a priest in uniform, and could be scornful about those who wanted an early peace. He could on occasion sound like any other conventional patriotic preacher of the period: 'You ask me what we are fighting for – I give it you in three words: Freedom, Honour, and Peace. You ask me what we are fighting for, and I give it you in one word: Christ.'[1] When he was attached to a School of Physical and Bayonet Training he sometimes went on a tour with an extraordinary collection of morale-boosters which included a champion boxer, two wrestlers, and an N.C.O. who had killed eighteen Germans with a bayonet. Geoffrey would asthmatically box with the boxer. Then he would get them ready for battle with a twenty-minute talk.[2] How else could a chaplain build bridges except by some type of costly yet ironic incarnation? When invited to preach before the King, he began his sermon, not with a text but with the statement: 'I have come from the bloody slime of the trenches'.[3] Sassoon wrote of a church parade which made the trenches seem 'very remote. What possible connection was there?'[4] But the best chaplains tried often desperately and in impossible circumstances to make some connection. Guy Rogers at one time had an almost daily assignment of giving the troops a three-minute message to soldiers before they entrained for the front from a reinforcement camp. At one stage, Studdert Kennedy would spend night after night at Rouen station, playing the piano in the coffee shop, leading the singing, offering to write home for them, praying with them, talking with them individually, and, as the train filled up, distributing New Testaments and packets of cigarettes, then at dawn going back exhausted to the canteen as the lights of the train disappeared.[5] He shocked the conventional (though there was a conventional side to his complex character), because he often played the fool for Christ's sake, giving himself to the needs of the men without a thought for any status, clerical or military. (Peter Berger has described the minister as a type of 'clown', for a clown is a sacerdotal figure in his absurdity and vicariousness.) General Plumer reported him for what he considered to be an outrageous sermon. A lecture he gave at B. K. Cunningham's school for chaplains made Cunningham angry. The war which he had entered with conventional patriotism, and for which he was prepared to be a morale-booster, shook his faith to the foundations. He shared in the attack on Messines Ridge in 1917, for his part in which he was awarded the M.C. It had been preceded by the explosion of mines in tunnels which had been dug beneath the German positions. Lloyd George heard the explosion in Downing Street. Studdert Kennedy said to a friend after the attack: 'You know, this business has made me less cocksure of much of which I was cocksure before. On two points I am certain: Christ and His Sacrament; apart from those I am not sure I am certain of anything. . . .'[6] In his poem 'High and Lifted Up', he began with Isaiah's vision of the glory of God in the Temple, then he wrote:

> God, I hate this splendid vision – all its splendour is a lie . . .
> And I hate the God of power on His hellish heavenly throne . . .
> Thou hast bid us seek Thy glory, in a criminal crucified . . .
> For the very God of Heaven is not Power, but Power of Love.

He expounded his understanding of the chaplain's ministry to Theodore Bayley Hardy (whom even Montague called a 'hero and saint')[7]

'Live with the men; go everywhere they go. Make up your mind you will share all their risks, and more if you can do any good. The line is the key to the whole business. Work in the very front, and they will listen to you; but if you stay behind, you're wasting your time. Men will forgive you anything but lack of courage and devotion.' . . . I said the more padres died in battle doing Christian deeds the better; most of us would be more useful dead than alive. He asked me about purely spiritual work. I said, 'There is very little; it is all muddled and mixed. Take a box of fags in your haversack and a great deal of love in your heart, and go up to them: laugh with them, joke with them. You can pray with them sometimes; but pray for them always.'[8]

In some cases Studdert Kennedy had to bury men where they fell, lying on his stomach to say the service. He would hold services for men with hands and faces blackened just before a raid. (There were many stories too of the lengths to which Hardy went in his caring; on one occasion he remained for nearly two days with a soldier who was three-quarters embedded in the mud of no-man's-land, and then he worked with those who came to extricate him. He won the D.S.O., the M.C., and the V.C. in ten months and died of wounds in 1918.)[9]

What did traditional religious teaching mean in such surroundings? What did the old teaching on prayer mean, Studdert Kennedy asked in one of his dialect poems, 'Thy Will be Done'?: the soldier prayed as he had been taught, but the gas still kept blowing over them. Studdert Kennedy asked what did the words from the Eucharist really mean: 'preserve thy body and soul unto everlasting life', when he came across a corporal terribly mutilated in a shellhole to whom he had said these words at Communion three days before? Only a God who not only suffered in Christ on the cross but who was still suffering now made any sense.[10] He wrote in 'The Suffering God':

> Father, if He, the Christ, were Thy Revealer,
>   Truly the First Begotten of the Lord,
> Then must Thou be a Suff'rer and a Healer,
>   Pierced to the heart by the sorrow of the sword.

In some sense the war re-enacted Christ's Passion: he wrote in 'Dead and Buried':

> I was crucified in Cambrai,
>   And again outside Bapaume;
> I was scourged for miles along the Albert Road,
>   I was driven, pierced and bleeding,
>   With a million maggots feeding
> On the body that I carried as my load.

The only way in which he could make any sense of so many deaths was to see them redemptively:

> He bled
> Horribly. Do you remember?
> I can't forget,
> I would not if I could,
> It were not right I should;
> He died for me.
> He was a God, that boy . . .
>
> ('Her Gift')

Only a God who was a 'Comrade God' (the title of another poem), who was involved in the suffering, was believable. The belief in a distant unknowable God, to whose will we must bow unquestioningly, he satirized in 'A Sermon' which ends: 'Deliver us from cant'. The Eucharist also spoke of a God who comes near:

> How through this Sacrament of simple things
> The great God burns His way,
> I know not – He is there.
>
> ('At the Eucharist')

The soldier on leave was drawn back by 'a stronger love' than even that of women:

> Your comrade Love is stronger love,
> 'Cause it draws ye back to 'ell
>
> ('Passing the Love of Women')

Why is this 'comrade love' so powerful? Because, Studdert Kennedy believed, it was a sacrament of the love of Christ himself:

> 'Ere we are now, stretcher-case, boys,
> Bring 'im aht a cup o' tea!
> *Inasmuch as ye have done it*
> *Ye have done it unto Me.*
>
> ('To Stretcher-Bearers')

Studdert Kennedy was not afraid to speak frankly of the reality of sexual temptation and to be understanding towards it in himself and others, though the language he used in his verse was sometimes rather Victorian and melodramatic. William Wand, who in style of chaplaincy and in general temperament was very different from Studdert Kennedy, like many others, recognized and was moved by his greatness: 'I never knew anyone who could speak so directly to the condition of his hearers.'[11]

F. R. Barry, in his autobiography, vividly described the theological, ethical and personal challenges that confronted the chaplains. They had to serve men under intense moral and physical strain. Much of what they had been taught to preach seemed almost totally irrelevant. The war revealed with 'a very heart-searching shock' what they ought to have known already: the alienation of the workers (and therefore the soldiers) from the Church. At first chaplains were worried by bawdy language and womanizing, but soon learnt that these were superficial matters:

> Our real problems were very much deeper than that. Religion apparently meant nothing to them. Was this something for which we should upbraid men who were enduring far more than we were? Or could there be something lacking in the religion? For we learnt in battle how splendid and how noble these apparently irreligious people were. How were these grand qualities related to the Gospel that we had been ordained to preach? We could not conclude, of course, that they did not need it: but what message had the Gospel for them and in what form ought it to be presented? And beyond all that, in so evil a situation, of which the devil seemed to be in control, how could we go on believing in God at all, as the Father of our Lord Jesus Christ? . . . We had to re-examine our fundamentals and to hammer out a working theology which could stand the test of battle-conditions and give men a faith that could overcome the world. . . . The question was: What is the Gospel really *about*? Only an other-worldly salvation? The troops were asking radical questions now about the social and economic structure which they were supposed to be fighting to preserve. Were they worth preserving? . . . The chaplains did what they could to guide these questionings.[12]

The fundamental issues which Barry describes were certainly agonized over by Studdert Kennedy. Charles Raven tackled many of them also, but in another key; indeed much of his life was devoted to an attempt to reconstruct the Christian message. When war broke out, Raven was Dean of Emmanuel College, Cambridge. He felt a compelling urge to enlist as a combatant, but was rejected four times on medical grounds. Instead, in 1917 he became a chaplain. Paradoxically, for one who after 1930 became one of the most influential of English

pacifists, he was never more eloquent than when he spoke and wrote –
as he did frequently over the years – about the spiritual meaning of his
war experiences. There is no evidence that Raven was ever particularly
aware of the paradox. Though he hated fighting, the polemical parts of
his books are some of the most memorable. To his temperament, as one
of the last great pulpit orators, the way to truth through paradox and
dialectic was uncongenial.[13] It was during his first night in France on his
way to Vimy Ridge in April 1917, that he had a decisive experience of
the reality of Christ:

> . . . when death looked me in the face, my manhood withered and
> collapsed. For what seemed hours I was in an agony of fear . . . and
> suddenly as if spoken in the very room His words 'For their sakes I
> consecrate myself' and the fragrant splendour of His presence . . .
> for the next nine months He was never absent, and I never alone, and
> never save for an instant or two broken by fear. If He who was with
> me when I was blown up by a shell, and gassed, and sniped at, with
> me in hours of bombardment and the daily walk of death, was an
> illusion, then all that makes life worth living for me is illusion too. . . .

He shared his troops' dangers to the full. He described spending an hour
with an unknown private, under fire from a howitzer in a small hollow.
Shells kept bursting near; he appealed to the private to stay still, then
suddenly realized 'that at each explosion he had put his body in the
mouth of the hollow between it and me, offering his life for mine many
times under conditions that try the manhood of the bravest'.[14] His
theology and temperament enabled him to see at times a cosmic glory in
all experience, however horrible: 'down the trench came a stretcher-
party and a shapeless bundle that an hour before had been a laughing
boy. And the presence enfolded him – plants and insects, the dead and
the living were all ablaze with the Shechinah of God.'[15] His war
experiences banished the physical fear which had haunted him from
boyhood. He grew near to officers and men. 'Pacifists and C.O.s may
talk of the sanctity of human brotherhood; we out here have discovered
something at least of its reality', he wrote in 1917.[16] War faced him with
the ultimates of human experience, and he felt for ever bound up in
fellowship with those who had shared the same experience: 'We have
seen death face to face; and no man who has entered into that fellowship
and kept his manhood, has much to regret.'[17] Theologically, the war
led Raven to be as highly critical of easy language about divine
omnipotence as Studdert Kennedy. In an essay largely written on the

battlefield, he showed himself to be powerfully drawn to Romans 8.18–28 with its language of cosmic conflict and struggle, and in the years to come he repeatedly expounded that chapter.[18] On another occasion he wrote that the war was neither a 'gallant adventure', nor 'a dance of devils': 'it is just an intensified and concentrated sample of the whole cosmic process', in which the Cross is central: 'It is in His agony that He is most manifestly divine.'[19] Raven wrote in 1919, from his experience as a chaplain, that a simple appeal to the authority of Church or Bible was not credible to the majority of men. But the liberal Christian is 'not hampered by having to enforce acceptance of much that is difficult if not impossible for the average man'. So the prospects for liberal Christianity were now 'incalculably brighter' than they had been before the war.[20]

Fr John Groser had been trained in the tradition of Catholic socialism at Mirfield. Later he was to become perhaps the greatest of East End priests of the inter-war period. From 1915 to 1918 Groser was chaplain to an infantry regiment in France, and lived with his men in the trenches. He taught a more sacramental religion than most chaplains, and this was thought narrow and exclusive by some. He did not spend much time in the mess when out of the line; he preferred to visit the men in the barns, or the French farm women in their kitchens. One Christmas in the mess, the doctor sang a particularly filthy song. No one knew what to do to stop him except Groser, who leapt to his feet and with a hefty push sent the doctor flat on his back. In a battle Groser drew a line with which his C.O. still disagreed fifty years later. After heavy casualties, he asked Groser to take command of a group of soldiers. He believed that the men would not hold their ground without an officer to command them. But Groser refused. He felt that as a chaplain he could not take any part in the killing; his C.O. tried to explain the gravity of the situation:

> I reminded him that scores of men he knew had fallen that day after having done their utmost; and I was conveying to him – in what words I cannot remember – my despair of a religion that could teach that such a patronizing stand-offish attitude was the right one, when my words were drowned by a terrific outburst of fire from our own guns, who had spotted a counter-attack forming up. When the firing was over Groser told me that he would do what I wanted provided he didn't carry arms. To that I readily agreed.[21]

In a situation where every moral boundary seemed to have been destroyed, was this not a gesture of hope, the refusal of *this* priest to bear arms, however right it may have seemed to other priests to become combatants? (Eric Milner-White, when a chaplain in 1917, was said to have agreed to take command when all the officers of his unit had been killed or wounded, and to have been sent back to base for so doing – but the precise facts are not clear.)[22] I am reminded of how E. M. Forster, working with the Red Cross in Egypt, came across some poems by T. S. Eliot and wrote:

> Here was a protest, and a feeble one, and the more congenial for being feeble. For what, in that world of gigantic horror, was tolerable except the slighter gestures of dissent? He who measured himself against the war, who drew himself to his full height, as it were, and said to Armadillo-Armageddon 'Avaunt!' collapsed at once into a pinch of dust. But he who could turn aside to complain of ladies and drawing-rooms preserved a tiny drop of our self-respect, he carried on the human heritage.[23]

In 1918 John Groser was sent home wounded, having been mentioned in dispatches and awarded the M.C. By then he was making it known that he was finding it difficult to support the allied cause. He was beginning to see the war as a crime against humanity.

A much less well known but equally impressive chaplain was John Michael Stanhope Walker. In 1915 he went straight from a Lincolnshire village incumbency to the western front. In three months at a casualty station he buried some 900 dead. In one 24 hours, 1,300 casualties arrived; one night 700 arrived after 11 p.m. 'Sometimes one was in the moribund tent practically all day and night.' He tried to minister to all, but he wrote despondently: 'Tommy does not want religion. I don't persuade him.' But still he went on day after day; he wrote on the first day of the battle of the Somme 1916:

> We have 1,500 in and still they come, 3–400 officers, it is a sight – chaps with fearful wounds lying in agony, many so patient, some make a noise, one goes to a stretcher, lays one's hand on the forehead, it is cold, strike a match, he is dead – here a Communion, there an absolution, there a drink, there a madman, there a hot water bottle and so on – one madman was swearing and kicking, I gave him a drink, he tried to bite my hand and squirted the water from his mouth into my face. . . .

He borrowed some morphine to deaden the cries and groans of two or three hundred wounded Germans who received less medical attention when the pressure was greatest. On another occasion he noted 'I have seventy-odd addresses still waiting for letters, so I should like a quiet day or two.' He would rig up a packing case for a Eucharist: 'With some it is difficult e.g. today one man had no underjaw, chin and all blown away.' He helped another who had never been confirmed to make his confession and prepare for Communion. In the middle of the burnt-down car factory which was the setting for the hospital he created a garden. 'It will be sad to leave the garden a blaze of colour, peas and beans just coming in and tomatoes and marrows doing grandly.' So both in his ministry and in his garden he was trying to create love, beauty, and caring, in a world full of ugly hatred. But the strain was enormous: 'it keeps coming over one like a wave, the madness and the folly of it all. Will the day come when men of all nations refuse military service. . . ?' But though the wounded were always eager for his care as a man, only a few came to services. 'They would come as a favour to me if I pressed them, at least some would, but what is the use.' He returned to his country parish feeling defeated.[24]

Neville Talbot described the work of chaplains as 'hens trying to lay eggs on moving staircases'.[25] Before going up to Oxford in 1903, he had fought in the Boer War, where his uncle, General Lyttelton, was Commander-in-Chief. When the Great War broke out he left his Balliol chaplaincy, and he and his brother Keble (of the Community of the Resurrection) became chaplains. On 23 August 1914 the two brothers sailed down the Seine to Rouen. Neville was a chaplain for the duration of the war and in October 1916 became Assistant Chaplain-General to the Fifth Army. Why was the Church of England pastorally so ineffective? he asked. The Prayer Book seemed so inadequate to the needs of ordinary men. He felt he was 'peddling unmarketable C. of E. goods'.[26] Both brothers felt that, by comparison, the Roman Church seemed so clear in its teaching, and its spirituality more fitted for the needs of the average soldier. Walter Carey felt much the same. He wrote to the *Church Times* from his chaplaincy on H.M.S. *Warspite* in 1915:

Two things are brought home to me through this war. Firstly, that an ordinary Anglican religion won't do: it doesn't save souls in any volume. That is sufficient condemnation, therefore it must be scrapped. Secondly, that the only forms of religion in the Anglican

Communion which have any life in them are the Evangelical and the Sacramental.[27]

To Neville, religion seemed so separate from the ordinary world. Perhaps the separateness of the ordained ministry should be abolished? Perhaps some priests, deacons, and deaconesses should earn their own livings in lay professions? 'They would be able to speak in "kingdom-vernacular".'[28] It was such a formidable task for the soldier to discover the true treasure of Christianity; he wrote in November 1917:

> Men must dig in that strange field of Christianity through its odd and in part misleading, part repellent surface: it is a mosaic of kill-joyism and Balaam's ass's ears, and Noah and Mothers' Meetings and Athanasian damns and the Archbishop of Canterbury with £15,000 a year – through to the treasure.[29]

Why is it that men who unconsciously show so much Christianity in their lives do not 'delight' consciously in Christ himself?[30] Neville was very popular. When in January 1916 he was awarded the M.C., his battalion, weary from the line, put their caps on their bayonets and gave him three impromptu cheers on meeting him.

Working under Neville Talbot in the Ypres Salient was Philip ('Tubby') Clayton. Together they rented a house in Poperinghe in 1915 and turned it into a club for troops. They called it Talbot House after Gilbert Talbot, Neville's younger brother, who had recently been killed. Soon it became known as 'Toc H', the signallers' shorthand for Talbot House. Clayton described it as 'a home from home where friendships could be consecrated, and sad hearts renewed and cheered, a place of light and joy and brotherhood and peace'. The house was full of notices in the humour of the time,'IF YOU ARE IN THE HABIT OF SPITTING ON THE CARPET AT HOME, PLEASE SPIT HERE'. On the Chaplain's door there was the legend 'ABANDON RANK ALL YE THAT ENTER HERE'.[31] A chapel was established in the loft; a disused carpenter's bench served as the altar; Bishop Talbot sent out some hangings. No communion rail or pulpit were allowed so that priest and people could be close to one another. On Easter Day 1916 there were ten celebrations of the Eucharist from 5.30 a.m. onwards. Many found peace and sanity in the 'Upper Room' as it was known; some were baptized and confirmed, some made their confessions, some found vocations to the priesthood. After the trenches it seemed a home of love, warmth and vision. In May 1916 Archbishop Davidson confirmed thirty-seven men in the Upper Room:

... the old Archbishop sitting in his chair, with the lighted candles behind him as the darkness came on, and the candidates kneeling before him, while outside in the street there was the ceaseless rumble of troops moving up to the Salient and the intermittent sound of firing.[32]

But Clayton also ministered to the troops on the battlefields in the area. Nothing deterred him. After celebrating the Eucharist in a trench for eighteen men, he discovered four signallers unable to leave their post on the embankment which was being heavily shelled. Clayton scrambled over to them and all knelt, taking off their helmets to receive Communion.[33]

By 1918, there were thirteen members of the Community of the Resurrection serving as chaplains. (Members of other religious orders in the Church of England, like the Cowley Fathers and the Society of the Sacred Mission, Kelham, also sent some of their members.) At that stage six were in France, one in Egypt, one in Palestine, one a prisoner in Germany, two in the navy, two in India with the Y.M.C.A. In addition, as we saw earlier, Fr Northcott had enlisted as a private soldier. By 1917, four had received the M.C. Extracts from their letters to their brethren at Mirfield were regularly printed in *CR*, the quarterly magazine of the Community.

Most of the men, said Fr King, were out of touch with the Church, and regarded the priest as 'a being of almost another race'. A. C. Headlam in the *Church Quarterly* had cited a chaplain who said that the men 'need to be convinced that he is really a man and a neighbour'.[34] Some chaplains chafed against their rank and found it an additional barrier. Some denied that they were looked upon as 'mere officers' and used their rank to help men in difficulties with the authorities. Edward Woods (Bishop of Lichfield 1937–53), when Chaplain at Sandhurst, wrote in his 'Spiritual Diary': 'Need to *deserve*, morally and every other way, this deference.'[35] After three and a half years as a chaplain, Oswin Creighton took a more sombre view. He noted that a number of officers had come to the Eucharists he had arranged for Easter Day 1918, but hardly any men:

The war is really breaking no barriers down. The hardest line ever drawn in human society is that between officers and men. Do what you will, you cannot destroy or even lessen it ... they live in two different worlds, and the chaplain lives in the officers' world.[36]

1 Bishop Winnington-Ingram in uniform as Chaplain of the
London Rifle Brigade, August 1914. See p. 35

2 'The Great Sacrifice' by James Clark: included in the Christmas
1914 number of the *Graphic*, it was soon hanging in many churches,
homes, and hospitals. The *Graphic*, offering further copies for sale in the
issue of 6 February 1915, called it 'The most inspired Picture of the
War'. See p. 191

The chaplains, wrote one of the Mirfield Fathers, received very few commendations from parish priests. One appeal in the two church newspapers produced only six replies for 15,000 men. Of course few soldiers held the Catholic view of the sacraments as taught by the Mirfield chaplains. Fr Keble Talbot contrasted the Roman Catholic soldiers with their basic knowledge of prayer and sacraments with the ignorance of these things among soldiers who described themselves as 'C. of E.' But 'while the Sacraments are esoteric enigmas to them, they respond very readily to direct appeals.' Fr Fitzgerald ministered to large numbers of Scottish and Irish Presbyterians who knew little or nothing about the sacraments, but 'one feels their whole life to be sacramental'. Fr King in Gallipoli reserved the sacrament in one kind, made a rule of four hours' fast, and then gave Communion at any time and in any place – for example under a tree twenty yards from the firing line. For three weeks he was unable to say Mass because of restrictions on groups meeting together. But he constantly went along the firing trench, chatting, offering cigarettes. caramels and instruction on prayer: 'Man after man will tell you how during the heat of an engagement he said his prayers for the first time since he said them at his mother's knee.' One fellow-chaplain had regularly to say Mass in a mortuary tent with around him sometimes as many as thirty bodies sewn up in sackcloth awaiting burial. Fr Rees described how in Egypt men had brought sheaves of lilies and roses to decorate the altar for Easter: 'Many of them told me afterwards what a difference that stately altar made to them . . . the garden of the Lord in the midst of the wilderness, and home in a barren land.' But the Mirfield Fathers with their experience of parish missions and the informal mission services in the Quarry at Mirfield, and carrying around the *Mirfield Mission Hymn Book*, were more able to meet the need for informal services than other chaplains who had been accustomed only to conduct strictly Prayer Book services in parish churches. When Fr King was at Grantham, he held each Sunday an early Eucharist, an informal parade service with cornet players to help the singing, and a mission service in the evening which included an appeal to sign the pledge. The war had broken down English reserve and religious formalism, he wrote, and informal prayer meetings had developed. When Fr Barnes said Evensong daily, it was punctuated with extempore prayers said by Nonconformists who were among his best supporters. In Gallipoli, Fr King trained subalterns to conduct prayer meetings when no chaplain was available.

The ministry of the chaplains took many varied forms. Fr King provided three tents at Grantham which were crowded every evening; pen, ink, and paper, newspapers, games, books, and magazines were provided, and every evening an impromptu concert was held. However much the chaplain might find the establishment of clubs and canteens wearisome and time-consuming, Fr Talbot believed that the whole man must be ministered to; religion must be shown to be concerned with the everyday. Chaplains were often given the chore of censoring letters; Fr Fitzgerald would censor 200 in a batch. It brought chaplains into intimate touch with what the men were feeling, though it could be inhibiting to the men to know that an officer would read their letters.

As members of a religious order, prayer naturally meant much to the Mirfield Fathers, and they tried hard to teach the men to pray. Fr King prepared the men for storming the Gallipoli beaches in 1915. From his ship, tied alongside a destroyer, he passed the word along about 1,000 men to use the silence by saying the Lord's Prayer at a fixed moment:

> . . . as I called them to prayer a deep and solemn silence passed along both decks, and General and Colonel and officers and men of their own accord stood up and with bowed heads joined with me. . . . Then a pause, followed by a short extempore prayer for pardon for the past and protection through all the dangers that awaited us, we commended our loved ones, our cause, and ourselves into God's hands. And so we closed our little service with the noble words of the Aaronic Blessing.

Then came the battle: 'One feels so helpless, there seems so little one can do, so much to be done; a clasp of the hand as the wounds are hastily bandaged, a muttered prayer, a drink of water and that is about all.' Next Sunday, having received Communion from the reserved sacrament, he went back to the battlefield and spent six hours burying the dead. When he had to cross the open plain in the dark he would say Compline from memory, and wrote how significant was Psalm 91 ('Thou shalt not be afraid of any terror by night', etc.).

Fr Talbot mused on the need for a wider, more flexible spirituality:

> . . . whence comes the generosity, humility, and devoted obedience characteristic of many whom one meets here, except from the Spirit of our Lord? and is that to be despised or accounted irreligious which shows itself supremely in action, while little aware of the more mystical or devotional ways of religion?

Some men, he said, would always be restive in a Catholic atmosphere;

we must not ask a man 'to develop gifts of the Spirit which are not his and never will be in this world'. In August 1916 he wrote that the chaplains were only beginning to realize the full extent of the obstacles to religion, to learn the point of contact, and to question many of their previous assumptions. One sergeant-major had told him that to most men religion meant nothing except the notion that there was One above, a sense of duty to live decently, and a belief that there would be a reckoning sometime. If the chaplain, Talbot comments, is there (as one General had asserted) to preach only on duty, honour, and discipline (that is to reinforce morale), then the result will be 'a shorn and pedestrian religion'; but perhaps this is the main avenue to God for many Englishmen.

Fr King at Gallipoli had told the men, 'This is a holy war', but he did not glorify war. It was 'Hell', and yet was 'instrumental in drawing from men deeds of unparalleled heroism and self-sacrifice'. Fr Talbot felt the same: 'The whole thing is very horrible, but it is shot through with grandeur and beauty. I don't suppose that many men will ever be so much alive if they live for fifty years more.' He believed that the incongruity between Christianity and war was being more and more felt. A young officer asserted almost violently that he would not dream of going to Communion in France, but if he went home on leave he certainly would. Another who had a passionate interest in music at home, felt that in France the world of music belonged to another life. 'War has come down like a screen', Talbot commented. Christ was reverenced, but teaching seemed like an impracticable dream. The desire to worship was nearly extinct. But there is a 'gentle wistfulness' in the faces of some of the soldiers: 'they are just nestling up in their hearts to the things and persons they love.' 'How long will Christianity countenance this way of settling disputes?' asked Fr Eustace Hill. He wrote of a Quiet Day he had conducted, and how he had told the men that 'Love of Right was to be our incentive, not Hate'. At lunch the Colonel commented pungently: 'Well, Padre, you think it all right sticking Germans. You love 'em and stick 'em?' Others came to the chaplains puzzled as to what to think of providence, when so many believed there was only fate and destiny.

In almost every village a crucifix stood somewhere, sometimes the only object left standing, and this was said to impress even the most callous, though some scorned the survival of crucifixes as evidence of the providential love of God. In 1916 a small book of meditations was published by A. H. Baverstock, a parish priest, (with a preface by G. K.

Chesterton) entitled *The Unscathed Crucifix*, which was interleaved with several photographs illustrating the title. Those who, like the Mirfield Fathers, had often meditated on the Passion and celebrated the Holy Week rites, now found themselves spattered with gangrene and real blood. Fr Fitzgerald reflected that he had often in pre-war days meditated through Maundy Thursday night, but he had never felt so close to the Passion as when he attended to the needs of the sick, wounded, and dying in Holy Week 1916. On Maundy Thursday 1919 he was able to say Mass at the little Russian church on Carmel; how different, he reflected, from the previous year when near the Jordan under the bombing he had been covered in blood helping to bring the wounded to hospital and the dead for burial. Fr Hill found the stretcher shoulder-strap 'a real priest's stole'. When Fr Talbot was extricating the wounded from a trench, a young soldier called out 'Are you our clergy?', and then 'put his arms round me and clung to me, feeling, I suppose, he was not alone in a friendless world'. In those less self-conscious days tenderness between men could be openly avowed – so superbly caught in Susan Hill's novel *Strange Meeting* (1971) – 'the dearest lot of young fellows are in now, mostly wounded', wrote Fr Fitzgerald, about his visits to the hospital wards.

But the strain on the chaplains was enormous. Dick Sheppard was instituted to St Martin-in-the-Fields in November 1914. But in August he had gone out to France to be a temporary hospital chaplain. He identified himself so deeply with the wounded that he had to return in the middle of October broken in body and mind. He would sit up all night with the dying, some in agony and terror from lockjaw.[37] Then there was the strain of being with men sentenced to death until the moment of execution; this too fell to chaplains. Though many death sentences for cowardice and desertion were commuted, on the average one soldier was shot by a firing squad every week. Guy Rogers wrote:

> It has just fallen to my lot to prepare a deserter for his death. That meant breaking the news to him; helping him with his last letters; passing the night with him on the straw of his cell (a wayside barn) and trying to prepare his soul for meeting God; witnessing the execution and burying him immediately.[38]

Sometimes chaplains appeared at courts martial to defend accused soldiers as the 'Prisoner's Friend'.

Archbishop Davidson and other bishops visited the chaplains and gave them much needed encouragement. Guy Rogers wrote about the Archbishop's visit in May 1916: 'I saw him in a motor in his archiepiscopal robes with a tin helmet on his head. That I think must surely be one of the sights of the war.'[39] Archbishop Lang had grasped something of the horrors of the war and the pastoral needs of the troops from the letters he had received from Dick Sheppard and others. In 1915 he spent a month with the Grand Fleet and two years later visited the western front. His main business in France was to attend conferences of chaplains; he found them in a critical mood. Harry Blackburne told Archbishop Davidson on one of his visits to France: 'The bishops are sitting like a lot of old hens on eggs which they do not know how to hatch.'[40] Lang thought that some chaplains displayed an attitude to the bishops which 'is unjust and not very seemly among men who ought to be learning the discipline of respect to senior officers'. Returning on the boat he encountered a more famous critic of the war, Ramsay MacDonald, who had been in France seeing Red Cross work; on the way out the crew had struck because of him; on his return he was smuggled aboard.[41]

But the chaplains needed more pastoral care than either resident or visiting bishops could provide. During 1916 a number of conferences were held for chaplains in France under the inspiration of Harry Blackburne, Senior Chaplain to the First Army, attended by Free Church as well as Anglican chaplains; the Roman Catholics declined the invitations.[42] In January 1917, Bishop Gwynne recommended the establishment of a permanent centre for instruction and prayer to help chaplains to do their work more effectively. B. K. Cunningham, who had already given addresses for Blackburne in 1916, was selected to be Warden. Cunningham had been Warden of the theological college at Farnham until it was disbanded with the coming of the war. Randall Davidson as Bishop of Winchester had appointed him and held him in high esteem. When the Secretary for War decided that he could not possibly accept a man as deaf as Cunningham – he would become a liability under war conditions – the King intervened and declared that Cunningham was to be accepted. The military authorities were sceptical about the venture, but helped to equip a large house at St-Omer, and this was opened in February 1917. During the next two years nearly 900 chaplains passed through the centre. Attendance was compulsory, and therefore some came with an initial resentment. But 'B.K.' (as he was known) won nearly everyone over by his simplicity and sanctity. The burden of continually running conferences and retreats for a different group of men every week was considerable. All were weary and in need of spiritual and physical refreshment. Some had grown slack and depressed, a few had fallen into grave sin. The romance of conducting services in barns and Eucharists on packing cases had palled. As 'B.K.' said, the combatant might try to shut his heart to all feeling; the chaplain could or should not. Most chaplains as Christian leaders inevitably felt more keenly than others the tremendous strain of constantly trying to reconcile their belief with the war.[43] The pressures on the chaplain to become merely the mouthpiece of the military authorities were very great. Sometimes unsure of his role, treated as a jack-of-all-trades, sometimes feeling neither accepted by officers nor by men as a priest, wearied with indifference and misunderstanding, tired of innuendoes that if he was a 'real man' he would be fighting, it was tempting for him to try to solve all these tensions by a display of bellicosity. Major-General Sir William Thwaites told a post-war soldiers' dinner how before an engagement he would gather the chaplains together and preach *them* a sermon:

> I told them on one occasion that I wanted a bloodthirsty sermon next Sunday, and would not have any texts from the New Testament. . . . On that Sunday I got hold by accident of a blushing young curate straight out from England – but he preached the most bloodthirsty sermon I had ever listened to.[44]

B. K. Cunningham in 1919 summed up the lessons he had learned from the experience of running the school:

> My own opinion is that the pre-war theological college system, as judged by the padres it produced, did not come well out of the experience of war; the devotional training had been along too narrow lines and depended too much on favourable environment, and when that was no longer given the padre was apt to lose his bearings.[45]

7

The Army and Religion

We have looked in some detail at the work of the chaplains against the background of critical comment from a number of sources. In this chapter we shall explore further the characteristics of the religion of the soldiers as it was revealed in the war.[1]

The chaplains of the various Churches were not the only Christian agencies working among the troops. S.P.C.K. and the British and Foreign Bible Society, with other agencies, distributed over forty million Bibles, prayer books, hymn books and tracts in the first two years of the war. In October 1914, Bishop Taylor Smith received half a million copies of the New Testament and individual Gospels for distribution to soldiers from the Scripture Gift Mission. Typical of their productions was a pocket-size copy of St John's Gospel bearing the inscription: '"ACTIVE SERVICE," 1914–1915. PLEASE CARRY THIS IN YOUR POCKET AND READ IT EVERY DAY.' On the front inside cover was a message from Lord Roberts dated 25 August 1914: 'I ask you to put your trust in God. He will watch over you and strengthen you. You will find in this little Book guidance when you are in health, comfort when you are in sickness, and strength when you are in adversity.' Verses that seemed to the promoters of particular importance were printed in black type, and the text was subdivided so that it could be read so much a day over two months. Some black and white illustrations in the familiar style of Sunday school prize Bibles were included. Hymns included 'Rock of ages', 'Sun of my soul', 'O God, our help in ages past', 'Abide with me', 'Eternal Father, strong to save' and 'Onward, Christian soldiers'. A Decision Form was also provided: 'Being convinced that I am a sinner, and believing that Christ died for me, I now accept Him as my personal Saviour, and with His help I intend to confess Him before men.' Stories were told of soldiers saved from death or wounding by shrapnel glancing off such breast-pocket bibles carried by faithful soldiers. The S.P.C.K. Foreign Translations Committee published tracts for German prisoners, and devotional books in African and Maori languages for troops from the colonies and dominions.

Like the Salvation Army, the Church Army provided tents and huts for canteens and recreation centres. Eventually there were about 2,000 centres run by the Church Army. It built up a fleet of fifty ambulances nearly all driven by clergy who acted as pastors as well as drivers. It organized visitors for the wounded, hostels for soldiers on leave in London, parcels for prisoners of war and recreation centres for wives of men at the front.[2] In the January 1916 issue of the *Church Quarterly*, an advertisement appealed to clergy and churchwardens to give money raised in Lent for Church Army recreation huts. Field-Marshal French was quoted as a supporter of the appeal. The Manchester diocese alone raised £10,000 to provide huts. Other appeals for both the Church Army and the Y.M.C.A. regularly appeared in the church press. Clergy went out to work with the Y.M.C.A., which in France and other countries provided recreational, worship and educational facilities for the troops on an interdenominational basis. One such clergyman was Percy Dearmer, who resigned from St Mary's, Primrose Hill, at Christmas 1915 to work in the Y.M.C.A. huts in France and India. Bishop Gore greatly admired the work of the Y.M.C.A. When someone asked him why the Church of England Men's Society had not done anything similar, Gore replied typically: 'I don't know; it's only another failure of the Church of England to seize an opportunity. I hate the Church of England.' However, his Oxford diocese provided recreation and refreshment huts in military camps in the diocese and through the Church Army also a centre in France.[3] Some churchmen were rather wary of what was called 'Y.M.C.A. religion' because of its interdenominational and non-sacramental character, though in fact Y.M.C.A. huts were regularly used by chaplains of all the Churches for their own services. *Challenge* defended Y.M.C.A.: it was a valuable clearing-house, not a new denomination.[4]

What was religion like at the front? Opinions differed greatly as to the value of church parades. James Jack was a Company Commander when he wrote in his Diary in October 1915: 'Today I attended church parade – as an example to those whose Faith is still intact. Besides, the practice helps to screw up one's sense of duty.'[5] Charles Carrington recalls the 'church parade conducted most seriously before the whole brigade in hollow square, and the communion administered after the service to a devout group in the corner of a field'.[6] For C. E. Montague one great advantage of going to France was that he and his fellows were delivered from formal church parades with all the cleaning of brasses and so on which preceded them, and the sermons from 'well-meaning divines' at the parades themselves.[7] Oswin Creighton tried to make services voluntary wherever possible in France, though at times he arranged compulsory parades so as to be able to speak to all the men together; some grumbled because they were compelled to attend, others grumbled if there were no compulsory parades because they said that no religious provision was being made for them![8] When Studdert Kennedy became chaplain of the Fourth Infantry School, Colonel Campbell told him that there would be no compulsory services, and that if he could not attract men voluntarily to services, he would be dismissed. Studdert Kennedy knew how to anticipate soldiers' reactions. When he spoke at a smoking concert he began 'I know what you're thinking: here comes a bloody parson', and then proceeded to grip his audience by the power of what he said.[9]

Very often the Church at the front had to function unprotected, lacking traditional sanctuary or atmosphere. R. H. Tawney recalled a typical Eucharist in 1916:

> The Priest stood in the door of a wooden shanty. The communicants stood and knelt in ranks outside. One guessed at the familiar words through the rattling of rifle bolts, the bursts of song and occasional laughter from the other men, as they put their equipment together outside their little bivouacs, bushes bent till they met and covered with tarpaulins, or smoked happily in an unwonted freedom from fatigues.[10]

Fr Waggett said Mass in his bedroom on occasion, and tried to create a more churchly atmosphere by using incense. Studdert Kennedy had startled his pre-war congregation at Rugby, where he had been a curate, by declaring that there were times when he would like to take a 'great sledge-hammer, smash every stained glass window in this church and go out and celebrate the Lord's Supper in the fields with a cup and platter'. It was therefore a liberation for him to celebrate the Eucharist in a French farmyard shed on Christmas Day – 'No lights, no ritual, nothing to help but the rain and the far-off roll of guns, and Christ was born in a cattle-shed on Christmas Day'[11] – but it is clear from the language he used that primitivism also had its romantic appeal. Oswin Creighton celebrated near Alexandria on an altar made out of coke-boxes, with broken beer bottles as vases and a Woodbine cigarette box for the alms. Harry Blackburne described a Eucharist in a barn ankle-deep in mud, and how the staff captain made kneelers from some blankets.

'Never were such hymn-singers known', wrote Scott Holland reassuringly to the people at home about the troops in France. 'They sing and sing for ever.'[12] Singing in general was very much a feature of this period as a villager recalls:

> There was such a lot of singing in the villages then. . . . Boys sang in the fields, and at night we all met at the Forge and sang. The chapels were full of singing. When the first war came, it was singing, singing all the time.[13]

Familiar hymns (and prayers) were a link with home. Almost every soldier would know well a dozen or so hymns from day school, Sunday school, church or chapel. Some had martial words and marching tunes. So hymns both bound the soldiers together and brought them into emotional touch with the world at home. Hymns like 'Onward, Christian Soldiers' and 'Fight the good fight' seemed to give religious sanction to the war, though the soldiers themselves were easily sickened by too many martial hymns, especially when they were urged to sing them by clergy who did not fight themselves.[14]

One picture postcard in a series entitled 'Just before the Battle, Mother' depicted a soldier on the battlefield thinking of his family at home. They appeared in a bright cloud (contrasting with the gloom of the soldier's surroundings) gathered round the harmonium singing hymns. A series of picture postcards illustrated 'Fight the good fight'. The first verse was printed below a drawing of a church parade being conducted in the battle zone by an immaculate chaplain in surplice, scarf and hood. The second verse, including the lines 'Lift up thine eyes, and seek his face', showed an extraordinarily tidy officer looking up to heaven with rapt gaze, hymn book in hand, standing among some generalized ruins. The third verse 'Cast care aside' depicted a spruce soldier, not a hair out of place, kneeling beside his cannon while the battle rages in the distance.

For many years the students at the Church of England Teachers' Training College for men at Culham sang a daily evening hymn (a version of the Compline Psalm 91):

> Holiest, breathe an evening blessing,
> Ere repose our spirits seal . . . .
> Though destruction walk around us,

Though the arrow past us fly,
Angel-guards from thee surround us;
We are safe if thou art nigh.[15]

In the magazine for summer 1915, a former student's letter was quoted in which he described how the 5th Oxford and Bucks Light Infantry were forty yards from the German trenches. On the Sunday evening the ex-Culham men sang their college evening hymn. After the 'Amen' a German called 'Encore'. Frederick Grisewood recalled the scene:

The effect of these men's voices rising up out of the ground in the still night air was startling. The Saxons evidently appreciated it, as they would shout across and demand our evening hymn every night. The hymn turned out to be an old German one which must have been familiar to our enemy opposite.

In return, the English would call 'Fritz' up to sing – he would stand on the German parapet in full view of everyone and sing aria after aria from German operas: 'While he was singing, it seemed almost as if the whole war had come to an end. For what seemed miles on either side there was complete and utter silence, broken only by the faint singing of the nightingales.' Saying a final 'Guten Abend Englisch' he climbed down, and gradually the war would begin again.[16] The second verse of a specially composed hymn celebrating 'Culham Restored' after the war included:

We thank Thee for our soldiers,
Whose glory death hath sealed,
Who sang the songs of Culham
In trench and battlefield.[17]

At home, 'God moves in a mysterious way' was a very popular hymn. At the front, 'Lead, kindly Light, amid the encircling gloom' was a favourite hymn before going up the line. To Huntly Gordon, a field-gunner in Flanders 1917–18, born in a Scottish manse and educated at Clifton, the lines from that hymn:

Keep thou my feet; I do not ask to see
The distant scene; one step enough for me.

meant a great deal as he faced the trenches. The Psalms also helped – 'particularly as they were written by a fighter who knew what it was to be scared stiff'. He quoted in the Prayer Book version (familiar from his time in the choir at Clifton) various verses which expressed his own feelings in the Ypres Salient:

> I stick fast in the deep mire, where no ground is. (Ps. 69)
>
> The earth trembled and quaked: the very foundations also of the hills shook. (Ps. 18)
>
> Our heart is not turned back: neither our steps gone out of thy way;
>
> No, not when thou hast smitten us into the place of dragons: and covered us with the shadow of death. . . .
>
> For our soul is brought low, even unto the dust: our belly cleaveth unto the ground. (Ps. 44)

Then he added self-consciously: 'Forgive this outpouring. It's good to get it off one's chest. Like the eels, I expect we'll get used to skinning; and it will be easier now to keep up the pretence that it's all quite good fun out here, with nothing to worry about but the mud.'[18] When Bishop Winnington-Ingram went out to France for a Holy Week and Easter Mission in 1915, he took with him a portable altar, copies of an adapted Russian litany, and large numbers of hymn sheets with four hymns: 'When I survey', 'Rock of ages', 'There is a green hill', and 'Jesu, Lover of my soul'.[19] The members of one division which was supposed to be silent before going over the top were heard singing quietly, 'Jesu, Lover of my soul'.[20] Robert Graves remembers Welsh soldiers singing hymns instead of music-hall songs, each taking a part, as they marched towards the shells, until the shells came so near that 'Aberystwyth' was broken up in the middle of a verse.

One odd legacy of the widespread knowledge of hymns was that well-known tunes were available to be set to comic or bawdy words. Frank Richards, a private soldier, said that soldiers like hymn tunes, but preferred their own racy words. To sing bawdy verses to hymn tunes was an example of that sceptical wartime humour which enabled men to cope, because by mocking the whole hierarchy of God, politicians, the Church, military authorities, and the romantic picture of soldiers as heroic knights, they were all cut down to size; hence too the popularity of Bruce Bairnsfather's cartoons. One soldier wrote that common songs, even dirty songs, moved him more than the 'divinest' music because of the men who sang them: 'The main thing is a love for, a passionate faith in, my fellow men.'[21] Charles Carrington, son of a priest, said that he enjoyed the bawdy songs, but that soldiers just as easily turned to *Hymns Ancient and Modern* because it was 'as genuine a part of our folklore'.[22]

Educated soldiers often quoted from Shakespeare (particularly *Henry V*) and from *Pilgrim's Progress*. Some carried Bunyan with them. After one soldier was killed in the battle of Loos his copy was returned to his parents, and they noticed that the passage beginning 'Then I entered into the Valley of the Shadow of Death' was marked.[23] Another soldier wrote: 'In our steel helmets and chain visors we somehow recall *Pilgrim's Progress*, armoured figures passing through the valley of the shadow.'[24] In one sentence Wilfred Owen used four literary references (one from Bunyan and three from the Bible) in trying to describe no-man's-land to his mother: 'It is like the eternal place of gnashing of teeth; the Slough of Despond could be contained in one of its crater-holes; the fires of Sodom and Gomorrah could not light a candle to it – to find the way to Babylon the Fallen.'[25] An Irishman described the sources of his spiritual nourishment: Holy Communion, *The Merchant of Venice*, Browning, Tennyson, and Isaiah 52 and 53.[26]

Some at home in the early days of the war, hearing all these stories of hymn-singing, Eucharists in barns, men praying for the first time since childhood before going into battle, concluded that at the front a religious revival was under way.[27] On 19 February 1915 *Challenge* reported that a 'Churchman's Battalion' had been formed consisting wholly of members of the Church Lads' Brigade. On 4 June it printed reports that in Germany too there had been high hopes for a revival of religion at the beginning of the war, but that the initially large church attendances had declined there also. Tom Pym pointed out in an essay written in 1916 that people considering the war's effects often discovered what they wanted to discover: the socialist talked of the war as bringing a new wave of socialism, the agnostic pointed to the failure of religion, the priest acclaimed a revival of the religious sense. But, he said, although under abnormal conditions people will often turn to religion, when they become accustomed to the new situation their concern for religion declines. Pym described the real situation pungently: 'good will not slide out of evil like mince out of a machine!'[28] F. H. Keeling, the Fabian, wrote from the Front in 1915:

> The yarns in some of the papers about the revival of religion at the Front amongst the English is all rot. . . . I don't think that there is much to be said for *le bon Dieu* after all this. I should think that humanism will gain considerably over theism after the war.

Religion, he felt, was like the whisky which so many drank to keep up their courage under the stress of battle. He hoped to be able to do without such 'physical or moral drugs'.[29] If by the end of the war anyone was still under the illusion that a religious revival had taken place or was about to take place, he would have soon had his wishful thinking dispelled by two symposia: *The Army and Religion* (1919) published by an inter-denominational group, and *The Church in the Furnace* (1917) a symposium by a group of Anglican chaplains. To these two books we now turn.

The Army and Religion was prepared under the chairmanship of Bishop E. S. Talbot. The membership of the Committee was drawn from eleven Churches, and included A. A. David (later Bishop of Liverpool), A. S. Peake, L. S. Hunter (later Bishop of Sheffield), Fr W. H. Frere, A. E. Garvie, John Oman, J. H. Oldham (later a leading ecumenical figure), Tissington Tatlow, B. H. Streeter, and E. S. Woods. Baron von Hügel, though not a member of the Committee, attended all the meetings and participated fully.[30] Through him and through correspondents, the Roman Catholic view was represented. It was at a base camp at Rouen that the idea of a committee of inquiry came into the mind of D. S. Cairns, Professor at the United Free Church College, Aberdeen. The idea arose out of his personal experience of soldiers, some remarks made by Neville Talbot, and the evidence given by chaplains to the Archbishops' Second Committee following the National Mission. Cairns, Tatlow and the leaders of the Y.M.C.A. agreed to approach Bishop Talbot to ask him to be chairman. 'If Donald Hankey were only still with us', wrote Cairns to Tatlow in November 1916.[31] Hankey's view that many soldiers were in some measure Christian without knowing it deeply influenced the Committee. It began its work (which was financed by the Y.M.C.A.) in 1917 and received nearly three hundred memoranda in response to its questionnaire. Three questions were asked of correspondents: (1) What are the men thinking about Religion, Morality, and Society? (2) Has the war made men more open to a religious appeal or has it created new difficulties for belief? (3) What proportion of the men are vitally connected to any of the Churches, and what do they think of the Churches?

The war, said the Committee, had brought to light both the strong and weak features of national life. Those who had survived owed it to those who died to create a better world. There had been a falling away from the Churches ever since the early days of the Industrial Revolution. Most of those who died had little use for the Church, and did not know Christ in the full sense, but there was a deep truth in the sentiment that had placed a cross on every grave: 'Is it not as if the Christ whom they knew not in life claims them in death?'[32] Men in the forces were not godless; most prayed before a battle, and thanked God when they survived. 'The soldier has got religion, I am not sure that he has got Christianity', said Neville Talbot.[33] Though belief in God and life after death was widespread, God seemed distant and helpless, and there was little understanding of the nature of life after death. So often when the immediate danger receded, a concern for religion receded with it. Nearly all the problems related to the problem of suffering: how could Christianity and war be reconciled? in what sense was God both loving and omnipotent? why should the innocent suffer with the guilty? how could human freedom co-exist with divine foreknowledge?

There was practically universal respect for Jesus, whereas the Churches were constantly criticized. Christ as the heroic fellow-sufferer in a good cause, depicted on the wayside crucifix, was reverenced; but turning the other cheek was considered unmanly. Hardly any had any belief in Jesus as the risen and living Son of God. The cross meant self-sacrifice, not atonement. Though the war had stimulated religious awareness and prayer, it was not connected with Christianity or the Churches. Perhaps as a result of the prominence of the Ten Commandments in the Communion service and elsewhere, Christianity was commonly thought of in negative terms – not swearing, not drinking, and so on.[34] The picture of a religious revival at the front was 'untrue and pernicious'[35] – the situation was much more complex than had been thought before the war. The war had revealed both the heights and depths of human nature; a Major commented:

It was a wet, cold morning, about 6.0 a.m. in winter, on the Somme. I saw half a dozen of my boys taking charge of two infantrymen at their last gasp from wet, mud, fatigue, and exposure. The poor fellows had actually lain down to die on the roadside by our battery. My men gave them their breakfast (we were short of rations in those days), their socks (we were short of these), shirts and everything; and rubbed them and lit fires all around them and sweated over them, and got them to hospital. Now they would be utterly surprised to hear that any of this had got to do with morality or religion. Morality has to do with not breaking laws.[36]

The economic system taught men to be materialistic. War imposed a continuous moral and physical strain producing numbness of the mind and fatigue of the soul. This encouraged the advocacy of any methods designed to shorten the war: 'an eye for an eye' was often quoted as a justification for reprisals. When soldiers were obsessed with whether their equipment was superior to that of the Germans, it was hard to see where the power of God came in. Could we expect men 'living together under the conditions of beasts' to have a lofty moral outlook?[37] Yet in spite of all this, the war had deepened both compassion between men and the spiritual life of some soldiers. One soldier described how he had been forced to think, because of nights on sentry duty in a ruined village with the noise of guns, the scuttling of rats, the tread of soldiers carrying rations and ammunition, the groans of a wounded man carried by on a stretcher, the sounds of the burying party digging a grave who then tried to drown their experience with rum, the scent of roses and flowers from uncared-for village gardens, a broken crucifix at the cross roads.

Men were poorly equipped spiritually for so sudden and terrible a crisis. The failures of education in general, and religious education in particular, were apparent.[38] The men were not thinking at all, just carrying on. The splendour of their heroism contrasted sharply with the poverty of their thought. The results of all the religious education were 'strangely small'.[39] The Churches' teaching had come over as externalized dogma; only hymns lasted and gave delight. For the type of Christian who believed that only through the consciously accepted grace of God could truly good deeds be done, or who thought in terms of 'good' and 'bad' men, the war produced many puzzling paradoxes. 'Unredeemed human nature is infinitely nobler than I had dreamed', said one chaplain.[40] The war produced heroism and comradeship but also encouraged swearing, drunkenness, dishonesty, gambling, and impurity. Yet the soldier who visited the brothels could also be a brave man in danger and go through fire for a friend. (The surprise with which such discoveries were greeted by the Committee suggests narrow acquaintance with the paradoxes of human nature.) The Churches had yet to realize the power of friendship: 'Friendship out here is one of the great sacraments of life', said a sergeant.[41] Surely Christ is the author of the 'Christ-like actions and ideals which every day transfigure the front line trenches'.[42] The war had broken down social barriers, and there was surprisingly little hatred of the Germans.

Fatalism seemed to be of more help to many soldiers than Christianity. 'If your name is on the shell you will get it' was a frequently asserted opinion among troops. Fatalism steadied the nerves. 'Soldiers are fatalists; otherwise they would be madmen', declared a lance-corporal.[43] *Omar Khayyam* was popular among the more educated. Men prayed under stress. They wanted to believe that there was Someone outside themselves who would keep them and their families safe. They were more ready to receive Communion before battle than at camps away from the fighting. The fact that there seemed no providential pattern discernible, when one was killed and another saved, encouraged fatalism or notions of predestination.[44]

Only about 20 per cent were in touch with the Churches, though the proportion was rather higher in Scotland. The Church was criticized on innumerable counts – it lacked reality and conviction: 'When you go to church the bloody thing they offer you is the most damned insipid thing imaginable', said one officer.[45] The divisions within and between the Churches produced confusion and rivalry. The clergy were out of touch; they were professional people, living in large houses, a cut above the ordinary people. In a chaplain, personality counted for everything; the fact that he was ordained counted for nothing. The Churches did not support social justice. The Church of England was state-endowed. Churches still had reserved pews. The Churches were autocratic bodies in a democratic world. The Churches seemed stuck in the 16th and 17th centuries, unable to recognize the Spirit in contemporary movements like that for the emancipation of women.

In its analysis of the evidence, the Committee seized upon the facts that the Churches had failed to attract four-fifths of the young men of the country; that despite all the religious education, there seemed to be so much fog surrounding Christian teaching; yet so many Christian qualities had been shown. So a great new effort of religious education (teaching, for example, the Bible as progressive revelation) must be made; the widespread desire for social justice must be harnessed; the fraternity between social groups must not be lost. The Church needed more fellowship in its life and more democracy in its government. The idea of a League of Nations was a Christian ideal. There was now a widespread loathing of war: 'Of what war has it been true that men have had to live for months among the unburied dead?'[46] The Churches had proved ineffective, not only because they could not prevent war, but that they had said nothing distinctive during it. In education, the Committee believed that there had been too much memory learning, too little exercise of the imagination, too much competitive, too little co-operative learning. Though religious education had borne inadequate fruits, perhaps it and baptism were the sources of the fraternity, heroism, and half-humorous humility at the front. Soldiers often used Christian standards by which to judge the Church. The most powerful humanizing and moral influence was the home. So the war did not create these virtues, rather it 'has broken the ice and set the waters free'.[47] Like others, the Committee felt that the well-known war poem by Lucy Whitmell 'Christ in Flanders' expressed the widespread conviction among Christians that the Christ who had been half-forgotten in the easier days of peace was being rediscovered in the testing days of war:

> *Now* we remember; over here in Flanders –
> (It isn't strange to think of You in Flanders) –
>   This hideous warfare seems to make things clear.
> We never thought about You much in England –
> But now that we are far away from England –
>   We have no doubts, we know that You are here.
>
> You helped us pass the jest along the trenches –
> Where, in cold blood, we waited in the trenches –
>   You touched its ribaldry and made it fine.
> You stood beside us in our pain and weakness –
> We're glad to think You understand our weakness –
>   Somehow it seems to help us not to whine.

Winnington-Ingram reprinted the poem from the *Spectator* (where it had originally appeared in September 1915) for his diocesan magazine, and quoted it in sermons.[48] Scott Holland quoted it in the symposium edited by G. K. A. Bell *The War and the Kingdom of God* (1915) and in a letter called it 'a wonderful poem'.[49]

The report ended with the type of expressions of hope for the post-war Church and world which we have encountered before. The Churches must draw together to promote the Kingdom of God – the Y.M.C.A. and S.C.M. had set an example. Pledges to serve Christ and his kingdom had been signed by no fewer than 350,000 men: men will serve sacrificially for war; why not for peace? 'The long battle of defence and retreat is over, the moment for a great common advance has begun.'[50] So the Committee added its influence to the movements which supported church reform, ecumenism, social concern, the League of Nations, and liberal theology, which were to be dominant in the post-war life of the Churches. The similarity of outlook and conclusions to those of the Archbishops' Committees will be noted; there was some overlap in membership; but in some ways the conclusions of this Report were more sombre than those of the

Archbishops' Third Committee on Evangelism. Even after four years of war the Committee believed that the Churches did not yet realize the extent of the lack of religious belief and practice: they were 'living in a fool's paradise'.[51]

The Report was notably defective on at least five counts. Firstly, it said little about the deeper causes of war. Secondly, having recognized the work of the incognito Christ, it was unable to explore the deeper implications of this fact for the mission of the Church. Thirdly, its psychological and ethical understanding of the nature of man was often naïve. Fourthly, despite all the sombre evidence, the Committee felt able to predict a fundamental change in the future: 'The future is lit up with promise.'[52] Fifthly, it did not listen to the advice of von Hügel, who distrusted the simplicity of 'our good Chairman' (Bishop Talbot), who, because he so much admired the virtues of the English soldier, was in danger of 'reducing our Theology to "Tommy-ness"':

> It is impossible to confine any at all adequate statement of the richness of life within the kind of formula that Tommy can understand; and, if we do not get him to feel that the richness is there, all round him and within him, we shall never have him; indeed it is not worth trying to have him. . . . There are things beyond Tommy, and the minute he wakes up to this primary fact, we shall have a sign that he is saved.[53]

Unwittingly, von Hügel pointed ahead to that emphasis upon the mystery and transcendence of divine truth which was to be at the heart of Karl Barth's theology and of the neo-orthodox movement.[54]

The Church in the Furnace was the title chosen for a collection of essays by seventeen chaplains, edited by F. B. Macnutt and published in 1917. The contributors included three D.S.O.s and four M.C.s; some of them became well-known names in the Church. F. R. Barry, one of the essayists, said that it was commonly known as 'The fat in the fire'. Macnutt wrote in the Foreword: 'The Church is in the furnace. We have felt the purging of the purgatorial fires . . . have seen the pure metal dropping apart from the dross.' Is such language, he asked, too flamboyant, melodramatic, apocalyptic? He answered that only the language of the Book of Revelation was adequate to express their experiences. We have already encountered many of the themes of the essayists; our summary of them may therefore be brief.

The life of the Church and the army were contrasted; the Church was individualistic, the army corporate; entry into and membership of the army made great demands; baptism and membership of the Church made few. Junior officers and N.C.O.s were ready to try to make up for the deficiency of an officer; the laity blame everything onto the priest. Soldiers could be daring and self-sacrificial; there was little of this spirit in the Church. Could the Church (following William James) find in a crusade transcending class the 'moral equivalent' of war in peacetime? The war had enabled the upper classes to come into daily contact with the poor; all shared the same dangers. The essayists strongly supported the type of church reforms being advocated at that time.

The war had shown the clergy to be amateurs. Theological colleges did not prepare men adequately. They made parsons out of men 'at the expense of their humanity and naturalness', wrote Neville Talbot; they 'produce the mind which is clerical and yet not truly professional'.[55] When the chaplains returned home, they would desire the same freedom in ministry that they had known at the front. They would have authority only in so far as they rang true, not because of any clerical status. They should be interpreters between the classes. If chaplains seemed to be remote, this was not because of their rank, but because they were suspected of being unable or unwilling to discuss matters man to man. Studdert Kennedy attacked the parsonic manner and 'dry rot in the pulpit'.[56]

Chaplains had widely felt the need for greater freedom in worship, and believed that the Eucharist should be restored to its central place in worship. The Prayer Book was too intellectual, lacked homeliness, and urgently needed revision – that was why so few soldiers carried Prayer Books for their own devotions. One chaplain painted a moving picture of informal Eucharists:

We have had our Communions in the orchards of little French villages, where we placed a borrowed table under the shadow of the fruit trees, while the men knelt here and there on the bare grass around, and the peaceful cows gazed wonderingly at the sight. We have celebrated behind our lines with an ammunition box for altar and a shell-hole for the Sanctuary, amidst the thunder of guns which ever and again drowned the familiar words, and when the time came for Communion we passed with the Bread of Life from man to man as they knelt in disorder where they could find kneeling space on the shell-torn ground. And whether in the peaceful orchard or on the field of battle, we all felt a reality in the service, a nearness to God, a true feeding upon Christ, an actual sharing of the one Bread which we have seldom experienced in the more formal celebrations of our churches at home.[57]

Differences of churchmanship between chaplains had often been overcome as Catholics had responded to pastoral need and become less rigid, and Evangelicals had been more ready to use ritual aids to worship. Thankfully, there had been much co-operation too between the Churches (and this must continue and increase); sadly, the Church of Rome had often stood aside. Eric Milner-White (himself a priest in the Catholic tradition) believed that the majority of Anglo-Catholic servers and laymen had failed the chaplains, because they found the 'surroundings too rough'.[58]

If soldiers had displayed the fruits of the Spirit, did not this mean that the Church had done a better job than had been realized? Yet there was the puzzling paradox of 'a Christian life combined with a pagan creed'.[59] The phrases which kept the soldiers going – 'Pack up your troubles in your old kit bag and smile, smile, smile', 'Carry On' and 'Keep Smiling' – were not these the equivalents of St Paul's exhortation to cast all care upon God? But prayer was often only for safety in danger, and phrases like 'Thy will be done' were often interpreted fatalistically. N.C.O.s were uneasy if a man became too religious because it might make him worry too much about dying. There could be no easy revival of religion as a result of the war, because war was a spiritual narcotic.

Two essays stand out. The first was by F. R. Barry: 'Faith in the Light of War'. The collapse of visible supports forces us back upon the invisible. War impels us to search for the meaning of horror as in a Shakespearian tragedy. In the midst of the battle of the Somme, feeling incapable of prayer, 'worn out and atheistic', Barry turned to the Epistle for Michaelmas Day (Revelation 12.7–12) and a 'rush of light' dawned. War compels us to adopt a 'Crisis-Ethic'. War unmasks the trivialities in religion; it impels one to take 'the devil' seriously, it sweeps away false ideas of divine omnipotence conceived of as Olympian and passionless: 'Our God *in His manward aspect* . . . is a Being who is limited and striving'. The worship of a sweet, gentle Jesus must surely disappear.[60] The second, by Studdert Kennedy, took a more clear-eyed view of soldiers than one essayist who had written that the present generation had 'entirely lost all sense of the awfulness of sin' – by that he meant bad language and visits to 'haunts of vice'.[61] Studdert Kennedy wrote:

Why are the men whose courage, good comradeship, gallantry and cheerfulness, we are bound to admire indifferent to Christianity? This is the question that all of us ask ourselves. . . .[62] The root of the soldier's blasphemy is the same as that of his humour, and that is why they are so often mixed. They are both efforts to solve a felt but unformulated contradiction in life, and they are both essentially Christian, the signs of a lost sheep of the Good Shepherd.[63]

The Church, he said, had often taught a muddled religion; for example, it taught prayer for protection rather than for strength for fighting and dying; it dismissed the idea of a literal six days for creation, but then recited the Ten Commandments which quoted it as the sanction for the sabbath rest. The basic religious difficulty for the soldiers was that of suffering, as revealed and intensified by the war.

Bishop Gwynne in his preface had rightly asserted that the discontent the chaplains expressed in this symposium was not a sign of weakness but of realism. The discoveries which the chaplains made about the complexities of their contemporary religious, ethical, and theological situation were as important for their day as were the discoveries made by the French worker-priests when they accompanied their deported fellow countrymen to work in Germany during the second world war. Milner-White declared:

We are a new race, we priests of France, humbled by much strain and much failure, revolutionaries not at all in spirit, but actually in fact; and while often we sigh for the former days, the processions of splendid offices and the swell of the organ, these will never again comfort us unless or until the great multitude also find their approach to God through them.

Kenneth Kirk asserted that some chaplains would never be able to accept the restraints of parochial life; those who returned to parishes would never 'fall into the old grooves again'.[64] The subsequent careers of Milner-White and Kirk indicate the ways in which the Church of England can neutralize radical aspirations.

8

Death, Bereavement, and the Supernatural

Preaching in St Paul's Cathedral on 9 August 1914, Bishop
Winnington-Ingram said that if a heathen poet could declare 'Dulce et
decorum est pro patria mori',[1] 'with how much more conviction should
a Christian parent say the same'. In another sermon he told of one who
was to have been ordained that autumn, but who was killed fighting, and
so 'received the even greater consecration of a martyr's death'.[2] At the
end of 1914 Austin Dobson summed up the feelings of many people in a
poem in the Christmas edition of *Sphere*:

> What do your clear bells ring to me
> In this glad hour of jubilee?
> Not joy, not joy. I hear instead:
> So many dead! So many dead!

In August 1915 when Michael MacDonagh, as a *Times* reporter,
attended the service at St Paul's to commemorate the first anniversary
of the war, tears came into his eyes when he saw that most of the
congregation were in mourning. But as the war went on and casualty
lists mounted, the feelings of many changed from a mixture of sadness
and pride to bitterness and horror, though some continued to speak the
language of simple patriotism. The change seems to have started after
the battle of the Somme which began on 1 July 1916. All the previous
week the sound of guns bombarding the German positions could be
heard in places along the South Coast and even in London. On the eve
of the battle Sir Douglas Haig wrote to his wife: 'Now you must know
that I feel that every step in my plan has been taken with the Divine help
– and I ask daily for aid, not merely in making the plan, but in carrying
it out. . . .'[3] But on the first day of the battle, of the 110,000 who
attacked, 20,000 were killed and 40,000 wounded, the heaviest losses
ever suffered in a single day by any army in the first war. The truth
about the slaughter on the Somme soon began to appear at home; for
the first time, casualty lists contained the names of everyone's friends

and relations. From Bradford alone there were 1,770 casualties after the first hour of the offensive. It was days before the wounded in no-man's-land stopped crying out. Even today the villagers in the Somme area are still turning up bones in their fields. 'Idealism perished on the Somme', writes A. J. P. Taylor.[4] To Edmund Blunden, the first day of the Somme offensive showed that no one had won, or could win. 'The War had won, and would go on winning.' Some began to feel that the war could last thirty years, or perhaps for ever.[5] Christopher Dowling, of the Imperial War Museum, writes:

> . . . in the final analysis, it was not the threat of punishment which kept the British army in the field, nor was it patriotism, which seldom survived the first tour of duty in the trenches. The war was the supreme test of an individual's physical and mental stamina, and there were few who failed to respond to its challenge. Men endured the horrors and privations of trench warfare because their self-respect and their sense of duty would not allow them to give in.[6]

After the Somme, some soldiers became convinced of the pointlessness of it all. A favourite piece of Tommy philosophy was expressed in the resigned phrase (humour keeping despair at bay): 'We're here because we're here.' Having endured the boredom and degradation and uncertainty of industrial employment, many an ordinary working-class soldier had developed a resilience which made him better able to cope with the trenches than those brought up in softer circumstances. 'You come into this world crying, you go out crying, don't cry in between' was a steel-worker's commentary on life.[7] But the clergy (as we have seen from the opening quotations from Winnington-Ingram) were eager to moralize and idealize. R. J. Campbell wrote that the war had 'forced us to lift our faces from the flesh-pots and visualise afresh – namely, that life is only gained in proportion as it is laid down at the call of the higher-than-self'[8] – note the echoes of St John's Gospel.

Wounded soldiers became a familiar sight all over the country. Visiting Brighton in June 1917, Caroline Playne wrote: 'the sight of hundreds of men on crutches going about in groups, many having lost one leg, many others both legs, caused sickening horror. The maiming of masses of strong, young men thus brought home was appalling.' Yet, she says, people, though at first horrified, got used to such sights, so that there was a 'hardening and coarsening' of national life.[9] In London's East End, street shrines sprang up carrying names of local soldiers surrounded by flowers and photographs of the Royal Family. They were said by Winnington-Ingram to have been started by the Rector of South Hackney and to be commended by the Queen.[10] In January 1916, Robert Bridges, Poet Laureate, issued an uplifting anthology *The Spirit of Man*; we need, he wrote in the Preface, spiritual nourishment, 'distraction from a grief that is intolerable constantly to face'. The old simple patriotism was in decline in the music-halls. At the front, said Robert Graves, patriotism was fit only for civilians or prisoners, and new arrivals who talked patriotically were told to cut it out. In an exhibition of paintings by war artists in 1918, Paul Nash depicted a waste land with terrible realism. Sassoon wrote in 'Counter-Attack':

> The place was rotten with dead; green clumsy legs,
> High-booted, sprawled and grovelled along the saps;
> And trunks, face downward, in the sucking mud,
> Wallowed like trodden sand-bags loosely filled;
> And naked sodden buttocks, mats of hair,
> Bulged, clotted heads slept in the plastering slime.
> And then the rain began . . .

A mixture of detachment and humour was one defence against such horrors. Wilfred Owen (who had just read Sassoon's poem), after lying under a soldier shot through the head whose blood had soaked into his shoulder, told Sassoon in October 1918: 'My senses are charred. I shall feel again as soon as I dare, but now I must not.' He no longer took the cigarette out of his mouth when he wrote 'Deceased' across letters he returned to their senders.[11] Macabre humour was another defence. A villager from Akenfield recalls how in the Dardenelles the corpses kept reappearing. 'Hands were the worst; they would escape from the sand, pointing, begging – even waving! There was one we all shook when we passed, saying, "Good morning", in a posh voice.'[12] Some soldiers searching for souvenirs soon overcame scruples about plundering the dead. One brought in a German skull; he had had to scrape off the flesh and hair. Coppard tells of men searching the corpses for tinned food and cigarettes. At first, letters of condolence were personally written to relatives of dead and wounded; as the losses mounted, printed forms took their place. But the amazing fact for those at the front was that the two worlds were physically so close. An officer could breakfast in the trenches and dine the same evening in his London club.

In the first war, 745,000 British soldiers died. In addition over one-and-a-half million were wounded, some seriously. Officer casualties were often three times greater than those of other ranks. Oxford

University's roll of honour contained 14,561 names; of these, 2,680 were killed or died of wounds or sickness. Trinity College, Cambridge, lost over 600 of its former undergraduates. Edward Lyttelton, Headmaster of Eton, recorded that for about fifteen pages of the leaving Register every single Etonian old and fit enough to serve had enlisted.[13] Across the nation as a whole nine per cent of all British men under 45 were killed. When the war was over, bewildered parties made melancholy visits to the devastated areas of the front, looking in some cases in vain for the burial places of relatives. The Jewish relatives of Isaac Rosenberg, who had paid 3s. 3d. to have 'Artist and Poet' inscribed on the gravestone, wondered whether the body under the Star of David was in fact that of another, and whether ironically Rosenberg lay somewhere else under a Christian Cross.[14] The memorial at Thiepval records the names of over 70,000 who were killed during the Somme offensive and had no known grave. Though on 11 November 1918 crowds danced and cheered, Robert Graves walked about alone along the dikes of Rhuddlan 'cursing and sobbing and thinking of the dead'.[15]

In 1929, I. A. Richards, the literary critic, puzzled over 'a widespread general inhibition of all the simpler expansive developments of emotion . . . among our educated population. It is a new condition not easily paralleled in history.'[16] In Chapter 27 of Ernest Hemingway's *A Farewell to Arms* (1929) a character remarks:

> I was always embarrassed by the words sacred, glorious, and sacrifice and the expression in vain. We had heard them, sometimes standing in the rain almost out of earshot, so that only the shouted words came through, and had read them, on proclamations that were slapped up by billposters over other proclamations, now for a long time, and I had seen nothing sacred, and the things that were glorious had no glory and the sacrifices were like the stockyards of Chicago if nothing was done with the meat except to bury it. There were many words that you could not stand to hear and finally only the names of places had dignity. . . . Abstract words such as glory, honour, courage, or hallow were obscene beside the concrete names of villages . . .

This inhibition about the validity of expansive or eloquent language has deepened, so it has now become very difficult to mint a convincing contemporary language to encompass love of country, religious belief or tragedy (for example) – hence our problem in finding a genuine language for the liturgy or for translations of the Bible, and the tendency to fall back on an uneasy pastiche.[17]

People in the first war inherited their attitudes towards death from the Victorian period. Most people still died at home, so that many had witnessed a deathbed before their 'teens were over. In the writings of Tennyson, Dickens, and Charlotte Yonge, death and bereavement had an important place. The Evangelical emphasis upon death as the moment of judgement, and the revival of Catholic rituals for dying and burial made the deathbed of crucial religious and moral importance; the pathos of the deathbed was believed to be morally purifying. The watchers at an Evangelical death waited for the final message to confirm faith before the soul passed over. Queen Victoria was eager to hear an account of the last days and hours of Archbishop Tait in 1882. Davidson, Tait's son-in-law and chaplain, replied in great detail much to the Queen's satisfaction.[18] The 'good' death had an important place in Evangelical tracts and exhortations. Death confronted the reader or hearer with the issue of his own eternal destiny, and the godly death was an empirical confirmation of belief. Though the growth of cremation had begun to change burial customs, the attempts to disguise crematoria as Gothic chapels and to conceal the chimney in a spire or tower indicated the tension between the utilitarian and the romantic, the modern and the traditional. It was some time before the practice of scattering ashes became popular; people liked to have a specific place to visit. After the burial scandals of the mid-Victorian period, much money, municipal and private, was devoted to the provision of adequate and seemly cemeteries. During the century social reforms had increased life-expectancy. During the nineteenth century an elaborate etiquette of mourning was developed, and people were prepared to spend considerable sums on elaborate funeral arrangements. Geoffrey Gorer remembers as a child walking on Hampstead Heath on the Sunday after the death of Edward VII, and noticing that nearly every woman was dressed in full mourning. Hearses drawn by horses with black plumes were a common feature of street life, and passers-by would take off their hats in respect. Mourners, easily distinguishable, had to be treated with special consideration. But by the middle of the war full mourning became exceptional, so great was the number of the bereaved. In any case, too ostentatious a display of mourning was thought unpatriotic and bad for morale.[19]

At the front, however much chaplains tried by burial rituals to maintain the significance of death, the elaborate Victorian burial customs were irrelevant. What did the 'resurrection of the body' mean to the soldiers who cleared and buried the rat-eaten pieces of flesh from the barbed wire? George Coppard describes how every square yard of the trenches seemed to be 'layered with corpses at various depths'. Protruding parts would be curtained off with a sandbag, but arms and heads kept reappearing. Sometimes the protruding putrid part had to be cut off and buried. 'So long as we were alive, we had to go on living, but it wasn't easy with the dead sandwiched so close to us. We took our meals and tried to sleep with them as our neighbours. Amid laughter and bawdy stories they were there.'[20] It is in this context that we should read Owen's poem 'Anthem for Doomed Youth':

> What passing-bells for these who die as cattle?
>   Only the monstrous anger of the guns,
> Only the stuttering rifles' rapid rattle
>   Can patter out their hasty orisons.
> No mockeries now for them; no prayers or bells,
>   Nor any voice of mourning save the choirs, –
> The shrill, demented choirs of wailing shells;
>   And bugles calling for them from sad shires.

At home, death bore heavily on the parish priests, both through the constant deaths of former parishioners, and through their own personal bereavements. Thirty per cent of the officers in the army were said to be sons of the clergy. By February 1916, thirteen sons from bishops' families had died in the war. Two of George Bell's brothers were killed within a few days of each other, and many of his former Oxford pupils were also killed; his horror of war and his determination to work for peace both arose from the sorrow he felt and shared during this period. That the clergy themselves were often mourners brought them into closer contact with their own people, and gave them a greater capacity to understand the sufferings of their parishioners.

Archbishop Davidson was unfailing in his sympathy for the bereaved. In a letter of sympathy in 1916 to a priest in his own diocese whose son had been killed, he told him how he had just come from sitting with Asquith 'whose frame is sore stricken, for he was wrapped up in Raymond. Tonight I go to see ——, whose son and heir, intensely loved, was killed yesterday – and so it is, day by day.'[21] Those like Henson who were accustomed to cover their vulnerability with a protective front found such letters of condolence difficult to write. Cyril

Garbett, then Vicar of the large parish of Portsea, insisted that though his staff was depleted (many had left to become chaplains) regular contact should be kept with every house from which a man had gone to serve in the forces. Any news of bereavement meant an immediate visit from one of the staff. The battle of Jutland in 1916 cost 6,097 British lives; there were several bereaved families in every street in the parish of Portsea as a result. The memory of this haunted him for the rest of his life. The constant strain on him, as on other parish priests, was enormous.[22] Peter Green recognized with characteristic pastoral sensitivity the special grief of those whose loved ones had died and been buried in a foreign land, far away from their families, and the need therefore of each bereaved family for its own special service in their parish church. He suggested that this should take the form of a burial service, with hymns, address, catafalque, wreath and Last Post.[23] Whenever possible, he took each such service himself. Winnington-Ingram frequently alluded in his sermons to the bereaved who 'poured' into his room: 'I spend much of my time, whenever I have a chance, with the widows and the mothers of those who are gone.'

> When I, an unmarried man, think to-day of my own spiritual sons, dear to me as if they were my own boys, who have month by month gone to their death, or come home maimed for life, it is almost more than I can bear, and I can do something more than merely sympathize with the father and mother who have given one, two, three and I have known even four sons in the same cause. I do more than sympathize: I feel with them; I suffer with them.[24]

But doctrinally, and therefore pastorally, the ministry of the Church of England to the dying and the bereaved was confused. Biblical criticism, emphasis on a social gospel, evolution, liberal views of the love of God, and a materialistic type of science had been steadily eroding the old clear-cut doctrines about heaven and hell which up to the mid-nineteenth century had been broadly held in common by the majority of Christians for centuries.[25] Some Christians preached that the war had at last brought men into contact with reality, by facing everyone with the fact of death and the issue of eternal destiny, and hoped that the Church and Christianity would thereby recover lost ground. R. J. Campbell wrote in 1916 that he believed the war would bring back a more definite doctrine of the Communion of Saints. He believed that Protestantism had 'little comfort to give to mourners, for it has been so sadly silent regarding the fate of our dead'. He drew by contrast a moving picture of French Catholics praying before the exposed Sacrament in a church on All Souls' Day. Through visiting French churches he had begun to realize 'the devotional value, the practical helpfulness' of the reservation of the Sacrament. 'It makes all the difference between a dead building and a place that is a sanctuary indeed, wherein worshippers feel that they are in immediate contact with the supernatural and divine.'[26]

In 1914 public prayer for the dead was uncommon in the Church of England; by the end of the war it had become widespread. After the war, *Songs of Praise* included a hymn for Funerals beginning 'How can I cease to pray for thee?' Though the 1549 Prayer Book had contained explicit prayers for the departed, they were modified almost out of existence in the 1552 and 1662 Books. Prayers for the dead, however, were included in 'A Form of Intercession' issued in 1900 during the Boer War, and in the 'Form of Service' for the commemoration of Queen Victoria in 1902. The Prayer Book of 1928 was later to include prayers for the dead in the Burial and Communion rites and in 'Occasional Prayers', propers for a funeral Communion, and for the observance of All Souls' Day.[27] On All Souls' Day 1914, the Archbishop of Canterbury preached a sermon on the subject which was much quoted (the *Guardian* printed it verbatim). He said that the abuses of the medieval system were clear, but went on:

> But surely now there is place for a gentler recognition of the instinctive, the natural, the loyal craving of the bereaved, and the abuses of the chantry system and the extravagances of Tetzel need not now, nearly four centuries afterwards, thwart or hinder the reverent, the absolutely trustful prayer of a wounded spirit who feels it natural and helpful to pray for him whom we shall not greet on earth again, but who, in his Father's loving keeping, still lives, and, as we may surely believe, still grows from strength to strength in truer purity and in deepened reverence and love.[28]

The writer of the article 'Prayers for the Departed' in the *Church Quarterly* for October 1916 pointed out that more than for many centuries past English people were finding that it was natural and right to pray for their departed; such prayer was a legitimate development of biblical teaching. Even the most reserved were moved by the universal grief. A. C. Headlam wrote of a service at All Souls College, Oxford, on 2 November 1917:

We had our service this morning. I do not think that I have ever felt the tragedy of the War more — the chapel filled almost entirely with old men and the roll of the killed and the feeling of sadness. At one point in the service a great sob came from Wilkinson, whose son was killed: and I did not know whether I should get through; but just when I thought I might fail I got stronger.

Yet Headlam was a man who usually had such a very tight rein on his feelings that he could appear impassive and forbidding.[29] Anglo-Catholics of course welcomed a much wider recognition of a practice that they had always strongly commended, and gladly prayed for the dead and offered Requiems.[30] Cards were issued depicting a priest celebrating a Requiem; above the altar was a cloud containing the faces of soldiers for whom the Requiem was being offered. Bishop Moule of Durham, a staunch Evangelical, though he deplored medieval practices, said that he gave 'perpetual greetings' to the departed; it was certainly 'no sin' to follow them with 'suspiria' that they might enjoy ever growing light and joy in heaven.[31] Bishop Percival of Hereford, a liberal with modernist sympathies and a fierce critic of Anglo-Catholicism, found no doctrinal problem about using an official form for commendation of the fallen. After the death of his son in the war, each day he personally read this commendation after the offices in his chapel. Harry Blackburne wrote from the front that at a burial in the line the men always asked him to say a prayer for the dead man and his relatives, 'and yet there are still some at home who quibble about prayers for the dead'.[32] Geoffrey Gordon said that no services were more willingly attended than the regular services of commemoration held as soon as possible after the battalion or brigade had been in action:

> Even those who would not ordinarily regard themselves as religious and who do not usually attend voluntary services seem then to feel the need of a religious expression for the sentiments of regret, affection, and respect which can find satisfaction in no other outlet.[33]

But when in 1917 Forms of Prayer issued by authority for the first time contained an explicit prayer for the departed, the evangelical Bishop Chavasse of Liverpool protested to Archbishop Davidson. Such prayers, he said, were causing 'distress and resentment' among large numbers of church people and were contrary to Scripture and the teachings of the Church of England. Davidson pointed out in reply that the prayer in question was discretionary; but in any case hundreds of thousands of people wished for prayers of this nature, and that he was often pressed to provide them officially. Many of 'marked Evangelical opinion would thankfully use it'. Knox, the evangelical Bishop of Manchester, was the only other bishop to protest.[34] Both were completely out of touch with popular sentiment; bereavement was sweeping away the latent Protestantism of the English people in this matter. Three chaplains on the Archbishops' Second Committee in an Appendix, and the Committee itself (with two dissentients) also wished that a revised Prayer Book should 'guide and satisfy the widespread desire for Prayers for the Dead'.[35] In a sermon in Westminster Abbey on All Saints' Day 1919, William Temple declared: 'Let us pray for those whom we know and love who have passed on to the other life. . . . But do not be content to pray for them. Let us also ask them to pray for us.' Death does not settle everything irrevocably. Growth continues beyond the grave. We do not pray for the dead because we believe that God will otherwise neglect them, but because 'we claim the privilege of uniting our love for them with God's'.[36]

If the needs of the bereaved made prayers for the dead a normal feature of the worship of the Church of England, they also weakened the Bishops' regulations about access to the reserved Sacrament which had been embodied in a draft rubric of 1911. The War had increased the need to give Communion at short notice, but some parishes had been reserving the Sacrament for private and public devotions as well. In 1915, Bishop Gore wrote to the Archbishop of Canterbury that as the Bishop of London had 'surrendered' and allowed access for prayer before the Blessed Sacrament, and that as this was also true of the Birmingham and Chichester dioceses, he also was considering abandoning his stand. In a debate in Convocation on reservation in February 1917, Bishop Winnington-Ingram 'frankly admitted' that the regulations had broken down in the London diocese: 'the tide of human grief and anxiety had been too great, the longing to get as near as possible to the Sacramental Presence of our Lord had been too urgent'. He could not promise that the chapels for reservation in his diocese would be inaccessible. In view of this, the meaning of the resolution which was passed reaffirming the regulations was unclear. A Memorial had been signed by nearly 1,000 priests asserting that they could not obey any rubric which forbade access to the place of reservation. Later that year the bishops formulated a more detailed policy forbidding permanent reservation, but it was as difficult to enforce as the previous

3 A solemn dedication of two Red Cross ambulances at St Paul's, Knightsbridge, in January 1915. The congregation had raised £1,300 for their cost

4 Bishop Winnington-Ingram conducting a service for the London Territorials from an altar of drums at St Paul's Cathedral, July 1915. See p. 252

5　Queen Mary visiting a street shrine in South Hackney, London, August 1916. See pp. 67, 170–1, 202, 295, 300

draft rubric.[37] The practice of permanent reservation (for which cautious provision was to be made in the 1928 Prayer Book) continued to spread gradually between the wars, and more rapidly during and after the second war.

The pressures of bereavement drove some mourners to spiritualism, and seances were resorted to by an increasing number of people. At one stage of the war there were said to be 118 mediums in the Kensington area alone. In 1916 Sir Oliver Lodge wrote *Raymond*, a memoir of his son killed the year before. It contained a number of 'supernormal communications' from his dead son. Lodge's scientific reputation gave spiritualism a new authority in the minds of many people. Lord Halifax criticized Lodge's spiritualism in an address at St Martin-in-the-Fields, given at the request of Dick Sheppard in February 1917. It was later published as *'Raymond' – Some Criticisms*. Bishop Talbot was engaged by Lodge in a detailed correspondence on the subject in the same year. Neville Figgis in a sermon that Michaelmas Day said that we should not be surprised by the rapid growth of spiritualism:

> The fact that with so many these things have taken the place of Christian Faith is a Nemesis on the Church for neglect. Religion has been to many either a thing of this world, or merely a system of ideas. Its accredited and official spokesmen have been so timid of all doings that make a concrete reality of communion with the world beyond, that our generation has turned otherwhere for the springs of consolation. Instead of getting angry, we should do better to revive our faith in the unseen presences. . . .[38]

Winnington-Ingram warned against spiritualism in general and criticized *Raymond* in particular in an All Saints' Day sermon in 1917 entitled 'The Blessedness of Seeing by Faith'. He commended the practice of remembering the dead on All Saints' Day. Systematically and vividly he taught what he believed to be the Christian doctrines about these questions to combat the growth of spiritualism.[39] When mediums offered to get in touch with Kipling's son killed in the battle of Loos, Kipling replied with his poem 'The Road to En-Dor', written in 1917.

When Basil Matthews edited a volume of sermons by distinguished preachers of the day in 1917, he wrote that the question of death and the future life was one of the most urgent issues thrown into prominence by the war. A. E. Garvie, Principal of New College, Hampstead, in one of these sermons regarded the question 'Is it well with those who have fallen?' as one of the four theological questions most frequently raised at that time.[40]

Could the politicians and generals on both sides have thrown so many millions of men into certain death without the widespread existence of a quasi-Islamic belief, encouraged explicitly or tacitly by many in the Churches, that soldiers dying nobly in a 'holy war' would immediately enter into everlasting life? No one preached this view more constantly and vividly than Winnington-Ingram; the qualifications which he added on occasion about the need for repentance, forgiveness and faith were too much in the nature of asides for them to have any real effect. The pressures of bereavement and patriotism made any mention of hell or even of an intermediate state rare on the lips of preachers. Cardinal Bourne said about the war 'God has peopled Heaven with saints who, without it, would hardly have reached Heaven's door-sill'.[41] If we are to comfort mourners, Winnington-Ingram said, 'we must go back to a much brighter view of death'; we have 'lost our faith in the beauty of death':

> . . . those dear young men, they are not dead. They were never more alive than five minutes after death . . . they love still those they have loved on earth, and they live a fuller life than this, a more glorious life.[42]

He often quoted a poem by Katharine Tynan beginning:

> Lest Heaven be for the greybeards hoary;
> GOD, Who made boys for His delight,
> Goes in earth's hour of grief and glory
> And calls the boys in from the night;
> When they come trooping from the war
> Our skies have many a new gold star.[43]

When he visited the front for a Holy Week mission in 1915, he took with him 10,000 booklets of 'Good Friday and Easter Day thoughts', written by himself. The soldier on Good Friday is asked to meditate: 'Christ died for others today; then if I am called to die for others I shall be only following Him; He will look on me as His comrade-in-arms and will be with me in the hour of death and afterwards.' Then he is asked to pray for forgiveness for his sins. On Easter Day: 'Christ rose from the grave today, then death is not the end. My dead comrade who lies on the stretcher will live again. . . . Death is the "gate of life".'[44] On another occasion he quoted approvingly the statement of a Colonel who had lost both sons in one day: 'CHRIST will welcome them as His comrades in arms as they come into the other world.' Winnington-Ingram commented:

> I believe that not only will CHRIST welcome them as comrades in arms, but over every one who dies in this war with his face towards the foe, if he dies in CHRIST, will be said those words: 'This is My beloved son, This is My beloved son. This is My beloved son, in whom I am well pleased.[45]

In another sermon he quoted a 'boy' who had said to him only the previous night: 'Do not think that if I am killed I shall be the least unhappy. I trust I shall have forgiveness of my sins and be admitted to Paradise.'[46] At the Canadian Memorial service at St Paul's in 1915, he preached on 'Thou gavest him a long life: even for ever and ever'. He quoted Rupert Brooke's 'The Dead':

> These laid the world away; poured out the red
> Sweet wine of youth; gave up the years to be
>   Of work and joy, and that unhoped serene,
>   That men call age; and those who would have been,
> Their sons, they gave, their immortality.

He assured his congregation:

> . . . the family circle is still complete. . . . Unseen hands uphold you; unseen spirits speak to yours; close by, though hidden by a veil, the real, lasting activities of the other world proceed apace. Death has been for them a great promotion. . . .[47]

This sermon was published separately (as well as with other sermons in a collection) with a space left for the portrait of the dead friend or relative to be inserted. He told the congregation at a Memorial Service for the London Rifle Brigade in 1915 that he had seen six bereaved mothers in one afternoon: 'the boys died in the most glorious cause for which a man ever died.' But they had not really died.

> JESUS CHRIST loved young men. . . . He knows how to make young men happy. He knows your boy. He knows what he can enjoy, and the sort of life he can live, and the company in which he will be happy; and He has got it ready for him. When that full-blooded, happy-starred spirit shoots into the spirit world, he finds

there the Lord who loved him, and Who has ready a life for him
which he can enjoy.[48]

Some churchmen felt uneasy about such language. Guy Rogers said
that men despised chaplains who watered down the Christian teaching:
it was absurd that under the stress of war we should say that dying in
obedience to duty 'atones for a life which may have been one long
dereliction of duty'.[49] Charles Raven scathingly criticized bishops who
'turned themselves into recruiting officers . . . and declaimed with an
almost Mohammedan fervour upon the bliss awaiting the dying
warrior'.[50] A. E. Garvie said in a sermon that, while the Christian gospel
does not warrant a declaration that those who have died without a
Christian belief simply perish, there is no warrant for believing that
those who die without any inward change are at once saved because
they died sacrificially. We are saved by Christ's sacrifice, not by self-
sacrifice.[51] An edition of St John's Gospel prepared for the troops by the
evangelical Scripture Gift Mission printed such texts as 3.36, 5.24,
11.25 in bold type; such texts emphasized the eternal consequences of
belief or disbelief in this life. But the Gospels were also an important
source of the imagery with which the more educated described both the
comradeship of the army and their willingness to die for their country.
A favourite text for memorials was John 15.13: 'Greater love hath no
man than this, that a man lay down his life for his friends.' When Owen
returned to France after his breakdown, he wrote to Sassoon (echoing
John 10.11 and Amos 7.14): 'And now I am among the herds again, a
Herdsman; and a Shepherd of sheep that do not know my voice.'[52] On
the title page of the *Letters of Oswin Creighton* edited by his mother,
another favourite text from the Gospels appears: 'He that loseth his life
for my sake shall find it.'

If the pressures of the war forced some Christians to modify
traditional doctrines about life after death, so it also impelled some
outside the Churches to adopt some type of belief in immortality. H. G.
Wells's Mr Britling in his own bereavement wrote a letter to the
bereaved parents of his former German family tutor: '"These boys,
these hopes, this war has killed." The words hung for a time in his mind.
"No!" said Mr. Britling stoutly, "they live!"' He felt the presence of
God: 'a voice within him bade him be of good courage'[53] – another echo
of St John's Gospel. Studdert Kennedy and other Christians made
much of the religious passages in *Mr. Britling*; he said it was widely
read in the trenches by officers.[54] Helen Thomas, widow of Edward

Thomas the poet, wrote an account of their courtship and marriage shortly after her husband was killed in 1917. A friend had suggested that it might help her to recover from the severe breakdown caused by his death. Her account was entitled *As It Was*. When she completed the story to include the later years and her husband's death, the second part was published as *World Without End*. It is significant that in these two titles she reached for the Christian affirmation of the *Gloria Patri* to convey her deeply moving conviction of the continuing presence of her husband:

> But the memory of the joy and hope and happiness of the reunions has stayed with me, and for ever, so it seems to me, part of me will stand at the gate and listen for his step, watch for his long stride; feel the strong embrace of his arms, and his kiss.[55]

In 1898 Gladstone wrote that the doctrine of hell had been relegated 'to the far-off corners of the Christian mind'. Men no longer were deprived of posts in theological institutions or faculties, or suffered ecclesiastical censure for teaching a tentative universalism or conditional immortality. The number of 'hell-fire' sermons had greatly diminished. The majority of the population were too sophisticated in an age of biblical criticism, or were too much affected by the conviction that the penal system should reform rather than punish, or were generally too 'progressive', to take hell seriously.[56] In any case during the war, even the most lurid pictures which any conservative preacher might conjure up would look stagy by comparison with the reality of what everyone called the 'hell' of the trenches. Studdert Kennedy in his poems 'Eternal Hope' and 'Well?' argued against popular pictures of hell and judgement. In 1929 Percy Dearmer published *The Legend of Hell*; in the Preface he wrote that during the war, when he worked for the Y.M.C.A. in France, the question he was most frequently asked was, 'How can a just God send people to everlasting torment?' In tracing the history of the doctrine of hell, he was glad to be able to record that though it survived in popular thought most theologians had abandoned it, as (in Hasting Rashdall's words written in 1916) 'clearly revolting to the modern conscience'.[57] R. J. Campbell in his liberal modernist period at the City Temple wrote that 'the Christian fundamental of the love of God renders the dogma of everlasting punishment impossible'.[58] But by 1916 he had revised his opinions to approximate them to those of his mentor Charles Gore, who ordained him: the 'moral order must be vindicated against those who seek to violate it'; there is, however, nothing in the New Testament to justify a belief in the everlasting punishment of sin.

> The doctrine of an intermediate purificatory state in which the souls of those who have not died in mortal sin are being cleansed from earthly stains, and are benefited by the prayers of the faithful on earth, is ancient and catholic and accordant to the feelings of most people.

When asked by a soldier at the front about the eternal fate of those who die for their country, though their lives have been a 'bit rackety', Campbell agreed with the soldier that God would give them a chance.[59] Charles Raven believed that experience at the front had shown that no sinner was wholly black; such experience made it much more difficult to believe that anyone could be damned.[60]

Horatio Bottomley echoed popular sentiment in rejecting any idea that soldiers needed to repent. Though Newman's *Dream of Gerontius* (set to music by Elgar in 1900) and some revisionist theology, both Catholic and liberal, encouraged belief in an intermediate state, few applied it to soldiers. One who did was Bishop Gore:

> I cherish the belief that the sacrifice of themselves which they make so cheerfully and which is so splendid will keep their hearts open enough to God for Him to do the rest in purgatory or paradise or whatever awaits them the other side.[61]

A sermon preached by Fr Cyril Bickersteth C.R. on All Souls' Day 1916 stressed the importance of the feast. It was impossible to believe that the many who die without faith or absolution went to hell. Christ went to preach to the spirits in prison. No one was ever beyond hope. Purgatory truly understood was a place of cleansing and preparation.[62] A soldier in R. C. Sherriff's popular play *Journey's End* (1928) mused:

> Supposing the worst happened – supposing we were knocked right out. Think of all the chaps who've gone already. It can't be very lonely there – with all those fellows. Sometimes I think it's lonelier here. (II. ii)

Tennyson had popularized this theme in *In Memoriam* (1850) which was still regarded as the classical statement about death and bereavement in the early twentieth century, and was frequently quoted by preachers:

And I shall know him when we meet:
And we shall sit at endless feast,
   Enjoying each the other's good:
   What vaster dream can hit the mood
Of Love on earth?

                              (XLVII)

It was impossible, wrote C. E. Montague, to believe that those who died fighting together could be separated in the life beyond by the closing of the gates on any of them; Donald Hankey, unlike Montague a churchman, agreed.[63] Whatever the Bible or the Churches might teach about separating sheep from goats, soldiers wrote about a comradeship so deep that it could not be broken by death or divided by Judgement, and, as we have seen, that comradeship was often described in language derived from the Gospels. The traditional Christian belief that the goal of man is the vision of God was largely superseded by the idea of heaven as a reunion of the dead. William St Leger was killed at the age of 23 in 1918. As his friends were killed one by one, he imagined himself reunited with them (echoes of Wisdom 3.9 and 1 Corinthians 13.12).

> But meantime Denis and Henry and all those others are happy together – supremely happy . . . and they are waiting for me to join them and when I do will give me a great welcome. Then I will understand everything and be happy and content.[64]

Kipling wrote a short story during the war depicting the crowds of war-dead arriving in heaven: 'On the Gate'. He delayed publication until 1926 on the advice of his wife. Those who superintended the arrival of the dead included Charles Bradlaugh and Judas Iscariot. A reason for including even the most unlikely was usually found: 'Q.M.A.' ('Quia multum amavit'), 'G.L.H.' ('Greater love hath no man'), 'I.W.' (Importunate Widow) or 2 Samuel 14.14:

> For we must needs die, and are as water spilt on the ground, which cannot be gathered up again; neither doth God respect any person: yet doth he devise means, that his banished be not expelled from him.

Many books appeared with titles like *Our Comradeship with the Blessed Dead* (1915): this was a collection of weekly addresses given by Bishop John Maud of Kensington at intercession services at St Martin-in-the-Fields. The Archbishop of Canterbury, preaching at a Memorial Service for Australians and New Zealanders in St Paul's in June 1915, said that it would be untrue to claim that all who gave their lives were stainless saints. But we should pray that they may 'pass onward in the new and larger life from strength to strength'.[65]

A memoir of Gilbert Talbot, a son of the Bishop of Winchester, killed in 1915, was written by his mother, at first only for private circulation. The copy in the library of the Community of the Resurrection, Mirfield, was given by Mrs Talbot to Bishop Gore, and inscribed by her: 'They are the living soul of England now.' In 1912, Gilbert had written a letter on the theme of self-sacrifice and (with slight inaccuracy) had quoted Browning's *The Ring and the Book*:[66]

> O lover of my life, my soldier-saint,
> Who put his breast between the spears and me.
>
> (Book VII)

In September 1914, he wrote to his parents about the war: 'It's all magnificent really – it's purging us all.' His Colonel had told him 'Remember you are responsible for 54 lives; not 55 – your own doesn't count.'[67] When he was killed, his brother Neville crawled out to his body under shelling into no-man's-land:

> He was lying almost on his face, obviously killed outright. I stroked his hair and commended his soul to the Father, Who made him, to the Son, Who redeemed him, and to the Holy Spirit, Who made him good, and prayed that we might meet again, and crawled away.

A few days later, when the fighting had subsided, with the help of some soldiers, he retrieved Gilbert's body. 'How strong is the sense of outrage at non-burial in one's blood!' Neville commented. He added later, 'In that moment I took the measure of death.' He told the men that it was the soul that mattered: 'Fear not him who can kill the body.'[68] To be able to assert that, was a way of coping with death, especially when it was linked with liturgical rituals of commendation and burial as traditional 'containers' of what could otherwise be an unbearable emotion. The themes that war cleanses and that only the body is lost in death found famous expression in Rupert Brooke's sonnet of 1914, 'Peace', with its image of the swimmers leaping gladly into 'cleanness', leaving behind the old and weary world, and its assertion that in death there is 'Naught broken save this body'. If human nature was being cleansed by war, and death only kills the body, then all the suffering had a purpose. Oswin Creighton wrote (echoing 2 Corinthians 4 and 6):

Surely death is not the horror of war, but the causes which contribute to war. The Cross is beautiful – the forces which lead up to it are damnable. It really does not in the least matter how many people are killed, who wins, whether we starve or anything else of a transitory nature, provided that in the process human nature is transformed in some way or another.[69]

The owner of one Prayer Book lovingly recorded the dates of the significant events of the war, and the deaths of relatives and friends who were killed, against the psalms of the day. On the flyleaf is written '1915. Genl. Sir A. W. Currie to the Canadian troops: – "To those who fall I say, You will not die, but step into immortality. Your mothers will not lament your fate, but will be proud to have borne such sons."' For the idealists it was a death for England, freedom, loyalty to friends and treaties, a blow against a devilish foe: 'The War is amazingly inspiring, and all the Belgian stories and all the devilish and damnable horrors that these swine inflict on the women and children make one long to get there. . . .' wrote Gilbert Talbot in September 1914.[70]

Basil Bourchier, Vicar of St Jude's, Hampstead, had served with the Red Cross in August 1914, had been captured in Belgium and after being condemned to death was released. The story was told, in the Preface to Bourchier's *For All We Have and Are* and by Winnington-Ingram in his sermon 'The Holy War', in the style of the adventure stories of Rider Haggard and George Alfred Henty. The *Graphic* (12 September 1914) popularized the story with drawings under the headline 'A London Vicar in the Hands of the Huns'. Bourchier was a friend and admirer of Horatio Bottomley, who waged a bitterly anti-German campaign in *John Bull* and elsewhere. He preached at Bottomley's funeral in 1933 and paid tribute to his efforts in sustaining the morale of the soldiers in wartime.[71] Bourchier frequently visited the troops at home and in France during the war. He was proud that so many English and continental royalty visited his church and the Garden Suburb. A history of the parish in 1923 devoted a number of pages to their names and those of the nobility. He was a fervent believer in Empire; British rule was 'invariably beneficent'; India for the Indians or Sudan for the Sudanese were 'impossible' propositions. The League of Nations was 'not nearly British enough' for his liking.[72] A friend and admirer of Winnington-Ingram, his bishop, he had a similar romantically religious attitude to the war. In 1915 he declared in a sermon (on the lips of Christ): 'to die for England is to taste the sweetest vintage of death that can be offered to English lips'.[73]

The conviction that pre-war England had been selfish, lazy, squabbling and morally enfeebled, and that war brought national unity, purpose and a new spirit of self-sacrifice, was widespread.[74] The idea that the shedding of blood would redeem, cleanse, purify the nations in an almost mystical manner had Christian, chivalric, and primitive roots. On the day war was declared, J. L. Garvin, Editor of *The Observer*, expressed this idea vividly:

> We have to do our part in killing a creed of war. Then at last, after a rain of blood, there may be set the greater rainbow in the Heavens before the vision of the souls of men. And after Armageddon war, indeed, may be no more.[75]

H. G. Wells wrote a series of articles a few days later entitled 'The War that Will End War': 'This, the greatest of all wars, is not just another war – it is the last war.'[76] This was subsequently often used to justify yet one more battle, one even greater effort. Winnington-Ingram in September 1914 had spoken of 'this Armageddon'.[77] Note Garvin's use of biblical language: God's covenant with Noah that a destroying flood would never again be sent; the references to Armageddon from Revelation 16, perhaps an oblique reference to the winepress of blood from Chapter 14, the end to death and suffering promised in Isaiah 25.8 and Revelation 21.4. Perhaps he had also in mind Bolingbroke's speech in *Richard II* Act III Scene 3:

> If not, I'll use the advantage of my power
> And lay the summer's dust with showers of blood
> Rain'd from the wounds of slaughtered Englishmen.

The Bible also supplied much of the phraseology for the idea of redemptive death; Moses had sprinkled the blood upon the people saying 'Behold the blood of the covenant' (Exodus 24); the New Testament, in expounding the death of Christ, used sacrificial imagery and ideas from the Old Testament. The haunting phrase from Hebrews 9.22 ('without shedding of blood is no remission') was often cited in the first war. Many outside the Church as well as inside turned to consider the crucifixion afresh. Neville Figgis said in a sermon in 1917:

> When the Cross of Christ is held before us, it is not as a strange, unique phenomenon. It is the inner meaning of all our struggles, the symbol of all sacrifice for distant ends.[78]

The desire for self-sacrifice is very evident in the letters of some of the idealistic young men of the period, at least in the earlier stages of their war experience. F. H. Keeling, the Fabian intellectual, had been haunted for years by the desire to earn his living as a manual worker. He joined up in August 1914 and eagerly shared the life of the ordinary soldier serving in the ranks.[79] On the eve of the Somme holocaust in 1916, one soldier described his preparations for the battle in language which owes much to the traditional stories of Christian chivalry, and something to the Scouting ethos:

> I took my Communion yesterday with dozens of others who are going over tomorrow; and never have I attended a more impressive service. I placed my body in God's keeping, and I am going into battle with His name on my lips, full of confidence and trusting implicitly in Him . . . should it be God's holy will to call me away I am quite prepared to go . . . I could not pray for a finer death; and you, my dear Mother and Dad, will know that I died doing my duty to my God, my Country and my King. I ask that you should look upon it as an honour that you have given your son for the sake of King and Country.[80]

Tennyson in *Idylls of the King* (1859), Charlotte Yonge in *The Heir of Redclyffe* (1853), and the Pre-Raphaelites had popularized the ethos of medieval chivalry. Edward Strachey's Preface to the expurgated *Morte d'Arthur* (1884) had called for a chivalric approach to modern social problems. In pre-war days many suffragettes described their campaigns in the language of righteous crusades against an evil and unscrupulous foe. The official organ of the W.S.P.U. on 17 October 1913 pictured the suffragette as a pure St George repulsing the libidinous attacks of the press portrayed as a dragon. Emily Davison, who threw herself under the King's horse in June 1913, wrote that personal friendship had to become 'a grim holocaust to Liberty'. Like the Christian disciple she must love the cause more than her family. Like Christ she had to drink 'this cup of anguish'. She described herself as re-enacting Calvary for unborn generations.[81] In November 1914 Mrs Pankhurst appealed to soldiers to fight like knights of old with unstained swords.[82] Studdert Kennedy in 'Patience' wrote of the frustration of wanting to do 'just one grand deed and die', but of having to climb to God, 'deed by deed, and tear by tear'. In Ireland during this period, rebels like Patrick Pearse proclaimed that a blood sacrifice like that of Christ was necessary to redeem Ireland. On the eve of his execution for his part in the Easter Rising in 1916, he wrote a prayer for his mother to be addressed to the

Virgin Mary who had also seen her son die 'amid the scorn of men / For whom He died'. James Connolly, also executed after the Irish rebellion, quoted: 'without the shedding of Blood there is no Redemption' in an article in February 1916.[83] One of the phrases that haunted Mr Britling, the liberal humanist, as he struggled to find the meaning of the war, was 'Redemption by the shedding of blood'.[84] Winnington-Ingram in Advent 1916 said: 'the precious blood of their dearest boy mingles with the Precious Blood which flowed in Calvary; again the world is being redeemed by precious blood. "CHRIST did what my boy did; my boy imitated what CHRIST did" they say.'[85] Fr Bull, convalescing after a chaplaincy in France, was overwhelmed with sadness at seeing young soldiers full of fun and laughter, knowing how so many of them would be killed. Then God rebuked his sadness with the words, 'Nay, they are lambs for the sacrifice.' Preaching in St Paul's in July 1915 on Hebrews 12.1 he asserted: 'after a year of crucifixion our Nation answers with unflinching resolution, "To the last drop of our blood"', and quoted Isaiah 50.7.[86] Caroline Playne was understandably concerned about the effect of the use during the war of the Christian language of redemption by blood.[87] Archbishop Söderblom of Uppsala was in a Bohemian village when war was declared. His German friend, Adolf Deissmann, spoke of a 'ver sacrum', a sacred springtime. Söderblom had heard England described as 'a people at prayer'. As a neutral he observed that the nations spoke of the outbreak of war as a cathartic experience.[88]

Sassoon's poem 'The Redeemer' tells of the Christ figure who appeared in the trenches, identified with all the human need and suffering:

> He faced me, reeling in his weariness,
> Shouldering his load of planks, so hard to bear.
> I say that He was Christ, who wrought to bless
> All groping things with freedom bright as air,
> And with His mercy washed and made them fair.
> Then the flame sank, and all grew black as pitch,
> When we began to struggle along the ditch;
> And someone flung his burden in the muck,
> Mumbling: 'Christ Almighty, now I'm stuck!'

All over France British soldiers came across crucifixes, often for the first time in their lives. An area of the Somme was called 'Crucifix Valley' because of the calvary which stood there. The wooden cemetery crucifix at Ypres had a dud shell lodged between the cross and the figure, prompting many comments on the apparently miraculous power of the cross. Field Punishment No. 1 (being strapped spread-eagled on a wheel or other object) was nicknamed 'crucifixion'. This was deeply resented. Once after a service for prisoners at which Passion hymns had been sung, one prisoner was overheard to say to another 'And now they're going to crucify us'.[89] (This punishment was abolished in 1923.) George Coppard on the way to the battle of the Somme passed what was called Crucifix Corner. He remembered looking at the sorrowful face on the cross. Many, he thought, who had passed a few hours before were now dead; many now passing would follow them.

On the eve of Passchendaele, Bishop Gwynne sat down by the roadside as the last of the troops had gone forward. He prayed hard to understand the slaughter he foresaw. He heard a voice say, 'Only the best can give the best'. He turned and found a crucifix standing alone in an otherwise totally ruined village.[90] But not all soldiers were so impressed; one said 'Who was he anyway? I bet I've suffered more than ever he did.'[91]

In 1917, a churchwarden presented St Mary's at Alsager with a copy of the popular picture 'The Great Sacrifice'. (It had originally appeared in the Christmas 1914 issue of the *Graphic*.)[92] It shows a dead soldier in the field, his uniform neat and tidy, his only wound the size of a small coin in his head; he lies with one hand on the feet of a spectral crucified Christ. Below the picture was written the text 'Greater love hath no man than this', and a poem which includes these lines:

> One more unflinching valorous soul hath sped
> To that far land whose shadowy paths unfold
> Beyond the posterns of the sunset-gold,
> Beyond the bourn to which our dreams have led
> One more true knight . . .
> The Army of the dear triumphant dead . . .
> Mothers and sons . . . Take hope, and see
> In the white book of Chivalry, set apart,
> The April glory of the dauntless heart
> Who fought and died that Freedom might be free.

A paragraph by the vicar in the October magazine expressed gratitude, and recalled that the Queen had made a similar presentation to a church in the south recently. But he added that while acknowledging with deepest reverence the self-sacrifice of the soldiers, 'one ought perhaps to point out that the Sacrifice made by our Lord and Saviour Jesus Christ upon the Cross must ever remain by itself infinitely above and beyond any sacrifice that could ever be made by men'. It is noteworthy that a priest who never for a moment (at least in the magazine) questioned the justness of the war or its conduct was only prepared to enter a note of dissent when he felt that a point of theology was at stake. Though some could use the language of Christian redemption to idealize the slaughter and to claim Christ as uniquely on the English side, many also reached for the language because it was the only one available which seemed to give some positive meaning to what was happening. Sir John Arkwright's hymn 'O Valiant Hearts', written in the war, is open to the charges that it idealized war, naïvely implied that the Allies were on the side of God and sentimentalized the fallen ('your knightly virtue'). But in praying to Christ 'to bless our lesser Calvaries', Arkwright was surely not denying the uniqueness of the Atonement (as some have suggested), but was trying to make the connection between Christ's sufferings and our own, which has some biblical authority, similar to that made by Neville Figgis in the sermon quoted above.[93]

Popular anecdotes stressed the heroism of the soldiers: 'Our captain was laid low, mortally wounded. He lay in the trench and just before he died we captured our last objective and he went west, saying "Bravo England".'[94] One soldier wrote that but for the war his life would have been a trifling affair, and that the world would have been made no different by his death: 'But we shall live for ever in the results of our efforts.'[95] The Principal of Culham, in his Christmas letter for 1915, wrote of the 'holy memories of brothers who fell in the high cause of righteousness' and gave vignettes of recent heroic deaths of former members of the college. But most ordinary soldiers resented such idealization. They felt that there was too much vicarious self-satisfaction in the civilian glorification of war: that such glorification was propaganda designed to prevent any talk of a negotiated peace. Some soldiers felt a deeper bond between themselves and their enemies sharing the same horrors than between themselves and civilians at home. Robert Graves tells how an officer gave orders that the next of kin of a soldier who committed suicide should be told that he died a soldier's death.[96] In 'Suicide in the Trenches' and 'The Hero' Sassoon wrote poems about similar situations. According to Charles Carrington, the lack of communication between those at home and those at the front was the reason why it took ten years before most of the classic war autobiographies appeared.[97] Donald Hankey believed that the Bairnsfather cartoons got closer to the authentic heroism of the soldiers than did the idealizers. Neither the heroic nor the satiric pictures were adequate to the reality of war.[98]

Temporary crosses, made out of two bits of wood from an ammunition box with the name scrawled in indelible pencil, were common sights. One rough memorial consisted of a bas-relief of Christ carved with a jack-knife in the chalk of the grave. Blackburne, when burying soldiers, always kept careful map references of the graves in case the names on the crosses became obliterated. In what was perhaps the most popular poem of the war − 'In Flanders Fields' (published in *Punch* in December 1915) − John McCrae wrote:

> In Flanders fields the poppies blow
> Between the crosses, row on row
> That mark our place . . .

If there were many images of death, there were also some of resurrection. Soldiers, consciously or unconsciously echoing biblical images of wastes turned into fruitful land as signs of God's covenant love and redemptive power, often described the ironic contrast between the constant killing and the beauty of sunrise and sunset, between villages with every building destroyed and their gardens full of spring flowers and the trees in blossom. The attentiveness to nature also reflected the deep influence of the Romantic movement. Oswin Creighton wrote:

> We are living on no-man's-land, a mass of shell craters and barbed wire, mazes of trenches and dug-outs. The soil is barren and chalky. I went over to see an Irish labour company near by, and found the officers contemplating a little dusty flower-bed in which they had planted a few seeds and quite excited to see some of them beginning to show.[99]

Harry Blackburne always asked that at funerals the trumpeters should sound the Reveille after the Last Post − before the war, he said, the service had ended with the Last Post. This was to become a normal and always moving part of post-war Remembrance ritual, an expression of general hope, or even of resurrection. The image of the Last Trump ('the trumpet shall sound, and the dead shall be raised incorruptible') was well known from the Burial Service (1 Corinthians 15) as well as from Handel's *Messiah*. Popular inscriptions for headstones included 'Till morning breaks' and 'Until the day breaks and the shadows flee', both owing something to biblical and romantic imagery and also to the popular hymn 'Abide with me'. When Edmund Blunden and a companion came out of shelling alive in enemy territory, he said, 'We were received as Lazarus was'; the march to a town behind the lines was 'our resurrection road'.[100]

A widely reported sermon by the Free Churchman Dr R. F. Horton in June 1915 helped to spread the story of the Angels at Mons; the *Guardian* was not impressed by the evidence adduced.[101] Hensley Henson believed that war stimulated superstition, and weakened faith.[102] When he criticized the story of the Angels at Mons in a sermon in Westminster Abbey in July 1915, he received a grateful letter from Archbishop Davidson, but a large number of protests. One woman signing herself 'A Daughter of the Church' wrote to Henson:

> If our dear lads who are giving their lives for England can visualize our Saviour and His angels come to help and comfort them in that hell of carnage . . . who shall be so cruel, CRUEL, as to tell them they are wrong? And they are NOT wrong, for where shall the aid and ministry of Heaven be found if not there? God works miracles of help and salvation even in our time.

Henson was depressed visiting Bishop Moule at Auckland Castle to find that he was 'deeply bitten by the Angelic legend'.[103] The day after the Armistice, Bishop Moule said in a Thanksgiving address:

> Let them also remember that there had been acts of God independent of the co-operation of man, manifest in the readiness and position of the British Fleet at the outbreak of war, and also during the retreat from Mons, while who could deny that during the last three months there had been a definite answer to National prayer. Since August 4, when at last the Nation knelt down in prayer, we had not sustained a reverse.[104]

(Moule was a conservative Evangelical who shrank from any engagement with new theological or biblical insights. When Principal of Ridley Hall 1881–99 his students were struck by his reluctance to meet the intellectual challenges of the time.)[105] The story of the Angels at Mons originated in an avowedly fictional short story, 'The Bowmen', published in the *Evening News* on 29 September 1914. To the great embarrassment of the author, the story quickly began to circulate as fact. An emotional version of the story, presented as fact and quoting eyewitnesses, was published by the Rev. A. A. Boddy, *The Real Angels of Mons* (1915). The permission of the official censor, which was displayed by the booklet, gave it further credence, and helped recruiting and morale. Like Gideon in Judges 6, people were eager for contemporary evidence of God's activity.

Stories of relics, sacred pictures and crucifixes miraculously preserved, circulated widely; alleged appearances of Joan of Arc were seriously discussed. Many soldiers carried talismans – New Testaments, texts worn round the neck, holy medals, lucky coins, dried flowers and so on. The inventor of a lucky charm for soldiers claimed in August 1915 that he had sold one million and a quarter since the outbreak of war. R. J. Campbell reported that soldiers had told him of the miraculous preservation of an altar crucifix while the whole church around it had been destroyed. The protection surrounding a statue of the Virgin and Child was shattered, while the figures remained untouched. An altar was demolished, while the Blessed Sacrament was left unharmed. Campbell did not know whether to believe such stories, but symbolically they were true, 'the ruin wrought by earthly evil reaches not so very far'.[106] Among the troops fatalism was widespread. 'If it's got your bloody number on it there's nothing you can do about it' was a constantly reiterated remark. It was widely considered unlucky to light a third cigarette from the same match. Superstition and fatalism were, like humour, ways of cultivating detachment and so strengthening morale – official army language and laconic understatement were other means of doing so. Fatalism helped people to cope with the unexpected deaths so frequently recorded. How can a man thank God, just after an engagement, for being spared, asked Tom Pym, when the shell which remarkably missed him killed his best friend? 'How can he attribute his own safety to God's protection and return thanks for it without at the same time attributing Harry's death to the same Agency and resenting it?'[107]

The readiness of both troops and those at home to believe in supernatural deliverances, to trust in superstition or fatalism, illustrates the fact that English people will often readily believe in the supernatural, provided it is not part of the Bible or the institutionalized supernaturalism of the Church.[108] So it was not because the Christian faith was too supernatural or mythological that the troops mostly had little interest in it. The many who were familiar with the Bible used Christian imagery and mythology to describe their experiences. The language of self-sacrifice from the Gospels and the language of 'comradeship' from the Fourth Gospel were at hand, together with the imagery of *Pilgrim's Progress*. Large numbers were ready to see supernatural significance in chance incidents or in the statue of the Virgin and Child bent low, probably by artillery fire, on the top of the basilica at Albert. But the Church of England was nervous of folk religion:[109] its evangelicalism was too puritan, biblicist and pietistic, its liberalism too detached and academic, its catholicism too self-conscious, dogmatic and nostalgic. In one sense it was too worldly (identified with the social and military establishment), in another sense it was not worldly, sophisticated enough. But then it was facing a situation for which it was as little prepared as the fighting men themselves. Without the biblical imagery purveyed through the Church directly or indirectly, and without the burial and memorial rituals of the Church, the men at the front and those at home would have had hardly any 'containers' at all to help them through those four years of constant death and bereavement. No wonder that through superstition, fatalism, spiritualism and supernatural stories, through creating gardens in waste places, as well as through Christian doctrine, prayer and ritual, people looked for a sign that there was some hope, some order, some loving providence, in the midst of such apocalyptic experience. But since the Churches became increasingly wary of locating the activity of God in miracles, contemporary or biblical, and found it increasingly difficult to preach wholeheartedly the old, simple understanding of providence and divine intervention, many people, as time went on, either rejected the supernatural altogether or sought it outside the mainstream institutional Churches.[110]

9

Patriotism is not enough

The function of nationality and its relation to religion was much debated in the nineteenth century. On the one hand, national religion was believed by many to be essential for national consciousness. On the other hand, the Christian faith seemed to imply some form of internationalism, and it sought to express this not only through the traditional role of the papacy, but also in new ways through the growth of world-wide confessional families (the first Lambeth Conference was held in 1867) and in the beginnings of ecumenism. But the Napoleonic conquests had created a deep fear of a super-power and had renewed desires for national independence. Those who valued nationality noted that the nation states of Italy and Germany were created through war. According to Hegel, war was a method of keeping nations from stagnation.[1] J. B. Mozley in his influential sermon on War in 1871 had proclaimed that nations were necessary barriers and breakwaters to contain the boundless ocean of humanity, for it was dangerous and impossible to conceive a universal empire. There were grave difficulties about any system of arbitration: 'thus every prospect which the progress of society appears to open of eradicating war . . . closes as soon as we examine it.'[2] A committee of the Lambeth Conference of 1897 declared that before a war was invoked it was 'the solemn duty of the people to make sure that it is a great principle and not a prejudice or object of pride which is at stake'. Though it hesitated 'to pronounce war, *per se*, to be immoral', the Church should familiarize people with the idea of arbitration. 'Christianity encouraged the nobler aspects of patriotism, but Christianity certainly proclaims the brotherhood of man.'[3] Meanwhile in 1864 the First Socialist International was held, the International Red Cross was founded and the First Geneva Convention was drawn up. Those Christians who opposed the Boer War and were critical of imperialism argued that imperialism was a form of nationalistic arrogance. Bishops Gore and Percival, both critics of the Boer War, supported Welsh Disestablishment because they believed in national self-determination.

On 14 August 1914, the liberal Anglican *Challenge* in a leading article on 'Patriotism' said:

> Among the first of the old ideas that we must be ready to give up is that of patriotism understood in its present narrow sense. . . . We must come to see that patriotism represents a national temper corresponding to a stage in the social evolution of the individual long left behind. It stands for the assertion of the self and the raising of the self at the expense of others . . . it must bar the way to the larger ideal of brotherhood.

At a more popular level, however, the *Graphic* on 21 November 1914 devoted a full page of photographs to the theme, 'The Activity of the Church in Time of War'. The photographs showed German, French, and Anglican priests serving as combatants and Belgian priests acting as Red Cross workers, and commented, 'In few wars has the Church taken such a unanimous stand for the God of Battle.' The previous two issues depicted a German priest blessing a regiment with a monstrance and a Russian priest leading soldiers into battle holding a cross aloft.

During the war the propagandists in the various nations made use of the differing religious allegiances of the warring powers to harness old antagonisms for the war effort. This had paradoxical results. While some English Protestants accused the Pope of being in league with the Central Powers, some Catholic Belgians saw themselves as victims of German Protestantism. Yet the Belgian Cardinal Mercier, during and after the war, forged close links with Anglicans in England and the United States. It was odd, as Peter Green pointed out in the *Manchester Guardian* of 17 September 1914, for Englishmen to find themselves allied to Russia – its history of Jewish persecution was particularly abhorrent to northern communities which contained strong Jewish elements – against Germany, which seemed to many in England a second Fatherland. Moreover, English Protestants felt close ties to Germany as the home of the Reformation. English theologians, especially Modernists, felt warmly towards Germany as the source of much biblical criticism and theological liberalism. If Orthodox Russia was fighting with the Allies, Orthodox Bulgaria was on the side of Germany. Turks might be able to claim that they were fighting for Islam against British Christians, yet the British Empire included more Muslims than the Ottoman Empire. German Protestants might regard themselves as menaced by Orthodox Russia and Catholic France, while some German Catholics could see themselves as fighting for Christianity against the anti-clerical governments of Italy and France. German army belts were inscribed: 'Gott mit uns'.

In this chapter we shall look at three areas in which the war challenged as well as expressed Christian nationalism: the ecumenical movement; British attitudes to Germany during the war; suggestions for a negotiated peace.

In this first section we shall survey the impetus given to ecumenism by the war. The first large-scale conference of the modern ecumencial movement had taken place at Edinburgh in 1910, but it was a conference between missionary societies rather than between Churches, and no Roman Catholics or Orthodox attended. The war interrupted plans for the first conference on Faith and Order and the creation of an international missionary council. English and German churchmen paid exchange visits in 1908 and 1909, and in 1910 a Council to foster closer relations was formed. The World Alliance was created in August 1914. Remarkably, its International Committee was able to meet in Switzerland in August 1915, with delegates not only from a number of neutral countries, but also from Germany, Britain, and Italy. The World Alliance undertook aid to interned civilians and prisoners of war under the name of *Caritas inter arma*; it attempted to keep up some contact between churchmen of the warring nations; it also did much to promote the ideal of a league of nations to promote international peace for the future.

Until the outbreak of war, German theology was widely, even uncritically, revered in England. But when the war came, the liberal Protestantism associated with theologians like Harnack became doubly suspect to many Catholic and Evangelical Anglicans. In *The Modern Churchman* for October 1914, Foakes-Jackson expressed his nervousness lest theological liberalism should be discredited by its German connections, and his fears were echoed in other issues. Allied propaganda fed the public with often tendentious selections from Nietzsche, Treitschke, and Bernhardi, and this trio was often quoted by churchmen and others as typical examples of the godless, militaristic philosophy of Germany. The average Englishman knew little about German history or culture. In education the classical languages were taught in preference to German or French.[4]

The Student Christian Movements in many countries coalesced into the World Student Christian Federation in 1895, and from 1911 began to include Eastern Orthodox members. The British S.C.M. had many contacts with German S.C.M. leaders before the war. When war came, members of the British S.C.M. were asked to pray for the continental leaders: 'Some of us know and love their leaders as well as our own.' The S.C.M. leaders of the warring nations tried through intermediaries to keep up some contact and to understand each other's views.[5]

The war stimulated ecumenical thinking and action in several directions. At the beginning of the war, R. J. Campbell made an appeal from the pulpit of the City Temple that the Pope should convene a Christian peace conference after the war. He reiterated the proposal two years later as an Anglican, and looked back nostalgically to the medieval world which had 'one visible seat of moral authority to which all men looked'. That system failed, but after the war could not there be a united action by the Churches through the Papacy to restore on better terms the old international amity?[6] But the fact that the Papacy did not condemn Germany in the manner they had hoped for led some English Christians to condemn the Vatican as pro-German.[7] In *The Neutrality of the Holy See* published by the Catholic Truth Society in 1915, the Roman Catholic Bishop of Northampton tried to explain why the Pope had not spoken out against German atrocities. To have done so would have placed German Roman Catholics in grave danger.

The report *The Army and Religion* summed up the situation in the forces: 'Seen against the vast and terrible background of the trenches and the battlefield, ecclesiastical divisions look spectral and unreal.'[8] One chaplain said, 'I have never laboured under such a sense of the disastrous divisions of the Body of Christ as during my service out here.'[9] Guy Rogers, an Irish Evangelical, felt the sadness of the Roman priest saying the Rosary with his men a few yards away from where he was celebrating Holy Communion.

> How pathetic in a way to an onlooker. Two 'rival' shrines and 'rival' priests; yet we were all seeking after God and seeking Him through Christ. One feels a close link of sympathy with anyone of any communion who stands for strong and definite belief – over against the kind of tolerant, half-patronising and wholly vague Christianity which is so characteristic of even a good type of officer.'

Many Anglican chaplains, he said, were led to practise intercommunion with the Free Churches.[10] (After the war, as Rector of Birmingham, he ardently promoted ecumenism.) In some places Anglicans, Free

Churchmen and Roman Catholics would use the same Y.M.C.A. hut for their services and hold a joint evening service on Sundays. In some parishes in France the local *curé* would not allow the use of the church for non-Roman Catholic services, and such a refusal caused bitterness; in other places the use of a temporary altar in the nave would be allowed. But in November 1914 Archbishop Davidson wrote to the Archbishop of Rouen to thank him for allowing Roman Catholic hospital chapels to be used for Anglican services. Bishop Russell Wakefield of Birmingham believed that, because of the recent separation between Church and State in France, some French bishops were nervous lest, if Anglicans were allowed the use of their churches, sects and secularists might also claim the right to use them as well.[11]

The Mirfield Fathers, with their strong concern for unity, particularly with Roman Catholics and Orthodox, often wrote of how this concern had been deepened into longing by the ecumenical contacts created by the war. Those in the Middle East enjoyed Orthodox hospitality and worship and were able to use Orthodox churches for services and Quiet Days. At Damascus the Greek Patriarch lent candlesticks and an altar frontal for a Confirmation in a Y.M.C.A. cinema marquee. Fr Freestone, in Salonika, shared his communion vessels with a Serbian Orthodox priest attached to the hospital. Oswin Creighton had found Roman Catholicism incomprehensible before the war. Now he and a Roman chaplain jointly organized the formation of groups of soldiers for Bible study. Neville Talbot wrote of the admiration he grew to feel for the Roman system:

> An indifference to the attraction, fullness, firmness, convenience, warmth, comfort, psychological power of Roman Catholic cultus implies, I think, a great insensibility to the needs of the average man. Many a time in hospitals in the War did I long that there had been in the hazy, muddled souls of C. of E. men the familiarity with and knowledge of their religion to be found in Roman Catholics.[12]

Though Anglican chaplains often rejoiced in the ways in which the circumstances of the front had broken down differences of Anglican churchmanship, it was not easy for minorities: Anglo-Catholic friends of Ronald Knox were distressed at finding themselves dependent on chaplains who celebrated in scarf and hood in Y.M.C.A. tents and who knew nothing about hearing confessions. On the other hand, Fr Groser, a priest in the Catholic tradition, came across a group of German prisoners of war, set up an altar, and gave them all Communion,

Lutherans, Calvinists, Baptists, and, for all he knew, agnostics too. Ironically he was severely rebuked for this by Bishop Taylor Smith, the conservative Evangelical Chaplain-General.

At home, in many parishes, united services were held, and it became customary to invite Free Church ministers to take part in national occasions in the parish churches; but it was not easy for groups totally unused to worshipping together to understand each other's styles of worship. Hensley Henson rejoiced: 'The blessed contagion of religious fellowship is flowing back from the Front to the parishes at home.' As Bishop of Hereford he welcomed the interchange of pulpits. As Dean of Durham in 1917 he accepted an invitation to preach in the City Temple. When the Bishop of London heard of this he wrote to deprecate his action, which seemed to invalidate Campbell's decision to seek ordination in the Church of England.[13] In Manchester, Bishop Knox's militant support of church schools before the war had antagonized many Free Churchmen. But the war led to joint prayer meetings in the Free Trade and Albert Halls, and the creation of a Council of Christian Congregations. Knox commented: 'The feuds of the Balfour Act were forgotten, and brotherly relations established.'[14] A writer in *Commonwealth* for June 1916 pointed out that not only was Britain fighting alongside Roman Catholics in a Roman Catholic country, in an alliance with Russian Orthodox, but that, whereas Nonconformists had given a somewhat hesitant support to the Boer War, in the present conflict they were united with the Church of England. In the presence of death, shared by all denominations, differences paled. The *Graphic* on 21 November 1914 published a full-page drawing of a Mass being said in an English mansion for Belgian refugees which by its style was clearly intended to evoke sympathy for both Mass and refugees.

The building of the Westminster Central Hall in flamboyant baroque in its challenging position opposite the Abbey and Parliament at the turn of the century had symbolized the conviction of many Free Churchmen that at last, after centuries of exclusion from the national life, they had arrived. Many Nonconformists rejoiced when in December 1916 Lloyd George became the first Free Church Prime Minister.

Some bridges were also built between Christians and Jews. Chaplains sometimes shared their ministry to the wounded and dying with rabbis. When Bishop Paget of Stepney dedicated a street shrine in Bethnal Green, the street was crowded with bareheaded Christians, and Jews with heads covered. He gave the blessing in English, then turned to the

Jews, thanked them for coming, and gave the blessing in Hebrew. In 1918, when Winnington-Ingram preached at a Thanksgiving service for the liberation of the Holy Land, he expressed his hope that the Jews soon would be able to have a home of their own.[15] The presence of so many foreign students in England stimulated student interest in other religions. An S.C.M. report in 1919 welcomed the interest, but warned against a too optimistic view of other faiths.[16]

The Serbian Orthodox Church, suffering greatly through invading armies, asked the Church of England to help to train seminary students. As a result, starting in 1918, some sixty students were trained at Anglican theological colleges at Oxford during the next two years. When Cuddesdon re-opened to welcome a band of young Serbs dressed in old clothes, tattered uniforms, and even sheepskins, together with their priests and professors, Bishop Gore was at the gate to welcome them. He took a keen interest in them and addressed them from time to time. A. C. Headlam, chairman of the committee which supervised their training and welfare, was given a free visit to Yugoslavia by its government and Church in 1926; he and Archbishop Davidson received Serbian decorations.

Archbishop Davidson rejoiced in the wider contacts between Christians of different traditions brought about by the war. In October 1914 he summoned a conference, to study the implications of the war, to which leading Free Churchmen and Quakers were invited as well as Anglicans. The statement supporting the King's appeal for total abstinence was signed not only by Davidson and Lang, but also by Cardinal Bourne and the President of the Free Church Council. Through the Archbishop's initiative, the first Sunday in 1915 was observed as a Day of Prayer by Roman Catholics and Free Churchmen as well as by the Church of England, and in France, Belgium, Russia and America as well. When Davidson visited France in 1916, he was delighted that Free Church and Church of Scotland chaplains attended his conferences together with the Anglican chaplains.

At various crucial times in the affairs of the Russian Church during the war, Davidson exchanged messages of prayer and goodwill, and after the Revolution he helped to promote a Russian Famine Relief Fund. When the Patriarch of Moscow died in 1925, a wreath from the Archbishop of Canterbury was the only tribute from a Church outside Russia. The participation of Russia on the Allied side during the war had given a great stimulus to Anglican interest in Russian Orthodoxy. 'Russian religious thought must become a constantly growing force in

Western religious life after the war', wrote Peter Green in the *Manchester Guardian* for 9 September 1915. He drew attention to the lectures on Russian Orthodoxy in Manchester Cathedral by Fr Frere. Frere had lectured in Russia in 1912 and spent three months there in 1914. He was in charge of the training of Serbian Orthodox students at St Stephen's House, Oxford, during the war. (In 1951 one of these students, now a bishop, visited Mirfield to pray at Frere's tomb.) In 1928 when the Anglo-Orthodox Fellowship of St Alban and St Sergius was formed, Frere became its first President.

Inevitably, German and English Christians, who had begun to draw closer before the war through their exchange visits and through meeting at various ecumenical conferences, were drawn apart by the war. In September 1914, the 'Appeal to Evangelical Christians abroad' from German theologians (including Harnack, Deissmann, and Loofs) reached Lambeth Palace. Recalling the happy relations established at Edinburgh in 1910, they repudiated charges of German aggression and asserted that Germany had gone to war to repel attack. The Archbishop, with a large number of leaders from several Christian traditions, who also signed the reply, said that he was amazed at the version of recent history produced by the German theologians, and in detail presented the British case. He also expressed his distress at being separated by war from those with whom there had been Christian co-operation and fellowship in the past, and his hope that this would be renewed in the future.[17] The Archbishop was not alone in thankfully recalling relationships established between English and German Christians before the war. Even Winnington-Ingram struck a hopeful note in 1915. People ask, he said, what was the good of the Edinburgh Conference or the exchange visits of German and English churchmen. But he was sure that they would bear fruit when peace returned and such men as they had met came to the fore in Germany. Dr John R. Mott, the American ecumenical leader, had met many missionaries in Berlin after war had broken out, and many of them had never even heard of Bernhardi.[18] Fr Bickersteth reminded readers of *CR* for Christmas 1914:

In the German hosts arrayed against us there are not only the disciples of Nietzsche and Bernhardi . . . there are gentle Christian men who love their wives and children, and connect, as we do, all the sanctities of home with Bethlehem and Nazareth; there are, for instance, our old friends from Ober-Ammergau, who have entered into the Gospel story with a passionate devotion.

During the war direct personal communication between English and German Christians was virtually impossible, but through Americans Archbishop Davidson was kept in touch and informed. In October 1914 he saw Dr Mott, who was on his way to a missionary conference in Berlin. Davidson wrote:

> . . . let it be made clear to them that I, for my part, am resolved not to let these terrible international strifes impair a friendship and a community of thought and prayer which I have valued beyond words. That our German brothers and friends in the Faith of our Lord Jesus Christ desire simply to be loyal to the cause of Our Master and of truth, I do not doubt for an hour. The incomprehensible thing to me is how it can come about that our views of plain historic facts and of prevalent teaching can differ so widely. . . . But I retain, through thick and thin, my belief in the honesty of those German friends . . .

In 1915 Davidson received a letter from Dr Deissmann complaining of British treatment of Germans in the Cameroons, and he discussed this with the Colonial Office. Receiving also from him a series of weekly letters sent to American churchmen, the Archbishop replied at length, affirming his belief that the bonds of Christian fellowship, though strained, still held, but asserting that with one exception (a sermon by a German pastor which Dr Deissmann had sent) hatred seemed to be the dominant spirit in Germany. Again he spoke of his bewilderment at the German version of recent history; he also referred with horror to the sinking of the *Lusitania* and to the Bryce Report. The Archbishop's letter obviously made a considerable impression on Deissmann who said in one of his weekly letters that, though discussion as to the merits of the German and British cases was now impossible, after the war he hoped for an open discussion, when 'the noble Christian spirit of the Archbishop. will be a guarantee for the helpfulness of such a discussion'.[19] *Challenge* regularly gave its readers what news it could about German church life in wartime. It also frequently pressed for officially sanctioned prayers for the German people.

In various areas of Africa and India the Anglican Church had to take over responsibility for German missions because German missionaries had been interned. In 1917 Archbishop Davidson and missionary representatives met with Government officials and succeeded in somewhat modifying a policy aimed at the virtual exclusion of German missionaries from work in certain areas after the war. Though the absolute exclusion of German missionaries was lifted in 1925, some restrictions remained. J. H. Oldham secured the modification of the Versailles Treaty so that German mission property was placed under trustees rather than being confiscated to pay war debts.

Thus, in many ways the war deepened the desire for fellowship between separated Christians. At home, the wartime practice of making important national appeals ecumenically, became customary in the post-war period. In October 1918 Davidson invited Free Church as well as Anglican leaders to a conference to organize Christian support for the League of Nations. In 1919 he joined with Cardinal Bourne and Free Churchmen to appeal for a settlement of the railway strike. When in May 1922 the Russian Patriarch was arrested, Davidson was supported by a large number of leaders of other Churches in an appeal to Lenin. In 1923 an even weightier group including Cardinal Bourne, Free Churchmen, General Booth of the Salvation Army and the Chief Rabbi signed a solemn protest against religious persecution in Russia. It was natural therefore that the Archbishop should seek ecumenical support for his proposals for a settlement of the General Strike in 1926. G. K. A. Bell wrote:

> During the War and the years that followed, the office of Archbishop of Canterbury gathered to itself a wholly new character in the international field. . . . During Randall Davidson's tenure of the archiepiscopal see the office of Archbishop of Canterbury acquired a commanding position in the communions of Christendom unprecedented in the previous history of the Church.[20]

When the war was over, ecumenical organizations began to resume their life and new ones were formed. In 1919 the leaders of the German and British S.C.M.s met in Holland and discussed the war, the blockade and the peace treaty. The first post-war conference of the World Alliance met near The Hague at Oud Wassenaar in October 1919. Tensions were considerable. Bishop E. S. Talbot made a deep impression. Dr Deissmann considered that the success of the conference was largely due to Talbot's deeply Christian outlook. When the German delegates arrived, they stood embarrassed, unsure as to how they would be received. Talbot went out to meet them, both hands held out in welcome. Walking in the park with Archbishop Söderblom, Talbot exclaimed, 'But look! my old friend Spiecker' (a German delegate). The two embraced. Söderblom commented: 'It was the first meeting after the War between Germany and England which I witnessed.'[21] The French and Belgians insisted that the Germans should recognize their war guilt. The German delegates issued a declaration condemning Germany's violation of Belgian neutrality. The conference eagerly welcomed the League, appealed for the rights of minorities affected by the Peace Treaty, and proclaimed the duty of the Churches to promote new developments in international and social relationships. The World Alliance met again in conference in Geneva in August 1920. The Archbishop of Canterbury was proposed as President. When the leader of the German delegation demurred at the election of the chief ecclesiastic of a former enemy power, a Serbian priest told the Germans, 'He has been a true friend to you. All through the War, though English, he has taken a more than English view of the War. He is the most internationally minded man in Europe. When I was in London he made two great speeches, all in support of you' – a reference probably to the Archbishop's speeches against reprisals. Great applause broke out and the election was carried without dissent, a remarkable tribute to the Archbishop's international standing.[22]

In the Michaelmas 1915 issue of *CR*, Fr Frere (later a participant in the Malines Conversations with Roman Catholics) wrote that all the Churches of Europe needed a change of heart: 'Europe cannot worship together. . . . It is necessarily easier to quarrel, and more difficult to agree, because we cannot pray together.' First we must seek for a united spiritual effort with our Roman Catholic allies in France, Belgium, and Italy, and with our Orthodox allies in Russia. But such a spiritual effort might unite us too 'with our foes, with the Roman Catholics and the Lutherans of the Central Empires'. The same width of vision characterized the 'Appeal to All Christian People' issued from the Lambeth Conference of 1920. The Appeal was perhaps the most significant result of the ecumenical spirit which had been so strongly quickened by the war:

> The time has come, we believe, for all the separated groups of Christians to agree in forgetting the things which are behind and reaching out towards the goal of a reunited Catholic Church. . . . The vision which rises before us is that of a Church, genuinely Catholic, loyal to all Truth, and gathering into its fellowship all 'who profess and call themselves Christians', within whose visible unity all the treasures of faith and order, bequeathed as a heritage by the past to the present, shall be possessed in common, and made serviceable to the whole Body of Christ.

Three of the immediate recommendations of the Conference arose out of the experience of war: the occasional exchange of pulpits, the admission of baptized non-Anglicans to Communion between the initiation of a unity scheme and its completion, and the formation of local councils of churches. The Encyclical Letter acknowledged the stimulus created by the war:

> The weakness of the Church in the world of to-day is not surprising when we consider how the bands of its own fellowship are loosened and broken. . . . But the war and its horrors, waged as it was between so-called Christian nations, drove home the truth with the shock of a sudden awakening. Men in all Communions begin to think of the reunion of Christendom, not as a laudable ambition or a beautiful dream, but as an imperative necessity.[23]

The response of the Free Churches was warm and immediate. One of those who had helped with the drafting of the Appeal was Neville Talbot, now Bishop of Pretoria. Bishop Weston of Zanzibar (who had been at the heart of the 'Kikuyu' controversy over the federal scheme of unity proposed in East Africa in 1913) gave it his enthusiastic support. For the first time an Orthodox bishop participated in the Conference. In 1921, the Ecumenical Patriarch came to London and twice visited Davidson; when he died during the visit, the Archbishop read the Gospel at the funeral service. In 1920 the Preparatory Conferences on Faith and Order, and Life and Work, were held in Geneva. Some German leaders were present at both conferences, though in an unofficial capacity. Cardinal Mercier of Malines, known for his courage during the German occupation, replied to the Lambeth Appeal with a cordial message to the Archbishop. The Cardinal's ecumenical spirit combined with the zealous initiative of Lord Halifax to inaugurate that series of unofficial meetings between Anglicans and Roman Catholics between 1921 and 1926 known as the Malines Conversations.

We turn now to wartime attitudes towards Germany. When war broke out, many turned with relief from conflicts in Britain to project their aggression on an external enemy. The fact that conscription was only introduced after eighteen months of war made it particularly necessary to whip up patriotic feeling and to moralize and ideologize the war. Herbert Butterfield wrote in *Christianity and History* that 'wars should be regarded as quarrels between allies who happen to have fallen out'.[24] But it is much more difficult to take this view when a war is moralized, as Alan Booth has pointed out:

Indeed there is a very strong case to be made for the contention that a situation which is already somewhat intractable between two parties to an international quarrel becomes utterly insoluble once it is moralised, and that this is the state of affairs in some of the most acute contemporary confrontations either of ideology or race. As soon as either side becomes convinced that its cause is the cause of righteousness, the only outcome which is tolerable is the unconditional surrender of the opponent. . . . It becomes, in a curious way, the task of the man of moral earnestness to deflate the moral pretensions of nations as a contribution to peace. In so doing, he can avoid becoming insufferable only if he accepts a measure of such deflation as applying also to himself.[25]

On the whole there seems to have been remarkably little hatred for Germans at the front itself. British soldiers were just as likely to swear heartily at generals behind the front, soldiers of other nationalities on their own side, pressmen or war profiteers, as at Germans themselves. Sassoon wrote a bitter poem 'Fight to a Finish' in which soldiers on a Victory Parade through London suddenly fixed bayonets and turned on the crowd of 'Yellow-Pressmen'. In an article for the *Westminster Gazette*, published in August 1916, R. H. Tawney deliberately rejected the popular picture of the war as a conflict between English knights and German devils. Most men, he wrote, have within them a savage beast which occasionally shouts to be given a chance to destroy with joyful cunning. German soldiers were 'brave as lions'. He described how he tried to hit a particular German with his gun. But he kept missing and became puzzled and angry. He did not really wish to hurt him or anyone else. It was just that he hated missing. 'That's the beastliest thing in war, the damnable frivolity. One's like a merry, mischievous ape tearing up the image of God. When I read now the babble of journalists about "the sporting spirit of our soldiers", it makes me almost sick. God forgive us all!' In another article, published in the *Nation* that October, Tawney asked the British public whether they realized that English soldiers regarded themselves and their enemies as victims of a common catastrophe, comrades sharing the same misery. This drew the soldiers on both sides closer to one another than to those at home. Those at home found it easier to hate the Germans than the soldiers who were actually fighting them. Those at home realized nothing of the moral contradictions, the sense of futility and the crushing of spiritual faculties which the soldiers experienced.

But it is not among those who have suffered most cruelly or whose comprehension of the tragedy is most profound that I find the hatred which appals. For in suffering, as in knowledge, there is something that transcends personal emotion and unites the soul to the suffering and wisdom of God. I find it rather among those who, having no outlet in suffering or action, seem to discover in hatred the sensation of activity which they have missed elsewhere. . . . You do not help yourselves, or your country, or your soldiers, by hating, but only by loving and striving to be more lovable.[26]

Both these articles by Tawney show great depths of wisdom, realism, and compassion about the human condition derived from a Christian faith which had been tested by the actuality of war.

C. E. Montague said that a man might come to the fighting line full of hatred, remembering, say, the *Lusitania*, but at the front 'the holy passion began to ooze out at the ends of his fingers'. When you had heard the Germans exchanging jokes across the firing lines with the English, when you had found in the dead German's pockets family photographs, tobacco, and a letter from his wife, when you had discovered his trench to be full of normal life, food half-cooked, muddy straw pressed flat by a sleeping man, then it seemed ludicrous to regard the German soldier as 'Incarnate Evil'.[27] F. H. Keeling wrote in a letter in December 1915 that he would go on fighting as long as necessary to force a decision, but after the war he expected 'a wave of practical pacifism from the ex-infantrymen of Western Europe that will sweep many barriers to progress away'. 'I will *not* hate Germans to the order of any bloody politician, and the first thing I shall do after I am free will be to go to Germany and create all the ties I can with German life.'[28] Rifleman Atkins even described an occasional collusion between the two sides, so that when the regulation patrols were sent out each side held their fire.[29] Gestures of an old-style chivalry occurred sporadically. Richthofen, a German ace pilot, who had shot down eighty planes in two years from his scarlet-painted aircraft, was himself shot down by an English pilot in 1918. Next day a message was dropped on the German base to inform the German Flying Corps that Richthofen had been buried with full military honours, and a photograph of the occasion was enclosed.[30] Yet Studdert Kennedy, in lectures given to soldiers in almost every part of France, purveyed a highly-coloured version of German history and their national characteristics – 'one of the most backward and barbarous in the world' is how he described the German people:

6   A New Zealand chaplain administering Holy Communion in a field near the fighting line, August 1917

7 Archbishop Lang visiting Admiral Jellicoe on board the *Iron Duke* during his tour of the Grand Fleet, July 1915. 'Church and State united in the Common Cause' proclaimed the *Graphic*

8 A chaplain preparing the altar for a service in a French casino, June 1916

'Germany does not believe in freedom. . . . We, on the other hand, are the pioneers of freedom. . . .'[31]

The humour of the soldiers, the nicknames they gave to enemies, weapons and trenches, the elaborate jokes in the *Wipers Times*, were all 'containers' for horrors otherwise too overwhelming to be borne, expressions of the human need to create boundaries in moral and physical chaos, ways of turning evil into a familiar and even comic friend. The humour was a kind of transcendence, a type of resurrection hope. Could you kill without hating? Wilfred Owen asked. He thought so. In 'At a Calvary near the Ancre' he spoke of the soldiers, who did not hate, as being closer to Christ than the Church which hated Germany:

> Near Golgotha strolls many a priest,
> And in their faces there is pride
> That they were flesh-marked by the Beast
> By whom the gentle Christ's denied.
>
> The scribes on all the people shove
> And brawl allegiance to the state,
> But they who love the greater love
> Lay down their life; they do not hate.

The stories about the Christmas Truce of 1914 were told not only because they were true, but also because soldiers and others wanted them to be true; they wanted to feel that somehow Christmas and Christianity could make some difference to human behaviour, that the old Christian military conventions still had some authority. The stories were also told by socialists to convey the comforting illusion that left to themselves the ordinary men would not fight, that the war was all the fault of the politicians and generals – forgetting the débâcle of international socialism at the outbreak of war. Neville Talbot described the truce as

> just spontaneous on the part of the rank and file on either side. The men, on their own, seemingly, had patched up a truce in the course of the night by dint of waving lights. Meetings, handshakings and exchange of smokes took place in the middle of the lines.[32]

Another account tells not only of the exchange of souvenirs, home addresses, cigarettes and presents, but also how the Germans brought out the bodies of twenty-nine English dead by agreement between the officers on both sides. They were buried exactly half-way between the two lines. But after strong reprimands from headquarters, firing gradually started again after Boxing Day. Next Christmas there were no truces, partly because of the strict orders from headquarters, partly because of increased bitterness. But this was not the predominant mood. Fr Northcott arriving in France in 1918 noted that there was 'little or none of the bitterness towards the Hun that the propagandist tries to stir up at home'. He instanced the fact that Germans buried the English as well as the German dead; over English graves they would erect crosses with inscriptions like 'Hier ruht ein unbek. Eng. soldat.'[33] Fr Bull described how an English soldier reacted to being wounded: 'You can't blame them, you see, sir, as they are only doing their duty same as we are, and they are suffering as much as we suffer.'[34]

By contrast, at home, anti-German feeling was often intense. George V did not share this hysteria. Five days after the outbreak of war he was surprised to receive a War Office proposal that the Kaiser and his son should be publicly removed from their honorary commands in the Army List. After further persuasion he agreed, but refused to give any publicity to their removal. For a time he withstood public agitation to remove the Garter Banners of enemy royalty from St George's Chapel, Windsor. He gave way in May 1915, but insisted that their name plates should remain on their stalls.[35] When the Kaiser's banner was taken down and lay on the floor, the workman asked the Dean, 'Wouldn't you like to spit on it, sir?'[36] Popular clamour forced the resignation of Prince Louis of Battenberg, the First Sea Lord, in October 1914. In July 1917 the name of the royal house was changed to Windsor after whispers had reached the King that he was thought to be pro-German because of the German names that he and his family bore. MacDonagh believed that though the 'die-hards' were only a comparatively small minority, they were in control of public opinion. One of the die-hards was Horatio Bottomley who was said to be more popular than any Minister of the Crown. As an orator and publicist he was skilful and unscrupulous. He wrote in *John Bull* about 'Germhuns' in England: '. . . you cannot naturalise an unnatural beast – a human abortion – a hellish fiend. But you *can* exterminate it.' 'Lock Up All Germans. Confiscate All Their Property' was another of his headlines.[37] That someone like Bottomley could be so popular and influential (he may actually have been offered a place in the government) is a measure of the society of the time.

In the Preface to *The Spirit of Man* Bridges wrote that the 'progress of mankind on the path of liberty and humanity had been suddenly arrested and its promise discredited by the apostasy of a great people'. Our 'cousins' were, we had thought, honest and virtuous, but we now see them 'all united in a wild enthusiasm for the great scheme of tyranny . . . and obedient to military regulations for cruelty, terrorism, and devastation'. Though 'our national follies and sins have deserved punishment', yet 'our country is called of God to stand for the truth of man's hope':

> Here we stand upright, and above reproach. . . . Britons have ever fought well for their country, and their country's Cause is the high Cause of Freedom and Honour. . . . We can therefore be happy in our sorrows, happy even in the death of our beloved who fall in the fight; for they die nobly, as heroes and saints die, with hearts and hands unstained by hatred or wrong.

In 1920, however, Bridges was responsible for a letter signed by a number of prominent academics which was sent to the heads of German universities to express the desire for a resumption of intellectual co-operation.[38] He was roughly treated for his initiative by those whose hatred of Germany he had helped to fan by his Preface of 1916. When Lord Halifax went to tea at Marlborough House in December 1914, the chocolate cake was decorated with figures of the Kaiser and the Crown Prince being blown to pieces by an Allied bomb. *Sphere* on 24 October 1914 published a drawing of German soldiers stabling horses in a church and cleaning their boots with surplices while the horses ate the altar flowers! Though Bishop Paget of Stepney found the East-Enders forgiving towards Germans, rioting crowds attacked German shops there, as in other places, after the sinking of the *Lusitania* in May 1915 and other disasters.

Atrocity stories seem to have been more easily believed in England and to have created more hatred of the Germans at home than at the front. Though some soldiers like George Sherston felt at first that it was unpatriotic to disbelieve the stories, many soldiers were increasingly sceptical about them. They became disillusioned about the press and allied propaganda when they saw the gap between newspaper reports and the actuality of events which they had experienced. 'You can't believe a word you read' became a catch-phrase. The discrediting of many of the atrocity stories after the war made it possible for both newspapers and the general public to disbelieve or ignore stories about the Nazi concentration camps in the 1930s. Archbishop Davidson seems to have accepted the Bryce Report on German atrocities without question when it was published in May 1915. Bryce had been a close friend since Oxford days when he had been Davidson's tutor. In a letter intended for publication, Davidson wrote to the Prime Minister on 15 May 1915 that the last few weeks had shown afresh 'the nature of the fight we have to wage against the unbridled forces of cruelty and wrong' – he instanced the German use of poison gas and the sinking of the *Lusitania*. These two events gave 'new evidence of the spirit which in the earlier stages of the War inspired the shameless horrors perpetrated upon helpless civilians under the authority, as we now know, of the officers of the German army'. But he stressed that the right reaction was not to use poison gas in retaliation, nor to indulge in 'contemptible' assaults on Germans in England, but to 'throw our every ounce of strength into the fight'.[39] (This published letter was more diplomatically restrained than the much more anguished private letters which he was writing to the Prime Minister and the King's private secretary, Lord Stamfordham, to protest vehemently against the suggestions being made that the British should also use poison gas.)[40] Dean Inge suspected that the stories of atrocities had been exaggerated for propaganda purposes, and asked Bryce whether they were true. 'He answered gravely, "The Germans are doing things which have not been done in civilised warfare for centuries." '[41] *Challenge*, which on 30 October 1914, had expressed its scepticism about atrocity stories, accepted the Report without query on 21 May 1915. It had published an address by Bryce on 'The Missionary Opportunity' to a group of Christian laymen on 11 December 1914. Lord Bryce had been a well-loved and deeply respected Ambassador in Washington. On 10 May 1915 the *Daily Mail* printed a photograph of some of the victims of the sinking of the *Lusitania* which included dead bodies of children. The caption read 'Whosoever shall offend one of these little ones that believe in Me, it is better for him that a millstone were hanged about his neck and he were cast into the sea.' Tom Pym took a more detached view. He quoted a Colonel whose battalion had suffered much from the Germans, including poison gas. 'People talk about German atrocities. . . . Well, I don't know. I've seen my own men commit atrocities, and should expect to see it again. You can't stimulate and let loose the animal in men and then expect to be able to cage it up again at a moment's notice.' Pym recalled the story when listening to a young well-educated private of eighteen who had been alarmed by the sudden onset of 'blood-lust' in himself. He experienced, said Pym, 'a sample of the force in human nature which may make a soldier of any nationality bayonet an old man or rape a woman'.[42]

Early in the war the Government had established a secret propaganda Bureau at Wellington House under C. F. G. Masterman, which systematically stimulated anti-German feeling. The war created an estrangement between Masterman and the Church of England. Busy making propaganda himself, he disliked it when the Church spoke with a propagandist voice. At one time he had seriously considered ordination. Having married one of the daughters of General Sir Neville Lyttelton he was related to the Talbots; one of his brothers was Canon Howard Masterman. Later Lloyd George created the Department of Information to supervise the Bureau and three other organizations, including a division for producing propaganda films. Rudyard Kipling, H. G. Wells and Arnold Bennett were among those who helped with propaganda.[43]

If Davidson was at times too ready to trust his friends in government circles, he was also ready to press politicians hard if he suspected them of giving false information to the public. In February 1915 he spoke frankly about this question with Asquith, who was 'taken aback by the bluntness of the form in which I put it', noted Davidson. The Archbishop met Americans from time to time who were also in touch with German religious leaders, and he was anxious to be able to rely on British statements when questioned.[44]

During the opening months of 1915, the first Zeppelin raids, the sinking of the *Lusitania*, the German use of poison gas and the publication of the Bryce Report all created intense anti-German feeling, accompanied by bitterness towards any suspected of less than wholehearted support for the war effort. In *The Times* for 19 February a 'Churchman' attacked the clergy for not enlisting, and complained about the 'very feeble attitude of the Church of England in regard to the war'. A fierce correspondence ensued in which some bishops joined. On 22 February a vicar wrote that the crisis was too big for the Archbishop to handle, and that only the Bishop of London had the courage of his convictions. *Challenge* also struck a more sombre note. It said of the Bryce Report: 'we were not prepared for the apostasy of the German Government from the faith in humanity which is partially expressed in international law.' It spoke of a new sense of 'the forces of evil, powerful and organised which are loose in the world', and considered that they needed exorcizing by more determined prayer.[45]

A distinct hardening of attitude (a reaction both to recent German actions and to the current criticism of the Church of England in *The Times* and elsewhere) can be discerned in the contrast between the Homily read in churches in January and the utterances of the bishops at Whitsuntide. The Homily included the statement: 'We shall have no desire to see our enemies crushed merely for the sake of their humiliation.'[46] But the Whitsun resolutions of the bishops called on 'the nation to concentrate upon the successful prosecution of the war the full power of its spiritual, moral and material resources', and pledged support for government measures to mobilize all the national energies. The Archbishops in their Pastoral said:

> The spirit arrayed against us threatens the very foundations of civilised order in Christendom. . . . On behalf of righteousness and in our country's cause there is no one, there is nothing, too dear or too sacred to be offered. . . . Are the Christian people of our land putting into the high service of prayer anything like the energy and resolution, or the sacrifice of time and thought which in many quarters are forthcoming with a ready will for other branches of national service?[47]

R. S. Eves, Chaplain of St John's, Cambridge, protested in the *Nation* for 5 June against the Pastoral with its 'open acceptance of a national Godhead' and its 'negation of the fundamental spirit of the Catholic Church'. He and others reiterated this criticism in *Challenge* for 11 June; the Pastoral was in effect 'the proclamation of a holy war'; it was 'apostasy' to class prayer with 'other branches of national service'. They received support from F. R. Barry in the issue of 25 June. The *Church Times* on 11 June, however, gave support to the Archbishops, and *Challenge* on 25 June spoke of a strong feeling that the Church of England had not been doing all she could to meet the crisis.[48] 'Spiritual mobilisation' became a popular slogan to describe the Church's function in some quarters, though some churchmen like Bishop Frodsham (*Guardian*, 1 July 1915) disliked the term which seemed to imply that the Church was merely a department of the state. Henson wrote:

> In their efforts to 'mobilise our spiritual forces' (a wholly preposterous phrase), many religious leaders, who ought to have

known better, seemed to be sanctioning doctrines of prayer which cannot really be reconciled with the Christian belief in God, or with the known method of His providential government.[49]

The formation of the coalition government in May 1915 demonstrated that political parties were willing to sink their differences for a united war effort. It was argued by some (e.g. in the correspondence columns of *The Times* in late July) that the Churches ought to do the same. On 11 June *Challenge* published a picture showing the Mohammedan community in Calcutta uniting in prayer for a British victory.

In a sermon on 9 August 1914 in St Paul's, Bishop Winnington-Ingram appealed to people to treat Germans in Britain with kindness, and though in another sermon that autumn he said that the war was a conflict between 'Christ and Odin', he again rejected any 'un-Christian hatred of the German people'.[50] He voted with other bishops against reprisals in the debates of 1916 and 1917. However, as we have seen, he, Basil Bourchier, and other clergy told atrocity stories with a naïve relish. On the first Sunday in Advent 1915 Winnington-Ingram preached a sermon in Westminster Abbey entitled 'Missionary work the only final cure for War'. His text was Isaiah 11.9 ('They shall not hurt nor destroy in all my holy mountain'). When we see after nineteen hundred years of Christianity 'an outbreak of viler passions than has been seen in this world for a thousand years', little wonder 'the cynics scoff'.

And first we see Belgium stabbed in the back and ravaged, then Poland, and then Serbia, and then the Armenian nation wiped out – five hundred thousand at a moderate estimate being actually killed; and then as a necessary consequence, to save the freedom of the world, to save Liberty's own self, to save the honour of women and the innocence of children, everything that is noblest in Europe, everyone that loves freedom and honour, everyone that puts principle above ease, and life itself beyond mere living, are banded in a great crusade – we cannot deny it – to kill Germans: to kill them, not for the sake of killing, but to save the world; to kill the good as well as the bad, to kill the young men as well as the old, to kill those who have shown kindness to our wounded as well as those fiends who crucified the Canadian sergeant, who superintended the Armenian massacres, who sank the *Lusitania*, and who turned the machine-guns on the civilians of Aerschott and Louvain – and to kill them lest the civilisation of the world should itself be killed.

He quoted 'the Prussian creed' compiled by an American, and went on:

> Now, I do not quote this . . . to stir up un-christian hatred of the German race, many of whom as individuals would repudiate such sayings as their own personal belief, but I do it to defend Christianity.

He had just heard of a son who had died in Germany and had spoken of the great kindness he had received in German hospitals. But 'only one nation has set at naught the Christian principles which have slowly been gaining ground in the conduct of war'. When the world is wholly Christian there will be no war, hence the urgency of the missionary task; we spend less than a million pounds a year on missions, yet we now spend five millions a day on the war, because of the 'neglect of our Christian duty'.

> No one believes more absolutely than I do in the righteousness of the present war; as I have said a thousand times, I look upon it as a war for purity, for freedom, for international honour, and for the principles of Christianity. I look on everyone who fights for this cause as a hero, and everyone who dies in it as a martyr. . . .

Since the war began 'all that was chivalrous and noble in Europe has suddenly leaped to light'.

> Christianity has been rediscovered. Censors have been converted by reading soldiers' letters. Many a man who professed himself an atheist has now seen what Christianity really means. . . . 'Could you sing me a hymn?' asked a young officer, dying in the last battle, of the chaplain, who in the very thick of the shells and the bullets was at his work. And, with his arm round him, the chaplain sang with him 'Jesu, Lover of my soul', until he died.[51]

Fortunately not all the leaders of the Church of England spoke with the accents of Winnington-Ingram. In November 1914, Archbishop Lang, entering a hall in York to address a meeting on war aims, was given a lampoon against the Kaiser. Lang reacted by adding to his speech an impromptu reference to a 'sacred memory' of the Kaiser kneeling beside Edward VII at the bier of Queen Victoria. Reporters neglecting the context of the remark (he had condemned the militaristic spirit of Germany and the Kaiser's advisers) telegraphed the phrase all over the world. In Lang's words:

Immediately there descended upon me a vast spate of letters, protesting and denouncing. It was a sad revelation of the hysteria already working in the public mind. One letter was significant: 'That the Kaiser's soul may rot eternally in Hell is the daily prayer of yours truly, A. B., Churchwarden and communicant for twenty-five years'. . . . the worst thing is that the storm has been a really woeful revelation of the spirit of hatred and malice which the War seems to have aroused. It is terribly hard to get even a hearing for some faint voices of the Christian spirit. . . . I doubt if we can throw stones at those German 'Hymns of hate'.

He received twenty-four iron crosses by post, friends cut him, and the royal family were said to be critical. Four years later the incident was still being thrown at him. The strain told; by 1916 he had lost most of his hair, which had gone almost white. (Ill-expressed phrases in his broadcast at the time of the Abdication in December 1936 aroused similar hostility.)[52] William Boyd Carpenter (Bishop of Ripon 1884–1911) had tried to promote Anglo-German friendship before the war with the encouragement of Edward VII. The bishop had been the Kaiser's guest on a number of occasions, and they had corresponded as close friends. In a letter of 3 August 1914 the bishop urged the Kaiser to exert his influence for peace. A stern letter he wrote to the Kaiser in December 1914 was never transmitted.[53] Courageously, Boyd Carpenter wrote in 1916 an essay about the Kaiser with a heart 'sore with the sense of bitter disappointment'. 'I thought I knew him well . . . I had learned to love him well. . . . And this is the pity of it all: he might have been so great.'[54] Before the war the Kaiser had been widely praised in England as a theologian and peacemaker; but after August 1914 he became the most hated of Germans. Bottomley in *John Bull* published an article entitled, 'The Kaiser certified Insane' and proclaimed, 'No Mercy for the Berlin Butcher'.[55] J. Cathcart-Wason M.P. wrote a pamphlet on the Kaiser entitled *The Beast* (1915) and prefaced it with a quotation from Revelation 19.20.

There were other churchmen who tried to stem the tide of hatred. Towards the end of 1914, William Temple said that certain members of his congregation at St James's Piccadilly were 'prepared to believe any evil of the Germans without a particle of evidence'.[56] The Collegium Group, of which Temple was chairman, issued early in the war several prayers for wartime, including this prayer for Germany:

Give thy blessing, O Father, to the people of that great and fair land, with whose rulers we are at war. . . . Grant that, united in a good understanding with those who are now become our enemies, though they are our brethren in Christ, they and we may establish a new order, wherein the nations may live together in trust and fellowship.[57]

An advertisement appeared in *The Times* in July 1917 appealing for people not to purchase anything made in Germany, nor to transact business with Germany for ten years after the war. In a letter to *The Times*, Temple condemned it as 'sentimental humbug, at once more dangerous and more contemptible because the sentiment is one of malignity and not of generosity'. Hatred 'makes people blind and leads them to ignore plain facts'.[58]

Official Forms of Prayer issued by the Church of England succeeded on the whole in striking an authentically Christian note, though they became rather more partisan as the war progressed. The service for 3 January 1915 exhorted the people to confess national sins including 'arrogance as a people':

> We shall have no desire to see our enemies crushed merely for the sake of their humiliation. We shall wish for them, as for ourselves, that their eyes may be opened to know what is true; and we shall pray that the day may come, by the mercy of God, when we may learn to understand and respect one another, and may be united as friends to pursue the common good.

This clause was added to the Litany: 'That it may please thee/To forgive our enemies, and to help us to forgive them.'[59] However, the *Forms of Prayer for Public Use on Fourth and Fifth August 1917* displayed a more sombre and militant tone. Revelation 19.11–16 was ordered for the Epistle at Holy Communion with its picture of the white horse ridden by 'Faithful and True' clothed with a vesture dipped in blood smiting the nations and ruling them with a rod of iron: 'he treadeth the winepress of the fierceness and wrath of Almighty God.' But the Gospel (Mark 11.22–25) reminded the people 'when ye stand praying, forgive, if ye have ought against any'. The Exhortation was openly political. The nation had not entered the war for 'gain' or 'self-preservation', but because of 'the open violation of a solemn compact between the nations and the cruel invasion of a small and neutral state'. 'We are fighting for truth, for justice, for decency in warfare, for the world's freedom from oppression, for the very possibility of its progress in the future.' The entry of the United States had, it asserted, confirmed the righteousness of Britain's cause. *A Form of Thanksgiving and Prayer* for 6 July 1919 showed that the passions of war had cooled. The Epistle was from Romans 12.15–end: 'Rejoice with them that do rejoice, and weep with them that weep. . . . Recompense to no man evil for evil . . . live peaceably with all men . . . avenge not yourselves . . . if thine enemy hunger, feed him; if he thirst, give him drink.'

In March 1915, Dr Edward Lyttelton, Headmaster of Eton, brother of General Sir Neville Lyttelton, and brother-in-law to Bishop E. S. Talbot, preached at St Margaret's Westminster on 'Love your enemies'. How could Britain so act towards Germany that their hatred of us could eventually be removed? he asked. If we urged that the Kiel canal should be internationalized, could Britain offer to internationalize Gibraltar as well?

> If we intend to hold fast to everything we have gained in the past – and some of them possessions which have been gained by very questionable means – and we say that we are not going to part with a single inch of territory or a single privilege, all I can say is we are abandoning the principle of Christianity and taking once more our stand on the principle of competition.[60]

The press erupted in uproar against the sermon. Among the church papers, the *Guardian* was fiercely critical,[61] but the *Church Times*[62] said that while there might be two opinions on his wisdom and the particular examples he had chosen, there could be only one opinion that it was the duty of a Christian priest 'in all circumstances' to preach 'Love your enemies'. It reproduced not only long extracts from the sermon, but also Lyttelton's explanatory letters in *The Times* and other correspondence. 'We have talked of warring for a principle. Is it quite mad, then, to think of acting on it?' Lyttelton asked. The Bishop of Birmingham (Russell Wakefield) on the other hand believed that 'the one thing we must do now is to bring Germany to her knees'; the sermon would convince Germany that Britain was weakening. Michael MacDonagh wrote in his diary: 'Magnanimous and courageous words! Worthily spoken from a Christian pulpit!'[63] When, despite protesting letters to the Dean (Bishop Welldon), Lyttelton preached at Manchester Cathedral a fortnight later, crowds outside sang 'Rule Britannia' and 'God save the King'. After the service he had to be smuggled out by a side door. Lyttelton commented in retrospect upon the whole episode: 'The incident, like many others in the war, was fruitfully instructive as to the psychology of a multitude trying to suppress its deep misgivings. . . .'[64]

Bishop Gore told his clergy in the autumn of 1914:

The Bible is full of patriotic emotion; but even more conspicuously the Bible is full of a great warning against the sufficiency of patriotism, against the sufficiency of the thoughts natural to flesh and blood. Some of the most conspicuous figures in the Bible, like Jeremiah, are called to the truly terrible vocation of appearing as unpatriotic. . . .

But today, he said, we are not called to play an 'unpatriotic part'. It was 'our duty to engage in this war'. Therefore, 'we can wholeheartedly yield ourselves to the stream of patriotic enthusiasm which is sweeping so mightily through the nation'. But the spirit which had led to the war was the same spirit of selfish acquisitiveness and competition which had been organizing class against class. Through the division of the Church we had lost the sense of the Catholic Church – 'a great fellowship with a common mind, inspiring and restraining nations as well as individuals'. Self-sacrifice for one's country is not distinctively Christian; but through it we are reminded that the Christian life is also to be sacrificial.[65] When in 1918 he visited America he declared that the object of the war was not to 'crush' Germany, but German militarism. Enemy nations would have to be admitted to the League of Nations.[66] Scott Holland advised his readers in *Commonwealth* to play German religious music to counteract 'carnivorous fury': 'This is the real Germany, and you love it. . . . How foolish and far-away, now, the rabid talk of your Treitschkes and Bernhardis.'[67]

Peter Green often used his weekly article in the *Manchester Guardian* to protest against anti-German hysteria, which he found so rife, not least in some church circles: 'the cause of religion is suffering very terribly from the almost total failure of the Church to make any effective protest against the spirit of hatred and falsehood', he wrote on 3 December 1914. A week later he pointed out that since Britain would have to deal with Germany after the war, it was good policy as well as good ethics 'to believe as little evil, and as much good of them as we can'. On 7 November 1918, after severely criticizing a bishop who had called for the punishment of Germany, he recalled: 'Early in the war I pointed out in this column that all the most offensive nouns, adjectives and adverbs which were being hurled at the Germans are from those in high ecclesiastical place.' In his preaching too he condemned the prevalent spirit of self-righteous hatred. 'Think ye the Germans alone are sinners? I tell you nay, but unless ye repent ye shall all likewise perish', he said in one sermon. When people were short of food in 1917 because of U-boat activity, he preached on 'Blessed are the peacemakers' in Manchester Cathedral. To illustrate the text he told the story of how he had heard a soldier from the front rebuking a civilian who had spoken of the Germans as 'swine'.[68] Though apparently he accepted the Bryce Report (*Manchester Guardian*, 20 May 1915), and though when Edith Cavell was shot he wrote of 'a deep-seated and apparently ineradicable strain of bestial savagery in the German character' (28 October 1915), he frequently exposed and ridiculed hearsay atrocity stories. For the independent stand he took in articles and sermons, he received constant criticism, and sometimes was at odds with the Manchester Cathedral Chapter.

The story of Edith Cavell deeply moved Peter Green, especially as she had been a member of his own congregation before the war. 'I realise that patriotism is not enough. I must have no hatred or bitterness towards anyone', she told the English chaplain at Brussels who celebrated the Holy Communion with her before she was executed on 12 October 1915. She was buried by the German military chaplain, who paid tribute to her bravery and Christian faith. How much of what she said did she owe to the teaching of Peter Green? Here was an Anglican nurse ministered to by English and German chaplains and in her last statement reaching out towards a larger loyalty than even her undoubted devotion to England. In the Preface to *St Joan*, Bernard Shaw in 1924 protested that the English in omitting her famous words from her statue in London had used her for anti-German propaganda. Dick Sheppard also campaigned for their inclusion. The Labour Government saw that her words were added to the pedestal.

In a sermon on the Day of Intercession at St Paul's on 3 January 1915, Archbishop Davidson warned:

Let me name one more peril against which our hearts and minds are, after today's prayers, to be garrisoned afresh. It is the peril of letting anger − even if it be righteous anger − be fanned and cherished into something like an un-Christian hate.

At Easter 1915 he preached in Canterbury Cathedral. On the one hand, he spoke of his conviction that it was morally right for Britain to fight. He asked each member of the congregation to question himself:

Should I feel happier now, more loyal to Christ and to His principles, if we in England were today standing on one side, mere lookers-on, bearing no part in the common suffering, while France and Belgium were trampled and devastated, and we expressed our sympathy and did nothing more? . . . We have no right to ask that we should escape our share of the burden or of the purifying discipline. Of course, it is not all quite simple. . . . One and all, the Christian nations of this century and last century have need of penitence. . . .

On the other hand, he pleaded strongly that the national moral currency should not be debased by a spirit of retaliation. He reminded his hearers of

thousands of our German fellow Christians in that great country, who would detest, as strongly as we can detest them, barbarities and cruelties against a foe. Fathers and mothers, wives and sisters there, are sending out their dearest with the thought and prayer that God will enable them to be valiant unto death for what they do believe – however strange that may seem to us – to be the cause of justice and right.

Such considerations, he said, should give more 'gentleness' to our thoughts about Germany.[69] In 1915 when government policy against aliens became more severe, he took up cases of hardship with the authorities. In 1916 he tried hard to secure clemency for Roger Casement, whom he had met when he (Davidson) had been protesting against Congo atrocities before the war. His pleas were rejected by the Cabinet. When anti-German feeling was running very high in 1918, and agitation against aliens was renewed, he preached on the fourth Anniversary of the war in St Margaret's Westminster in the presence of the King and Queen and members of both Houses of Parliament. He distinguished between 'a righteous wrath' and 'a form of wrath which may degenerate into a poisonous hatred', and 'corrupt and defile': 'we have to see to it that the spirit of hate find no nurture in our hearts.' He noted in his diary that he had tried to avoid 'the comparatively easy and certainly popular course of beating the big drum, and simply belauding ourselves and our cause'. Looking to the post-war period he believed that it was unworkable and impolitic to regard Germany as outside the pale of civilized nations.[70] Preaching on Matthew 6.9 in Westminster Abbey on 10 November 1918 he asked the nation to remember that when the 'Our Father' was said, the words helped to crumble the barriers: '"Our Father", "Pater Noster", "Notre Père" – yes, and "Unser Vater" . . .'[71]

In July 1917, when heavy daylight raids on London were creating widespread popular demands for revenge and causing anti-German riots, the Canterbury House of Laymen passed with only two dissentients this resolution proposed by Lord Hugh Cecil:

> That in view of the example of Germany, and of the tendency of the war to inflame national sentiment, it was necessary to reaffirm that Christians owe their first and highest allegiance to the Catholic Church which is the Body of Christ, and that they were bound to love all the disciples of Christ of whatever nationality as brethren.[72]

But if anti-German hysteria was all too common at home, at least in death Germans and English were to some united at last. Mr Britling oscillated between various attitudes to Germans. They could seem ridiculous or devilish. When an aunt was killed in a raid he comforted himself by thinking of cruel retaliations. He contemplated writing an essay on 'The Anatomy of Hate', but he was moved to say of the Zeppelin raiders, 'Father, forgive them, for they know not what they do'. After his own son had been killed, he heard of the death of his former German family tutor, and he wrote to his parents as 'England bereaved to Germany bereaved'.[73] In 1915, New College, Oxford, was criticized for including on a list of the fallen, three former undergraduates who had been German soldiers. The three German names were added in 1930 to the permanent memorial of 1921 with the following inscription: 'In memory of the men of this College who coming from a Foreign Land entered into the inheritance of this place and returning fought and died for their country . . .'. The names of the dead on the panels in St Catharine's College Chapel, Cambridge, were carved in the 1920s. Some years later the name of a former German undergraduate who had died serving in the German Air Force was added with this enigmatic inscription: 'Hostis Amicus'. At Theberton parish church in Suffolk, a large board commemorates sixteen German airmen who were buried in the churchyard after a Zeppelin was shot down in 1917. Part of the Zeppelin still hangs in the church porch. Before the bodies were removed in 1963 to a war cemetery in Staffordshire, local people at Remembrance-tide decorated the German graves as generously as they did their own War Memorial. 'The graves were always a treasured possession.' The commemorative board reads:

'Who art thou that judgest another man's servant? to his own master he standeth or falleth' (Rom. 14.4).[74]

If the war was a crusade, a holy war, a war to end war, a battle against anti-Christ, how possibly could there be any kind of negotiated peace with the forces of evil? For the Christian was pledged in baptism 'manfully to fight' under Christ's banner 'against sin, the world and the devil, and to continue Christ's faithful soldier and servant unto his life's end'. So argued the majority in both Church and State. The *Guardian*, which had praised the restraint of official war prayers at the beginning of the war, by mid-1917 thought them too indefinite: victory should be prayed for directly.[75]

Immediately after the outbreak of war, Nathan Söderblom, recently elected Archbishop of Uppsala, issued an appeal for peace, and tried to persuade churchmen in various countries to sign it. But only those in neutral countries signed. Archbishop Davidson in declining to sign explained that the war had to proceed 'for the bringing to an issue the fundamental moral principle of faithfulness to a Nation's obligation to its solemnly plighted word'.[76] In August 1917 the Pope issued a bold appeal for peace and set forth definite proposals including renunciation of indemnities, mutual disarmament and the return of occupied territories – themes which had also been in the minds of the Stockholm conference of labour leaders that summer. *Challenge* welcomed the papal initiative, though with reservations.[77] But most Anglican reactions were dismissive. The *Guardian* was contemptuous of any suggestion of 'compromise',[78] and even *Commonwealth* was sceptical.[79] A. C. Headlam wrote in the *Church Quarterly* that the Pope was 'an innocent and unworldly man who mistakes the wolf for a sheep'; if his proposals were followed the Germans would have the chance to recuperate, and then, when the occasion came, would be able to resume their previous policies. 'It only remains for the Allies to have the courage, the resolution and determination to continue to the end, to ensure that the punishment shall be complete.'[80] At Whitsun that year Söderblom issued another appeal signed by church leaders in neutral countries. In July, the British Council for Promoting an International Christian Meeting was formed. Though led by Quakers (who had been in close touch with Söderblom), it drew in the Bishops of Southwark and Oxford, Dean Inge, Lord Parmoor, E. W. Barnes, William Temple, and Alfred Garvie. But the English Archbishops refused invitations to a conference proposed for December 1917. In any case the British Government was opposed to their participation and was not prepared to issue passports. When in February 1918 Davidson received another invitation he sent a temporizing reply after consulting leading English politicians. In November he declined a further invitation from Söderblom. Davidson believed that a conference could be held after peace had been concluded, but not during the negotiations. He was wary throughout of Söderblom's initiatives, too ready to accede to the views of government ministers he consulted and trusted. When Davidson was appointed Archbishop in 1903, Scott Holland had voiced his anxiety lest he should be beguiled by the 'sirens' of the Athenaeum, for he believed that Davidson had 'a deep veneration for the judgement and the wisdom of important laity of this type'.[81] Some politicians nicknamed him 'God's own Butler'.[82]

In so far as Davidson consistently avoided supporting any group which tried to enlist his support for a peace initiative, he was thoroughly representative of the majority opinion in Church and State. The League of Nations Society, formed in 1915, carried on its business quietly because people were suspicious of peace talk. In August 1917 Arthur Henderson, the Labour politician, was forced to resign from the Cabinet because he favoured participation in a socialist conference to which neutral and German delegates would also be invited. In 1915 Winnington-Ingram said that Germany could not at present be trusted to keep any treaties; after their use of poison gas, and the sinking of the *Lusitania*, 'no laws, human or Divine, at present bind her, and no promise, however sacred, is considered at present to be anything but empty words'. Germany was now 'the enemy of the human race'.[83] '"On to the end"; listen not for one moment to proposals for a patched-up peace,' he said in a National Mission sermon, 'which would only mean those children of ours now in the cradle will have to do it all over again in a few years' time.'[84] In an address in 1915 on the feet of Jesus, Basil Bourchier spoke of the determination of Jesus to go to Jerusalem; similarly, nothing must be allowed to divert us from Berlin:

> Silenced must be these ill-conceived overtures. If need be, these untimely pacificists [*sic*] must be firmly dealt with. . . . Berlin is our objective, and only when our feet, and those of our Allies, are planted there, with our enemy, whose infamy has for all time dishonoured the annals of warfare, beaten to his knees – then, and only then, will we discuss the terms of peace.[85]

Churchmen like Winnington-Ingram, Bourchier, and A. C. Headlam were in tune with the opinions of political leaders. Lloyd George said in September 1916: 'Britain has only begun to fight. . . . The fight must be to a finish – to a knock-out' – words echoed by Asquith that autumn when he denounced 'a patched-up, precarious, dishonouring compromise, masquerading under the name of Peace'.[86] As late as October 1918 Kipling wrote in 'Justice':

> Heavy the load we undergo,
>   And our own hands prepare,
> If we have parley with the foe,
>   The load our sons must bear.

A peace initiative from a surprising quarter was made when Lord Lansdowne (a Conservative peer, formerly Foreign Secretary 1900–5, and member of the Cabinet 1915–16) argued in a letter to the *Daily Telegraph* for 29 November 1917 that to prolong the war would mean the collapse of European civilization. The Allies must clear the air by stating clear terms, and by reassuring the Germans that they did not wish for the annihilation of the German nation. The Government quickly dissociated itself from the letter. *Challenge* (7 December 1917) and *Commonwealth* (January 1918) agreed that an ill-considered peace was impossible, but that the question of negotiations should be discussed; the latter declared: 'The letter breathes a better spirit than that of the "knock-out blow".' But the *Guardian* (6 December 1917) and the *Church Times* (7 December 1917) denounced Lord Lansdowne for undermining the war effort. *The Times* (30 November 1917), to which the letter had been originally sent, explained that it had declined to publish it because it did not reflect any responsible body of opinion. Bishop Gore, a relative of Lord Lansdowne's, also thought that the only security would come from a victory over militarism. Davidson believed that the abuse which had greeted the letter was 'monstrously unfair'. Lansdowne himself had the impression that the Archbishop was on his side.[87] But Davidson gave no public indication of his attitude, though he told Asquith in February 1918 that in general he was in favour of Lansdowne's position. When Lansdowne published further proposals in 1918, Davidson privately agreed that the Allies ought to be discussing whether peace terms were obtainable. But Davidson noted of himself: 'there is no outstanding controversial matter in which I find myself brimming or effervescing with thought, or controverting vehemently a current view'.[88]

Just as Dick Sheppard had invited Edward Lyttelton to preach at St

Martin's after his sermon, so now he publicly expressed his agreement with Lansdowne. In December 1917 Oswin Creighton wrote from the front:

> I wish people would act on Lansdowne's letter and hurry up and discuss peace. . . . We cannot hope to destroy Germany without destroying ourselves, and why go on destroying each other? I don't so much mind people being killed as the fact that the survivors will have gone back so much. Think of the mental stagnation of the last three and a half years . . . people giving their minds solely to destruction and no thought of construction.[89]

Tissington Tatlow also supported Lansdowne who, he wrote, had expressed thoughts which had been in the minds of many for several months.[90]

The outlook of English churchmen, though widened and challenged by the first war, was much narrower than during the second war. On 25 August 1939, on the eve of the second war, Henson wrote in his diary:

> What can I say to these young soldiers which is fitting, helpful, and definitely Christian? The conventional patriotic tub-thumping is out of the question. We have got past that phase. As Nurse Cavell said, 'Patriotism is not enough'.[91]

The real development of internationalism in general, and ecumenism in particular, took place only in the inter-war years. Moreover, whereas in the first war there was no church or political opposition within Germany which was perceptible to English eyes, both before and during the second war some opposition to Hitler was obvious. In the second war, Bonhoeffer sent his last message to a leading bishop in an enemy country, George Bell of Chichester. Simply to recall that one incident is to realize how much was accomplished ecumenically in the inter-war period, and how much more parochial in comparison was the general vision of the Churches in the first war, when 'Christendom stood fragmented before the catastrophe, its impotent little pieces adhering to the warring local nationalisms'.[92] Nevertheless the power of Christianity to evoke a more than merely national loyalty was sometimes evident in the life of the Churches in the first war. This might be symbolized by Alfred Garvie reading daily his German New Testament, while his close friend Adolf Deissmann in Germany read the New Testament in English in order to remind themselves of their common fellowship in Christ.[93]

10

Faith and War

E. R. Wickham rightly asserts that the major defect of the Churches in the nineteenth and twentieth centuries has been 'a failure of prophecy, a failure to understand and interpret the phase of history into which the age had come'. So the Christian laity have been left morally and intellectually unsustained:

> The First World War raised the question of Providence, of the relation of God to History and of His character and very existence, in perhaps the most acute way that has ever happened, and certainly in the most public way. Not merely with religious men and serious thinkers, but quite literally with every Tom, Dick and Harry. Questions were wrung out of people that only a prophetic Christianity at close grips with the secular problems of the age had the slightest chance of meeting. And the word was not forthcoming.[1]

Though the Church did not fully realize it at the time, the war created a situation in some ways as catastrophic as that which faced the Jews during and after the exile in Babylon, who were forced to ask fundamental questions about their inherited mode of faith, forced to reconsider their understanding of their own history.

Because the ordained leadership of the Church of England was never involved in the actual experience of work in an industrial society, its efforts to understand the industrial revolution were not only belated, but also almost always external to the inner experiences of those actually working in the system. So likewise, because most clergy did not share the actual experience of the trenches – only a proportion of the chaplains was actually with the fighting men, only a few actually lived in the trenches, and only a few fought as combatants or worked as noncombatants – the majority of clerical reactions to the war came from people who were far removed from its daily actuality. After the war the Church was an obvious target. Caroline Playne had helped at one stage in the work of the Church of England Peace League. In *Society at War* (1931) she devoted a chapter to 'The Failure of the Clerics'. 'Clerics no longer lead the masses, they are led by them', she wrote. Though she appreciated the 'state of torment' of clergy like Bishop E. S. Talbot, Neville Talbot and William Temple, she condemned the 'general complete failure of clerics to walk in the way of Life', and 'the enthusiasm with which they adopted the aberrations of belligerent madness'. She told a wartime story, the popularity of which was significant. A clergyman got into a carriage full of soldiers returning to the front. He enthusiastically exclaimed, 'So you are going to fight God's war.' No response; he repeated his statement. Again silence. Then he asked, 'Don't you believe this is God's war?' Silence, broken after a while by: 'Sir, hadn't you better keep your poor Friend out of this bloody mess?'[2]

The three major modes of thought in the nineteenth century — Romanticism, Liberalism and Evangelicalism, together with their counterparts in the Church of England — were all weighed in the balances between 1914 and 1918 and found wanting.

Romanticism, despite Wordsworth's proposal that the natural and the everyday should be the material for transfiguration, taught men to experience life in a profoundly split and nostalgic way. 'Nineteenth century poetry', wrote Dr Leavis, 'was characteristically preoccupied with the creation of a dream-world.'[3] Pugin and his followers provided the architectural equivalent of this. Wemmick in *Great Expectations* retreated at week-ends from the harsh, cruel world of his work into fantasies, pastoral and Gothic.[4] The Romanticism of Scott, Young England, Kenelm Digby, Tennyson, William Morris, the Pre-Raphaelites and Charlotte Yonge created a fantasy world of chivalry, and so eventually provided imagery for patriots like Bishop Winnington-Ingram and Mrs Pankhurst to use. Sometimes the language of chivalry was put to serious and practical use, as when in 1904 the Chantry Group was founded as an order of Christian chivalry, drawing its inspiration and imagery from Tennyson and Bunyan; its annual meeting was called Camelot; its 'knights' (women as well as men) unite in prayer, social work and reconciliation. It still continues.[5] Scott Holland, in *Commonwealth* for October 1914, called the Sermon on the Mount 'the book of Christian Knighthood'. Edward Woods, when Chaplain at Sandhurst during the war, wrote a book for the cadets which he called *Knights in Armour*. Some of the stories of the miraculous deliverance of sacred objects in France reminded R. J. Campbell of Sir Galahad's vision at Mass as described in

Idylls of the King.[6] A bereaved mother writing to Winnington-Ingram described fallen soldiers as 'that great band of brave, shining knights who have given all'.[7] Georgian poetry mostly concentrated upon an idyllic, static, pastoral scene – the countryside to which H. G. Wells's Mr Polly escaped. Romanticism also taught men either to hope or to despair; life was to be lived with strong, simple emotions. Romanticism disliked ambivalence as much as Evangelicalism. It encouraged men to adopt a highly selective view of the world – 'All things bright and beautiful'; this could not cope with the Somme and Passchendaele any more than could romantic notions of chivalry.

Despite heroic figures among its priests, monks and nuns, emotionally Anglo-Catholicism was fired by romantic nostalgia. A newspaper described the restored parish church at Barrow Gurney, Bristol, re-dedicated in 1889:

> Upon entering the church . . . one steps, as it were, into the Middle Ages. Is it possible, we ask, that we are living in the 19th century, and that we are within a few miles distance of a great city of grime and dust, and toil and many ugly things?[8]

Even the evangelical Church Pastoral Aid Society, which aimed to supply staff for industrial districts, pictured on its monthly magazine cover a medieval church in a tiny village.[9] It is ironically characteristic that the two enduring nineteenth-century liturgical creations were both romantically nostalgic. The Harvest Festival became popular in the latter half of the century just when England had become predominantly an industrial society. The service of Nine Lessons and Carols, devised by the Revd G. H. S. Walpole for use at Truro in 1880, spread through the influence of E. W. Benson (Bishop of Truro 1877–83, Archbishop of Canterbury 1883–96). It influenced Eric Milner-White when he created the Carol Service at King's College, Cambridge, first held on Christmas Eve, 1918. Though poignantly beautiful, it was almost totally encapsulated from any contact with the modern world. The ethos of his *Cambridge Offices and Orisons* (1921), with its medieval title, was amazingly remote from the trenches which had been his world only a short time before.[10] More Anglo-Catholic energy was channelled into the battle to revive medieval rituals or to import them from the continent than into theology or the creation of a new spirituality for an industrial society.

The real life of the Victorian period went not into poetry but into the novel. The best novels of Dickens, Hardy, Conrad, and George Eliot certainly tackled the ambivalence of life and action, and encouraged men to look below the simple labels of 'innocent' and 'guilty', but how many churchmen were prepared to grapple with the ambiguities which the great novelists felt and described? Appendix I to *Lux Mundi* (1889) contained a depressingly negative paragraph about the arts and literature, but Fr Neville Figgis said in a sermon in 1917:

> The most dangerous notion that modern Christianity has to combat is that it means a shrinking from life, that by its moral system it closes the avenues of human experience, and that in that it is wedded to the tradition which starves the mind.[11]

The English novel of the twentieth century which communicates the vibrant reality of God more profoundly than perhaps any other – D. H. Lawrence's *The Rainbow* (1915) – was prosecuted for obscenity.

Reasonable-minded liberalism and rationalistic utilitarianism also were judged and found wanting: the liberalism typified in the remark of Matthew Arnold that when we read the Gospels, and need a principle by which we may distinguish between the true Jesus and the misunderstandings of him by his followers, 'the more reasonable Jesus is likewise, surely, the more real one'.[12] I think too of the rationalism of Bernard Shaw, dazzlingly but frantically keeping all the verbal balls spinning in the air, lest one genuine, heartfelt feeling about the complexity of human experience should touch the earth. H. G. Wells's Mr Britling discovered that his easy-going liberalism could not cope with the unexpected revelation of the power of evil. Was it only a stage in evolution? He discovered that man was not a reasonable creature. Could we look forward to an age when a new democratic order, ending the rule of kings, emperors, priests, and commercial greed, would banish war? He came to believe in God, but only a finite, suffering, struggling God was credible. It was hard for him to believe that the best qualities in the heart of man would eventually win through to victory.[13]

Theological liberalism secularized, domesticated and academicized Christianity, yet paradoxically refrained from interacting with the real, hard, fruitful centre of secularity in, say, Ibsen or Strindberg. So often, in order to maintain the optimism that the Kingdom was ever advancing, Christians (and non-Christians) of a liberal outlook tended to blacken the German people; it is not man that is guilty and twisted, but only the German people, or anachronistically despotic rulers; war was abnormal, a temporary set-back; the comforting rationale that this was the last war, a war to end wars, was thankfully adopted. The liberal exemplarist view of the atonement made it much easier to identify the self-sacrifice of the soldier with the sacrifice of Christ. Liberal preachers were anxious to relieve God from any responsibility for the dark side of life. Karl Barth had been deeply disillusioned with liberal theology when ninety-three German intellectuals, including almost all his theological teachers, had proclaimed their support of the Kaiser's policy in August 1914. He wrote in 1921:

> Whenever men claim to be able to see the Kingdom of God as a growing organism, or – to describe it more suitably – as a growing building, what they see is not the Kingdom of God, but the Tower of Babel. There is, no doubt, a great and universal 'building' at which we all in our various ways labour in fear and trembling; but it is a work in which the will of God at no single point touches or overlaps with the will of man.[14]

Evangelicalism was found wanting too. The first world war found it still, on the whole, clinging to most of the features of biblical literalism, unreconciled to evolution and proclaiming a stern theodicy, a type of predestination and a substitutionary theory of the atonement. Its puritanism regarded secular life as an enemy to be fought. Its picture of salvation and evangelism was atomistic, it had no understanding of the larger work of Christ expressed in Logos theology, and therefore could not comprehend the claims that the character of Christ was being exhibited by soldiers who were right outside any overt Christian allegiance. Anglican Evangelicals were usually among the most conservative of churchmen politically and ecclesiastically, and often held a nationalistic and erastian view of the Church. Thinking in terms of simple antitheses between good and evil, innocent and guilty, purity and impurity, a kingdom of light and a kingdom of darkness, Evangelicalism could not cope with the ethical and theological ambiguities encountered in the daily life of the soldier – the swearing, drinking, brothel-visiting soldier who might perform acts of heroism in battle, be tender to the wounded friend and be singularly lacking in bitterness towards the enemy. (The Group Brotherhood, a study society of Anglican liberal Evangelicals, was formed in 1906, but did not become influential until the inter-war period.)

In trying to assess the theological temper of the period it is depressing but salutary to recall a religious best-selling novel of the time, *When It Was Dark* by Guy Thorne (1903). The praise lavished on it by Winnington-Ingram in a sermon in Westminster Abbey was quoted by the publishers in subsequent editions; he also commended it to ordinands. The Bishop of Exeter (Archibald Robertson) also praised it, and Field-Marshal Montgomery in 1970 said that reading it had been a major turning-point of his young life. The novel tells how a Jewish multi-millionaire – there is a strong strain of sadistic anti-semitism in the book – blackmails the head of the Palestine division of the British Museum into faking archaeological evidence to prove that Christ never rose from the dead. On this news being made public, the morals of the world collapse, the Russians mobilize, India revolts, criminal assaults on women in England rise by two hundred per cent, and Consols fall to sixty-five. Without the literal truth of the Resurrection, upon which the whole of Christianity depends, there is no longer anything to hold civilization together. Winnington-Ingram agreed:

> It paints, in wonderful colours, what it seems to me the world would be if for six months, as in the story is supposed to be the case, owing to a gigantic fraud, the Resurrection might be supposed never to have occurred. . . .

But the scheming Jew is exposed by a heroic and gentlemanly Anglican curate, and slowly the world returns to faith, morality and prosperity.[15]

Poets like Owen, Sassoon, Rosenberg and T. S. Eliot found a new language wrung out of them by experience. This new language tried to express the paradoxes and the ironies of human experience. But contemporary reviewers did not usually approve of poets who wrote too realistically about the war. On 3 October 1914, the *Spectator* proudly printed a previously unpublished patriotic poem by Tennyson, and commented that it might have been written for the present crisis.[16] Much of the best poetry of the war arose from the gap between war as actually experienced and the romantic, religious and chivalric images which dominated the imaginations of the conventional. Michael Ramsey has described those, who in the great turmoil of mind created by the war, felt acutely a theological gap: 'If Modernism failed to meet their deepest needs, orthodoxy had scarcely found an idiom in which to speak to them.'[17]

Oswin Creighton's letters provide a telling and moving documentation of that theological gap and the failure of ethics and theology to find a new language. His father had been the noted church historian and Bishop of London. Oswin was educated at Marlborough and Keble. After spending a year at Farnham under B. K. Cunningham and after a curacy in Notting Hill, he worked as a mission priest in Canada for four years. In November 1914, at the age of 31, he became a chaplain, serving in England, Gallipoli, and later in France where he was killed in 1918 visiting men in a battery position. He wrote in 1915:

> Last night I had a long talk with the adjutant. . . . He had been an acolyte in a spiky church for six years, and at the time believed everything and found the greatest comfort in the Church. Now he finds that he cannot honestly believe anything he was taught. Such a common story . . . I am becoming terribly unorthodox. There is a rooted idea among officers and men alike that religion is concerned almost solely with the next world. . . . All evangelical teaching, which is rife in the army, seems to have gone in this direction.

When he preached about the establishment of the Kingdom of God here and now, rather than in heaven, the men were surprised:

> I really don't know which does more absolutely to stultify all true religion, spikery or evangelicism . . . they must be slain if the Church is to have any meaning for the majority of thoughtful, natural men.[18]

Though always a questioning priest, his early letters as chaplain exhibited a fairly conventional patriotism ('one feels the greatness of England and all that she stands for')[19] and a rather condescending pastoral outlook. ('The men are just like children. The officers are all delightful.')[20] But with great pain he discovered, stage by stage, that neither his inherited patriotism matched the actuality of war, nor did his inherited ethics, spirituality or theology match the reality of the men as they turned out to be. The old clear boundaries between Church and world did not correspond to reality:

> The pious, narrow, self-satisfied, exclusive, moral world within – the weak, kindly, happy, loose-moralled, generous, spontaneous, tolerant world without. Which is better? Can the National Mission break down the barrier?[21]

He gave up his habit of trying to anticipate Judgement Day by separating men into sheep and goats: 'Men are not good and bad. But I think they are wise and foolish.'[22] He tried to teach about the Kingdom, but felt it sounded so 'vague and incoherent'.[23] He grew to understand the officers who on their leaves in Paris tried to enjoy every pleasure to the full. He imagined one such officer saying to God:

You have allowed the world to become an impossible place – a mass
of contradictions. . . . We have had the most terrifying experiences.
How can You blame us if as an antidote to them we avail ourselves,
when opportunity arises, to the utmost of the pleasure the world can
give us? And don't say they are not pleasures, because we have tried
them and know they are. And don't say the best men are not the
same, because the best men we know, the finest and bravest and most
capable soldiers, are the same.

Even if we can distinguish between wheat and tares, how can we pluck
up one without the other – and 'the best soil always produces the
healthiest weeds'.[24] And why do 'ecclesiastical people so often become
less believing than the profane'?[25] He felt uncertain as to whether to
give a blessing (as a fellow chaplain did) to the troops as they went into
battle 'as though it were a little charm'.[26] So few took any real interest in
the Church, the Bible or the sacraments, whether the services were
voluntary or compulsory; they were glad to crowd the canteen which he
ran, but they did not want the Bread of Life. Perhaps the professional
ministry should be abolished and clergy should work for their living:
unless we know 'what is in man' we cannot tell men about God. The
whole Church must be active instead of leaving everything to the
parson. 'This solitary business is impossible.'[27] He began to be able to
talk frankly with the men about sex, but again he is baffled: 'What to do
with a really passionate nature is a question which never seems to have
been properly solved. The teaching of mere self-suppression is in most
cases mischievous.'[28] He refused to tell the men to hate the Germans or
the Kaiser: 'We are always being taught to hate the Germans, and to
refuse to think or speak of peace. We are told about our glorious cause,
till it simply stinks in the nostrils of the average man.'[29] Nine months
before he was killed, he wrote:

I sometimes feel inclined to wonder why God hides Himself so
inscrutably from our experience. Or is it that the Church has taught
us for so long to look for Him in the wrong places? . . . No one out
here thinks at all, but they rub along and learn a lot about human
nature and lose a great deal that is false in their judgements and
standards. They learn how rotten conventions are and what a lot of
bunkum we have allowed ourselves to swallow. . . . It is as though we
had been violently seasick and were getting to the stage of feeling
very empty and ravenously hungry. . . . I don't quite know where I
find things that stand the test.[30]

But for him the Cross makes some sense of the continuous slaughter, and 'ideals are indestructible, because man who conceives them is indestructible'.[31] A nation that consisted of independent, thinking individuals would never desire to fight. 'And the Church has been such a foe to independent minds, with its fettering creeds and formulas.'[32]

Creighton's answers to the questions sent out by the committee preparing *The Army and Religion* were said by J. H. Oldham, one of its members, to go more to the heart of the situation than other contributions they had received. Creighton concluded his evidence:

> The war reveals that the Englishman is the best-hearted, most enduring, and most ignorant and least original man in the world. The work of the Church is to help him to build up what he has not got on the basis of what he has. An understanding Church is our great need.[33]

But the theological training of ordinands at this period was not conducive to the creation of an 'understanding Church'. The theology of Oxford and Cambridge (in which many ordinands were reared) was dominated by an analytical biblical criticism and the history of Christian origins, though at Cambridge an annual series of lectures in pastoral theology was established in 1883. At Oxford and Cambridge theology was unrelated to other disciplines. It was taught without reference to faith in as 'scientific' and objective a way as possible, to gain respect for theology as an academic subject, and to win the trust of the increasing number of Nonconformist undergraduates.[34] Many of the theological colleges were small and badly staffed. Some lasted only a few years. Between 1890 and 1902 no less than eleven new places for training were created, and five others closed. Typical of the smaller ventures was one begun in 1900 by Bishop Chavasse, in Liverpool next to the Palace, to take five or six graduates at a time. There was endless discussion in Convocations, committees and Church Congresses for many years about the need to improve standards, but the Central Advisory Council of Training for the Ministry was not established until 1912.[35] The theological colleges of the Church of England were all created by local diocesan or party initiatives. In 1900 Henson wrote that the English form of establishment had

> declericalised the clergy beyond all precedent or parallel. . . . The normal training of the English clergy, at school and university, is entirely non-professional, hence they are the most theologically

ignorant and the best educated ministry in existence, and the worst informed on all matters of ecclesiastical technique; but hence also they are the most vigorous and healthy in moral tone, and the sanest in political action. They think, and speak, and act in ways which are essentially similar to those of their Christian neighbours. . . . [36]

We must allow in this passage for the fact that Henson enjoyed cramping reality into an antithetical style. But the picture that he drew tallies with the frequent criticism at the front that Anglican chaplains were often amateurish and lacked a proper professionalism as priests.

Theology before the war was on the whole complacent. Even Mandell Creighton in 1896 believed that the attack on Christianity had been intellectually repulsed.[37] The deeper implications of, say, the growing challenges from the study of comparative religion and psychology were hardly realized. By 1914, liberal and Catholic theology had now for some time accommodated itself, at an intellectual level, to evolution by revised attitudes to Original Sin and the creation narratives (though these attitudes had hardly percolated down to more than a fraction of the laity); but the fact that evolution revealed a God who chose a long-drawn-out and bloody method of creation was not treated with the heart-searching it deserved. It was more consoling to teach the evolution of the Kingdom of God. Indeed evolution could be used to justify not only *laissez-faire* economics, but also war itself. Basil Wilberforce, Archdeacon of Westminster and Speaker's Chaplain, told soldiers in Westminster Abbey on 9 August 1914: 'The war to which you are called is a direct co-operation with the spirit of evolution which advances and educates humanity.'[38] J. B. Mozley's views on war expressed in a famous sermon in 1871 were often cited during the first war. He had seen war as an essential element in human progress; conflict was necessary for the *status quo* to be changed. The spirit in war which enabled men to give their lives sacrificially for others was especially harmonious with Christianity.[39] But few clergy, and even fewer laity, read theological books in the normal course of events. To them theologians seemed to be obsessed with the minutiae of biblical criticism and to be out of touch with pastoral realities. The average churchman learned his theology from hymns and the Book of Common Prayer. But what probably chiefly determined his theological attitudes was what he had learnt in public, day or Sunday school. Army chaplains frequently despaired of the actual results of the religious education of the time, as they saw them exemplified in the troops to whom they tried to minister. And much popular folk religion and superstition was passed down through traditions affected but little by the Churches.

If the intelligent chaplain or layman had taken *Lux Mundi* (1889) or *Foundations* (1913) into the trenches – and Paul Fussell has reminded us that soldiers read a wide variety of serious literature[40] – what help would he have found them? In limited areas he would have found a good deal of help from *Lux Mundi*. After all, it was the most intelligent re-statement of the faith for half a century or more. It would have helped him to come to terms with biblical criticism and evolution, and to comprehend both Christ in his real humanity and in his wide activity as Logos; he would have received some aid in relating Christianity to other religions; he would have received a large picture of the Church as transcending nationalism. Nevertheless, the evolutionary optimism of Illingworth might have jarred, and the neglect of any real study of evil and the lack of fresh thinking on ethical questions would have made it all seem very remote. He would, I think, have been even less helped by *Foundations*, liberal and questioning though it aimed to be. He might wonder why its publication had been attended by such clamour. Though the essayists attempted to restate doctrine in the light of the contemporary situation, the atmosphere of the book is academic and remote; it seems very much the expression of an in-group re-arranging the traditional theological furniture. The essayists seem unaware of the real challenges of the secular world, not least in the sphere of ethics, which is totally neglected. These two collections indicate how theologically unprepared the Church of England was for the war.

Equally in 1914, despite all that had been done by the Christian Social Movement in the nineteenth century, the social thinking of the Church of England was often naïve and confused, though much more expert work was done towards the end of the war and after it. The Guild of St Matthew (founded 1877) had expired in 1909. The Christian Social Union (1889) as an organization had sadly declined. The Church Socialist League (1906) was still finding its feet – Conrad Noel split away in 1916 and founded the Catholic Crusade. Though in the later years of the nineteenth century the mild collectivist ideas of the C.S.U. had been widely espoused by the younger leadership of the Church of England, most of the clergy failed to understand working-class culture. The Christian radicals themselves were almost entirely upper-class clergy with little experience of industrial or commercial life. The Guild of St Matthew never had a membership of more than 400, none from the working class. The C.S.U. had at one point about 6,000 members, but again none from the working class. But the C.S.U. ideals did have a very considerable influence on the post-war leadership of the Church of England. As contrasted with the continent, the clergy of the Church of England refused to side with any particular political party, and declined to teach the laity about their political conduct; only the small number of committed socialists among the clergy preached about politics directly.[41]

Yet the theological climate was not wholly depressing and unprepared. The much derided R. J. Campbell was in a fumbling, naïve, yet adventurous way trying to locate God's activity in the world. A Congregationalist minister at the City Temple from 1903 to 1915, he was received into the Church of England by Gore in 1915, and was ordained by him. When Campbell became an Anglican he disowned and bought out the rights of *The New Theology* (1907) to prevent its reissue. In it he had written that if the Christian faith was rearticulated in terms of divine immanence and 'monistic idealism', it would once again lay hold of the civilized world. Traditional language of divine transcendence promotes dualistic thinking and the belief that God intervenes only occasionally in history.[42] Traditional doctrines about the Bible, the Fall, Atonement, Heaven, and Hell are not only misleading but unscientific and unethical. Psychology teaches that the rational self is only part of the human personality. Evil and good are necessary to each other:

> sin itself is a quest for God – a blundering quest, but a quest for all that. The man who got dead drunk last night did so because of the impulse within himself to break through the barriers of his limitations, to express himself, and to realise more abundant life.[43]

The New Theology is the gospel of the Kingdom. The Church exists to prepare men not for another world but for this: 'Slowly, very slowly, with every now and then a depressing set-back, the race is climbing the steep ascent towards the ideal of universal brotherhood.'[44] The Labour Party is a church, for it gathers together those who want to try to bring in the Kingdom of God. Since humanity is 'the expression of one being', Christ is seeking expression through each soul: 'There is no life, however depraved, which does not occasionally emit some signs of its kinship to Jesus and its eternal sonship to God.'[45] The atonement needs to be 'repeated on the altar of human hearts': 'Go with J. Keir Hardie to the House of Commons, and listen to his pleading for justice to his order, and you see the Atonement.'[46] The Bible is not exclusive: 'We are writing a Bible with our own lives today.'[47]

Campbell's naïve optimism would have looked absurd to many in the trenches, but at least he was trying to break out of that inherited transcendentalism, moralism and biblicism which the more sensitive chaplains found to be such an obstacle. By 1916 he had changed his mind on many of these issues, and was writing an essay on 'The Illusion of Progress'. To work for progress was a noble but inadequate aim:

> To talk of progress as sufficient in itself as a dynamic to human devotion and enterprise is like saying it is worth setting a prairie on fire in order that possibly some people a thousand miles off in the direction the wind is blowing may be able to cook their evening meal.

Only the final consummation of all things can be the ground of our hope.[48]

To read P. T. Forsyth's *The Justification of God* (1916) after Campbell's *New Theology* (both were Congregationalists) is to move into a totally different atmosphere. Forsyth's subtitle was 'Lectures for War-Time on a Christian Theodicy'; the 'passion' for a theodicy was, he believed, the keynote of religion for multitudes of people.[49] The awful nature of evil was now being revealed. No evolutionary process can save us, only redemption. The war is a judgement on a godless civilization. The faith of some had hitherto never been tested; their religion had been aesthetic, pietistic, sheltered, with only a limited awareness of wickedness:

> When a sudden crash brings such people face to face with tragedy in its ghastliest and most inhuman forms, a faith which was only humane or serene in its note is apt to give way. It had but a divine atmosphere rather than a divine foundation. . . . It is a staggering blow to a faith that grew up in a long peace, a high culture, a shallow notion of history, society, or morality, and a view of religion as but a divine blessing upon life instead of a fundamental judgment and regeneration of it.[50]

The confident rhetoric of Forsyth's book sweeps on to the end, but the splendidly transcendent assertions in the end become unconvincing because they do not stoop to take into account the actual messiness and complexity of life as both Campbell and *The Army and Religion* attempted to do. Deutero-Isaiah exhorted the exiles to lift up their eyes

9   A chaplain writing letters for the wounded, 1916

10   A chaplain conducting a burial service in the trenches, 1918

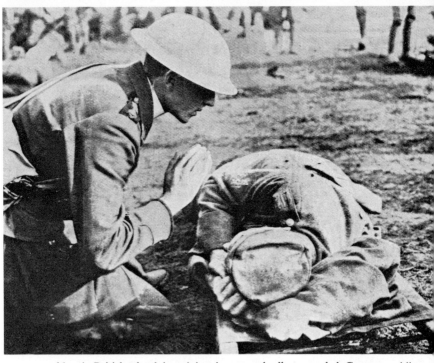

11 A British chaplain ministering to a badly wounded German soldier, October 1918

12 The Bishop of Dover (H. E. Bilbrough) dedicating a war memorial to 556 men of the South-Eastern and Chatham Railway Company at Dover Marine Station, 1922

to the transcendent Creator-Redeemer, but he was prepared to chance his arm by being very specific about the role assigned to Cyrus – as God chanced his arm in the contingency of the Incarnation.

Over against the liberal, reasonable Jesus, Albert Schweitzer in *The Quest of the Historical Jesus* (1906; English translation 1910) proclaimed a strange eschatological figure. Some liberal Anglicans were horrified. Temple was disquieted by Schweitzer's influence on Streeter, Rawlinson, and Parsons, fellow contributors to *Foundations*. [51] Figgis and Hoskyns were among those who felt that Schweitzer's strange, unexpected Jesus was exactly the challenge that was needed.[52] Streeter in *Foundations* pointed out that evolutionary theories obscured the fact that the greatest advances often occurred through crises and catastrophes which can 'take even the wisest by surprise'.[53]

Bishop Gore was one of the few churchmen to see the significance of the Boer War as a challenge to easy-going evolutionary optimism.[54] (By contrast Winnington-Ingram saw it as a fight for freedom, and the soldiers as tasting the 'joy of sacrifice' in a 'labour of love'.)[55] Not only had Gore a wide vision of the *Una Sancta*, not only did he proclaim a higher vocation for the Church than to be merely the religious icing on the erastian cake, but he taught also an appropriately sombre view of human nature:

> ... human nature, as we have had experience of it in history, presents in great measure a scene of moral ruin, so that Christ enters not merely to consummate an order but to restore it, not to accomplish only but to redeem.[56]

Sin could become so engrained that it prevented the forgiveness of God, and so became an 'eternal sin'; some doctrine of hell was therefore inevitable, but in terms of extinction rather than torment.[57] In the Preface to *Belief in God* he wrote characteristically that 'the only very difficult dogma of the Church' was that God is love.

The theology of F. D. Maurice (1805–72) was hardly known at all, though he deeply influenced Hort, Stewart Headlam and Conrad Noel. Maurice taught that war created and preserved national identity. If undertaken to sustain truth and order, it could be a participation in God's own war against evil. Soldiers have a vocation as real as the clergy, lawyers or doctors.[58] But his theology of Christ and the Church, if it had been known, could have helped those in wartime who wrestled with these doctrines. The Church, Maurice believed, was not simply the home of the redeemed, but a sign that the whole human race was potentially in Christ; he crossed swords therefore with Pusey, who saw baptism as the transfer of a person from the sin-dominated world into the ark of salvation. He was also at variance with the Evangelical scheme of salvation which started with the depravity of man; through his part in the creation, according to Maurice, Christ was Lord of all before he came in the flesh; there is goodness in the world as well as worldliness in the Church.

Studdert Kennedy began the war with a simple, even bloodthirsty patriotism; but experience of the war, at first hand, forced him to discard, even to loathe, such views. At a popular but deeply felt level (unlike academic theologians, he really was in touch with ordinary men) he explored most of the central themes for theology, ethics, and spirituality. Is God beyond or involved with the suffering of the world? (Both Streeter and Fairbairn had taught that God suffered with the world.) Does the Cross make sense of suffering? How are we to understand the Bible, the boundaries of the Church, sexual ethics, the Eucharist, heaven and hell, the unseen and unrecognized Christ who is present in acts of human compassion as well as in the sufferings of the world? He wrote in 1919:

> It is never pleasant tearing clinging ivy from old walls and breaking down the homes where many noble people have lived and died content, because time has rendered them not fit for habitation. . . . For me and for a good many others this work of destruction was finally accomplished during the past four years in a brutal, cruel, and merciless fashion.[59]

'Never such innocence again', writes Philip Larkin in his poem 'MCMXIV' published in 1967. William Empson's *Seven Types of Ambiguity* (1930) would have been inconceivable before 1914. Through the writings of Empson, I. A. Richards, F. R. Leavis, and T. S. Eliot, and the discoveries of psycho-analysis, words like 'undertones', 'paradox', and 'ambiguity' ceased to be equivalent to deceit and double dealing, and became terms implying praiseworthy richness, depth, and comprehensiveness. In the post-war period also, logical positivism made people more attentive to the capacity of language to deceive. But much of theology before, during and after the war lacked the qualities of ambivalence, paradox, irony, tragedy, grief, sophistication, which are necessary to cope with the complexity of experience. The poet sometimes seemed abler to cope with ambivalence than the theologian. Wilfred Owen was quite aware of the ambiguity of his own position.

When he was returning to France (for the last time) after his convalescence, he quoted to his mother some favourite words of Tagore, full of ambiguity: 'When I go from hence let this be my parting word, that what I have seen is unsurpassable.' He could perceive the possible presence of God in blasphemy and its possible absence in prayer.[60] Churchmen were usually too earnest, too unsmiling, too 'yea, nay' to allow such thoughts past their internal censor. Just as divorce courts still thought in terms of 'innocent' and 'guilty', and clergy debated whether they should re-marry the 'innocent party', so it was not easy for people to acknowledge that religion could be both truly nourishing, yet also devilishly corrupting, or that war could be evil, yet also exhilarating, so stretching to every sinew that those who survived sometimes never got over their guilty sense that this was the only time they had really lived. It is always a temptation for churchmen to identify faith with a willingness to man the institutional pumps. The need to maintain the institution, to justify a stipendiary ministry, and to salve an uneasy conscience about mission, can turn the evangelist into the propagandist, who then finds it hard to listen to the 'common religion' of ordinary men because it is expressed in unorthodox and anti-institutional terms.[61] It becomes therefore difficult to face the implications of Reinhold Niebuhr's remark: 'The Church can be Anti-Christ, and if and when the Church fails to admit this, it is the Anti-Christ.[62] Bernard Shaw in his wartime postscript to *Androcles and the Lion* exposed what he felt to be the tribalism of the Churches:

> They have turned their churches into recruiting stations and their vestries into munition workshops. But it has never occurred to them to take off their black coats and say quite simply, 'I find in the hour of trial that the Sermon on the Mount is tosh, and that I am not a Christian. I apologise for all the unpatriotic nonsense I have been preaching all the years. Have the goodness to give me a revolver and a commission in a regiment which has for its chaplain a priest of the god Mars: *my* God.' Not a bit of it. They have stuck to their livings and served Mars in the name of Christ, to the scandal of all religious mankind. When the Archbishop of York behaved like a gentleman and the Head Master of Eton preached a Christian sermon, and were reviled by the rabble, the Martian parsons encouraged the rabble.[63]

Shaw saw the scandal with characteristic clarity; but he perceived neither his own delight in pillorying the Churches, nor the painful dilemmas they were facing. Shaw here is just as damagingly naïve, just as blind to the dangers of the unequivocal language of self-righteousness as was, say, Winnington-Ingram on the other side.

In the post-war period most theologians reacted to the war either with outbursts of fervent optimism, or withdrawn despair, or by simply carrying on with the old issues as if nothing untoward had happened in the meantime. On the one hand there was *Songs of Praise*, or some features of the 1928 Prayer Book – for example its excision in the Alternative Commination Service of the phrase 'Cursed is he that putteth his trust in man, and taketh man for his defence'. On the other hand there was the pulling up of the drawbridges by Barthianism and biblical theology. This type of transcendentalism became imperialist and elitist in the hands of some churchmen (for example in the less attractive side of the writings of C. S. Lewis). The most considerable and representative achievement of Anglican Catholic theology in the immediate post-war period, *Essays Catholic and Critical* (ed. E. G. Selwyn, 1926), was a powerful reply to liberalism. Yet despite the presence of two ex-chaplains among its contributors (Milner-White and K. E. Kirk), its world is self-enclosed; the essayists seem unaware of the theological and ethical challenges of the war. When set in its historical context, the painlessness of its theology is extraordinary.

In the post-war world, few were able to hold transcendence and immanence together. Was it not possible to combine a transcendence which alone gives perspective with a generous and grateful recognition of God's activity and presence right outside the religious camp, a recognition that normally God comes to us incarnate? Without such a combination, transcendentalists become elitist and escapist, and immanentists become pelagian, sentimental, and tyrannized by the contemporary. To go deeply into the reality of human experience is to be forced to question all neat black-and-white categories of 'good' and 'evil'; painfully, yet hopefully, we are drawn to recognize 'the fundamental part which evil seems inescapably to play in the production of good'.[64] I do not mean only that Vaughan Williams's experiences on active service in France, say, enabled him to produce the first sketches of his Pastoral Symphony, but rather that, in Shakespeare's words,

> There is some soul of goodness in things evil,
> Would men observingly distil it out;
>
> (*Henry V* IV:i)

There is also some soul of evil in things good. One thinks of the tragic irony that the Fourth Gospel, which has done more than perhaps any other document in the New Testament to nourish and widen Christian experience, has also been regularly used in Christian history to create a theologically based anti-semitism. When Bruno Bettelheim was in German concentration camps he kept secret psycho-analytic observations; he discovered how much of the brutality around him expressed what was going on inside himself. Another analyst pointed out that refugees from the holocaust were often oppressed with guilt, not only because they had escaped, but also because the Nazi programme of extermination expressed some of the deepest and most horrifying drives within themselves.[65] Nazism intuitively found a way of utilizing the dark symbols of sado-masochism; hence its enduring appeal to the subterranean layers of the human mind. That is why religion and theology, if they function only at the level of the conscious mind, effect less than men imagine. In a crisis, much of the determinative action takes place below stairs. So 'Onward, Christian Soldiers', 'Abide with me' and 'Lead, kindly Light', and the wide range of biblical imagery available, were part of religion in the first war in a way that *Lux Mundi* or *Foundations* or the sober statements of Randall Davidson could never be. Winston Churchill recognized the ambivalences of the year that war broke out:

> But there was a strange temper in the air. Unsatisfied by material prosperity the nations turned restlessly towards strife internal or external. National passions, unduly exalted in the decline of religion, burned beneath the surface of nearly every land with fierce, if shrouded, fires. Almost one might think the world wished to suffer. Certainly men were everywhere eager to dare.[66]

We have surveyed the general theological scene. I want to look more closely now at some churchmen's reflections on the relationship of faith and war. It is easy to criticize churchmen for offering opinions identical to, or overlapping to some extent with, those outside the Church. But churchmen had to rely on the same censored information as everyone else. There was no authoritative independent ecumenical source of information available. Even the S.C.M., with its tradition of inter-nationalism and social thinking, had hardly considered questions of peace and war before 1914. Therefore we find that churchmen in some respects argued like other citizens: Britain had gone to war to defend Belgium and to be loyal to treaties, to defend the small nation against the large; to prevent the triumph of militarism which committed atrocities; to defeat the ideas of Nietzsche, Treitschke, and Bernhardi. The evidence available convinced Davidson, Lang, and other churchmen that it was a 'just war' as defined by Christian tradition. Von Hügel (whose father had been an Austrian ambassador) agreed.[67] Many Christians saw the war as a judgement – on Christians for failing to make the world Christian, and for failing to live up to their profession; on the godless who broke the Sabbath, promoted the disestablishment of the Church in Wales; on immorality, drunkenness, prostitution, the competitive system, class conflict; on erastian Lutheranism, Prussianism and liberal German theology. Watts-Ditchfield, the Evangelical Bishop of Chelmsford, in a much discussed sermon in Holy Week 1916 at St Paul's, saw the war as a judgement on all the nations, including the Allies:

> Had not the Allies much to answer for in the past – Russia for her treatment of the Jews, Belgium for the Congo atrocities, France for her overthrow of God and religion. . . . We should look on our own sins – the opium traffic forced on China, our refusal to interfere when Armenians were massacred, the neglect of Sunday, the prevalence of intemperance and impurity, the hastening to be rich, the division among the classes and the masses, the unhealthy public spirit as shown in the press, the neglect of the housing question, the begrudging of money for old-age pensions, and the removal of slums.

The Church of England had lost its hold on the nation; after sixteen centuries of influence, only five per cent of men were communicants.[68]

Henson, though an enthusiastic speaker at recruiting rallies, was aware of the dangers of unreflecting patriotism and tribal religion. In the Preface to *War-Time Sermons* (1915) he showed himself sensitive to the temptations of the preacher in wartime to give way to 'vehemence and violence' and to eschew 'moderation, charity or justice'. The preacher's words should be of such a character that when war was over he could read them without shame. Like Davidson he aimed to hold before his hearers the dangers of hatred and revenge and the duty of forgiveness.[69] In the *Church Quarterly* of October 1914 he wrote that there was happily no dispute as to the justice of England's cause, now that the diplomatic correspondence had been published, and the conduct of German armies in Belgium had been revealed. War demoralizes and encourages superstition, but creates national unity. In the present state of civilization war was inevitable, therefore Christian morality had to face this fact: 'once bind the Christian profession to an impossible morality, and you destroy its value as a redemptive instrument. . . . Armies and navies have precisely the same title to exist in a sin-disordered world as policemen, judges, and clergymen.'[70]

Neville Figgis had never shared the conventional liberal optimism of many of his contemporaries. He was much more widely read in history, politics, and literature than most churchmen. In a Cambridge University sermon in 1915 he proclaimed that the war would bury conventional religion, 'the tepid weak tea of choristers' Anglicanism'. The Church would be less extensive in the future, but more intensive. In a sermon in 1917, he outlined the various effects of war on faith. Men had learnt the reality of evil. The notion of automatic progress had gone. The idea that culture would ameliorate all our ills had been exploded – no country was more cultured than Germany. The Atonement must now become more central than the Incarnation. The war demonstrated the bankruptcy not of Christianity but of naturalism. The 'Alexandrian age' of English religion dominated by Westcott had closed; we now needed to emphasize the distinctiveness of Christianity. In another Cambridge University sermon in 1918 he compared the situation with that which Augustine faced and for which he produced *The City of God*. We find it hard to accept the message of the Cross that loss may bring real gain:

> In words we believe that, but we find it hard in act – in our own case. Still harder is it in the national cause. Yet nations, like individuals, may be the greatest when they have to tread the *via dolorosa* like Belgium now. The age-long triumph of English freedom might conceivably come, not after a victory but out of disaster unparalleled. I am not saying that this need be, or that we should not strain every nerve. Only let us not cease to remind ourselves that our faith in God's love as the ground of life must not be made dependent on the issue of any actual struggle.[71]

Other churchmen were also moved to adopt a similarly transcendent faith. Fr Herbert Kelly S.S.M. wrote in the *Church Quarterly* for January 1915 that to go back to scripture produces a different perspective. (The war was pressing him, like Scott Holland[72] and other theologians, towards a more eschatological faith.) Perhaps, he wrote, we are at the beginning of the end of European civilization. 'I know no reason in Scripture or out of it, why things should come to our ideal, least of all in our time.'[73] Fr Kelly was critical of some of the literature associated with the National Mission for its lack of a theocentric faith; he was also uneasy about a too ready recourse to the language of patripassianism.[74] In the *Church Quarterly* for October 1916, H. L. Goudge (Regius Professor of Divinity at Oxford 1923–39) declared that the Apocalypse was coming into its own. 'The old world, which we seemed to understand, has given way beneath us, and we have fallen through it into the world of the Bible.'[75] Churchmen often adopted a type of patripassianism. In 1918, Bishop Furse's daughter died, not quite fourteen years old; his deep grief mingled with his sorrow about the war; in his Pretoria diocesan letter he grappled with the questions about the meaning of prayer, evil and suffering. The war for him was 'the concentrated manifestation' of the universal battle between good and evil. In this, God had the hardest part of all. 'I believe He is suffering over the sorrows of the war, and over every single sorrow here, brought to birth by the sin and disorder and disease of the world.' It was not reasonable to pray that no one should be killed in the war. Was it not more pagan than Christian, he asked, to pray that your own son should be spared, which inevitably costs the life of someone else? We pray that the Army as a whole may conquer, not that individual lives may be spared, for 'there are worse things than death'.[76] W. R. Matthews experienced the full range of human reactions to war when he saw a Zeppelin crash in flames near Potter's Bar; he heard the shouts of triumph from the crowd mingling with the cries of agony from the crew being burned alive: 'the picture remains and symbolised for me the whole war period: fear, relief, joy in victory and the intolerable pain of all the defeated and injured.'[77]

By contrast, Darwell Stone, to judge from his biography, remained extraordinarily detached. The only reference to war in the index is 'War-bread, Consecration of' – he promised a correspondent to find out the precise constituents of war-bread so that he could decide whether it could be used for Communion. Most of the letters reprinted from this period deal with ecclesiastical minutiae. His biographer (writing in the middle of the second world war) considered that the 'most pressing' of the theological controversies of the first war was that of reservation.[78] At the other end of the ecclesiastical spectrum, Bishop Knox devoted a mere half-dozen out of three hundred pages in his *Reminiscences* to the war period, and there are no signs of any heart-searching, no hint of the theological and ethical issues which the war had raised. He concluded his descriptions of the Church in wartime with the words: 'It is high time to return to the most significant of all the changes in diocesan life, the story of the development of the Diocesan Conference.'[79]

The voice which rose above those of all other churchmen was that of Bishop Winnington-Ingram. He was an experienced missioner with a flair for publicity. He united the Victorian, romantic, and chivalric images of war with themes of sacrifice and fellowship from the Gospels. During the Boer War, Bishop Gore had tried to get him appointed Chaplain-General: 'The army wd. love Ingram.'[80] Bishop Wand remembers how Oxford undergraduates before the war would pack St Mary's to hear him: 'the handsome and glamorous Bishop of London, with his cockney accent and ready eloquence, his exuberant friendliness and all the romance of the East End. It would be safe to say that at that time for the average undergraduate he represented religion in general, and the Church of England in particular, at their very best.'[81] He was always intensely patriotic and a lover of Empire. He was happy singing 'Land of Hope and Glory' and speaking from a platform covered with a Union Jack. He believed that British rule was beneficent; the 'cubs' happily followed the British lion into war. 'There is no other country in the world that can make people so happy under its rule as our country.' Whereas the English loved freedom, the Germans were a down-trodden race. He told an audience how he had preached on Psalm 137 before the London Rifle Brigade ('my men') went into battle. Jesus too had loved his city, and was 'a patriot at heart'. The Bible taught that love and defence of one's country was 'a primary religious duty'.[82] His autobiography was full of ingenuous vanity, the honours he had received, the great ones who were his friends. In an address at the Guildhall in Advent 1914 he described how he had listened to a speech by Sir Edward Grey ('that dear old man'): 'we had tea together in the House of Lords afterwards and talked it over'.[83] He spoke with ready sentiment about quiet homes, bereaved widows, the refugee girl with her treasured violin, the glorious dead welcomed by Christ, girls mutilated by atrocities, the child with its arm blown off by a bomb who said, 'They've killed daddy and done this to me', and about the weeping father in the railway carriage whose five sons had been killed and whose wife was in a lunatic asylum as a result.

Both world wars, he believed, were great crusades. He never seemed to have been troubled by doubts as to the rightness of his stance. He believed that God worked slowly; it had taken 1800 years to abolish slavery. He quoted J. B. Mozley: 'even God can only get out of each age the morality of which the age is capable'.[84] As late as 1917, he could still declare: 'the good old British race never did a more Christlike thing than when, on August 4th, 1914, it went to war.'[85] He had an instinct for dramatic gestures. On Sunday 25 July 1915 he marched from Trafalgar Square to St Paul's in the pouring rain leading 3,000 troops. His publishers wrote proudly of the pleasure in publishing 'the remarkable sermon' this 'Bishop of the Battlefields' preached on the steps of 'the National Valhalla'.[86] He said in May 1919: 'the Church of England is national and patriotic to its core.'[87]

Frequently during the war, Winnington-Ingram assured everyone that a religious revival was under way or just round the corner; it was uncongenial to his temperament to contemplate depressing or complex facts. Hyperbole was his natural *métier*. He had a romantic and over-trustful view of human nature, hence his incapacity to create the type of discipline in his diocese which the Archbishop and other bishops pressed for. But at the same time there is no doubting his pastoral warmth, his capacity to voice patriotic sentiments and to clothe them in Christian phraseology, his determination that the Church of England should serve the nation. So he turned Fulham Palace into a hospital (financed by the Freemasons), paid frequent visits to the troops, at home and overseas, sent a personal message to all in service hospitals and toured the country on behalf of the National Mission. During his visit to the Fleet in 1916, the crew of the *Iron Duke* sang 'Should auld acquaintance be forgot' as he left the ship. The visits to the troops were given wide publicity. His chaplain wrote *The Bishop of London's Visit to the Front* (1915). In the Introduction, Winnington-Ingram wrote: 'I have not removed the kind expressions occasionally used about myself, as I know that the writer would feel hurt if I did.'

He tried to uphold the tradition of the Just War, however bellicose his language.[88] Speaking in Advent 1914, he urged the Third Battalion of the London Rifle Brigade (and the nation) to observe the Christian principles of the Hague Convention – shield and guard women and children; look after wounded enemies; mines were not to be laid in neutral waters; never fire on a white flag; never place machine-guns in ambulances.[89]

Winnington-Ingram did much to popularize the belief that the nation was engaged in a Holy War. Sometimes this term was used by people quite precisely to mean a crusade with God against the powers of darkness; sometimes it was used simply to convey a general conviction that England was on the side of right. (Mrs Pankhurst had described the Suffragette campaign as a 'Holy War' in June 1913.)[90] As early as 6 September 1914 Winnington-Ingram preached a sermon to soldiers at Bisley entitled 'The Holy War'. He began with stories of German brutality told him by Basil Bourchier, which he repeated in the language of a boy's adventure story. He quoted the Kaiser, Treitschke, and Bernhardi from a recent issue of the *Daily Mail* and Rudyard Kipling's 'For All We Have and Are'. After a brief conventional confession of national and personal sins, he then said:

> But when we have said all that, this is an *Holy War*. We are on the side of Christianity against anti-Christ. We are on the side of the New Testament which respects the weak, and honours treaties, and dies for its friends, and looks upon war as a regrettable necessity. . . . It is a Holy War, and to fight in a Holy War is an honour. . . . Already I have seen a light in men's eyes which I have never seen before.

He quoted a poem by Newbolt, told the congregation 'It is Christ then who calls us round the standard to fight', reminded them 'He that is not with me is against me', and appealed to them to say 'Here am I, send me'.[91] In the *Guardian* for 10 June 1915 he gave this message:

> I think the Church can best help the nation first of all by making it realise that it is engaged in a Holy War, and not be afraid of saying so. Christ died on Good Friday for Freedom, Honour, and Chivalry, and our boys are dying for the same things. Having once realised that everything worth having in the world is at stake, the nation will not hesitate to allow itself to be mobilised. You ask for my advice in a sentence as to what the Church is to do. I answer MOBILISE THE NATION FOR A HOLY WAR.

F. R. Barry in *Challenge* for 25 June called it an 'astonishing' message: 'From God's own standpoint perhaps all the belligerents are equally wrong.' Scott Holland and Walter Lock (Warden of Keble) expressed their great alarm in the *Guardian* for 17 June. Scott Holland appealed to the bishop to withdraw the term 'Holy War' which had such 'ugly and sinister associations'. The clergy should not be asked to become 'Mad Mullahs preaching a Jehad, but, at the most, very humble and penitent policemen. . . .' Had we not condemned the Kaiser for such language? But on 24 June Winnington-Ingram was unrepentant; he was a Christian bishop not a Mohammedan, therefore it could be taken for granted that he wanted people to fight as Christians, without bitterness, and with mercy towards the wounded and prisoners, and chivalry towards women and children. Subsequent issues contained large numbers of letters supporting the bishop, including a long contribution from Bishop Furse. Only one correspondent supported Scott Holland

and Lock. But when an Editorial on 1 July declared that the two protesters had 'carried with them neither the clergy nor the laity', A. E. J. Rawlinson, an Oxford theologian (Bishop of Derby 1936–59) disagreed. He wrote in the issue of 8 July that many soldiers were disappointed in the clergy for yielding to the temptation to act as recruiting sergeants, for issuing so few warnings against vengeance and hatred, and for not saying more about 'the difficult duty of loving our enemies'.[92]

But Winnington-Ingram was not alone in using the term 'Holy War'. On 6 September 1914, H. C. Beeching, Dean of Norwich, preached (and the S.P.C.K. later published) a sermon entitled 'Armageddon'. Germany was no longer a Christian nation: 'It is a holy war in which we have taken our part; a war of Christ against anti-Christ . . . the battle is indeed for the Cross . . . it is indeed Armageddon. Ranged against us are the Dragon and the False Prophet. . . .'[93] Basil Bourchier in 1915 published ten addresses in *For All We Have and Are*, its title derived from Kipling's poem. General Smith-Dorrien, who was at one stage Commander of the Second Army, in his Foreword wrote of Bourchier's 'unrivalled experiences of the devilish deeds of our foe' when he was captured in Belgium in August 1914. He was one of the two Generals who had used Winnington-Ingram so effectively to persuade Territorials to volunteer. Bourchier was also a friend and admirer of his bishop and wrote: 'During the last fifteen months the Bishop's efforts to stir the Church of England to rise to its God-given opportunity have won the approbation of all men. It is for us, clergy and laity alike, to back him up.'[94] In one of his addresses Bourchier told the troops that the belief that warfare was irreconcilable with Christianity was not tenable at the present time:

We are fighting, not so much for the honour of our country, as for the honour of our God. Not only is this a holy war, it is the holiest war that ever has been waged. The cause is the most sacred that man has been asked to defend. It is the honour of the most High God which is imperilled. Our enemies have done despite to His Name. The Christian man never had less cause for misgiving for being a soldier. This truly is a war of ideals. Odin is ranged against Christ and Berlin is seeking to prove its supremacy over Bethlehem. Every shot that is fired, every bayonet thrust that gets home, every life that is sacrificed, is in very truth 'for His Name's sake'. Have no misgiving. The Huns have dishonoured His Name. Have I not seen it with my own eyes? Almost a year ago I was a witness of their open hatred of the Christ.

He went on to describe how he had witnessed churches in ruins or in flames. 'We have it on indisputable authority' that the Germans had burnt crucifixes, mutilated Madonnas, converted churches into stables and raped women in 'sacred edifices'.[95] In another address he commended the *Church Times* for encouraging Christians to regard the operations in the Dardanelles as 'the latest of the Crusades'. These operations might lead to the capture of Constantinople so that it would be a Christian city again, and also to the rescue of the Holy Land 'from the defiling grip of the infidel'.[96] In the last address Bourchier pleaded with the soldiers to deepen their 'sense of immortality'; they might not be mentioned in the press or be decorated,

> but in the presence of a multitude that no man can number, in the Presence of God, His angels, and His saints you shall receive the reward of faithful service and hear yourself called to greater dignity, promoted by the Great Commander Himself, decorated by the one and only Ruler of Princes.[97]

Of course this kind of full-throated patriotism was not confined to Christians, but churchmen were more familiar with the whole range of powerfully emotive biblical imagery than those who were not in such daily contact with the Bible.

By contrast, the agnostic F. H. Keeling, who fought with enthusiasm to defeat militarism, wrote to Canon William Danks of Canterbury, a leading Modern Churchman, in December 1915:

> I hope you aren't one of these ecclesiastical German-haters – I am sure you aren't. Few Englishmen out here hate their enemies – I feel as sorry for the Germans as for our own men in the bombardments. . . . The 'Holy War' idea is Christian cant of the worst kind. It is all rot to suppose we are white and the Germans black.[98]

I want now to look at three books which from different points of view tried to work out a relationship between Christian faith and war.

Anglican pacifism was not fully articulated until the 1930s through such clergy as Charles Raven and Dick Sheppard. A survey of Christian reactions to the war, however, would be incomplete without an example of pacifist attitudes in the period of the war itself. *Christ and War* (1913) by William Wilson, a Quaker, was used by Friends' Study Circles. Dr Rendel Harris commended it warmly. When it was republished in November 1914, significantly few modifications seemed to the author to be necessary; he believed that the coming of war had confirmed his chief contentions. The subtitle 'The Reasonableness of Disarmament on Christian, Humanitarian and Economic Grounds' indicates the outlook of the author, who had been much influenced by Norman Angell. War, incompatible with Christ's teachings, could be abolished because it was clearly to the advantage of all men to do so: 'all that stands in the way is human ignorance and prejudice, and in every department of life these are constantly being overcome.'[99] War, far from being in accord with evolution, resulted in the survival of the least fit; far from being natural, it was becoming increasingly difficult to persuade men to fight. War was unfitted to be an instrument of justice and could never advance the Kingdom of God. If the passion for revenge moved a nation towards war, 'reason, humanity and religion may restrain it by showing that war can only bring material and moral loss'.[100] Violence was playing 'a gradually decreasing part in human life. War itself is already playing a decreasing part in international affairs.'[101] Nevertheless, advance was not automatic; nations must realize the 'reasonableness of arbitration and the foolishness of war' and work towards world federation.[102] Lovers of peace should support foreign missions; only Christianity could give unity to mankind.

Theologically, the book is open to various criticisms: the dismissal of the Old Testament, which unlike the New Testament is an explicitly political document; the neglect of eschatology; the *simpliste* attitude towards the new relationship between Church and State inaugurated under Constantine. Wilson failed to grasp the tragic element in human history (a dominant theme in the Deuteronomic history of the Old Testament) and he had a naïve faith in man's reasonableness. The book indicates the incapacity of progressive liberalism to cope adequately with the deeper issues raised by the war.

The War and the Kingdom of God (1915) was edited by G. K. A. Bell. All the contributors were convinced that England had been morally bound to go to war, but were sensitive to those who asked, 'Was Christianity discredited as a practical force?'[103] Bell movingly articulated the tension for the sensitive Christian conscience between duty to country and allegiance to the Kingdom of God beyond national loyalty. H. L. Goudge stressed that prayer for the Kingdom went beyond nationalism. Since the Church was Catholic, no nation could claim to be 'God's peculiar people'.[104] Recognizing that many felt that justice was not being done to Christ's plain teaching, he devoted an essay to discussing the complexity of the evidence.

In the most original essay of the book, 'The Humiliation of War', Peter Green asserted strongly that Christ's teaching was not an interim ethic; Jesus never showed more understanding of man than in his teaching about non-resistance.

> I profoundly disbelieve in the possibility of any good coming of war, and I regard all talk about war in itself being a moral purge, and a wholesome discipline, and a school of character, and all the rest of it, as being either profoundly immoral and anti-Christian, or mere moral platitudes.[105]

How, then, could we reconcile the belief that to go to war was right with the belief that war was always wrong? Only by recognizing that it is not always possible to act rightly. Because of our own sins 'there was no right course open' any longer.[106] We could not isolate the final German act from the forty years which had led up to it, for which we all had ample cause for repentance. The war was a judgement from God; when war broke out, the Church should have summoned the nation to a searching self-examination leading to a deep penitence. Sins such as hatred, drunkenness, lust, gambling, commercial dishonesty, neglect of spiritual things, were common at all times. The sins that the Church should be attacking now were those which had specifically led to the war. The Churches of Europe had failed to give their whole support to peace movements, to the reduction of armaments and to international arbitration and had acquiesced in terrible social inequalities. The Church had failed to put into practice Christ's teaching on non-resistance and evangelical poverty. In controversies about education, Home Rule or Welsh disestablishment, Christians had fought each other to the last ditch:

> And is it not true that in all these disputes the most intractable factor was the religious one, and that the *odium theologicum* was always the chief source of heat and of hatred? . . . It is surely absurd to maintain that Christianity cannot be applied in our public life in England and then to fall into transports of surprise, indignation and grief when it proves unworkable in the public life of Europe.[107]

The same spirit in which we had conducted our disputes at home in every sphere of public life was now devastating Europe. (Many themes of this essay had already appeared in his weekly articles in the *Manchester Guardian*.)

Canon J. G. Simpson of St Paul's believed that the clergy should not bear arms because war belonged to the secular process, not to the Kingdom of God. Though soldiers' self-sacrifices had resemblances to the death of Christ, the two were distinct because Christ never took up the spear. The preacher was tempted to become a recruiting sergeant, as published sermons showed, though men of God should not be fanning hatred or righteous indignation:

> Patriotic zeal must never be allowed to betray the clergy into creating the impression that death on the battlefield is a passport to heaven. That is the danger of harping upon such phrases as 'holy war'. The man in the trenches is probably the last person to be deceived by any such language.[108]

'The voice of the superman is heard in much of our popular imperialism. Treitschke is not the only pagan philosopher, nor Prussians the only megalomaniacs.'[109] The Church must proclaim the need for a united and effective Catholic Church which would be the 'surest pledge' for 'a warless world'.[110]

Scott Holland considered that we would emerge from the war with two contrary convictions. Firstly, we now knew that war is a hell, not a romantic, glamorous adventure: 'All chivalry, all generosity, all the glory of the strife has gone. . . . It is insane.'[111] But secondly, 'Right in the heart of hell, men have found a strange heaven. They have been nearer to the mind and heart of Christ than they had even attained to in the life of peace. They have known what it was to give away their hope of life out of love of others . . . they have been initiated into the secret of sacrifice, into the inner meaning of life through death.'[112] 'That which has been revealed through war declares the coming death of war.'[113] The more men were drawn to an alliance with the crucified, the more impossible would it be to express sacrifice in terms of killing. When the pressure of war was removed, how could we retain the spirit of heroic devotion? It was untrue that the self-assertion of strength in war or industrial strife was a fulfilment of Darwinian law. Huxley had taught us that it was man's task to control the cosmic process. The species which co-operated to strengthen the weak and change the environment would be the best fitted to survive. Therefore, after the war there must be an extension of co-operative industrial enterprise. The Church too must ask for sacrificial heroism from its members. 'There has been only a smug invitation to come to a comfortable seat and hear a sung mattins.'[114] The clergy were depressed; the whole Church needed 'Sons of Thunder', those in monastic communities who could 'afford to take on their lips the language of the Sermon on the Mount without offence', so presenting Christianity in its 'most romantic and heroic shape'.[115]

This is still an exciting book to read. Much of it stems from the Catholic socialism exemplified in the Christian Social Union, which was critical of the social and religious establishment, and of a merely national Church. If its hopes for the future now seem over-sanguine, that is because we have discovered how hard it is to achieve ideals in political life, and how unexpected so often are the results of reforms which seemed so obviously desirable; we have grown too accustomed to living with perpetual international crises to be able to envisage a 'warless world'.

The other symposium to be considered is *The Faith and the War* (1916) edited by F. J. Foakes-Jackson, Dean of Jesus College, Cambridge; over half the essays were written by members of the Churchmen's (later Modern Churchmen's) Union, which had commissioned the book. All believed that the Church had not yet risen to the challenge of war, and that England's cause was just. One of the recurring themes of the book was how the outbreak of the war could be reconciled with a belief in progress. 'If military imperialism is utterly defeated and exposed now, that will be a move on for the world.'[116] Percy Gardner wrote that the divine Power was not 'victoriously omnipotent, but works gradually, makes its way by slow progress, often suffers partial defeat from the hostile forces of evil'.[117] Foakes-Jackson pointed out that because the English had never experienced 'a great tragedy', the country had 'witnessed a steady peaceful progress' and assumed that this was the will of God.[118] Dean Inge did not believe there was a 'law of progresss'. But though pessimism was excusable, it was 'unnecessary', despite the transformation of one of the most civilized nations into 'a horde of Huns'. On Germany 'rests the sole guilt of this war'.[119] The pacifism of the new democracies was proof that barbarian passions could be contained. If we could get rid of false and anachronistic attitudes which encouraged territorial greed, military glory and the worship of the state, 'we could keep the ape and tiger in their cages'.[120] There was no biological law of international conflict; if we wanted peace we could have it. Military absolutism could not permanently maintain itself before the internationalism of the labour movement. We should not easily forget the lessons of war. It was a matter for shame that 'no one looks to organised Christianity as a probable saviour of society'. French and English churchmen had reacted as enthusiastic citizens; the German State Church had 'justified or brazenly denied every atrocity'; the Papacy had 'sold itself to Pan-Germanism'.[121] Before the war the Churches had done little to promote peace. It is we who have failed, not our religion.

A. E. Taylor in his essay on 'Immortality' did not engage at any point with the acute questions raised by the war on this subject. E. A. Burroughs considered that the war had not disturbed the ground of faith. C. W. Emmet surveyed the teaching of the New Testament on war, and Michael Glazebrook dealt with the nature of Christian citizenship.

Henson wrote the final essay on 'The Church of England after the war': 'Organised Christianity does not come well out of the world crisis.'[122] Christendom had been swayed by un-Christian principles; the ready and undiscriminating advocacy of war by some clergy had provoked repugnance. After the war, the Churches would be criticized because they had failed to bear witness to the Gospel, were disunited and were preoccupied with trivialities; Faber's hymn would be the core of the Creed:

> For the love of God is broader
>   Than the measures of man's mind;
> And the heart of the Eternal
>   Is most wonderfully kind.

The originality of Christianity lay not in its institutions or its theology, but in its moral expression; so after the war Christianity would be far more closely tied to the person of Christ. It would be more widely grasped that all who did the will of the Father and lived by the Spirit were Christ's brethren. The Church of England was capable of adopting and expressing this wider type of Christianity:

As a National Church it conciliates the patriotic sentiment which the war has stimulated, and escapes the aspect of sectarianism which the war has made repulsive. The name of England will emerge from the world-conflict with fresh titles to human veneration, dearer than ever to the thought of Englishmen, more richly freighted than before with associations of public service, and glorious memories of personal heroism. The Church of England will catch a certain lustre from its historic character as a national institution. Men will be disposed to give it a fair trial, willing to admit its right to express the Christian religion to and for Englishmen. The ancient churches, where the flags of the regiments have been treasured, and whose walls will carry many names of comrades sleeping on the battlefields abroad or beneath the ocean, will seem the natural homes of religion to the soldiers and sailors returning at last from the long war. A new link between the Church and the nation will have been forged in the furnace of affliction.[123]

How could the crucifix, seen so often at the Front, ever be thought of again as 'popish superstition'? How could old theories about schism and heresy be retained among those who have 'witnessed the sublimely simple faith of illiterate Salvationists and Methodists'? After the war 'a genuine cosmopolitanism' ought to emerge both ecclesiastically and internationally.[124]

This symposium is more detached, complacent, and narrowly patriotic, and less engaged with the realities of war than *War and the Kingdom of God*. One misses the passion and grief of Bell, Peter Green, and Scott Holland. *The Faith and the War* shows more readiness to transfer guilt on to German shoulders, and less willingness to see the war as a judgement on a whole civilization. Henson's essay is still fresh, but despite his (condescending) gestures towards non-Anglicans, he is really moved only when he paints that romantic picture of the Church of England as a great shrine for Englishness; he displays no vital interest in a world-wide Catholic Church. The Christ of his essay seems remote and hellenic compared with the Christ whom Sassoon met stumbling under his load of planks along the trenches in the pouring rain.

11

Preparing for Peace

Eleven o'clock struck on 11 November 1918: 'It seemed almost as if one heard a dead silence and then that the whole nation gave a sigh of relief. A few moments later the people had gone mad.'[1] Church bells, long silent, rang out. At the Baltic Exchange they sang the Doxology, and 'O God, our help in ages past' at the Stock Exchange. Crowds poured into St Paul's, Westminster Abbey, and churches throughout the country. At St Martin-in-the-Fields services were held almost continuously from 11.30 a.m. to midnight. At Birmingham people queued outside the cathedral to take part in one of the three thanksgiving services. Members of both Houses of Parliament attended a service at St Margaret's, Westminster, at which the Archbishop of Canterbury read the lesson from Isaiah 61 which included the verses:

> he hath sent me to bind up the brokenhearted, to proclaim liberty to the captives, and the opening of the prison to them that are bound; . . . And they shall build the old wastes, they shall raise up the former desolations, and they shall repair the waste cities, . . .

At Southwold, Suffolk, the Mayor read the official telegram from the balcony of the Swan, soldiers burned the Kaiser in effigy, and crowds filed into church. But relief was mingled with sadness for the dead and the bereaved, and for the passing of a unique experience. Michael MacDonagh wrote in his diary:

> I sorrowed for the millions of young men who had lost their lives; and perhaps more so for the living than for the dead – for the bereaved mothers and wives whose reawakened grief must in this hour of triumph be unbearably poignant. But what gave me the greatest shock was my feeling in regard to myself. A melancholy took hold of me when I came to realize, as I did quickly and keenly, that a great and unique episode in my life was past and gone. . . . Our sense of the value of life and its excitements, so vividly heightened by the War, is, with one final leap of its flame to-day, about to expire in its ashes.

Tomorrow we return to the monotonous and the humdrum, 'So sad, so strange, the days that are no more.'[2]

Some realized that the post-war world would be a difficult one with many problems. Dean Inge wrote: 'the situation is so perilous that only thoughtless people can be lighthearted over our victory, complete as it is.'[3] Henson later recalled the mood of the time in which the 'ecstatic rejoicings' at the end of the war were replaced by disillusionment, as troops returned to find a shortage of homes and jobs. The situation was worsened by 'the reckless self-indulgence' of those who had become rich through the war. Conventional morality seemed to be collapsing. 'War enfeebles *all* the cementing factors of ordered society.' The process of social disintegration was 'disastrously stimulated' by 'the so-called emancipation of women' and by the triumph of Communism in Russia. The one had bad effects on sexual morality. The other 'kindled in the public mind the panic fears and perilous dreams of revolution'. The contrast between 'the normal hardships of the toiling masses and the ostentatious luxury of the privileged few' became more 'grossly apparent since it was no longer softened and shrouded by the cautious reticences and decent conventions of settled habit. An epidemic of strikes broke out in the country.'[4] But in October 1920, visiting Germany shortly before his enthronement as Bishop of Durham, he was in a different mood; being driven in the Commander-in-Chief's car filled him with patriotic exultation: 'It was with a certain irrepressible pride that I found myself being driven through the streets of Cologne in a car with the Union Jack flying before it.'[5]

Free Churchmen felt recognized at last when in November 1918 the King and Queen attended a Solemn Service of Thanksgiving, arranged by the Free Church Council, in the Albert Hall – the first time a reigning monarch had attended a Free Church occasion. Dr John Clifford wrote: 'It is the beginning of a new day in the relations of the State to "dissent". It is the lifting to a slight extent of the social stigma.'[6] The Free Churches felt that through the war their communities had been brought into the main stream of the national life: 'Even if we should be called upon to oppose, we shall still be a recognised part of "His Majesty's Opposition"', wrote a Primitive Methodist historian in 1919. Just as some Free Churchmen pointed to their titled laymen as indications that their tradition was at last recognized in national life, so now they could instance the size of their Rolls of Honour to demonstrate their patriotism.[7] But though dissenters now preferred the more positive title 'Free Churchmen', to have to some degree joined the social and religious establishment prepared the way for assimilation and therefore decline.

When the Peace Treaty was signed on 28 June 1919, Thanksgiving Services were held throughout the country. Randall Davidson preached in the presence of the King and Queen at St Paul's on 6 July. He spoke of the horrors of war as well as its heroism, the need for peace, the significance of the League of Nations and among the immediate problems 'the scourge of impending famine' in Europe.[8] Henson found the service 'impressive' but he warned against overestimating 'these outbursts of popular religion'.[9]

There was a good deal of unease in the Church about the terms of the peace settlement, but those who had taken a hard line against Germany during the war called for hard peace terms. Bishop Moule wrote in the middle of October 1918:

> I think peace is really near. But to be a blessing, it must be a peace secured by Germany's real submission – and I am deeply sure that she must not go without some retributory pains and penalties as will mark her awful wrongdoings with a brand of solemn condemnation.[10]

Bishop Chavasse, preaching at a civic thanksgiving service in Liverpool in November, was reported as declaring: 'For the horrors inflicted upon humanity the evil doers must be punished and reparation made. They must listen to no weak and misleading phrase that we ought in Christian kindness to let bygones by bygones and forget the foul and dreadful deeds of shame and violence. The world must learn that the way of the transgressor was hard.'[11] In November 1918, Archbishop Davidson bitterly disappointed the German Church leader Dr Deissmann, who had asked Davidson to use his influence to ensure a conciliatory peace settlement. Davidson pointed out that England did not choose the war, went on to recite the 'savagery' with which the Germans had prosecuted the war, and regretted that Christian circles in Germany had not protested against 'these gross wrongs'. Therefore while the Allies had no wish to crush Germany, 'righteousness must be vindicated, even although the vindication involves sternness'. Davidson missed another opportunity in the General Election of 1918 when a flood of hatred was let loose on the hustings; he was disturbed by it, but did not criticize it in public.[12] He also deplored some features of the peace terms, but Lord

Robert Cecil and others counselled that to make a public criticism might give the Germans the excuse for not signing and so prolonging the blockade. In May 1919, however, Davidson wrote privately to Lloyd George to express the disquiet and anxiety of many people about the terms.[13]

Henson wrote in his diary that he thought that the terms of the Versailles Treaty were 'too hard, but what would have been the terms of the treaty which victorious Germany would have imposed on her defeated foes?'[14] In 1919, Neville Talbot, now back at Balliol, presided over a meeting at the Corn Exchange; the speakers included George Lansbury. The resolution declared that the meeting believed that the Peace terms offered 'no guarantee of a lasting peace'. There was a good deal of disorder. When Talbot spoke of the 'winning-over of the German people', a voice shouted, 'We don't want them'; but Talbot continued: 'Were they not tired to death of the barrenness and feebleness of hatred, fear and stupidity? Were they going to get any moral satisfaction from that which might be bought by money and super-indemnities?'[15] Peter Green believed that unless the Allies made a generous peace, the seeds of an even greater war would be sown. 'A sore, bitter and hostile Germany will be no benefit to the community of European nations', he wrote in the *Manchester Guardian* on 21 November 1918. Though Lord Halifax and A. C. Headlam criticized the proposal to try the Kaiser, the *Guardian* thought that he should be put on trial.[16] *Commonwealth* expressed its concern that the financial penalties imposed on Germany would cripple her and voiced doubts about other features of the Treaty.[17] But both the *Guardian* and the *Church Times* supported heavy indemnities. Germany's wealth, said the *Church Times*, is 'ample enough to keep her in comfort after she has indemnified us all'.[18] Winnington-Ingram was one of those who, having viewed the war in black-and-white terms, continued to cast the Allies in the role of instruments of divine justice. In a sermon preached on the First Sunday in Advent at the Abbey in 1918, he strongly urged the need to punish Germany 'for the greatest crime committed in the world for a thousand years'. God 'looks to us now to punish the wrongdoer'. This is no more revengeful than a court sentence. Advent reminds us of Judgement. Punishment is necessary to deter the wrongdoer and to maintain the moral standards of the world. He strongly rejected the view that all nations were 'more or less equally to blame'. The war had been created 'entirely by one nation to satisfy its pride and lust for power. We look upon it as deliberately planned for forty years, and carried out with diabolical craft and cunning.' After spending a good deal of his sermon emotionally cataloguing the war-crimes of the Central Powers, he urged the setting up of a Commission of Inquiry to bring the guilty to justice.[19] In 1932, William Temple, by then Archbishop of York, preached before the International Disarmament Conference in Geneva. His sermon was broadcast in a number of countries. Towards the end he denounced the War Guilt clause. 'We have to ask not only who dropped the match but who strewed the ground with gunpowder.' For this he was severely criticized.[20]

The Churches became aware of the immediate social problems in post-war Europe. Quaker relief teams were quickly at work. Some Christian voices were raised against the policy of continuing the blockade until the Treaty was signed. Davidson tried to help German prisoners still held hostage in France in December 1919, and actively promoted the Save the Children Fund, securing wide ecumenical support for it. When Bishop E. S. Talbot, at a meeting to promote the S.C.F. soon after the Armistice, spoke of 'poor downtrodden Germans', he received over 800 letters of protest.[21] Davidson, in the Lords in February 1920, called on the government to provide help, but he did not, like some speakers, blame the terms of the Peace Treaty for the distress. In February and April, debates were held on the subject in the Upper House of Canterbury Convocation. Davidson criticized the poor response of the British public in contributing only £100,000 in special church collections on Holy Innocents' Day.[22] The European Central Bureau for Inter-Church Aid was created in 1922, and through it much help was given to Churches facing distress in sixteen countries.

The S.C.M. had much work to do after the Armistice. Students flocked into universities and colleges. Some distrusted organized Christianity; some believed it more useful to work for the League than for the Church overseas. In the immediate post-war period, compulsory chapel was modified or abolished in many Oxford and Cambridge colleges under pressure from war veterans and the general climate of opinion. The S.C.M. became less Evangelical. The watchword ('The Evangelisation of the World in this Generation'), so confidently adopted by the Student Volunteer Missionary Union in 1896, was dropped; the S.C.M. basis of membership was revised to make it more acceptable to the many students who were less willing to use traditional theological language after the war.[23] The World Student Christian Federation started a programme of student relief, and students in forty-two countries contributed over half a million pounds for the relief of students in nineteen lands.

The League of Nations was the focus of much hope, inside and outside the Churches. The history section in Arthur Mee's *Children's Encyclopaedia* (1925) was entitled 'The March of Man from the Age of Barbarism to the League of Nations'. When *Songs of Praise*, edited by Percy Dearmer, was published in 1925, its liberal, optimistic tone proved so popular, both in churches and schools, that an enlarged edition appeared in 1931. Its non-sectarian type of Christianity, made popular by the war, was expressed, for example, in its modernist approach to sacramentalism, its liberal attitudes to other religions, and its benignly immanentist theology which made it attractive to those in the post-war period who were impatient of creeds, dogmas, religious and social divisions, and traditional language about sin. The section on 'Social Service' reflected the idealism of the time, both Christian and humanist; in it a group of 'National' hymns was followed by an 'International' group.[24] This latter collection begins with a hymn by Laurence Housman (composed for the Life and Liberty Movement) including the line:

> Races and peoples, lo, we stand divided   (326)

The refrain of the next hymn by Whittier begins:

> The dark night is ending and dawn has begun!   (327)

This is followed by Frederick Tennyson's

> The night is ended and the morning nears   (328)

and the group is concluded by Clifford Bax's hymn:

> Turn back, O Man, forswear thy foolish ways . . .
> Earth shall be fair, and all her people one   (329)

The section 'Social Service: General' includes Whittier's 'O brother man, fold to thy heart thy brother' (307), Shelley's 'The world's great age begins anew' (311) and Whitman's 'All the past we leave behind' (304). Perhaps the most popular hymn to come out of the war was Blake's 'Jerusalem' (446), set to music by Parry for a celebration of the granting of the vote to women. (The first number of *Challenge* on 1 May 1914 carried Blake's poem on its cover.) Nearly all these particular hymns were new to English congregations.

From early days, the leadership of the Church of England gave the idea of a League of Nations strong support. This was to be expected. It was easy to see it as the political equivalent of ecumenism. In pre-war days, liberal Christians had preached arbitration as the right way to settle international disputes, and as the next stage in the evolutionary process. Canon W. L. Grane of the Church of England Peace League had written in 1913: 'The next great step onward and upward in the social evolution of mankind consists in the establishment of Law and Justice on the throne now occupied by Violence as the final arbiter and last resort in the settlement of the world's affairs.'[25] The term 'League of Nations', unknown in the autumn of 1914, had become common by the spring of 1915. The Pope in his message of 1917 proposed a compulsory system of arbitration, with sanctions against recalcitrant states. In May 1917, the League of Nations Society held a meeting in London with Lord Bryce in the chair and the Archbishop of Canterbury as one of the chief speakers. In February 1918, the Upper House of the Canterbury Convocation warmly welcomed the proposed League:

> We desire to welcome in the name of the Prince of Peace the idea of such a League as shall promote the brotherhood of man, and shall have power at the last resort to constrain by economic pressure or armed force any nation which should refuse to submit to an international tribunal any dispute with another nation.

In the same month, Davidson headed a manifesto signed by leaders of the Church of England, the Free Churches, and the Roman Catholic Church, urging that the League 'should be put in the very forefront of the peace terms as their presupposition and guarantee'. In September Lord Robert Cecil wrote a confidential letter from the Foreign Office appealing to the Archbishop to write to the press to urge support for the League in response to a speech by President Wilson and to counter coolness in conservative circles.[26] Davidson immediately wrote a letter to *The Times*. The letter was widely approved, and a few days later Davidson attended a meeting addressed by Lord Grey to promote the League. In October, Davidson convened a meeting of Anglican and Free Church leaders to organize church support.[27]

In 1922 the Archbishop of Canterbury was invited to preach in St Peter's Cathedral in Geneva before the opening of the Third Assembly of the League. It was a sign of the times that an Anglican Archbishop should preach in Calvin's pulpit. He spoke of the constructive work done by the League, and ended with a deeply-felt appeal for an end to war, linking it with an ecumenical vision:

> We have seen with our own eyes, we have heard in our own homes and hospitals, its unspeakable, its illimitable horrors. And deliberately we say that, God helping us, there shall be no 'next time'. The foremost thinkers and statesmen and rulers now alive in Christendom have thrown their strength into devising plans – by tribunals, by delays, by pledges, by conditions, by sanctions – to make the thing impossible. And meantime we may surely say that militarism has fashioned its own coffin. We are here to clinch the nails. . . . It is, or it ought to be, unthinkable that we fail. . . . We are here to-day as Christians. If only every man and woman who holds that holy faith, could realize for himself, for herself, what the love of Jesus Christ our Saviour means, would there be need for a League of Nations? . . . Once let the Christian men and women upon earth, West and East, North and South, kneel to God side by side, stand shoulder to shoulder before men, to say what they mean shall happen, or rather, what shall not happen, in the round world again, and they are irresistible.

But when in 1924 William Temple, by then Bishop of Manchester, suggested that the bishops should commit themselves to a statement about war guilt which seemed to Davidson to place England on the same level of responsibility as Germany, he declined to support him.[28]

Other leading Anglicans also gave the League their support; so did the Lambeth Conference of 1920 which urged relief-work and the admission to the League of former enemy nations. Henson, like Davidson and many others at this period, took a sanguine view of the prospects for peace and of the power of Christian influence: 'I don't see why war between nations should not come to be as obsolete as the duel between individuals', he wrote in 1919.[29] Winnington-Ingram, with typical hyperbole, said in a sermon at Christmas 1919 that the League might 'hasten by five thousand years the advent of peace on earth'. It was 'the one hope of this tired and distracted world', he said in 1920.[30] Gore was another ardent advocate, and believed that Germany should be a member of the League (as did *Commonwealth*).[31] He hoped that as democracies replaced dynasties the spirit of peace would grow. He told the Lords in June 1918 that the League would only work if there was a mortification of national pride and a policy of effective sanctions, military and economic. In a visitation charge in the early summer, he stressed that three ideas were daily taking stronger hold of the imagination of the general public: the equal right of everyone to the opportunities of life; the supremacy of communal welfare over selfish individual interests; the fellowship of nations as supreme over sectional ambitions. Later he joined in signing an appeal for the amendment of the Versailles Treaty on the ground that certain articles were unjust and created a serious obstacle to international understanding.[32] Lord Charnwood, in an article in the *Church Quarterly* for July 1920, asserted that it was the special task of the Churches to ensure that the Government kept its pledges under the Covenant; if it did not, they should make loud and continued protest. But some Christians showed a naïve idealism in opposing the conviction of Gore and others that the League needed effective sanctions to impose its decisions.

It was widely felt that the League was the next stage in the evolution of international co-operation. It was often assumed that the Great War was a set-back to progress rather than an argument against an evolutionary view of history. In November 1918, Lloyd George asked: 'Are we to lapse back into the old national rivalries and animosities and competitive armaments, or are we to initiate the reign on earth of the Prince of Peace?'[33] The strength of popular jingoism was demonstrated in the 1918 election when Ramsay MacDonald, Lord Kerry (son of Lord Lansdowne), and Asquith were defeated; Sir Eric Geddes during the election had called for Germany to be squeezed 'till the pips squeak'. Parliament was not notably enthusiastic about the League, and the League of Nations Union had a hard struggle against the prevailing apathy. By strongly supporting the League, the leadership of the Church of England was courageous enough to stand against such narrow nationalism. Some of the language used by Christians, however, suggests that the recent revelation of human wickedness had not really been grasped.[34]

In his autobiography, Dean Matthews looked back at the idealism of those early post-war years and wrote with deep feeling:

> In one respect I shared in the illusions of my companions. In those days, we felt no anxiety about world war. We had fought the war to end war and the League of Nations was the guardian of Peace. We thought, or at least I thought, that the League of Nations was the triumphant creation of Liberal Christian idealism . . . for a Christian it was a plain duty to support the League, because it was consonant with the prayer 'Thy Kingdom come on earth'. Even now, with 'all

passion spent', I am unable to write on the failure of this faith and hope without bitter pain and resentment.[35]

Pressures for various types of reform in the Church of England had been greatly strengthened by the war as part of the general desire for a renewed Church representing all classes to serve the post-war world, and as an earnest of the repentance and hope proclaimed by the National Mission. Early in 1918, Neville Talbot wrote to his father, then Bishop of Winchester, that the chaplains had no wish to return to the old pattern of being able to discuss problems without any real power to act:

> So, before we come back, make a fundamental change. Act on the Life and Liberty Appeal. I feel that the Church is kind of ditched like an old vehicle without wheels. So, put wheels on the bus.[36]

For some years the pressure for the granting of more self-government to the Church of England had been growing. In 1895 the Church Reform League was founded, with Gore, Scott Holland, and Bishop Talbot as members. In 1903 the Representative Church Council was created, to combine the four houses of the Convocations and the two houses of laymen, into three houses of bishops, clergy and laymen. In June 1913 some church peers wrote to the Archbishop to urge that only devolution would solve the severe problem of getting ecclesiastical legislation through the crowded parliamentary timetable. In the summer of 1916 the Archbishops' Committee on Church and State, under the chairmanship of Lord Selborne, proposed a pattern of devolution similar to that established by the Enabling Act of 1919. The National Mission and its Committees of Inquiry had encouraged the Church to be more self-critical. The Fourth Committee believed that the Church should be granted more self-government. All these various factors provided the impetus which created the Life and Liberty Movement.

Temple wrote to the Archbishop of Canterbury, referring to friends like Dick Sheppard: 'The War and the Mission have brought them to boiling point. It is a psychological necessity that they should explode.'[37] Temple told the inaugural meeting of the Life and Liberty Movement in July 1917: 'We demand liberty for the Church of England because we believe that liberty is essential to fullness of life.'[38] He and his friends believed that they had the chaplains and members of the forces behind them. When Davidson seemed over-cautious, the leaders of Life and Liberty became impatient. In December 1917, its Council issued a long letter protesting that many churchmen in the forces were almost in despair. In one area of national life after another, reforms were being pressed forward; could church reforms really wait until peace came? Davidson, in a speech to the R.C.C. in February 1919, agreed that the work of the Church was hampered, but believed Parliament to be too busy at the moment, and warned the more enthusiastic supporters that more life and liberty (which he also desired) would not come 'by the waving of a wand or by the mere adoption of a scheme'.[39] The R.C.C. adopted the constitution of the new Church Assembly and the provisions of the Enabling Bill almost without disagreement. But it voted for a Baptismal rather than a Confirmation franchise. Bishop Gore felt he had been defeated on a crucial question and decided to resign the see of Oxford. Gore believed that a Baptismal franchise had been adopted in order to maintain the concept of the 'national church', whereas he conceived the Church as a more distinctive eucharistic community. Though he was often depressed by the Church of England, he valued it, not because it claimed to be the national church (he believed that establishment was 'inconsistent with the actual state of beliefs in the nation' and hampered religion) but because it stood for a reformed Catholicism.[40] He wrote to the Archbishop (who deeply regretted Gore's decision) that he felt also that he could better 'serve the causes of reconstruction' by thinking, study, writing, and preaching than by continuing as a diocesan bishop.[41] Life and Liberty had accepted Baptismal franchise partly because it believed that it would give the working classes more chance of representation in the Church's government, and partly because a Confirmation franchise would have alienated many broad churchmen whose support was needed.

From exactly the opposite standpoint to that of Gore, Henson disagreed sharply with the whole Life and Liberty movement, which he caricatured as 'Gore's crowd'. He opposed the Enabling Bill (and those whom he called 'the "Life and Liberty" dervishes') in every possible way, not least by ten letters he wrote to *The Times* in 1919. He believed that with the passing of the Bill the ideal of religious comprehension which had appealed to Englishmen for four centuries had passed away. Whereas previously every baptized Englishman was *ipso facto* a member of 'the National Church', after the Enabling Act came into force only those who had signed the new electoral roll forms would be so reckoned.[42] Bishop Knox, Canon Streeter, and some Free Churchmen also opposed the Bill, as did *The Times*. The socialist sympathies of the Life and Liberty movement alienated some conservative churchmen. But Percy Dearmer, then working in India, wrote in February 1918 that Life and Liberty did not go far enough. The State connection kept the clergy from turning the church into a sect. No movement of church reform would be blessed by God unless it began 'by repudiating the worldliness of the Church':

> O! and I do love the C. of E. so much. She *might* be what no other church in Christendom is. I believe she could even still be, if she came right off her pedestal – down from her thrones and palaces, and laid her jewels at the feet of the poor.[43]

When the Central Church Fund was created, organized largely by businessmen, it appealed to investors in these terms:

> The Church of England Central Fund is the most profitable investment that the nation through its citizens – whether Churchmen or not – can make. The dividends will be paid in the cure of social mischiefs, the growth of better and more efficient citizenship, the birth of better ideals, the stabilization of the social order.[44]

Commonwealth in March 1919 strongly criticized the phrasing of the appeal: this kind of statement would undo all the good work of chaplains who had led the men to think that the Church shared their aspirations; but now they read an appeal to the rich to support the Church as 'the bulwark of the existing social order'. It also reprinted a protest from the Church Socialist League: the appeal made the Church appear to be 'the obedient watchdog of the bourgeoisie'.

In his speech in the Lords in June 1919, Archbishop Davidson asked that the Enabling Bill should be passed 'to enable the Church of England to do its work properly'; he considered its opponents were unnecessarily alarmist; but he could not share all the hopes of its supporters.[45] However, when the Bill was passed, the vision of a more untrammelled Church, both more supernatural and more in touch with ordinary people and their concerns, began to seem almost as far away as ever. Temple had said that there would have been no Life and Liberty movement without Dick Sheppard; yet one of its most obvious products, the Church Assembly, infuriated Dick Sheppard; his feelings about it propelled him towards an increasing distrust of institutional religion. He was bitterly disappointed by the actual results of all the enthusiasm and idealism which had gone into the movement.[46] In the event, Davidson's temperate estimate of the benefits of the Act was proved accurate. The issues raised by the war were more theological and ethical than administrative, though clearly a reform of the government of the Church of England was long overdue. The Act was a necessary step along the way as the Church began to search for the right relationship with an increasingly secular and pluralist society. The rejection of the 1927 and 1928 Prayer Books in Parliament were bitter reminders to many churchmen that an erastian view of the Church was widely held, and that it could still be enforced. Equally the strong opposition to Welsh Disestablishment (passed in 1914, effected in 1920) indicated the reluctance of many Anglicans to come to terms with the religious pluralism which had been growing for a century. The aims of Life and Liberty were wider than the achievement of a degree of self-government for the Church. But once the Act was through, the movement was unable to continue its initial impetus. In 1920 William Temple accepted the see of Manchester, and soon he was preoccupied with the preliminary work of C.O.P.E.C. and with the duties of his episcopal office.

The unrest among chaplains was an important factor in the movement of opinion which led to the Enabling Act. At the front they discovered how pastorally ineffective the Church of England was: 'we are incapable of acting corporately. No rules are binding, and each member interprets them in his own way. . . . We are securely founded on the rock of Individualism, and upon that rock we are always splitting.'[47] Walter Carey and Harry Blackburne, both chaplains, were among the speakers at the inaugural meeting of Life and Liberty on 16 July. On 20 June *The Times* had published a letter from the Council of Life and Liberty which made its aims public for the first time. In response, the chaplains of the Seventh Division wrote to Temple to pledge their support:

> No matter what type or party we belonged to of old, we are now all haunted by the fear that the Home Church cannot see, and will not rise up to meet, the needs which have shocked each of us on entering, as minister of Christ, this huge intermingling of all sorts and conditions of our countrymen.[48]

The chaplains had developed their own form of 'We and They' which was common at the front, and felt pessimistic about the likelihood of speedy reform. Some published a manifesto that they would not go back to work in the parishes until certain conditions were fulfilled. Some wanted to equalize all stipends, others proposed squads of mobile missioners, others believed that some of the clergy should take up industrial work.

One chaplain who saw more deeply than most was Oswin Creighton. His mother was a member of the founding group of Life and Liberty. Oswin Creighton was more in touch with the central theological and pastoral realities revealed by the war than was Temple, who, unlike Creighton, had not known (and never knew) what it was to be stripped of theological and ecclesiastical certainties.[49] Creighton wrote to a sister in August 1917 (he had been telling her that it was as though they had all been 'violently seasick' and did not know where to find the things that would now stand the test):

> Well, how are we going to fill these empty stomachs with the food that will really satisfy? The Creeds, ministry of women, Prayer Book reform, *Life and Liberty*, the whole caboodle have all gone overboard as far as we are concerned. We don't really care about any of them. 'Well, you are a beastly, destructive, negative lot.' Granted. 'You don't care about anything.' No; false, quite false. We are sick – this is my point – sick to death of *abstractions*. We are learning that it is only human beings that count, and that if the Christian religion is to prosper on earth, it can *only* be by Christians understanding and serving their fellow-men. Discussions, conferences, inquiries, etc., simply do not interest or move us. But if a soldier hears the vicar has been looking after his wife and children in his absence – if the wife hears from the chaplain when her husband is killed – if there is any touch of human friendship and understanding, then we get near the foundation of all things, the heart of man.[50]

When a few months later he answered a memorandum from Life and Liberty he wrote to his mother:

> If the Church is to be self-governed, I do not want the governors to be the ecclesiastically minded, or necessarily the kind of people who are capable of thinking out things. . . . What can [the Kingdom] mean to the ordinary unthinking man?[51]

In April 1918, he had spent one afternoon and evening in the drenching rain helping to load up the ambulances with the wounded:

> Then I get a memorandum from *Life and Liberty* asking what the men are thinking about the self-government of the Church. People

meet in committees and conferences in London and the Provinces, and discuss these things, and wonder we do not thrill with excitement over their audacious proposals. They get wildly excited because they have heard of a brothel kept for soldiers in some small place, and they think that by shutting it they will save our pure-minded young men from temptation.[52]

After the war, some of the chaplains, not least a number of those who had been most vocal in urging widespread reform in the Church, were soon occupying positions of influence in it. Neville Talbot became Bishop of Pretoria in 1920, Walter Carey Bishop of Bloemfontein in 1921, Edward Woods Bishop of Croydon 1930–37, then Bishop of Lichfield. Fr Keble Talbot was Superior of the Community of the Resurrection from 1922 to 1940. B. K. Cunningham became Principal of Westcott House in 1919. F. R. Barry became Vicar of St Mary's Oxford in 1927 and Bishop of Southwell in 1941. Mervyn Haigh became Bishop of Coventry in 1931 and Bishop of Winchester in 1942. William Wand became Archbishop of Brisbane in 1934, Bishop of Bath and Wells in 1943, and Bishop of London in 1945. Kenneth Kirk was Regius Professor of Moral and Pastoral Theology at Oxford from 1933 to 1937 when he became Bishop of Oxford. Harry Blackburne was Dean of Bristol from 1934 to 1951. Eric Milner-White was Dean of King's College, Cambridge, 1918–1941, then Dean of York. Studdert Kennedy became Messenger (i.e. chief missioner) of the Industrial Christian Fellowship in 1922. Tubby Clayton became the Leader of Toc H. Charles Raven became a Canon of Liverpool Cathedral in 1924, and Regius Professor of Divinity at Cambridge in 1932.

When Canon Peter Green published *The Town Parson* in 1919, he dedicated it:

> To all those who
> having served their King and Country
> in the Great War
> desire now to serve the King of Kings
> in the Ministry of His Church
> and to the
> Memory of the Fallen

In the post-war period, the shortage of clergy became acute. In 1914, 610 deacons were ordained in the Church of England. In 1919 only 161 were ordained. Since then, the number ordained in any one year has never, except in 1962–3, exceeded the 1914 total, despite the considerable increase of population. In 1976 only 281 were ordained to the stipendiary ministry. Whereas in 1911 there was one clergyman for every 1,457 of the population, by 1951 the proportion had dropped to 1:2,111. The average age of the clergy increased considerably during the whole period.

When Hensley Henson became Bishop of Durham in 1920 he concluded that two major problems confronted him: the shortage of clergy and the relations of Church to Labour. He was startled by the poor quality of candidates, due partly to the war and partly to the policy of his predecessor, Handley Moule. Henson caused something of a sensation by declaring that he would normally require that candidates should be 'sound in wind and limb', for Moule out of the kindness of his heart had ordained a number who were physically handicapped. When Henson was Dean he had remarked to Bishop Moule at an ordination: 'Bishop, when you come here for an Ordination, the Cathedral acquires the aspect of the Pool of Bethesda.'[53]

During the war, the criticisms which were levelled against the Church, its parochial clergy and chaplains, often included criticism of the standards, length and content of ordination training. It was urged that a greater number of working-class ordinands must be secured both by new methods of training and by financial assistance to those in need. In the spring of 1916, the Archbishop of Canterbury began to consider the question of a special call to the ministry for those in the forces. In February 1918, he informed Convocation of his assurance to candidates in the forces through the Chaplain-General that financial difficulties would be no bar to ordination. After the war, government grants met a large proportion of the cost of the training of ex-service candidates, but the Church itself spent in addition £378,000 on the training of the 1,039 candidates from the services. Nugent Hicks, later Bishop of Lincoln, was Secretary of the Service Candidates' Committee. By November 1918, over 2,700 names of service candidates had been sent to Hicks by the Chaplains' Department.[54] Tubby Clayton had kept a roll at Poperinghe. The pledge which candidates signed at Poperinghe stated: 'If God decides to bring me through this war, I vow to take it as a hint from Him that I shall help and serve the Church in future throughout the life that He gives back to me.'[55] When Edward Woods interviewed candidates, he discovered that many felt that they had been spared for a special purpose.

In France a School of Instruction for candidates, numbering 250 men, was established shortly after the Armistice at Le Touquet, under

F. R. Barry. Archbishop Davidson visited the School, reiterated the pledge of financial assistance and told the men that they were called to help in laying foundations on the 'ruins of a broken civilisation'.[56] A similar school for officers was established under Fr Keble Talbot. But about half of the candidates had not reached the required educational standards, so a 'Test School' was needed. Tubby Clayton discovered that the only place immediately available was the prison at Knutsford, Cheshire. The prison was emptied of its German prisoners – it had previously housed conscientious objectors – and in six weeks it was prepared for the 150-odd men who arrived for the first term in March 1919. When Barry arrived in February to take up his duties, he found the building 'damp, filthy and forbidding – desolate galleries of dismal cells, desperately unlighted and unfurnished. Everything was beastly and repulsive.'[57] The beds did not come until the last minute; each person as he arrived at the station had to carry his own from the goods yard. At the first Evensong they sang Psalm 126:

> When the Lord turned again the captivity of Sion:
>   then were we like unto them that dream.
> Then was our mouth filled with laughter:
>   and our tongue with joy.

Here, for three years, a total of 675 men (of whom 435 were eventually ordained) were trained by an outstanding group with F. R. Barry as Principal and Mervyn Haigh, Tubby Clayton, and Robert Moberly among the staff, which also included some distinguished laymen. All types of men, and of churchmanship, had to be welded into one community. The Sunday Eucharist at 9.0 a.m., sung to Merbecke, foreshadowed the style of the Parish Communion which has gradually over the last fifty years become the main service of most parishes.

Though there were difficulties – some men found it very difficult to settle to study after service life, others suffered from psychological problems caused by the war – it was an exhilarating time. (After the initial rush of service candidates had been trained, the school moved to a large house near by; later its work was transferred to Hawarden.) F. R. Barry recalls the early days:

> It seemed altogether too wonderful to be true. The horror was over, a brighter dawn was breaking like the sun on the lilies in the Easter Garden. Surely a new world lay before us and a new pattern of brotherhood in freedom sealed by all that agony and sacrifice. Any

further war seemed unthinkable. An age – almost a Messianic age – of creative reconstruction beckoned us. 'He that sitteth upon the throne saith, Behold I make all things new.' No text was more frequently on our lips than that.[58]

Mervyn Haigh also wrote of the experience many years later:

It was no false dawn; mankind was then given a fresh chance and a finer morning could have followed had the chance been taken. . . . It is difficult for me not to become lyrical when I speak of the life which we were given to share at 'K' . . . I had part in such a manifestation, such a living embodiment, of the Fellowship of the Spirit, as I had never had part in before nor have I ever quite had part in since to the same extent. . . . All those at 'K' had been delivered in varying degrees from the same fiery furnace, held more or less the same beliefs, had before their eyes the same goal of Christian ministry, were living together and felt the desperate need of mankind for what the Gospel alone offered. We had been gathered out of the heart of a great tragedy into the heart of a great opportunity.[59]

The chaplains, said Barry, had discovered the presence of Christ 'in some of the most unlikely situations . . . and wonderful revelations of Christian quality sometimes in men who never came near their services and perhaps would not have described themselves as Christians'. How were they to relate all this to the organized Church? Was the Church wide enough in its outreach and theology to comprehend such 'diffused Christianity'?[60] But B. K. Cunningham, despite his wartime experiences, found ex-Knutsford men a trial when they arrived at Westcott House. He preferred men from the public schools. At Farnham before the war they had all dined every night in 'boiled shirts'.[61] Mervyn Haigh at Knutsford became involved in two characteristic products of the post-war Church. The first was *Songs of Praise*, which Haigh believed expressed some of the insights in theology which came out of the war. It became *the* hymn book for parishes trying to be modern and to reach from the inner circle to the outer fringes. Haigh also helped to produce the 'Grey Book' (1923) with F. R. Barry, Leslie Hunter, F. W. Dwelly, and Percy Dearmer. William Temple wrote the preface. It had originated in the Life and Liberty movement, and was the liberal attempt at Prayer Book revision.

The new intake of men from Knutsford saved the parochial system from a severe crisis. Barry believed that from that time there developed a greater theological realism, 'a wider vision of Christianity in its bearing on secular affairs'. The new system of church grants for training was 'the beginning of the end of a class-ministry in the Church of England'.[62] This latter claim is only partially true; though the creation of a system of grants was a great step forward, the Paul Report in 1964 demonstrated the continuing dominance of the public schools and Oxbridge in recruitment for the ministry.[63] Before the war ended, some chaplains suggested the revival of minor orders for men who wished to minister but were not suitable for the priesthood. In 1921, a Canterbury Convocation Committee proposed that men should be ordained to a permanent diaconate, while being employed in secular occupations. But neither proposal was put into effect.[64] Prefaces in *Crockford's Clerical Directory* in the 'twenties spoke with alarm about the clergy shortage. In 1924 the Editor pointed out that nearly all the service candidates had by now been ordained, and therefore government grants were also ending. The average number of ordinations for the last six years had been 287, while the average loss by death and retirement each year was about 700.[65] But the ex-service candidate brought into the ministry an experience of life very different from that of the pre-war ordinand, who usually came straight from school and university, unaware of the realities of working-class life until parish work forced them upon his attention.

'It is difficult for people who no longer believe in "a war to end war" to realise the hopes that people cherished of a new heaven and a new earth after the war of 1914–1918' wrote Guy Rogers.[66] Donald Hankey had eloquently expressed such a vision in 1916, in Chapter II of *A Student in Arms*, using language reminiscent of Old Testament prophecy: 'In those days there shall be no more petty strife between class and class, for all shall have learnt that they are one nation, and that they must seek the nation's good before their own.' But he feared that the lessons of the war would be forgotten and that people would simply slip back into the old grooves.[67] In 1918, when morale was low, Bishop Gwynne proposed to Haig that a card should be drawn up and distributed to the troops to state the objective of the war. It read:

Better homes where the children could grow up healthy and strong; better education which gave a child full opportunity for developing the faculties implanted in him by God; a fair deal for labour, giving to the worker a fuller life; justice for women and a resolute stand against prostitution; a discipline which keeps a man at his best and maintains holy matrimony as the ideal of family life.

Ironically, most of the cards were captured before distribution by the Germans when they broke through in March.[68] In 1923, Tom Pym, by then Head of Cambridge House, said in an Armistice Day sermon in the Abbey that in 1915 he had tended a dying soldier who asked whether his suffering was going to do any good. 'I pledged him my own word and told him I was sure that those for whom he died would try to make the world a better place.'[69] In the autumn of 1917 Archbishop Lang assured restive chaplains that the Church would ensure that post-war problems were tackled. As a result the Church Council on War Problems met at Lambeth on 26–27 April 1918; it had more than 100 members, with clerical and lay representatives from all the dioceses and some nominees including the Bishop of London and the Chaplain-General. Archbishop Davidson, who presided, declared that the Church must concentrate not merely on reconstruction but on a 'new birth'. He regretted the almost total absence of representatives from the Labour movement at the conference, 'as in every large church gathering'. The Bishop of London led off a discussion on 'Moral Problems' with a denunciation of lust, venereal disease, and the way in which both were linked with alcohol; a 'crusade' must be mounted against contraceptives. Bishop Taylor Smith also spoke about the need for purity. Mrs Creighton urged clergy and parents to inquire whether bridegrooms were free from venereal disease.[70]

One speaker pointed out that there was also such a thing as commercial immorality. Another discussion focused on the pastoral opportunities facing the Church following demobilization. Seventy per cent of soldiers were alienated from Christianity, and therefore, so far as religion was concerned, they were 'in precisely the same condition as they were in when they went out'. On the second day the conference discussed social reconstruction: wages, housing, and the need for worker participation; there should be a council for social questions in each diocese. The right deployment of returning chaplains was also raised. The Bishop of Winchester urged the Church to co-operate with societies like Y.M.C.A. (which was determined not to become a new sect), S.C.M., C.E.M.S. and the Church Army.[71] Early in 1918, Cardinal Bourne's Pastoral Letter was devoted to the 'New Order' of society which must be created when the war was over. But Frank Richards and George Coppard, as ex-private soldiers, recalled in their memoirs the bitter contrast they felt between unemployed ex-servicemen begging on the streets and the huge sums granted to high-ranking officers, between the promises made by politicians and what actually happened.

Various groups made their contribution to post-war Christian social thinking. Social concern in the S.C.M. had been greatly stimulated by the Matlock Conference (1909) of which Temple was chairman; one result was the formation of the Collegium group. Its book, *Competition* (1917), was a plea for a more collectivist society. During the war, members of the S.C.M. deepened their commitment to the social gospel of a more corporate society, a new awareness of the role of women, a new concern for education and the arts. Many spoke eagerly of a post-war social revolution.[72] Gore regarded the war as indicating the collapse of the old style of competitive society. He welcomed the new emphasis on the primacy of corporate over individual interest, and in his retirement tried to play a leading part in promoting Christian social thought and action along these lines. R. H. Tawney in *The Acquisitive Society* (1921) argued for the organization of industry as a service to the community. His *Religion and the Rise of Capitalism* (1926) was dedicated to Gore. It sought to give Christian socialism a convincing historical perspective. Both books had a wide influence, not least on William Temple. Throughout the war *Challenge* and *Commonwealth* reiterated the need for a reconciliation between the Church of England and the Labour movement. E. A. Burroughs, whose letters to *The Times* in the early part of 1915 had given him the status of a wartime prophet, in 1915 founded 'The League of the Spiritual War' for servicemen. Scott Holland was chairman. The members, eventually numbering 5,000, reaffirmed their baptismal promises, and pledged themselves, if their lives were spared, to 'take an active part in the Spiritual War which lies ahead of us'. But Burroughs's sheltered background, his upper-class mentality, and his lack of *rapport* with ordinary people, disabled him from comprehending many of the features of the post-war world, not least the power of economic forces to mould men's lives. The League fizzled out in 1920. 'No fresh inspiration came to him' in the post-war period, wrote his biographer.[73]

Christian socialists of Conrad Noel's persuasion regarded much of the talk of Christian reconstruction as a deception aimed at deferring the radical upheaval of society that was needed. 'Reconstruction without revolution is evil' he told the midsummer festival at Thaxted in 1917. Some priests were on the platform at the huge rally organized that

year in the Albert Hall to celebrate the Russian Revolution. George
Lansbury was in the chair. Clara Butt led the audience in the hymn
'Give peace to us in our time, O Lord', concluding:

> Through the thick darkness Thy Kingdom is hastening;
> Thou wilt give peace in our time, O Lord!

On the Sunday after the Armistice, Conrad Noel preached in the
Congregational Chapel at Thaxted that unless the Empires of the world
were brought down, all the promises of a better world would remain
unfulfilled, and evil men would restore the pre-war world with all its
poverty and bitter conflicts.[74] None the less, he enjoyed dining off gold
plate at the home of Lady Warwick, his socialist patron, and Edward
VII's former mistress. When he stayed there, he breakfasted 'in a
luxurious canopied bed with logs blazing on an open hearth, and then
slippers and dressing gown provided, and a large desk with blotting-
paper and my typewriter and every inducement to work under the most
comfortable conditions', he continued his writing of the life of Jesus 'the
revolutionary'.[75]

Co-operation rather than competition was to be the basis of society,
declared the Fifth Committee, the Lambeth Conference of 1920, and
other Christian groups. The task of spreading this message was given
by the Church of England to the Industrial. Christian Fellowship
created in 1919 out of the Navvy Mission and the C.S.U. Studdert
Kennedy was its chief missioner. Though not a trained social thinker, he
brought great eloquence and passion to his work. His wartime fame
ensured an entrance into the hearts of many working men. 'That chap
must have been on the dole or he could never talk like that' was one
comment. He was now moving towards pacifism. The titles of two of his
post-war books, *Lies* (1919) and *Food for the Fed-up* (1921), reflected
his mood. He shared the doubts of the doubters too keenly to be able to
preach a glib gospel. In his last article for the I.C.F. journal he wrote:

> Every man, whether Christian or not, must sooner or later stand in
> the last ditch face to face with the final doubt. I know that last ditch
> well. I have stood in it many a time; and I know that before I die I
> shall stand there again – and again.

He believed that a moralized capitalism was preferable to socialism, and
was deeply suspicious of any reformism which neglected to take
account of man's need for redemption. Another sign of the new level of
social concern in the Church of England was the creation in 1923 of a

permanent Social and Industrial Committee of the Church Assembly.[76] Winnington-Ingram argued that social reform was necessary to avoid in England what had happened to the Church in Russia.[77]

Some Catholics in the Church of England continued to preach and practise the social and political implications of their sacramental doctrines. In 1923, Bishop Frank Weston made his famous challenge to the Anglo-Catholic Congress: it was 'folly' and 'madness' to look for Jesus in the reserved sacrament without looking for him in the slum, in the poor, the oppressed and the despairing.[78] This speech inspired the establishment of the Anglo-Catholic Summer School of Sociology which began meeting in 1925; despite its title, it was open to all schools of thought. When Fr Basil Jellicoe (founder of the St Pancras House Improvement Society) helped at St Martin-in-the-Fields, a high church critic asked him 'How can you go to a church where the Blessed Sacrament is not reserved?' Fr Jellicoe replied: 'Because the crypt is reserved for Christ's poor.'[79] Some Catholics were teaching that variety of the modes of Christ's presence which many had also discovered in the trenches.

The Church of England was the main force behind the ecumenical conference C.O.P.E.C. (Conference on Christian Politics, Economics and Citizenship), first mooted in 1919 by the Collegium group. Temple, Gore, Raven, and Tawney played a leading part in the preparations, which started in 1921 with the appointment of twelve commissions on a wide variety of social questions. It culminated in a conference of 1,500 delegates in Birmingham under Temple's chairmanship in 1924. Its social thinking followed the general lines of recent Anglican thinking. Though Davidson found a reason for not attending, and Henson scornfully called it 'Christian Socialism in its latest phase',[80] the delegates confirmed and deepened the commitment of many within the Churches to a social and political application of Christianity, though there were differences of emphasis. The Commission on Christianity and War was divided between pacifists and non-pacifists, but the Conference united in condemning war as 'contrary to the spirit and teaching of Jesus Christ' (Resolution 1). Resolution 3 asked the Churches to refuse to support a war waged before, or in defiance of, arbitration. Resolution 7 stated:

That the Churches should hold these principles, not only in times of peace, when their practical denial is not threatened, but also, when war is imminent, they should dare to take an independent stand for righteousness and peace, even if the Press and public opinion be at the time against them.[81]

The new Christian internationalism created by those who, reacting to the war, combined the new social concern with the new ecumenical vision, was also evident at the Universal Christian Conference on Life and Work held in Stockholm in 1925. Its message stated:

> The sins and sorrows, the struggles and losses of the Great War and since, have compelled the Christian Churches to recognize, humbly and with shame, that 'the world is too strong for a divided church'.[82]

G. K. A. Bell was one of several Anglicans who took a prominent part. A sharp division soon became apparent between those who, like Bishop Theodore Woods, spoke about building the Kingdom of God on earth and took an optimistic view of the prospects for peace, and those (particularly from the continent) who criticized false optimism about the brotherhood of man, and the idea that it was possible for the Kingdom of God to be created on earth. One German delegate reiterated Luther's doctrine of the two kingdoms: 'in the present state of the League we cannot find religious power or any communion with the Kingdom of God'.[83] Bell pointed out that 'the rank and file of the churches, taken as a whole, are hardly alive to the international character and obligations of the Christian religion'.[84]

The Churches served the post-war world well by promoting a high ideal of peace and support for the League (called 'that Christian movement' by Lord Parmoor at C.O.P.E.C.).[85] They insisted that there were higher loyalties than those merely to the nation; Harold Buxton said at Stockholm, 'a church which is only *national* is a contradiction in terms'.[86] Lambeth 1930 and Stockholm grasped earlier than most the growing problem of what was called at Stockhom 'the rising tide of indignation and resentment among all the coloured races against the white'.[87] But in some of their utterances the Churches encouraged men to believe that the war had made any future war almost unthinkable, that it was an untypical activity for modern man,[88] and that the new ecumenical movement was a more powerful barrier to war than it really was. In the laudable desire to put past enmities behind them, Christians tended to underestimate the irrationalities and complexities of human nature.[89]

Bishop Theodore Woods in many ways typified the new, more politically committed, style of leadership which some bishops exercised in the period of post-war reconstruction. In May 1917 he moved a resolution in Convocation that the Church should carefully consider its contribution to preparations for peace. In February 1918 he reiterated his call for a new fellowship in industry, and strongly supported railway nationalization. A year later, against a background of strikes and unemployment, he called on employers to give workers a greater share in management, and on the government to convene an industrial peace conference. In March 1919 he urged in *The Times* the nationalization of mines and railways; it was 'simply the projection into the paths of peace of the spirit which captured our industries, and still more our armies, in war-time, when no man thought of personal profit, but all of the common weal'. In September he visited the T.U.C. in Glasgow in preparation for his presidential address to the Church Congress in October.[90] In 1917, Archbishop Lang, in a speech in the Lords, spoke about post-war issues to be tackled, including the unequal distribution of the rewards of industry and the dehumanizing way in which industry was organized; labour should share in management and profits. C. F. Garbett (who was to become Bishop of Southwark in 1919) called, in Convocation in May 1918, for a national minimum wage and for state provision against unemployment; he was vigorously supported by Temple.[91] Led by Garbett, the Convocations and Church Assembly frequently debated problems of housing and unemployment. The work of two priests – Basil Jellicoe through the St Pancras House Improvement Society, founded in 1924, and Charles Jenkinson through the Leeds city council in the 'thirties – showed what could be achieved by determined Christian social action.[92] After the war, some Anglican leaders attempted to intervene in industrial disputes in a manner which suggested more sympathy for the working class than had been shown in some pre-war interventions. In 1919 and 1921, Archbishop Davidson offered to mediate in the railway and coal strikes. Bishops Kempthorne, E. S. Talbot, and Garbett were highly critical of the Government during the Miners' strike in 1921. When, during the General Strike of 1926, Davidson addressed an appeal from the Churches to the Government, the T.U.C., and the employers, both the B.B.C. and the official *British Gazette* refused to publish it. The continuing efforts at mediation by 'The Standing Conference of the Christian Churches on the Coal Dispute' (which included Gore, Temple, Woods, other bishops, and Free Churchmen) aroused great hostility in government and other circles. The adoption of a moderate type of Christian socialism by influential Anglican leaders also angered politically conservative churchmen such as Henson, Headlam, and Inge.[93] In 1923, Davidson contemplated resignation because he wondered how far he could support the current social interpretation of Christianity.[94]

But not all churchmen reacted to the war by siding either with some kind of Christian socialist programme or with the conservative opposition to it. Percy Dearmer, once the Catholic socialist vicar of St Mary's, Primrose Hill, author of *The Parson's Handbook* (1899) and editor of the Anglo-Catholic *English Hymnal* (1906), was now editor of the liberal *Songs of Praise*. A friend wrote:

> After the cataclysm of the War, I have the impression that he more and more felt that there was no cut and dried programme adequate to the needs of humanity, no party that had more than a particle of the truth, no creed that did not require to be tested by the full fire of doubt, experiment and increasing knowledge.[95]

His books, *The Sin Obsession* (1927), *The Truth about Fasting* (1928), and *The Legend of Hell* (1929), were severely critical of Catholic orthodoxy, and in large measure arose out of questions raised by soldiers when he worked for the Y.M.C.A With Maude Royden, he established the interdenominational Guildhouse in 1920 for discussion and worship, though no morning services were held to avoid competing with the parish churches. It was deliberately self-governing. After a period in Kensington Town Hall, a permanent building was secured in Eccleston Square. Royden and Dearmer explained their plans in a statement: 'Our feeling is that the Church of England, like other Churches in the country, is at present appealing to that minority of English people who go to church on Sunday – a minority which appears to be decreasing.' They believed that the Church of England ought to make an effort to appeal to a wider public, especially students and younger people, who were estranged from the Churches, and who were at home neither in church nor with the Prayer Book. They proposed the creation of 'free centres' in every large city for experimental worship, addresses, and discussion. Such centres would create a deeper Christian fellowship, would make more use of the laity (especially the ministry of women) and would further Prayer Book revision by enabling proposed changes to be tried out in public. The resources of music and the arts would be fully employed. Free Church men and women would be invited to participate fully. 'As it happens, the Church of England has made us both something in the way of free lances. . . . Let her then use our experiments and our experience if she will.'[96] The Bishop of Kensington, Fr Bull, Mrs Creighton, Hewlett Johnson, George Lansbury, Tissington Tatlow, Dick Sheppard, Scott Lidgett, Cecil Sharp, Martin Shaw, Neville Talbot, William Temple, and Edward Woods were among the sponsors. Dearmer's experiences during the war deeply influenced him in this experiment, which tried to put into practice many of the convictions expressed by chaplains. The names of the sponsors indicate how greatly the project appealed to those who were most aware of the challenges of the war to traditional church divisions, theology, clericalized church government, pastoral methods, roles of women, and worship.

In 1923, Bishop David of Liverpool was deeply impressed by the 'Order of Solemn Ceremonial and Service' drawn up by F. W. Dwelly, Vicar of Emmanuel, Southport, for the dedication of the town war memorials. This led him to appoint Dwelly to draw up the form for the consecration of the new Liverpool Cathedral in July 1924. In 1925, Dwelly was appointed a Provisional Canon and in 1931 became Dean. In 1926, Dearmer visited Raven, who in 1924 had also been appointed a Provisional Canon, and was consulted by Dwelly about dress and ceremonial. Dearmer worked closely with Dwelly over *Songs of Praise*, which was used in the new Cathedral before its publication. Liverpool Cathedral became for many a symbol of the new liberal forward movement in the Church of England, though architecturally it was the final great expression of Victorian Gothic, and its physical liturgical arrangements owed more to Anglo-Catholicism than to the liberal modernism which it came to represent. Gore, when visiting the Cathedral, inspected the bookstall, and growled about the 'rotten' books on sale; 'I wonder what is going to be the end of this American religion?' he asked.[97] The ceremonial was original and splendid, and crowds (especially the young) travelled from all over Merseyside to hear Dwelly, Raven, Maude Royden, and other preachers at the famous 8.30 p.m. Sunday service. Raven supervised the training of the newly ordained in the first systematic diocesan post-ordination training scheme in the Church of England.[98]

In England, as in other countries, the war inevitably created a new emphasis upon national identity. This is very evident in, for example, many passages in H. G. Wells's *Mr. Britling*. The principle of national self-determination, which was proclaimed in January 1918 in President Wilson's Fourteen Points and enshrined in the League of Nations, also encouraged national self-consciousness. Ernest Barker's *National*

Character and the Factors in Its Formation (1927) is characteristic of the quest by that generation for the sources of national identity. In the Church of England the new feeling for the international dimension of Christianity was counterbalanced by a new and deeper awareness of the richness of the specifically English religious tradition. Thus those who wished to 'catholicize' the Church of England along English lines largely succeeded, whereas those who tried to promote Latin Catholicism as the norm failed to win any large-scale support among Anglicans. Some of the most creative features of English church life and English music in the twentieth century have resulted from attempts to recover and restate characteristic elements of of the English heritage, many of which were intertwined with the English religious tradition. The war considerably increased the number of people, not least churchmen, who turned to this heritage for fresh inspiration. This heritage included, for example, St Thomas Becket, Julian of Norwich, medieval drama, John Bunyan, George Herbert, John Donne, the Little Gidding community, William Wordsworth, William Blake, F. D. Maurice, William Morris, and the traditional folk songs, rituals, and carols of England.

In 1919 T. S. Eliot published his influential essay, 'Tradition and the Individual Talent', in which he wrote:

> The poet must be very conscious of the main current, which does not at all flow invariably through the most distinguished reputations. . . . He must be aware that the mind of Europe – the mind of his own country – a mind which he learns in time to be much more important than his own private mind – is a mind which changes, and that this change is a development which abandons nothing *en route*. . . . What is to be insisted upon is that the poet must develop or procure the consciousness of the past and that he should continue to develop this consciousness throughout his career.[99]

George Bell, when Dean of Canterbury, pioneered the revival of plays in churches with Masefield's *The Coming of Christ* performed in the Cathedral in 1928. It was through Bell that in 1933 an invitation came to Eliot to write a pageant ('The Rock') for the London church building scheme, and *Murder in the Cathedral* for the Canterbury Festival of 1935. Vaughan Williams's specially commissioned *Te Deum* enriched the enthronement of Archbishop Lang at Canterbury in 1928. He and Martin Shaw were musical editors of *Songs of Praise* and of the *Oxford Book of Carols* (1928), both edited by Dearmer. Vaughan Williams's spiritual pilgrimage has a representative significance. Son of a priest, he ceased to be a practising Christian in his 'teens, but continued to draw deeply upon the specifically English Christian tradition in his music. The 'new' music and rituals at Thaxted were in fact just as deeply traditional and English as *The Oxford Book of Carols*. Before the war, Noel had been a part-time curate with Dearmer at Primrose Hill, where the 'English' ceremonial, vestments and music were first put into practice.[100] Cecil Sharp, the collector of English folk songs, and Gustav Holst, a disciple of William Morris, were friends both of Conrad Noel and Vaughan Williams. It was Cecil Sharp who, with Scott Holland, in 1905 suggested Vaughan Williams to Dearmer as Musical Editor for the *English Hymnal*. Sharp lectured in Dearmer's time at St Mary's. Thus the Catholic socialist movement in the Church of England was a very English phenomenon. Fr Groser, the politically radical East End priest, wove his own vestments in the William Morris tradition. The processions he organized against social injustice were often preceded by a crucifix, and sometimes included a statue of St Thomas Becket. (In 1949 he played Becket memorably in the film of *Murder in the Cathedral*: that it was the duty of the Church to defy the State on occasion was a consistent theme of his teaching and actions.) Conrad Noel dedicated a Chapel at Thaxted church to John Ball, the priest leader of the Peasants' Revolt of the 14th century.

Stephen Koss in *Nonconformity in British Politics* (1975) declares roundly – and echoes many other commentators:

> However much a commonplace, it is no exaggeration to say that war, when it came unexpectedly in August 1914, dealt a shattering blow to organised religion. The churches never recovered from the ordeal, either in terms of communicants or self-possession. Thereafter, men looked elsewhere, if anywhere, for their moral certainties. Yet we must remember that here, as in other social situations, wartime experiences only hastened and intensified trends that were already under way.[101]

This has much truth in it, yet it is oversimplified. David Martin points out that men, not least Christians, like to believe they are living on an inclined plane where the trends are all one way.[102] The thesis that during the last hundred years, say, English society has undergone a rapid, simple and uniform secularization is now widely criticized.[103] If some were alienated from the Church of England by its support of the war, others were attracted by its support of the League of Nations or by the growth of Anglican pacifism. If some through the war became disillusioned with the Church, others through Toc H, British Legion and Remembrance rituals were drawn into some sort of relationship with it. T. S. Eliot, C. S. Lewis and later C. E. M. Joad found their home in the Church of England because of its Catholic and conservative orthodoxy. Others were drawn in, or retained, through modernism by the new liberal Evangelicalism, or by the social gospel preached by Temple, Gore, Tawney (and later Cripps).

On the other hand, as David Edwards puts it,

> The humiliation of the Christian Church is the great fact which stands out, and it often seems that the only solid achievement by Christians in our age has been their acquisition of a spirit of penitent humility.[104]

Mandell Creighton could say in 1899, echoing Hooker, that 'Church and State are not contradictory things. Church and State are the nation looked at from different points of view'.[105] Bishop Gore fiercely criticized that mythology when he spoke in the debate on Welsh Disestablishment in 1913 about 'a piecemeal Disestablishment which is continually going on . . . and we are finding ourselves disestablished almost everywhere except in the lunatic asylums'.[106] Since then English society has become even more pluralist, and the pace of 'piecemeal disestablishment' has quickened. One result is that, compared with the beginning of the century, the bishops of today have far fewer connections with the landed gentry, the peerage or the ruling classes, but come to a far greater extent from clerical families: 'a shift from a situation where the episcopate was part of a broader social élite to one where it is a more narrowly defined ecclesiastical élite'.[107]

This period has also been characterized by what David Edwards terms 'the decline and fall of Christian dogmatism'. One factor responsible for eroding or even destroying attitudes of automatic deference to statements made by those in authority was the widespread disillusionment with established leaders, political, ecclesiastical and military, during and after the first war. If the official Report, *Doctrine in the Church of England* (in gestation from 1922 to 1938), dismayed conservatives by the plurality of its views, *Christian Believing* (1976), from the recent Doctrine Commission, is even more tentative and pluriform. In 1907, many Anglicans were deeply distressed by the legalizing of marriage to a deceased wife's sister, and strenuously opposed it as bringing the law of the State for the first time into direct conflict with the law of the Church. But in 1966, the Archbishops' Commission in *Putting Asunder* recognized the Church of England's new type of relationship with a more secular society, and proposed a root-and-branch reform of the divorce law, so ending the largely defensive policy with which for a century it had met proposed changes in the law on divorce.

Thus, such generalizations as those of Stephen Koss are not altogether adequate to the complexity of the evidence. In some ways the Church of England emerged from the first war greatly strengthened, in other directions it had been gravely weakened. Outwardly at the annual Armistice Day services, for example, it still appeared as the staunch Church of the nation. But in its heart it knew, or ought to have known, otherwise. The war had revealed again and again how much weaker was its hold upon the nation than it realized. (This realization was the main impetus behind the post-war programmes of church reform and renewal which we have surveyed in this chapter.) During the inter-war period the hold of the Church slackened further. Since the 1930s, fewer and fewer English people have thought it worth while to express whatever faith they possess in terms of either regular or minimal commitment to the Church of England; nor has the story been any more cheering for other Churches, though the erosion of Roman Catholic loyalty has been slower and longer delayed.[108] Consider but one set of statistics: between 1885 and 1928 the proportion of the population in England of the age of fifteen and over who were Easter Day communicants in the Church of England never fell below 84 per 1000, and indeed reached 98 per 1000 in 1911, and even in 1925 was 90 per 1000. But since the early 1930s there has been a steady decline: by 1939 the proportion had dropped to 73 per 1000, by 1958 to 63 per 1000, and by 1973 to 42 per 1000.[109] Though English society was to become much more pluralist and secular than the leaders of the programmes of church reform after the first war had ever envisaged, nevertheless Christian imagery continued to have a considerable, even astonishing resilience, despite the fact that orthodox beliefs inside and outside the Church continued to crumble. And whatever the Church did, it could never re-establish its old type of authority in the nation. During the first war Davidson was in constant touch with ministers of state; during the second, Churchill saw little of either Lang or Temple.[110]

Certainly there was no simple religious revival either during or after the first war; but equally neither was there a process of simple secularization. The typical religion of Englishmen was less and less expressed through the institutional Church. But however diluted its content, it owed something to the continuance of the loose association of large numbers of the population with the Church, as well as to the persistence of religious worship and education in the schools. As Edward Norman wryly put it, 'Thus the Church today, in terms of regular and committed support, is not dissimilar from what it was in the later years of the eighteenth century.'[111]

12

Remembrance

They shall grow not old, as we that are left grow old:
Age shall not weary them, nor the years condemn.
At the going down of the sun and in the morning
We will remember them.

Laurence Binyon's lines in his poem 'For the Fallen' were first published
as early as September 1914 in *The Times*, but they caught with
remarkable prescience what most people wanted to say about
Remembrance in the post-war period, and they have been regularly
used ever since at memorial services for the war dead.

In the ancient world, war memorials usually conveyed a different
attitude to war from those in twentieth-century England. The famous
Black Obelisk of the Assyrian king Shalmaneser III in the ninth century
B.C. depicts Jehu of Israel kneeling in submission and offering gifts. The
Standard of Ur depicts on the War panel a procession of fully armed
troops, and on the Peace panel a splendid royal celebration banquet. In
more modern times it was thought sufficient to commemorate wars
fought by professional armies by erecting monuments to commanding
officers or by placing cairns or crosses on battlefields. But wars fought
by citizen armies, theoretically, at any rate, motivated by conscience
and ideology, demanded a different type of memorial. It is said that the
first occasion that monuments were erected in every town and village
listing the names of all who had been killed from the locality, was after
the American Civil War. The Great War produced far more
monuments than any previous single event in history. The war
memorials of twentieth-century England were erected not to celebrate
the triumphs of war, but to mourn the dead, individually as well as
corporately, with sadness and pride. The dedication of innumerable
memorials filled the engagement books of the bishops immediately after
the end of the war. Henson had hoped in a wartime essay that the
churches would become the 'natural homes of religion' to those who
returned, because they would contain the regimental banners and the

names of the dead.[1] In a farewell letter to the diocese of Hereford he wrote in September 1920:

> I am persuaded that the Memorial Crosses, in the Churchyards, on the village greens, where the roads meet, will for many years to come cry eloquent but silent protest against all that divides and degrades village life.[2]

Soon every city, town, and village had its own memorial. In 1919, exhibitions of designs for memorials were held at the Victoria and Albert Museum and at the Royal Academy. *Crockford's* advertised sketches of memorial stained glass windows. By contrast, memorials to those who died in the Boer War are few; it is rare to find one either in a public place or in a parish church. But the memorials of the Great War are strikingly communal and prominent monuments, the central focus of some open space like Whitehall, or St Peter's Square, Manchester, or many a village green. The erection of these memorials was much influenced by the wayside crucifixes in France, which made such a deep impression upon English soldiers, though only a minority of the memorials in England included a crucifix. Many English memorials took the form of a cross (often with a sword affixed). In the centre of St Albans, each of the streets of the Abbey parish had its own stone memorial plaque fixed to a house wall. Each plaque records the names of those killed from that street under a crucifix – a permanent form of the temporary street shrines erected during the war in London and elsewhere. Each plaque was dedicated with an individual service conducted by the Dean with the choir, relatives and neighbours present. By contrast, the standard national memorial placed in every French school and institution contained no religious symbolism at all – merely national emblems surrounded by the four neutral words 'Sacrifice, Devoir, Liberté, Droit.' The union of the cross with the sword in English war memorials and in hymns like 'O valiant hearts' caused concern to some churchmen, particularly as the war receded. The growing number of internationalists criticized it as jingoistic, and others (especially Evangelicals) criticized it for obscuring the uniqueness of the sacrifice of Christ. In a sermon in January 1920, Bishop Moule criticized the opinion that the soldier was a saint who went to heaven cleansed by his own blood. Therefore, he said, when he dedicated war memorials, he emphasized that heaven was not a reward for suffering. But then his patriotism and tender heart came into conflict with his Evangelicalism, and he added: 'I do not mean that God does not care for the brave sacrifice our sons have made. They who enter that world, because Jesus died, find the Father and the Son attentive to every tear.' But he was apprehensive lest anything should obscure the need for individual salvation by faith in Christ.[3]

Apart from national and local memorials, particular groups wanted their own memorials. Not only did the railway companies arrange a special service for their own 19,000 dead in St Paul's in May 1919 (at which Bishop Woods of Peterborough preached in the presence of the King) but memorials also were erected in the station precincts of the main line termini. In June 1922, Field-Marshal Sir Henry Wilson unveiled a war memorial to the employees of the Great Eastern Railway at Liverpool Street station. Returning home, he was attacked by two I.R.A. men, and though he tried to defend himself with his sword, he was fatally wounded by their bullets. The impotence of the sword against the terrorist bullet was grimly prophetic. Public schools had lost large numbers of their former pupils. At Repton, the memorial contained 355 names. At King's College, Cambridge, a side chapel was transformed under the direction of Milner-White into a memorial chapel. His own conviction that he had been miraculously delivered from death when repeatedly under fire as a chaplain caused him to have engraved on the window a verse from Psalm 140: 'O Lord God, thou strength of my health: thou hast covered my head in the day of battle.' At Sandhurst, a new east end for the chapel, as a memorial to over 4,000 cadets, was dedicated by the Archbishop of Canterbury in 1921. The question of erecting a memorial in Liverpool had been raised as early as 1916. It was resolved that the north-east transept of the new Cathedral and its furnishings, when complete, should be dedicated as a war memorial. In the transept a marble cenotaph was placed – the first in the country to be suggested as a Great War memorial; on the top of the cenotaph is a book containing 40,000 names written on vellum. The cathedral also provides a photographic copy of the Roll of Honour in three volumes, indexed so that any name can quickly be found. Each day a different page is exposed to view. Hanging above the galleries are many regimental colours. Above the chapel altar rests a marble sarcophagus. Sculptured figures of the New Testament centurions stand in niches in the reredos. On either side of the altar are two figures, a sailor and a soldier, nearly life-sized, and 'treated with great skill, as the intrusion of figures in modern uniform might well be expected to have an incongruous effect', says Dr V. E. Cotton in *The Book of Liverpool Cathedral* (1964).[4] One receives the impression from this and many other memorial chapels that their chief purpose is to convey an atmosphere of repose by clothing everything in archaic dress and language; war memorials were not erected to disturb, dismay or even warn.

During the war, parishes compiled and framed lists of those on active service. These lists were prayed over at daily intercession services and week by week at the Eucharist and other services. In a few churches the lists can still be seen, now faded, but still eloquent. At St Mary's, Sandbach, Cheshire, it is obvious that the names were written at first in neat alphabetical order on the customary printed Roll of Honour; but as the numbers grew, the spaces grew less and, all order swept away by the tide of concern, names had to be squeezed into every available gap. The fact that, half a century later, such lists still hang in some churches, in addition to the permanent memorial, is an indication of the emotion which still adheres to them.

The inscriptions on the memorials used elevated heroic language, and soldiers were often represented in windows and sculptures as knights in armour with drawn swords; sometimes St George and the dragon were pictured, following a well-known wartime poster. One of the favourite texts to be used was 'Greater love hath no man than this, that a man lay down his life for his friends'. So the nation strove to find a way of expressing its grief, its pride, its bafflement. There is a particular pathos in those who die young, far from home and family; and they had died in such vast numbers. The size of the memorials and the importance of their sites indicate that the community believed that it was indeed 'The Great War'. 'Their name liveth for evermore.' Though, after the second war, Armistice Day was renamed Remembrance Day and transferred to the nearest Sunday to 11 November (and so became more marginal to national life), the commemoration is still expressed in ritual and symbolism created during and after the first war. There were few separate memorials erected specifically for the dead of the second war. The normal practice was to inscribe new names on an existing or extra panel of the first war memorial. The village of Alsager in Cheshire recorded its forty-one names from the first war with their ranks; the eleven names from the second war were added without any such differentiation. In the second war there was not quite that absolute division either between ranks, or between civilians and fighting men, which characterized the first war. To those who erected the first war memorials, the war was a unique and unrepeatable catastrophe; perhaps there would never be another war again. To us it looks rather more like the first war in a continuing world crisis.

On 6 November 1919, George V sent a special message to the Empire: 'I believe that my people in every part of the Empire fervently wish to perpetuate the memory of that Great Deliverance, and of those who laid down their lives to achieve it.' He went on to hope that there would be 'a complete suspension of all our normal activities' for two minutes at 'the eleventh hour of the eleventh day of the eleventh month' so that 'in perfect stillness the thoughts of everyone may be concentrated on reverent remembrance of the Glorious Dead'.[5] The two minutes' silence had been suggested to the Colonial Secretary by Sir Percy Fitzpatrick, a South African leader, as late as October 1919. He had been deeply impressed during the war by the daily pause in South Africa for three minutes' silence at noon, when an intense communion between the living and the dead seemed to be established. His own son had been killed in the war. The Cabinet adopted the suggestion but thought that three minutes was too long.[6] During the war some in England had adopted a suggestion of pausing to pray each day as noon struck. On 11 November 1919 when eleven o'clock struck, large congregations were attending memorial Eucharists at St Paul's and the Abbey. At the Abbey the Communion of the people had just concluded when the hour struck, and after the silence the service resumed with the saying of the 'Our Father'. At St Paul's the hour bell interrupted the singing of 'Let saints on earth in concert sing':

> Men became as motionless as the marble figures which surrounded them. If women moved it was because they shook with emotion. . . .
> In an interval of seconds, men must have revisited the torn and blasted fields of France, the ridges of Flanders, the beaches of Gallipoli, and many a cemetery where long rows of wooden crosses mark the resting place of those who fell.[7]

In 1920, an Army Chaplain, David Railton, suggested to Dean Ryle, of Westminster Abbey, that an unknown soldier should be buried in the Abbey among the great names of the nation. In 1916, Railton had noticed a grave with the pencilled inscription on a wooden cross, 'An Unknown Soldier of the Black Watch'. A committee under Lord Curzon recommended that an unknown soldier should be disinterred in France; the King, however, at first disliked the idea.[8] The soldier was to be called the 'Unknown Warrior' so that he might represent all who had been killed, whether as soldiers, sailors or airmen. Four bodies were brought from the main battle areas to a chapel at St-Pol. There one body was selected at midnight, 7/8 November. A destroyer carried the coffin to Dover. On board were six barrels of earth from the Ypres Salient for the burial, so that the body should rest in the soil on which so many English troops were killed. The coffin was draped with the Union Jack which Railton had frequently used as an altar and coffin covering in France. On 11 November 1920, the King, after unveiling the new Cenotaph in Whitehall, walked behind the gun carriage which bore the coffin to the Abbey. The appropriateness and impressiveness of the ceremony removed the initial apprehensions which the King had felt. The Prayer Book burial service followed. The hymns included 'O valiant hearts', the Russian Contakion for the Dead, 'Lead, kindly Light', 'Abide with me', and Kipling's 'Recessional'. A piece of music by Beethoven was also played.[9] C. F. G. Masterman, who disliked the romantic language used about the Unknown Warrior, nevertheless commented: 'We were burying every boy's father, and every woman's lover, and every Mother's child.'[10] The whole concept (subsequently followed in several other countries), carried out at each stage with elaborate, even esoteric, ceremony (for example, the selection by a blindfold officer of one of the bodies at midnight in a guarded chapel), illustrated the way in which the desire for Remembrance moved the nation towards mythology, symbolism, and ritual.[11] The tombstone of Belgian marble was unveiled on 11 November 1921. The texts were all biblical: 'Greater love . . .', 'Unknown and yet well known', 'Dying and behold we live' and 'The Lord knoweth them that are His'. These were chosen by Dean Ryle from the texts on the wreaths laid a year before. 'They buried him among the kings, because he had done good toward God and toward his House' was suggested, from 2 Chronicles 24.16, by a northern Archdeacon. On 22 November 1921 Dean Ryle received a letter from Mr S. I. Levy, Principal of the Liverpool Hebrew Schools, protesting at the inclusion of the text 'In Christ shall all be made alive'. He told the Dean that a text should have been selected which 'would not have offended the living religious susceptibilities' of the dead soldier, and asked him to change it. The Dean replied that the text did not 'define the faith of the dead man, but the faith of those who buried him and who are responsible for his grave', and declined to make any alteration.[12] In 1931, David Railton wrote about the significance of the Unknown Warrior, whom Railton would have preferred to have been called the 'Unknown Comrade'. People learn 'the unity of all types of men at that grave. They see that in the long run, all men of goodwill are comrades in Life, Death and the Hereafter.' The dead man, he wrote, might be a public schoolboy or a gypsy, an officer or from the ranks, from Britain or the Empire, a clergyman, an Anglican, a Roman Catholic, a Nonconformist, a Jew, or one of no religious persuasion.[13] As F. H. Keeling wrote in 1916, surveying the future of religion in the post-war world: 'ritual can unite us, speculation must divide us.'[14] Archbishop Davidson had been involved in some controversy with the Cabinet over the nature of the ceremony at the unveiling of the Cenotaph. Its members (or at least Lloyd George) wished for an entirely secular service, on the grounds that Muslims and Hindus were among those commemorated. But the Archbishop prevailed, and prayer was offered and 'O God, our help' was sung.[15] Baron von Hügel had been asked by Bishop E. S. Talbot for his opinion about a suitable text for the Cenotaph and agreed to one from Revelation, but wished that it had been possible to inscribe the words from 2 Maccabees: 'It is a holy and wholesome thought to pray for the dead'.[16] But in fact no text appears on the Cenotaph. Some objected that it did not explicitly assert the Christian faith about the dead, but a correspondent in *Challenge* saw the empty coffin as an emblem of the Resurrection.[17] Until the 1930s men passing by the Cenotaph would raise their hats.

So during and after the war, the Church of England evolved a series of rituals for 'containing' the experiences of war in consultation with a society which, though increasingly secular and aware of its growing religious diversity, still found it necessary to turn to the resources of Christian ritual and imagery to express what it felt. The Archbishops' Third Committee in 1919 pointed out how deeply valued had been the wartime shrines erected in streets and public places:

> They serve the double purpose of keeping in mind the absent and the departed, and of bringing the recognition and remembrance of God and of the Cross of Christ out into the open. Intercession services, such as have often been held at these shrines, have influenced many people. . . . In these days of sorrow and danger the spectacle of men and women in the street engaged in prayer, it may be as night is falling, has often brought to the passers-by the atmosphere of the unseen world, and the sense of the presence of the great Father in Whom is their consolation and defence.[18]

Over the years, there has often been a tension between the outlook of the parish clergy and local representatives of the British Legion. On occasion clergy have tried to tone down the nationalism of the occasion, and have tried to delete, say, the singing of 'O valiant hearts' on the one hand, while on the other hand the British Legion has endeavoured to maintain the heroic and patriotic imagery in the face of the increasing internationalism of the clergy and the increasing disinterest of the general population, at least in urban areas. In the villages like Akenfield, Remembrance Day even today still draws large congregations; at Akenfield in 1967, roughly twice as many people attended the Remembrance Service, the Carol Service or the Harvest Festival as were in church for Christmas or Easter. But then in Akenfield the passing bell still tolled for the dead until the second war, and people would stop in the fields to count the strokes. In many country parishes there has been a continuing devotion to the resting places of the dead which long ago disappeared in the cities.[19] Remembrance Day at the Cenotaph is one of the few surviving occasions when one is most conscious of the Church of England endeavouring to act as the national Church; the hymns are interdenominational, and the language, prayers and ritual have been little affected by liturgical change. It is congruent with the traditionalism which Remembrancetide evokes that Benjamin Britten's *War Requiem* (1962), though musically contemporary, should have used as its main texts the Latin of the Requiem Mass and the poems of Wilfred Owen. Replicas of first world war poppies are still the most characteristic emblems of Remembrancetide. Symbols of repose and oblivion, in the period before the first war they were also symbols of homosexual love.[20] Many soldiers noted the flowering poppies in trenches and the fields around. John McCrae's immensely popular poem 'In Flanders Fields', published in *Punch* on 6 December 1915, made poppies inseparable from the experience of the first war. Herbert Read in 'A Short Poem for Armistice Day' meditated on the symbolism of disabled soldiers making artificial flowers 'of paper tin and metal thread' which have no scent and no power to fertilize.

In May 1917 the British Government decided that a National War Museum should be created to collect and display material relating to the war. The interest taken in the scheme by the Dominions led to its being given the present title of 'Imperial War Museum'. In 1920 George V opened the Museum in temporary quarters at the Crystal Palace. It moved to its present home in 1936. An official outline of the original scheme dated August 1917 shows that it was originally intended to become 'the National War Memorial':

A War Museum that did not record and honour the brave who sacrificed their lives for their country would be constructed on a fundamentally wrong principle. The very heart and focus of the building should be of a memorial character. This might take the form of a Hall of Honour as rich and beautiful in character as artists can devise, and adjacent to it a gallery devoted to the separate memorials of the Navy and Army by Ships, Regiments and Contingents. The Hall of Honour could be designed to bear on its walls painted portraits, and on its floors pedestals carrying busts or sculptured figures of such eminent individuals as the people as a whole may delight to single out for special honour.

But this grandiose scheme was never carried out, partly owing to the economic depression, but also no doubt partly because the idea of a National War Memorial had already been superseded by the Shrine of the Unknown Warrior, the Cenotaph in Whitehall, and innumerable memorials throughout the country.[21]

There are some 2,000 British war cemeteries in France and Belgium. In 1917, Kipling was approached to become one of the Imperial War Graves' Commissioners. Ironically, the body of his own son, killed in the battle of Loos, was never found. He worked diligently for the Commission for the remaining eighteen years of his life. It was he who suggested most of the inscriptions (though Lord Hugh Cecil objected that Kipling was not a known religious man) – 'Their Name Liveth For Evermore' (Ecclus. 44.14) on the 'Stone of Remembrance' in each cemetery; the words:

A Soldier of the Great War
Known unto God

above unidentified bodies; 'Their Glory Shall Not Be Blotted Out' (Ecclus. 44.13) in the case of graves obliterated by bombardments; the inscriptions on British memorials in French and Belgian cathedrals. It was Kipling too who suggested the daily ceremony of the Last Post at the Menin Gate: 'Sixty years after Passchendaele, the daily evening sounding at the Menin Gate of the Last Post and Retreat, echoing in the great hall with its remorseless decoration of columns of names, can still induce anguish, outrage, and a sense of hopeless loss in the visitor.'[22]

The architecture of the British war cemeteries was predominantly neo-classical. The funerary symbolism was derived mostly from pagan sources as was the symbolism of the Cenotaph in Whitehall, designed by Sir Edwin Lutyens, one of the principal architects for the War Graves Commission. Despite some protests, officers and men were buried in the same cemeteries; the comradeship of the trenches lived on. Private exhumations were not allowed. All were to rest together. At the request of relatives, religious symbols could be carved on headstones. But in spite of pressure from religious quarters, headstones rather than crosses were chosen to mark the graves, because the dead belonged to many religions. Respect for different creeds was a fundamental principle of the Commission. A shared death took precedence over a shared religion. The inscription from Ecclesiasticus on each Stone of Remembrance deliberately omitted a previous phrase which might have offended Hindus. However, a large free-standing 'Cross of Sacrifice' with a bronze sword affixed was erected in each cemetery, though some wondered whether it was too Catholic a symbol. The Stone of Remembrance in each cemetery (in shape and position suggesting an altar) was less explicitly Christian. Though the Commission went to unprecedented lengths to locate graves, to identify bodies, and to re-inter them in the new cemeteries, in fact nearly half the total dead of the British Empire have no known resting place. They were commemorated in huge memorials like the ones at Thiepval and the Menin Gate, powerful reminders of the mass slaughter which had been such a numbing feature of the war. As early as 1916 the planting of grass, shrubs, and flowers had been systematically undertaken, natural sacraments of hope. Lord Hugh Cecil's proposal, however, that a text should be inscribed on each Cross of Sacrifice, from 1 Corinthians 15.55, 57: 'O grave where is thy victory? Thanks be to God which giveth the victory through our Lord Jesus Christ.' was turned down, though it had been approved by the Archbishop of Canterbury. Even when the cemeteries and memorials were at last completed, this huge work of Remembrance covering many countries required, and still requires, costly maintenance. No sooner had the Menin Gate been completed than some of the 54,000 names became illegible. But it was claimed that the monuments themselves would last several hundred, even two thousand, years.[23]

Some visited the battlefields as sightseers. Others went as pilgrims. In 1919, the *Illustrated Michelin Guides to the Battlefields* were published. Travel agencies offered three-day cheap visits. Philip Johnstone wrote a sardonic poem, 'High Wood', in 1918. He imagined tourists being shown round the battlefields and being sold souvenirs, and offered refreshments in a dug-out; they were requested not to leave litter behind. The *Illustrated London News* for 14 June 1919 published a picture of picnickers on the battlefields. In the Spring of 1922 the King and Queen made a solemn pilgrimage to the cemeteries. 'In the course of my pilgrimage,' said the King, 'I have many times asked myself whether there can be more potent advocates of peace upon earth through the years to come than this massed multitude of witnesses to the desolation of war.' He hoped that these memorials would draw all peoples together on 'the deep-rooted basis of a common heroism and a common agony'. For Kipling the regular tours of the cemeteries as a Commissioner uncovered old wounds:

> 'I plough deep' said the car,
> 'I plough old wounds afresh –
> 'What you thought was a scar,
> 'I will show you is stricken flesh. . . .'[24]

One of Kipling's best short stories, 'The Gardener', was written after he had visited the Rouen cemetery in 1925. It tells of a mother making a pilgrimage across the Channel to visit the grave of her illegitimate son whom she had always passed off as her nephew at home. When the news of his death had reached her, the 'ritual', which the village had 'evolved' to deal with the bereaved, left her detached and distant. 'So Helen found herself moved on to another process of the manufacture – to a world of exultant or broken relatives, now strong in the certainty that there was an altar upon earth where they might lay their love.' Visiting the grave was for her, as for Mary Magdalene, a moment of revelation:

A man knelt behind a line of headstones – evidently a gardener, for he was firming a young plant in the soft earth. She went towards him, her paper in her hand. He rose at her approach and without prelude or salutation asked: 'Who are you looking for?'

'Lieutenant Michael Turrell – my nephew,' said Helen slowly and word for word, as she had many thousands of times in her life.

The man lifted his eyes and looked at her with infinite compassion before he turned from the fresh-sown grass toward the naked black crosses.

'Come with me', he said, 'and I will show you where your son lies.'

When Helen left the Cemetery she turned for a last look. In the distance she saw the man bending over his young plants; and she went away, supposing him to be the gardener.

But remembrance was not only a matter of erecting cenotaphs and laying out war cemeteries. As in any bereavement, the desire to mourn conflicted with the desire to go on living in the present and to move on to the future. Bereavement produces both idealization and anger. If anger is not allowed to be directed towards the deceased, it is channelled into other directions. Some of those who survived wished they too had been killed, some resented the idealization of the dead, some directed their anger at those who had been left untouched, or even had profited from the war. Sassoon in 'Aftermath' (1919) as the world 'rumbled on' appealed:

> Look down, and swear by the slain of the War that you'll never forget.

Studdert Kennedy in 'If Ye Forget' struggled between the yearning to forget – 'I am weary of remembrance' – and the duty to tell children so that war would be avoided in the future. Kipling in 'A Dead Statesman' expressed the anger of those who felt betrayed by the 'lies' of the politicians. Sassoon treated the squire in 'Memorial Tablet' with humorous sadness. But 'On Passing the New Menin Gate' was written with blazing anger:

> Well might the Dead who struggled in the slime
> Rise and deride this sepulchre of crime.

Soon after the war, the Rector of Islip asked Robert Graves, resident in the village, to speak from the chancel step at a War Memorial Service, and suggested he should read some war poems. Instead of choosing from the poems of Rupert Brooke, he read from Owen and Sassoon. He suggested that those who had died were like the men of Siloam, not particularly wicked or virtuous, and that the survivors should thank God they were alive and try to avoid wars in the future. The 'Church party', apart from the Rector, was scandalized, though the ex-service men 'liked to be told that they stood on equal terms with the glorious dead'.[25] Some ex-soldiers found the annual remembrance ceremony increasingly repellent. On Armistice Day 1921, thousands of unemployed marched towards the Cenotaph with pawn tickets instead of medals. For some years Charles Carrington held a party on Armistice Day, but the increasing solemnity of the occasion turned it into 'a day of mourning'. Many ex-soldiers, he said, found the Cenotaph ritual increasingly discomforting.[26] Sir Llewellyn Woodward, the historian, grew bitter about

the hollow words used too often at the unveiling of war memorials.

Glib words about the 'Great Sacrifice'. I know that in many cases these words were used with deep feeling by men who had lost their own sons. They became almost a *cliché* in the oratory of politicians. . . . As time went on, I began to dislike more and more the celebration of Armistice Day. I wished that all the formal ceremonies might be abandoned. . . . It was too easy for the older generation to find a convenient anodyne in the formal politeness of a two-minutes' silence, in the weaving of wreaths, in the provision of adequate pensions for widows and orphans.[27]

The mood of some in the post-war world was increasingly anti-heroic. It is impossible to think of Leopold Bloom of James Joyce's *Ulysses* (1922) as being the chief character in a pre-war novel. Studdert Kennedy introduced his book *Lies* (1919):

The post-war world is black with lies. . . . There's a bad smell about – a very bad smell; it is like the smell of the Dead – it is the smell of dead souls.

But of all the evocations of that grief which Church and nation tried fumblingly to express, re-live and assuage, few are more moving and authentic than the one given by A. L. Rowse in *A Cornish Childhood*. The school war memorial had just been unveiled. After the National Anthem, Last Post and Reveille,

A little man came up to me and started talking in a rambling way about his son who was killed. I think the poor fellow was for the moment carried away with sorrow. He said 'Sidney Herbert – Sidney Herbert – you know they called him Sidney Herbert, but really he was called Sidney Hubert: he was my boy. He was killed in the War – yes: I thought you would like to know.' And he went on like that till I dared not stay any longer with him.[28]

Some felt that for them the most abiding experiences of the war – the comradeship of the trenches – must somehow be kept alive.

How shall I say goodbye to you, wonderful, terrible days,
If I should live to live and leave 'neath an alien soil
You, my men, who taught me to walk with a smile in the ways
Of the valley of shadows, taught me to know you and love you, and
    toil
Glad in the glory of fellowship, happy in misery, strong

In the strength that laughs at its weakness, laughs at its sorrow and
    fears,
Facing the world that was not too kind with a jest and a song?
What can the world hold afterwards worthy of laughter or tears?
                        (Edward de Stein: 'Envoi')

Though the vast majority were only too glad to be demobilized, Charles
Carrington, like many others, felt 'a little scared' of civilian life; he could
not help looking back to the comradeship he had known.[29] Before the
end of the war, two associations of ex-servicemen were founded – the
'National Federation of Discharged and Demobilized Soldiers and
Sailors' for those in the ranks, of a rather left-wing colour, and the
'Comrades of the Great War' which was more conservative. Under
Haig's influence they were combined into the British Legion which
received its constitution in 1921.[30] In addition there were other
associations like the Ypres League and the Old Contemptibles
Association. Every branch of the latter (motto: 'God, King and
Country') held a church parade; until quite recently they also held two
national parades, one at the Cenotaph and one in St Paul's Cathedral. A
Padre's Fellowship was created in October 1918 with B. K.
Cunningham, F. B. Macnutt, Guy Rogers, Eric Milner-White, Walter
Carey, and E. S. Woods among its members, but it lost momentum as
Toc H grew, and ex-chaplains in any case became immersed in the post-
war tasks of the Church. It had aimed at conserving and applying the
results of their experiences as chaplains, maintaining the bond of
fellowship, keeping in touch with ex-soldiers and working for social
change and the reform and unity of the Church.[31]

In the April 1919 issue of *St Martin's Messenger*, Tubby Clayton
wrote a description of Talbot House at Poperinghe, at the suggestion of
his cousin, Dick Sheppard. 'What, then, is to happen to the fellowship of
Talbot House?' Clayton asked. 'It is plainly too great to lose.'[32] Clayton
had discussed with Sheppard the idea of a London house. The first
£10,000 came from two worshippers at St Martin's in memory of
Oswin Creighton.[33] At the end of 1919 Clayton left Knutsford to start
Toc. H. The first house was visited by some 1,600 men in the twelve
months, and some 400 had stayed there, so a second house was opened
in London. In 1920 Clayton began to campaign all over the country for
the establishment of other houses. Toc H was not intended simply as a
fellowship for ex-servicemen, but also aimed to attract the younger

generation to teach them the principles of the movement. These were summarized in the Four Points of the Toc H compass – Fellowship, Service, Fairmindedness and the Kingdom of God. In 1922 Clayton accepted Archbishop Davidson's proposal that he should become Vicar of All Hallows by the Tower, which then became the spiritual centre of the movement. In that year a lamp based on the type used in the catacombs was adopted as the emblem of Toc. H. On the lamp was inscribed *In Lumine Tuo Videbimus Lumen* from Psalm 36.9. The double Cross from the arms of Ypres was included in the design, for in the Ypres Salient Toc H was born. The original lamp was given by the Patron, the then Prince of Wales, and replicas were sent to all branches. It was thought of as a Lamp of Maintenance rather than of Remembrance. The Ceremony of Light which opens every meeting is held in a darkened room. It begins with a remembrance of 'our Elder Brethren': after a recital of Binyon's lines there is a minute's silence. A new member is admitted by a dialogue which opens with the Chairman asking 'Who goes there?' The candidate for admission states that the lamp was lit by 'Unselfish Sacrifice', and that 'Unselfish Service' will maintain it, which is 'The rent we pay for our room on earth'. 'Toc H', declared the Prince in 1921, 'is plainly one of the best things of its kind emerging from the years of sacrifice.' After Clayton's institution to All Hallows, 2,000 people gathered in the Guildhall; the Prince lit the lamp that he had given, never to be extinguished, and from it were lit the forty similar lamps for the various branches of Toc H. In the gathering were Bishop E. S. Talbot and Bishop Neville Talbot, links with Gilbert Talbot in whose memory the original house at Poperinghe had been founded. Bishop E. S. Talbot confirmed at All Hallows every year. At Poperinghe there had been an Open Communion, but at All Hallows only confirmed Anglicans could communicate. George Macleod protested, and for a while virtually withdrew from the movement. On the other hand, some Anglo-Catholics were also worried lest Toc H became Pan-Protestant. It was also decided that Unitarian ministers could not act as padres to branches, and of course Roman Catholics felt unable to join in Communion. However, Toc H remained an interdenominational movement, and so continued to express something of that ecumenical spirit which had been one of the fruits of the war.[34]

Toc H was given a Royal Charter in 1922. Its first aim was stated to be:

To preserve among ex-service men and to implant and preserve in others and transmit to future generations the traditions of Christian fellowship and service manifested by all ranks of the British Army on Active Service during the war.

Its other three aims were to promote social service, to foster a sense of mutual responsibility, and to mitigate 'the evils of class-consciousness'.[35] In 1926 the house at Poperhinghe was purchased for Toc H and several thousands of pilgrims from Toc H branches all over the world began to visit it each year. Clayton conducted regular pilgrimages to it. An ex-sapper on the 1931 Eastertide pilgrimage, who had himself been in the Salient, described how he knelt in the Upper Room at the house:

> I felt that I was standing in the presence of a great company of free men, free through Christ, and in some way their agony linked up with His. . . . There was the sense of being uplifted in that Great Company, my unworthiness to be of their company eliminated; but what, I think, shook me was the realisation, in some measure, of the agony they had known.[36]

The Great War continues in all kinds of ways to haunt the memory, and this has been superbly and movingly documented by Paul Fussell in *The Great War and Modern Memory*. Vernon Scannell said in a poem written out of the second war experience:

> Whenever war is spoken of
> I find
> The war that was called Great invades the mind . . .
>
> ('The Great War')

F. R. Barry in 1963 wrote that every 27th Evening of the month, when Psalm 126 ('When the Lord turned again the captivity of Sion') was appointed in the Prayer Book, something of the hopes and visions that arose in the hearts of men at the end of the war returned.[37] To re-enter the torments and the longings of the period, even sixty years later, even only through the imagination, is still a searing and searching experience. The Great War still focuses so many of the problems of the human predicament, in all its baffling paradoxes, still raises so many of the basic issues about human nature, ethics, nationality, religion, Christianity, the Church and theology. So there is still much to be learnt from it, still much for society and Church to digest and assimilate. 'When some great loss or reverse radically changes life for us it is absolutely necessary actively to re-negotiate life on a new set of terms.'[38] The fact that the Great War still haunts the communal memory suggests that we still have not yet completed our work of remembrance. If we have not already discovered it through other means, the Great War confronts us with the fact that there are no easy human or Christian answers to life, with its extraordinary mixture of tragedy and comedy, brutality and compassion, rationality and irrationality. It is the greatness of Christianity at its best that it affords no easy answers, but rather points us to the heart of the darkness unflinchingly, enables misery to be transmuted into pain and, by making the darkness tangible, turns the apparent absence of God into a presence, however paradoxical and elusive that presence has to be, God being God.

> Who then devised the torment? Love.
> Love is the unfamiliar Name
> Behind the hands that wove
> The intolerable shirt of flame
> Which human power cannot remove.
> We only live, only suspire
> Consumed by either fire or fire.[39]

Notes

INTRODUCTION

1 See Alan Webster's comments on A. J. P. Taylor's *English History 1914–1945* (1965), in 'The Taylor Cut Church', *Theology*, September 1966.

2 See John Kent, 'The Study of Modern Ecclesiastical History since 1930', in *The Pelican Guide to Modern Theology* (1969), ii, 243–8.

3 *The Secular Promise* (1964), p. 148.

4 D. M. MacKinnon (ed.), *Making Moral Decisions* (1969), p. 90.

5 *Theology*, August 1972, p. 417.

6 *A Church by Daylight* (1973), p. xvii; cf. Charles Elliott, 'Institutional Repentance', in *Theology*, January 1976.

7 A. D. Gilbert, *Religion and Society in Industrial England* (1976), p. 29.

8 *Church Congress Report* (1906), pp. 21–6. Cf. Bishop E. S. Talbot: '. . . there is among us a sense of discouragement. We doubt whether we are making way. There is a sense that we are not on the flow of the tide, and perhaps feel its ebb' (Sermon in *Church Congress Report*, 1902, p. 5).

9 C. F. G. Masterman, *The Condition of England*, ed. J. T. Bolton (1960), pp. 204–13.

10 Between those dates Inner London attendance dropped from 28·52 per cent of the population to 21·98 per cent, and the Church of England share from 13·52 per cent to 9·43 per cent; see Hugh McLeod, *Class and Religion in the Late Victorian City* (1974), p. 314.

11 *The Victorian Church* (1970), ii, 232.

12 ibid., 257.

13 Gilbert, p. 202.

14 I am indebted in this section to Olive Anderson, 'The Reactions of Church and Dissent towards the Crimean War', in *Journal of Ecclesiastical History*, October 1965.

15 Eric James (ed.), *Spirituality for Today* (1968), pp. 41–2.

16 James Obelkevich, *Religion and Rural Society* (1976), p. 281.

17 See Stephen Koss (ed.), *The Anatomy of an Anti-War Movement* (1973); Peter d'A. Jones, *The Christian Socialist Revival* (1968), pp. 198–205, 231–6.

18 p. xii.

19 *Church Congress Report* (1900), pp. 190–1.

20 *Under the Dome* (1902), pp. 245, 254.

21 Alan Hyman, *The Rise and Fall of Horatio Bottomley* (1972), pp. 150, 158.

22 Reginald Pound, *The Lost Generation* (1964), pp. 264–5.

23 See David Newsome, *Godliness and Good Learning* (1961), Chap. IV.

CHAPTER 1 THE COMING OF WAR

1 'The Leaning Tower', in *The Moment and Other Essays* (1947), p. 111.
2 Donald Read, *Edwardian England* (1972), pp. 17, 239–40, 248–51.
3 *Retrospect of an Unimportant Life* (1943), i, 173; cf. his *War-Time Sermons* (1915), pp. vii–viii.
4 *The Culham Club Magazine*, Autumn 1914.
5 Thomas Jones, *Lloyd George* (1951), p. 47.
6 Albert Marrin, *The Last Crusade* (1974), p. 71.
7 G. S. Spinks, *Religion in Britain since 1900* (1952), p. 65.
8 *The Story of the Student Christian Movement* (1933), p. 506.
9 Stephen Paget, *Henry Scott Holland* (1921), pp. 312–14.
10 pp. ix, 91.
11 Canon H. Roland Bate, 'Sixty Years Ago', in *Blackwood's Magazine*, November 1975, p. 385.
12 *Anti Christ and Other Sermons* (1913), p. 31.
13 Constance Padwick, *Temple Gairdner of Cairo* (1929), p. 235.
14 Adam Fox, *Dean Inge* (1960), pp. 131–2.
15 H. E. Sheen, *Canon Peter Green* (1965), p. 72.
16 Gwendolen Stephenson, *Edward Stuart Talbot* (1936), pp. 221–2.
17 G. L. Prestige, *Charles Gore* (1935), pp. 224–5, 369.
18 *Commonwealth*, October 1914; *Guardian*, 20 August 1914.
19 Quoted by John Nias, *Flame from an Oxford Cloister* (1961), pp. 128–30.
20 G. K. A. Bell, *Randall Davidson* (1952), pp. 731–5.
21 *'Quit You Like Men'* (1915), pp. 4–8.
22 (1969 edn), p. 172.
23 Harold Owen and John Bell (eds), *Collected Letters* (1967), p. 282.
24 *The War and The Soul* (1916), pp. 31, 35–6.
25 e.g. *Modern Painters* (1843–60), III, iv, Chap. xviii, §33.
26 Commended by Scott Holland in G. K. A. Bell (ed.), *The War and the Kingdom of God* (1915), p. 150.
27 See the tribute in *The Modern Churchman*, June 1916, p. 96.
28 *The Battle of the Lord* (1915), p. 165.
29 Nicholas Mosley, *Julian Grenfell* (1976), pp. 51, 89, 116, 122–3, 231–43.
30 *In London during the Great War* (1935), p. 60.
31 *The Times*, 5 April 1915.
32 Michael Hastings, *Rupert Brooke* (1967), p. 166; for tributes by Churchill and others, see pp. 182–5; cf. Paul Fussell, *The Great War and Modern Memory* (1975), Chap. VIII.
33 *With a machine gun to Cambrai* (1969), p. 1.
34 *The Six Lambeth Conferences* (1920), pp. 186, 207, 258–64, 312, 329.
35 See, for example, *Church Congress Report* (1896), pp. 422–41.
36 *Peace and the Churches* (1909), p. 63.
37 p. 202.
38 p. 191.
39 p. 61.
40 p. 122.
41 p. 136.

42 pp. 240–1.

43 *Friendly Relations between Great Britain and Germany* (1910), p. 69.

44 p. 210.

45 p. 11.

46 Donald Read (ed.), *Documents from Edwardian England* (1973), p. 330.

47 Jon Stallworthy, *Wilfred Owen* (1974), p. 104.

48 *Father Figures* (Penguin 1969), pp. 39–40.

49 William Temple, *Life of Bishop Percival* (1921), pp. 201–7.

50 pp. 356–8.

51 pp. 360–3.

52 Caroline E. Playne, *Society at War* (1931), p. 184.

53 *Three Sermons* (Church of England Peace League 1914), p. 9.

54 J. H. Fowler, *The Life and Letters of Edward Lee Hicks* (1922), pp. 171, 250–1, 283.

55 John B. Harford and Frederick C. MacDonald, *Handley Carr Glyn Moule* (1922), pp. 272–3.

56 Marrin, p. 64.

57 Kenneth O. Morgan, *Keir Hardie* (1975), pp. 181, 260–4; Georges Haupt, *Socialism and the Great War* (1972).

58 *Manchester Guardian*, 13 July 1916.

59 Reg Groves, *Conrad Noel and the Thaxted Movement* (1967), pp. 155–6, 174–5; Conrad Noel, *An Autobiography* (1945), p. 107; P. d'A. Jones, pp. 273–5.

60 Marrin, p. 250.

61 Bell, pp. 736–7.

62 13 August 1914.

63 *Manchester Guardian*, 20 August 1914.

64 F. H. Brabant, *Neville Stuart Talbot* (1949), p. 58.

65 e.g. Psalm 121; John 2.15; Mark 9.2–9; Isaiah 24.18; Hebrews 12.27 etc.

66 Frank Owen, *Tempestuous Journey: Lloyd George* (1954), p. 276.

67 H. G. Mulliner, *Arthur Burroughs* (1936), pp. 34–5; E. A. Burroughs, *The Valley of Decision* (1916), pp. 6–7. Canon H. D. Rawnsley also quoted the speech approvingly in a sermon, and in a speech to the York Convocation: *What the War is All About* (1915), pp. 52, 57.

68 *Christianity and War* (1916), p. 1.

69 K. W. Clements, 'Baptists and the Outbreak of the First World War', in *Baptist Quarterly*, April 1975. For Nonconformist attitudes, see Stephen Koss (ed.), *Nonconformity in British Politics* (1975), Chap. 6; C. Binfield, *So Down to Prayers: Studies in English Nonconformity 1780–1920* (1977), Chap. 11; Basil Willey, *Spots of Time* (1965).

70 For English Roman Catholic attitudes, see Ernest Oldmeadow, *Francis Cardinal Bourne* (1944), ii, Chaps. XIV, XV, XVII.

71 *Manchester Guardian*, 28 October 1915.

72 Cf., for example, the celebrated passage in Chapter XVII of Charles Kingsley's *Yeast* (1851), in which Kingsley pointed out the political significance of the cathedral choir singing the Magnificat.

73 e.g. the sermon by the Revd Samuel Hemphill, preached on 9 August 1914, in *Sermons for the Times, No. 4: Sermons on the Holy War* (1914).

74 See, for example, Norman Goodall, quoted in F. W. Dillistone, *C. H. Dodd* (1977), p. 84.

CHAPTER 2   THE CHURCH AND THE WAR EFFORT

1 F. R. Barry, *Period of My Life* (1970), p. 51.
2 Bell, pp. 740, 764.
3 *Guardian*, 31 December 1914.
4 J. B. Lancelot, *Frederick James Chavasse* (1929), p. 191.
5 Harford, pp. 272–80.
6 *Retrospect*, ii, 67; iii, 3.
7 *Retrospect*, i, 174–5.
8 *The Battle of the Lord*, pp. 40, 91.
9 Later reprinted in *A Day of God* (1914).
10 *A Call to Arms* (1914), pp. 7–8, 10–15; A. F. Winnington-Ingram, *Fifty Years' Work in London* (1940), pp. 108–10.
11 *Guardian*, 22 July 1915.
12 *The Potter and the Clay* (1917), p. 64.
13 F. W. B. Bullock, *A History of Training for the Ministry* (1976), p. 58; see *Guardian*, 27 May 1915, for the application of this policy in the London diocese.
14 J. R. H. Moorman, *B. K. Cunningham* (1947), pp. 69–70.
15 *Memories and Meanings* (1969), pp. 86–7.
16 *Retrospect*, i, 175–6; Tatlow, pp. 530–1.
17 The *Guardian*, 27 May 1915, supported his campaign.
18 Furse, *Stand Therefore!* (1953), pp. 75–7.
19 *Go Forward: Thoughts on the National Crisis* (1915).
20 *For All We Have and Are* (1915), p. 67.
21 *Old Soldiers Never Die* (1964 edn), p. 301.
22 Bell, pp. 739, 762, 765–6, 775–6.
23 Marrin, p. 191.
24 F. A. Iremonger, *William Temple* (1948), p. 193.
25 See the lengthy statement in the *Guardian*, 27 September 1917.
26 Bell, p. 817; J. G. Lockhart, *Cosmo Gordon Lang* (1949), p. 247; Marrin, pp. 195–7; R. C. D. Jasper, *A. C. Headlam* (1960), p. 102; P. E. Matheson, *Hastings Rashdall* (1928), pp. 152, 156.
27 Bell, pp. 887–90.
28 Prestige, pp. 370, 404; Gore, *War and the Church* (1914), pp. 60–6.
29 Stephenson, p. 230; Moorman, p. 71; E. S. Talbot, in *Contemporary Review*, February 1916.
30 F. L. Cross, *Darwell Stone* (1943), p. 119.
31 Evelyn Waugh, *Ronald Knox* (1959), p. 133.
32 Moorman, pp. 71–2.
33 *Church and Nation* (1916), pp. 96–7.
34 Harford, p. 273.
35 Nicolas Corte, *Pierre Teilhard de Chardin* (1960), p. 15.
36 See, for example, Henri Perrin, *Priest-Workman in Germany* (1948).
37 John Laffin (ed.), *Letters from the Front 1914–1918* (1973), p. 67.

38 *CR*, St John Baptist 1916; St John Baptist 1918; Michaelmas 1918; Christmas 1918; Lady Day 1919.
39 Thomas Jones, p. 93.
40 Winnington-Ingram, *The Church in Time of War*, pp. 314–17; Marrìn, pp. 199–200; MacDonagh, p. 185.
41 Lockhart, pp. 259–61.
42 Prestige, pp. 411–19.
43 G. H. Hardy, *Bertrand Russell and Trinity* (1970); A. R. Vidler, 'Bishop Barnes', in *The Modern Churchman*, Spring 1975, pp. 88–90.
44 John Rae, *Conscience and Politics* (1970), p. 134. I am indebted to this book for much of the detailed information in this section about conscientious objection.
45 Of 307 in various prisons in 1917, 109 were Quakers, 84 Nonconformists, 27 agnostics, 17 Anglicans, 14 Unitarians, 13 Jews, 7 Roman Catholics, and 36 miscellaneous – Margaret Hobhouse, *I Appeal unto Caesar* (1917), pp. 16–17.
46 *Times Recruiting Supplement*, 3 November 1915; *The Potter and the Clay*, pp. 11, 36.
47 Cf. Henson's defence of such metaphors: *War-Time Sermons*, p. 66.
48 Stephen Hobhouse, *Forty Years* (1951). It has been suggested by J. Newberry that most of *I Appeal unto Caesar* was written by Bertrand Russell – *Russell* (the *Journal* of the Bertrand Russell Archives, McMaster University, Ontario), Autumn 1974.
49 Lord Hugh Cecil frequently championed the cause of the conscientious objector: see Kenneth Rose, *The Later Cecils* (1975), pp. 264–5.
50 pp. ix, xiii.
51 Arthur Marwick, *The Deluge* (1973 edn), p. 82.
52 *The Times*, 8 October 1917. For a biographical sketch of Lord William Cecil, see Rose, Chap. 5.
53 11 October 1917.
54 Harold Nicolson, *King George the Fifth* (1952), p. 255.
55 *I Appeal unto Caesar*, pp. xiii–xiv.
56 Hansard XXV, col. 333.
57 Bell, pp. 817–22, 840, 953.
58 Prestige, pp. 388–9.
59 Iremonger, pp. 187–8.
60 *Prisoners of Hope*, pp. 41–3; J. T. Wilkinson, *A. S. Peake* (1971), pp. 152–5.
61 Tatlow, pp. 586–8.
62 William Purcell, *Fisher of Lambeth* (1969), pp. 55–7; Victor Gollancz, *More for Timothy* (1953), pp. 195, 289–309.
63 Siegfried Sassoon, *Complete Memoirs of George Sherston* (1937), pp. 496, 539–42; Robert Graves, *Goodbye to All That* (Penguin 1960), pp. 209–17; Stallworthy, pp. 205–11.
64 *Soldier from the Wars Returning* (1965), p. 222.
65 *The War and the Soul*, p. 60.
66 Private communication from his son, the late Canon Philip Cecil.
67 Harford, pp. 273–6.
68 p. 86.
69 *Challenge*, 18 September 1914.
70 pp. 7, 66, 77, 105, 122; on Fr Bull, see P. d'A. Jones, pp. 229–37.

71 *The Modern Churchman*, April 1916, p. 58.
72 Cf. January 1918, p. 3.

CHAPTER 3   THE CHURCH'S MINISTRY AT HOME

1 (Fontana edn 1957), pp. 170–1.
2 Letters from Birmingham, Alabama, Jail, 1963, in Martin Luther King, *Why We Can't Wait* (1964), p. 91.
3 Cf. the headline in *Sphere*, 15 May 1915: 'The Capture of the Garden of Eden'.
4 *The Church and Nation* (1901), p. 48.
5 *The Church in Time of War*, pp. v–vi.
6 *Retrospect*, i, 177.
7 Prestige, p. 372.
8 *The Church in Time of War*, pp. 271, 311–17.
9 *Memoirs*, pp. 448–9.
10 Bell, p. 832.
11 p. 900.
12 p. 318.
13 pp. 776, 815, 837, 899.
14 Leslie Paul, *The Deployment and Payment of the Clergy* (1964), pp. 282–5.
15 Prestige, p. 218.
16 Bullock, pp. 53, 84.
17 Cf. the Principal of Cuddesdon's protest at this situation: *Church Congress Report* (1902), p. 399.
18 Elma K. Paget, *Henry Luke Paget* (1939), p. 195.
19 Stephenson, pp. 229, 319.
20 A. W. Hopkinson, *Pastor's Progress* (1942), p. 126; Lockhart, p. 247; Moorman, p. 73.
21 Stephenson, p. 239.
22 Bell, pp. 313, 736, 752, 827–8.
23 Paget, pp. 197–9, 206–7.
24 Groves, pp, 159, 170–1.
25 R. Ellis Roberts, *H. R. L. Sheppard* (1942), p. 105.
26 Sheen, pp. 86–7.
27 20 August, 10 September 1914.
28 Waugh, pp. 134–7; Knox became a Roman Catholic in 1917.
29 A point made strongly by Dean Ryle in *The Attitude of the Church towards War* (1915), p. 8. The belief that Britain was an instrument of divine justice against the evil deeds of Germany was commonly expressed by churchmen.
30 Bell, pp. 886–7; Bell withheld Winnington-Ingram's name (see Davidson Papers, vol. 13); cf. Dean Inge, January 1918, on a sermon preached by Winnington-Ingram: 'The Bishop of London preached a most unchristian sermon, which with a few words changed might have been preached by a court chaplain at Berlin' (*Diary of a Dean*, 1949, p. 43).
31 E. S. Woods and F. B. Macnutt, *Theodore, Bishop of Winchester* (1933), p. 56.
32 See, for example, Peter Green, in *Manchester Guardian*, 9 December 1915.
33 Bell, pp. 767–8; Iremonger, Chap. XIII.
34 William Temple, *A Challenge to the Church* (1917), pp. 4–6, 34–5, 37–9, 60–1.

35 p. 5.
36 p. 43.
37 p. 302.
38 p. 52.
39 Bell, pp. 770–4.
40 Prestige, pp. 383–6.
41 E. A. Knox, *Reminiscences of an Octogenarian* (1935), pp. 272–5.
42 Harford, pp. 222–4.
43 Woods and Macnutt, pp. 69–75, 81, 226; Charles Smyth, *Cyril Forster Garbett* (1959), pp. 149–50, 216.
44 William Purcell, *Woodbine Willie* (1962), pp. 124–5, 127–9, 139.
45 *CR*, Lady Day 1917.
46 H. C. Jackson, *Pastor on the Nile* (1960), pp. 160–3.
47 *Fifty Years*, pp. 126–8; Iremonger, pp. 209–10.
48 *Rays of Dawn* (1918), pp. 16–29, 34.
49 Lockhart, pp. 254–5.
50 Iremonger, pp. 210–12.
51 Paget, p. 320.
52 April 1917.
53 April 1916, pp. 44–5.
54 Paget, p. 321.
55 19 May 1916.
56 *Retrospect*, i, 177–80.
57 *Letters*, ed. E. F. Braley (1950), pp. 14–15.
58 Groves, p. 176.
59 Maurice B. Reckitt, *P. E. T. Widdrington* (1961), pp. 64–5.
60 p. 214. This might also be a just comment on the fortnight's 'Crusade' at Woolwich in September 1917. The speakers included the Archbishop of Canterbury, the Chaplain-General, and six bishops. Each 'Crusader' wore an emblem of St George and the Dragon. Despite the ecstatic description in the *Guardian* ('The scenes in Woolwich are unparalleled in our history'), *Commonwealth* said that the Mission had 'brought to light the undisguised and palpable hostility of the workers against the church'. *Challenge* recorded the controversy as to whether the Woolwich munition workers had been actively hostile to the Church, but was clear that the Crusade had demonstrated that there was a continuing gap between Church and workers, that the Church had not yet found a means of presenting the Gospel to them, and that this underlined the need for church reform. If the workers at Woolwich had shown hostility, it said, it was to the Church rather than to Christianity (*Guardian*, 13 September 1917; *Commonwealth*, November 1917, p. 325; December, p. 382; *Challenge*, 7 September 1917, p. 296; 14 September, pp. 302–3, 312; 21 September, p. 318; 9 November, p. 27; 31 May 1918, p. 67).
61 Hobhouse, *Forty Years*, p. 143.
62 p. 3.
63 p. 6.
64 p. 2.
65 p. 5.
66 p. 1.
67 p. 1.

68 p. 3.
69 p. 4.
70 p. 5.
71 p. 61.
72 p. 169.
73 p. 13.
74 p. 32.
75 p. 33.
76 p. 35.
77 pp. 37–8.
78 p. 40.
79 p. 2.
80 p. 3 – an often-used phrase at this time, derived from Donald Hankey's *A Student in Arms* (1916), Chap. VII. Hankey is quoted on p. 32 of the Report, where it is stated that it is the duty of the Church to proclaim Christ to men, whom 'unknowingly they already worship'; cf. Acts 17.23.
81 p. 4.
82 p. 13.
83 p. 14.
84 p. 15.
85 p. 17.
86 pp. 62–4.
87 p. 65.
88 Cf. Gore, *War and the Church*, p. 72, and Chap. V: 'Church Reform'.
89 pp. 12, 20.
90 p. 22 (italics in the original).
91 p. 2.
92 p. 1.
93 p. 7.
94 p. 49.
95 p. 52.
96 pp. 60, 66, 68.
97 pp. 89–90.
98 p. 138.
99 p. 108.
100 *Retrospect*, i, 318.
101 p. 23.
102 E. R. Norman, *Church and Society in England* (1976), Chap. 6; P. d'A. Jones, p. 164.
103 Cf. Gore's lecture, 'Christianity and Socialism', given to the Pan-Anglican Conference of 1908, with its confession, 'How vast has been our failure!' and its call for repentance and reparation (P. d'A. Jones, pp. 215–16).
104 *The Doctrine of the Trinity* (1943), p. 35.
105 *Waiting on God* (1951), p. 26.
106 Chap. VII.
107 Isaiah 45.
108 See J. A. T. Robinson, *The New Reformation?* (1965), pp. 47–8; Karl Rahner, *The Christian of the Future* (1967).

109 *Church and People in an Industrial City* (1957), p. 230.
110 *Memoirs*, p. 449.

CHAPTER 4 MORAL ISSUES IN WARTIME

 1 p. 29
 2 Andrew Rosen, *Rise Up, Women!* (1971), p. 251.
 3 See Arthur Marwick, *Women at War 1914–1918* (1977).
 4 Marrin, pp. 56–9.
 5 Tatlow, pp. 596, 620.
 6 Bell, pp. 663–70.
 7 Bell, pp. 768–70.
 8 Iremonger, pp. 236–8.
 9 Cross, pp. 269–71.
10 p. 93.
11 Iremonger, pp. 257–8.
12 *A Day of God*, p. 51.
13 Marrin, p. 185.
14 *The Church in Time of War*, pp. 55, 181.
15 *For All We Have and Are*, p. 13.
16 *Papers from Picardy* (1917), p. 89.
17 Laffin, p. 105.
18 *The Army and Religion* (1919), p. 148.
19 Laffin, p. 119.
20 Graves, p. 204.
21 F. W. Dillistone, *Charles Raven* (1975), Chap. 15.
22 Rowland Ryder, *Edith Cavell* (1975), p. 229; cf. Bernard Shaw's Preface to *Saint Joan* (1924).
23 Graves, pp. 188–9.
24 *The Woman's Part* (1914), p. 16.
25 Kenneth Brill (ed.), *John Groser* (1971), p. 23.
26 Laurence Housman (ed.), *War Letters of Fallen Englishmen* (1930), pp. 80, 82, 83.
27 *So As by Fire* (1915), pp. 16–27.
28 Nicolson, pp. 272–3, 317.
29 On the doctrine of the Just War, see, for example, Sydney D. Bailey, *Prohibitions and Restraints in War* (1972).
30 Bell, pp. 777–8.
31 Bell, p. 781.
32 See, for example, a sermon in Canterbury Cathedral, Easter 1915; in '*Quit You Like Men*' (1915), pp. 59–62.
33 Bell, pp. 831–5. In the second world war Bishop Bell (chaplain to Davidson 1914–24) was able to draw upon Davidson's stand in his own campaign against reprisals: see R. C. D. Jasper, *George Bell* (1967), Chap. 14.
34 Prestige, p. 389.
35 Caroline E. Playne, *Britain Holds On* (1933), pp. 112–13.
36 p. 269.
37 July 1917, p. 155.

38 August 1917, pp. 212–13; cf. *Church Times* on reprisals, 21 May 1915. H. D. A. Major was Principal of Ripon Hall, Oxford 1919–48.

39 Marwick, *The Deluge*, p. 65.

40 Bell, pp. 746–9; Davidson, '*Quit You Like Men*', pp. 64–5; Marwick, *The Deluge*, pp. 62–8.

41 J. G. Lockhart, *Charles Lindley, Viscount Halifax* (1936), ii, 237.

42 Prestige, pp. 373–4.

43 *Retrospect*, i, 182–6.

44 pp. 392–3.

45 Lancelot, p. 194.

46 *Manchester Guardian*, 1 April, 14 October 1915.

47 Bell, pp. 749–50.

48 January 1915, pp. 359–62; the *Guardian* was also outraged: 25 March 1915, etc. But cf. *Challenge*, 11 December 1914.

49 A. J. P. Taylor (ed.), *Lloyd George: A Diary by Frances Stevenson* (1971), pp. 6–7.

50 Pym, p. 89.

51 Tresham Lever, *Clayton of Toc H* (1971), pp. 161–2.

52 Matthews, p. 91.

53 Bell, pp. 891–7.

54 Coppard, pp. 56–7.

55 Bell, pp. 822–7, 837–8.

56 F. S. Temple (ed.), *William Temple: Some Lambeth Letters 1942–1944* (1963), pp. 33–5.

57 *Memoirs*, p. 455.

CHAPTER 5 THE CHURCH AT THE FRONT

1 (Everyman edn 1969), pp. 281–2.

2 (Penguin edn 1960), pp. 157–9.

3 Fussell, pp. 204–7.

4 Guy Chapman, *A Kind of Survivor* (1975).

5 *A Passionate Prodigality* (1965 edn), p. 117.

6 *Memoirs*, p. 220.

7 p. 269.

8 p. 282.

9 Note the echoes of Galatians 6.5; Mark 2.27; John 15.13.

10 p. 274.

11 p. 275.

12 *Memoirs*, pp. 404–5.

13 p. 435.

14 p. 447.

15 pp. 631–2; for a discussion of Sassoon's religious development, see Dame Felicitas Corrigan, *Siegfried Sassoon* (1973).

16 *Letters*, pp. 126, 175.

17 See Hilda Spear, 'I too saw God', in *English,* Summer 1975; *Letters*, p. 461.

18 *Letters*, p. 285.

19 Note the echoes of the traditional ascription then often used by the Anglican preacher at the end of his sermon.

20 *Letters*, pp. 461–2.

21 p. 483.
22 p. 580.
23 p. 544.
24 p. 590.
25 p. 582; cf. p. 498.
26 p. 458.
27 p. 562.
28 p. 534.
29 pp. 69–70, 79.
30 pp. 76–9.
31 *Morale* (1967), pp. 204–11.
32 *This Also Happened on the Western Front* (1932), p. 93.
33 *A Student in Arms*, pp. 34–5.
34 Fussell, pp. 83–4.
35 For example, Guy Rogers, *A Rebel at Heart* (1956), p. 121; Pym, p. 106; *Archbishops' Third Committee*, pp. 3, 32; A. F. Winnington-Ingram, *The Spirit of Peace* (1921), p. 74.
36 David Edwards, *Ian Ramsey* (1973), p. 67.
37 *A Student in Arms*, pp. 114–15.
38 p. 202.
39 p. 206.
40 p. 221.
41 p. 70.
42 Coppard, p. 73.
43 (1964 edn), pp. 85–6, 239, 301–2, 324.
44 pp. 339–40.
45 Ronald Blythe, *Akenfield* (1969), pp. 38–40.
46 Laffin, p. 66.
47 Pym, p. 157.
48 *Musings and Memories* (1931), pp. 159–71.
49 *The Attack* (1953), pp. 21–2.
50 R. H. Preston, in *Theology*, April 1966, p. 158.
51 *Father Figures*, p. 155.
52 John Smyth, *In This Sign Conquer* (1968), pp. xviii-xix, 156, 198, 202–3; Bell, p. 850. (Their statistics differ slightly.)
53 Communication from the Royal Army Chaplains' Department.
54 E. L. Langston, *Bishop Taylor Smith* (1939), p. 73.
55 p. 125.
56 p. 128.
57 Jackson, pp. 149–50.
58 Bell, pp. 739, 751.
59 Lockhart, ii, 246–8.
60 Waugh, p. 135.
61 Information from Fr Justin Pearce, C.R., nephew of Canon E. H. Pearce (Assistant Chaplain-General 1916–1919, Bishop of Worcester 1919–1930).
62 See, for example, Peter Green in *Manchester Guardian*, 19 August 1915.
63 *Guardian*, 17 June, 8 July 1915; *Challenge*, 16 July 1915.
64 Jackson, pp. 138, 145, 149–51, 155–6.

65 p. 178.

66 *Period*, pp. 58, 60.

67 Jackson, pp. 162–5.

68 English Church Union: *Religious Ministrations in the Army* (1916).

69 Bell, pp. 848–9.

70 Woods and Macnutt, pp. 94–5.

71 Rogers, p. 92.

72 John Smyth, pp. 168–9.

73 F. R. Barry, *Mervyn Haigh* (1964), p. 43.

74 *Period*, pp. 52–3.

75 *Goodbye to My Generation* (1951), p. 38.

76 Nias, p. 130.

77 Purcell, p. 98.

78 *Period*, p. 54.

79 John Smyth, p. 157.

80 *Period*, pp. 60–1.

81 John Smyth, pp. xvi, 164–80; R. L. Barnes, *A War-Time Chaplaincy* (1939), p. 53.

82 *Challenge*, 11 September 1914.

83 Jackson, p. 146; P. B. Clayton, *Tales of Talbot House* (1919), p. 7; *Guardian*, 8 April 1915.

84 Brabant, p. 59.

85 Bell, p. 783.

86 John Smyth, p. 169.

87 Bell, p. 783.

88 John Smyth, p. 203.

89 Enid Porter, *Tales from the Fens* (1963), pp. 97–8.

90 P. d'A. Jones, pp. 75n., 181–3, 186–8; Bell, pp. 488–92. It is significant that the only occasion on which Davidson is mentioned in Donald Read's *Edwardian England* (p. 56) is in relation to this latter incident.

91 An old man in a country parish in the 1960s told me that he thought Holy Communion was 'reserved for the gentry'; cf. Obelkevich, pp. 271–2.

92 A. O. Rahilly, in *Father William Doyle S.J.* (1920), gives a description of the work of one Roman Catholic chaplain.

93 Oldmeadow, ii, 121.

94 24 June 1915.

95 *Aspects of the Church's Duty* (1915), p. 10.

96 *Memoirs*, p. 238; cf. the soldiers' opinions of the clergy in Louise Creighton (ed.), *Letters of Oswin Creighton* (1919), p. 169.

97 *Not the Whole Truth* (1971), p. 63.

98 March 1972, p. 104.

99 His general line was approved by Oswin Creighton, *Letters*, pp. 196–7.

100 Pym, pp. 107–15, 143.

CHAPTER 6 SOME CHAPLAINS

1 *Rough Talks by a Padre* (1918), pp. 66–7; cf. pp. 61, 130–1.

2 J. K. Mozley, *G. A. Studdert Kennedy by His Friends* (1929), p. 129.

3 W. H. Elliott, *Undiscovered Ends* (1951), p. 217.

4 *Memoirs*, p. 240.
5 Purcell, pp. 106–7.
6 Mozley, p. 154.
7 Montague, p. 67; but cf. Chapman, *A Kind of Survivor*, pp. 68–9.
8 Purcell, p. 118.
9 M. Hardy, *Hardy, V.C.* (1920), pp. 69–70.
10 Studdert Kennedy, *The Hardest Part* (1919), pp. 10, 118.
11 *Changeful Page* (1965), p. 85.
12 *Period*, pp. 56–7, 63.
13 Dillistone, pp. 73, 213, 312, 423.
14 *A Wanderer's Way* (1928), pp. 156–8, 168.
15 Dillistone, p. 299.
16 ibid., p. 86.
17 *Musings*, p. 162.
18 Dillistone, pp. 87, 428.
19 *Musings*, pp. 171, 180; cf. Teilhard de Chardin, *Writings in Time of War* (1968), for similar themes and reflections.
20 *The Modern Churchman*, January/February 1919, pp. 522–4.
21 Brill, pp. 27–8.
22 Patrick Wilkinson, *Eric Milner-White* (1963), p. 12.
23 *Abinger Harvest* (1946 edn), p. 88.
24 Michael Moynihan (ed.), *People at War 1914–18* (1973), Chap. 3.
25 Brabant, p. 57.
26 ibid., p. 65.
27 Carey, p. 100.
28 *Religion behind the Front and after the War* (1918), pp. 111–12.
29 Brabant, p. 67.
30 *Religion*, p. 67.
31 Clayton, pp. 36–7.
32 Bell, p. 780.
33 Lever, p. 67.
34 October 1916, p. 17.
35 Oliver Tomkins, *Edward Woods* (1957), p. 39.
36 *Letters*, p. 219; cf. pp. 229–30.
37 Ellis Roberts, p. 84.
38 Rogers, pp. 117–18.
39 Rogers, p. 113.
40 Barry, *Period*, p. 62.
41 Lockhart, pp. 257–8.
42 Blackburne, pp. 87, 99–100.
43 Moorman, pp. 80–93.
44 Playne, *Society at War*, pp. 209–10.
45 Moorman, p. 103.

CHAPTER 7 THE ARMY AND RELIGION

1 For a picture of religion in the Navy, see Henry Baynham, *Men from the Dreadnoughts* (1976), Chap. 18.

2 A. E. Reffold, *Wilson Carlile and the Church Army* (1956 edn), Chap. XIV.

3 Prestige, p. 372.

4 20 November 1914; cf. Appendix II of *The Army and Religion*.

5 John Terraine (ed.), *General Jack's Diary* (1964), p. 116.

6 *Soldier from the Wars Returning*, p. 185.

7 Montague, p. 66.

8 *Letters*, pp. 166, 178, 201.

9 Purcell, pp. 144–5.

10 Tawney, p. 11.

11 Purcell, pp. 62, 98.

12 *So As by Fire*, p. 116.

13 Blythe, p. 48.

14 *Challenge*, 23 October 1914.

15 *Culham Club Magazine*, Summer 1973.

16 *The World Goes By* (1952), pp. 110–11.

17 *Culham Club Magazine*, October 1922.

18 *The Unreturning Army* (1967), pp. 59, 80–1.

19 G. Vernon Smith, *The Bishop of London's Visit to the Front* (1915), pp. 11–12, 37.

20 Playne, *Britain Holds On*, p. 209.

21 Laffin, p. 108.

22 *Soldier from the Wars Returning*, p. 228.

23 Laffin, p. 15.

24 Housman, p. 69.

25 *Letters*, p. 429.

26 Housman, pp. 186–7.

27 For example, Winnington-Ingram, *Day of God*, p. 65.

28 Pym, pp. 6–9, 14–17.

29 *Letters and Recollections* (1918), pp. 239, 255.

30 In a letter to his old friend Bishop Talbot, von Hügel asked leave to explain to the Committee why obedience to his Church would not allow him to join in corporate prayer with them (*Selected Letters*, ed. Bernard Holland, 1933 edn, p. 245).

31 Tatlow, p. 589.

32 p. xxviii.

33 p. 9.

34 A point made strongly by Geoffrey Gordon in Pym, pp. 125–7, 134; cf. Gore's criticism of the use of the Ten Commandments in Communion and Catechism in *Archbishops' First Committee*, pp. 166–8; A. C. Headlam, in *Church Quarterly*, October 1916, pp. 13–15.

35 p. 74.

36 p. 68; cf. E. R. Wickham's comments on this passage: 'men discovered values which they never associated with religion or morality – again a characteristic evidenced in a thousand ways in working-class life back home, and throughout the years before – that comradeship and solidarity were the essence of life, that the damning sins were not "wangling", drunkenness, impurity or profanity, but cowardice, selfishness, snobbishness and tyranny' (p. 208). Chaplains (and men) often contrasted the comradeship of the trenches with the lack of fellowship within and between the Churches, and longed for a cause in the post-war world which

would elicit a similar spirit of self-sacrifice (e.g. Gordon, in Pym, pp. 191–2, 205–21).

37 p. 92.

38 Cf. Kenneth Kirk, *A Study of Silent Minds* (1918), summarized by E. W. Kemp, *Kenneth Escott Kirk* (1959), pp. 31–46.

39 *The Army and Religion*, p. 108.

40 p. 127.

41 p. 131.

42 pp. 134–5.

43 p. 164.

44 Cf. Kenneth Kirk, as quoted by Kemp, op. cit., p. 33: 'two things specifically connected with religion always come to him [i.e., the soldier] with the surprise of a miracle: the often repeated phenomenon of the crucifix standing untouched among ruins; and the strange vagaries of Providence, or fate, by which others have been struck down whilst he so far has been spared.' An Irish soldier on the Somme wrote: 'Somewhere the Choosers of the Slain are touching, as in our Norse story they used to touch, with invisible wands those who are to die' (Laffin, p. 70).

45 *The Army and Religion*, p. 57.

46 p. 332.

47 p. 365.

48 *The Potter and the Clay*, pp. 70–2.

49 Paget, p. 317.

50 *The Army and Religion*, p. 444.

51 p. 422.

52 p. 443.

53 Michael de la Bedoyere, *Baron von Hügel* (1951), pp. 298–9.

54 Henson criticized the Report for its 'mood of self-condemnation', its 'strain of half-ecstatic exaggeration' and its misunderstanding of both religion and society, in a sermon, 'A Kingdom That Cannot Be Shaken' (1919).

55 p. 275.

56 p. 403.

57 p. 234; cf. Henri Perrin, a French worker-priest, writing home from Germany in 1944: 'how could I have any nostalgia for the services we knew only too well in France – those "private" and mechanical prayers which are mostly routine, those low Masses said by a solitary priest and attended by a few of the faithful, lost in the four corners of an almost empty church, or, almost worse, those worldly Masses with the spirit of prayer almost gone out of them.' *Priest and Worker*, tr. Bernard Wall (1965), p. 36.

58 p. 200. The more rigid Anglo-Catholics had been brought up to despise Protestantism and to mock other forms of churchmanship. They were more adequately trained to fight for the triumph of Anglo-Catholicism than to struggle for the development of a spirituality tough enough to cope with the rigours of the front. Comprehensive churchmanship ('Y.M.C.A. religion') was aesthetically distasteful and theologically anathema to them: cf. Waugh, pp. 137–8.

59 p. 54.

60 pp. 38, 39, 45.

61 pp. 76, 79.

62 p. 376.

63 ibid., p. 378; cf. Coppard: 'in most of the situations that Tommies had to contend with, bad language was the only kind that made sense' (p. 46); cf. Harry Williams: 'There is often more love in a "Christ Almighty" than there is in a spiritually castrated "Alleluia".' *Tensions* (1976), p. 34; David Jones, *In Parenthesis* (1963 edn), p. xii.

64 *The Church in the Furnace*, pp. 176, 409.

CHAPTER 8   DEATH, BEREAVEMENT, AND THE SUPERNATURAL

1 The words were inscribed in letters of gold above the sanctuary in Sandhurst Chapel just before war broke out; cf. Owen's bitter poem, 'Dulce et Decorum Est'.

2 *Day of God*, pp. 5, 43.

3 Duff Cooper, *Haig* (1935), i, 327–8.

4 *The First World War* (Penguin 1966), p. 140.

5 Fussell, pp. 13, 72–3.

6 Coppard, p. viii.

7 Wickham, p. 209.

8 *The War and the Soul*, p. 36.

9 *Britain Holds On*, pp. 76–7.

10 *Rays of Dawn*, pp. 8–10.

11 *Letters*, p. 581.

12 Blythe, p. 40.

13 *Memories and Hopes* (1925), p. 184.

14 Joseph Cohen, *Journey to the Trenches: The Life of Isaac Rosenberg 1890–1918* (1975), p. 6.

15 Graves, p. 228.

16 *Practical Criticism*, p. 269.

17 See Ian Gregor and Walter Stein (eds), *The Prose for God* (1973).

18 Bell, pp. 53–5.

19 Geoffrey Gorer, *Death, Grief and Mourning* (1965), pp. 1–6.

20 Coppard, p. 46.

21 Bell, p. 790.

22 Charles Smyth, pp. 131–4.

23 *Manchester Guardian*, 1 July 1915.

24 *The Church in Time of War*, pp. 19, 226; *The Potter and the Clay*, pp. 234–5.

25 See Geoffrey Rowell, *Hell and the Victorians* (1974).

26 *The War and the Soul*, pp. 9, 13.

27 See Paul Welsby, 'Prayers for the Dead', in *Theology*, June 1966.

28 Bell, pp. 830–1.

29 Jasper, pp. 102, 353.

30 e.g., Paul Bull, *Peace and War*, pp. 86–92.

31 Harford, pp. 220–1. Mrs Moule took a more strict Evangelical view – see her letter in *Challenge*, 20 November 1914, and subsequent correspondence.

32 Blackburne, p. 32.

33 Pym, p. 221.

34 Bell, pp. 828–31.

35 pp. 26, 39, 41.

36 *Fellowship with God* (1920), pp. 78–9.
37 Bell, pp. 806–13.
38 *Hopes for English Religion* (1919), p. 182.
39 *Rays of Dawn*, pp. 179, 185–6; *The Spirit of Peace*, pp. 155–65.
40 *Christ: and the World at War*, pp. vi, 56.
41 Oldmeadow, ii, 108.
42 *The Church in Time of War*, pp. 234–6.
43 *Rays of Dawn*, p. 14; *The Potter and the Clay*, pp. 192–3.
44 Included in G. Vernon Smith, *The Bishop of London's Visit to the Front*.
45 *The Church in Time of War*, pp. 211–12.
46 p. 135.
47 p. 288.
48 pp. 297, 299.
49 Rogers, pp. 124–5.
50 *Musings*, p. 165.
51 Basil Matthews, pp. 71–2.
52 *Letters*, p. 571.
53 pp. 409–10; H. G. Wells's statement of his religious beliefs in *God the Invisible King* (1917) was much discussed in the religious press.
54 *The Church in the Furnace*, p. 381.
55 *As It Was and World Without End* (1972 edn), p. 161.
56 Rowell, p. 212.
57 pp. 127–8.
58 *The New Theology* (1907), p. 207.
59 *The War and the Soul*, pp. 76–7, 154, 162–3; cf. von Hügel, *Essays and Addresses*, first series (1921), Chap. 7: 'What do we mean by Heaven? What do we mean by Hell?' (1917).
60 *The Modern Churchman*, January/February 1919, p. 527.
61 Prestige, p. 373; cf. *War and the Church*, p. 22.
62 *CR*, Christmas 1916.
63 Montague, p. 73; Hankey, pp. 70, 128–9, 215–21; cf. C. F. G. Masterman, *Tennyson As a Religious Teacher* (1900).
64 Moynihan, p. 59.
65 '*Quit You Like Men*', p. 76.
66 Sent to Charles Carrington by his brother Philip, Browning's poem became a favourite in the mess (*Soldier from the Wars Returning*, p. 146). Another poem often cited was Wordsworth's 'Happy Warrior'.
67 *Gilbert Walter Lyttelton Talbot: A Memoir* (1916), pp. 37, 42, 47.
68 Brabant, pp. 62–3.
69 *Letters*, p. 185.
70 *Memoir*, p. 42.
71 Hyman, p. 290.
72 *Safety Last* (1927), pp. 42, 93.
73 *For All We Have and Are*, pp. 48–9.
74 Cf. R. T. Davidson, *The Testing of a Nation* (1919), p. 56. Ruskin, *The Crown of Wild Olive*, Lecture III (given in 1865) was frequently cited in the first war on this theme: 'war was the foundation of all great art'; 'all great nations learned their

truth of word, and strength of thought, in war . . . they were nourished in war and wasted by peace' (§§ 87, 94).

75 Marwick, *The Deluge*, p. 48.

76 Read, *Edwardian England*, p. 251.

77 *Sermons for the Times No. 4: Sermons on the Holy War* (1914), p. 3.

78 *Hopes for English Religion*, p. 129.

79 Keeling, p. 183.

80 Laffin, p. 6.

81 Rosen, pp. 199–200.

82 Arthur Marwick, *Women at War 1914–1918*, p. 32.

83 Robert Kee, *The Green Flag* (1972), pp. 531, 569; Guy Chapman, *Vain Glory* (1968), p. 377.

84 p. 274.

85 *Rays of Dawn*, p. 66.

86 *Peace and War*, pp. 49, 81.

87 *Britain Holds On*, pp. 406–7.

88 Bengt Sundkler, *Nathan Söderblom* (1968), p. 162.

89 Pym, p. 118.

90 Jackson, pp. 154–5.

91 *The Army and Religion*, p. 289.

92 'It most powerfully expresses a message of Christianity to our soldiers', said one chaplain (*Graphic*, 5 December 1914).

93 See p. 188, above.

94 Christopher Martin, *English Life in the First World War* (1974), p. 37.

95 Housman, p. 278.

96 Graves, p. 89.

97 *Soldier from the Wars Returning*, pp. 14, 264.

98 Hankey, pp. 284–8.

99 *Letters*, p. 198.

100 *Undertones of War* (1930 edn), pp. 147, 153.

101 17, 24 June 1915.

102 See, for example, *War-Time Sermons*, pp. ix–x, 231.

103 *Retrospect*, i, 176, 180–2.

104 Harford, p. 282.

105 Woods and Macnutt, pp. 29–31.

106 *The War and the Soul*, pp. 126–8.

107 Pym, pp. 44–5.

108 In England much superstition and folk religion is passed on from one generation to another through the rhymes and rituals of childhood. See Iona and Peter Opie, *The Lore and Language of Schoolchildren* (1959), especially Chaps. 11–12.

109 See Obelkevich, Chap. VI.

110 See Owen Chadwick, *The Secularization of the European Mind in the Nineteenth Century* (1975), Chap. 10.

CHAPTER 9 PATRIOTISM IS NOT ENOUGH

1 See Chadwick, *Secularization*, pp. 129–34.

2 *Sermons Preached before the University of Oxford* (1876), pp. 111–14.

3 *Six Lambeth Conferences*, pp. 259, 262.

4 See Marrin, pp. 97–118; W. B. Selbie, *The War and Theology* (1915).

5 Tatlow, pp. 509, 517–21.

6 *The War and the Soul*, pp. 78–9, 83–4; cf. Figgis, *Hopes for English Religion*, pp. 66–9.

7 See, for example, Henson, *War-Time Sermons*, p. 217.

8 p. 421.

9 *National Mission of Repentance and Hope: A Report of the Chaplains' Replies* (1916), p. 37.

10 Rogers, pp. 120, 129, 175.

11 *A Fortnight at the Front* (1915), pp. 16–17. Douglas Haig told Randall Davidson during the latter's visit to France in 1916 that he strongly disapproved of bishops coming out 'for joy rides about the country' and then writing books: 'We don't want our men and their ways exploited.' He was referring specifically to Russell Wakefield. (Bell, p. 783; Davidson Papers: *Visit to the Front 1916*: Bell concealed Russell Wakefield's name with asterisks.) Haig wholly approved of Davidson's visit, which was of a quite different character.

12 Brabant, p. 154.

13 *Retrospect*, i, 193–201, 299.

14 *Reminiscences*, p. 276.

15 *Victory and After* (1920), p. 30; cf. *Church Quarterly*, April 1919, p. 120.

16 Tatlow, pp. 616–19.

17 Bell, pp. 740–3. See also *To the Christian Scholars of Europe and America: A Reply from Oxford to the German Address to Evangelical Christians* (1914).

18 *The Church in Time of War*, pp. 238–9.

19 Bell, pp. 917–25.

20 Bell, p. 1153.

21 Stephenson, p. 251; Sundkler, p. 226.

22 Bell, pp. 1036–7.

23 *The Six Lambeth Conferences*, pp. 11, 27–8, 30–1.

24 p. 135.

25 *Not Only Peace* (1967), pp. 44–5.

26 Tawney, pp. 15–16, 25, 27, 28.

27 Montague, pp. 141–3.

28 Keeling, p. 259.

29 Moynihan, pp. 90–1.

30 J. C. King (ed.), *First World War* (1972), pp. 188–9.

31 *Rough Talks*, pp. 45, 79.

32 Brabant, p. 60.

33 *CR*, Christmas 1918.

34 *CR*, Christmas 1914.

35 Nicolson, pp. 249–50.

36 Henson, *Retrospect*, ii, 88.

37 Julian Symons, *Horatio Bottomley* (1955), pp. 166, 185–6; Hyman, p. 160.

38 Edward Thompson, *Robert Bridges* (1944), p. 92.

39 *Challenge*, 21 May 1915; cf. Bell, p. 924.

40 Bell, pp. 757–60.

41 *Diary*, p. 30.

42 Pym, pp. 25–31; cf. Studdert Kennedy, *Rough Talks*, p. 221.

43 Lucy Masterman, *C. F. G. Masterman* (1939), Chap. 11.

44 Bell, pp. 753–4.

45 21 May; cf. 28 May 1915.

46 Bell, p. 756.

47 *Guardian*, 27 May 1915.

48 See Temple's approval of the Pastoral, and his programme for united action by church and state, in his sermon, *Go Forward*, summarized above, pp. 38–9.

49 *War-Time Sermons*, pp. ix–x.

50 *Day of God*, pp. 10, 41, 42, 58; see also Winnington-Ingram, in Basil G. Bourchier (ed.), *What Is Wrong* (1916), p. 9. 'Christ or Odin' (like 'Christ or Nietzsche') was a popular slogan. It was widely believed that Germany had abandoned Christianity for the old Teutonic gods.

51 *The Potter and the Clay*, pp. 41–2, 46–7, 49–50, 53. This sermon was discussed in *Theology*, January and June 1971.

52 Lockhart, pp. 248–53, 261–2, 406.

53 H. D. A. Major, *Life and Letters of William Boyd Carpenter* (1925), pp. 248–50.

54 *Further Pages of My Life* (1916), pp. 288, 294.

55 Symons, p. 164.

56 Iremonger, p. 171.

57 Quoted and commended by Gore, in *War and the Church*, pp. 38–9.

58 Iremonger, p. 187.

59 *Forms of Prayer for Private and Public Use in Time of War* (1915).

60 *Church Times*, 1 April 1915.

61 31 March 1915.

62 1 April 1915.

63 MacDonagh, pp. 89–90.

64 Lyttelton, p. 187.

65 *War and the Church*, pp. 2, 4–5, 10, 12, 18, 60.

66 Prestige, p. 412; cf. von Hügel's attempts to distinguish the 'true Germany' from German militarism – Bedoyere, pp. 281–3.

67 *So As by Fire*, pp. 104–5.

68 Sheen, pp. 74, 79–80.

65 *'Quit You Like Men'*, pp. 44, 57–62.

70 Bell, pp. 757, 786–9, 903–5.

71 *The Testing of a Nation*, p. 157.

72 *Guardian*, 12 July 1917.

73 pp. 68, 260–1, 281–7, 401.

74 Information from the Rector of Theberton.

75 13 August 1914, 12 July 1917.

76 Bell, pp. 743–4.

77 24, 31 August 1917.

78 30 August 1917.

79 September 1917.

80 October 1917, pp. 139–40, 147.

81 Bell, pp. 406, 884–7, 940–1; Sundkler, Chap. 5.

82 *Lloyd George: A Diary by Frances Stevenson*, p. 40.

83 *The Church in Time of War*, pp. 275–6.

84 *Rays of Dawn*, pp. 6–7.

85 *For All We Have and Are*, pp. 72–3.

86 Thomas Jones, pp. 75–6; cf. Canon H. D. Rawnsley, *Against a Premature and Inconclusive Peace* (1917). A. J. P. Taylor (*English History 1914–1945*, pp. 65n., 115) questions whether the Germans in 1917 could have agreed to a negotiated peace acceptable to the Allies.

87 Lord Newton, *Lord Lansdowne* (1929), p. 472.

88 Bell, pp. 847–8, 886–7, 901.

89 *Letters*, p. 211.

90 *Challenge*, 7 December 1917.

91 *Retrospect*, iii, 47.

92 Leslie Paul, *A Church by Daylight*, p. 96.

93 Alfred E. Garvie, *Memories and Meanings of My Life* (1938), p. 166.

CHAPTER 10 FAITH AND WAR

1 Wickham, pp. 191, 204.

2 Chap. VI.

3 *New Bearings in English Poetry* (1950 edn), p. 10.

4 Chap. XXV.

5 Dillistone, pp. 265–73.

6 *The War and the Soul*, p. 128.

7 *The Potter and the Clay*, p. 98.

8 Barrow Gurney parish records.

9 K. S. Inglis, *Churches and the Working Classes in Victorian England* (1963), p. 24.

10 See Patrick Wilkinson, *Eric Milner-White* (1963); Philip Pare and Donald Harris, *Eric Milner-White* (1965).

11 *Hopes for English Religion*, p. 43; cf. H. E. Root, in A. R. Vidler (ed.), *Soundings* (1962), pp. 17–18.

12 *Last Essays on Church and Religion* (1877), Preface.

13 Cf. Leonard Woolf, *Downhill All the Way* (1967), p. 9; Kingsley Martin, *Father Figures*, p. 123.

14 *The Epistle to the Romans*, tr. E. C. Hoskyns (1933), p. 432.

15 Claud Cockburn, *Bestseller* (1972), pp. 1–2, 19–42; S. C. Carpenter, *Winnington-Ingram* (1949), p. 152.

16 Mildred Davidson, *The Poetry is in the Pity* (1972), pp. 136–40; cf. H. L. Elvin, 'Eagles and Trumpets for the Middle Classes', in *Scrutiny*, i (1932), 147–63.

17 *Gore to Temple* (1960), p. 62.

18 *Letters*, p. 127.

19 ibid., p. 121.

20 ibid., p. 125.

21 ibid., p. 159.

22 ibid., pp. 155, 193.

23 ibid., p. 214; cf. pp. 127, 131.

24 ibid., pp. 196–7; cf. pp. 181–2.

25 ibid., p. 210.

26 ibid., p. 131.

27 ibid., pp. 171–2, 176–7, 179, 187, 205, 209.
28 ibid., p. 200.
29 ibid., p. 187.
30 ibid., pp. 202–3.
31 ibid., p. 185.
32 ibid., pp. 210–11.
33 ibid., pp. 229, 233.
34 Owen Chadwick, *The Victorian Church* (1970), ii, 450–1; Barry, *Period*, pp. 46–7; Dillistone, p. 114.
35 Bullock, pp. 43, 48, 55; Wand, pp. 43–5.
36 H. H. Henson (ed.), *Church Problems* (1900), p. 21.
37 Louise Creighton, *Life and Letters of Mandell Creighton* (1904), ii, 191; cf. L. E. Elliott-Binns, *English Thought 1860–1900* (1956), Chap. 16.
38 G. W. E. Russell, *Basil Wilberforce* (1917), p. 163.
39 J. B. Mozley, pp. 104–6.
40 Fussell, Chap. V.
41 Norman, Chaps. 5–6; P. d'A. Jones, Chaps. V–VII, X.
42 pp. 3–5, 221.
43 p. 153.
44 p. 63.
45 pp. 108–9.
46 p. 173.
47 p. 185.
48 *The War and the Soul*, pp. 94–8.
49 p. v.
50 p. 99.
51 Iremonger, p. 163.
52 Figgis, *Civilisation at the Cross Roads*, p. 147; Ramsey, pp. 171–4.
53 pp. 120–1.
54 Prestige, p. 225.
55 *Under the Dome*, pp. 72–3.
56 *The Incarnation of the Son of God* (1891), p. 36.
57 ibid., p. 124; *Belief in God* (1921), Chap. VI (ii); *The Holy Spirit and the Church* (1924), Chap. IX (vi).
58 Frank M. McClain, *Maurice: Man and Moralist* (1972), pp. 130–4.
59 *Lies* (published in 1919; 1932 edn), p. 72.
60 *Letters*, pp. 430n., 534.
61 On 'common religion', see Robert Towler, *Homo Religiosus* (1974).
62 Quoted by H. A. Williams from an unpublished lecture of Niebuhr's: see A. R. Vidler (ed.), *Objections to Christian Belief* (1963), pp. 54–5.
63 See also his *Commonsense about the War* (1914).
64 H. A. Williams, *Tensions*, p. 39.
65 Bruno Bettelheim, *The Informed Heart* (1961); A. Alvarez, 'Beyond the Gentility Principle', in *The New Poetry* (Penguin 1966).
66 *The World Crisis* (1931 abridged edn), p. 107.
67 Von Hügel, *Letters*, pp. 211–12.
68 E. N. Gowing, *John Edwin Watts-Ditchfield* (1926), pp. 194–5.
69 pp. xi–xiii.

70 pp. 120–34.
71 *Hopes for English Religion*, pp. 16–24, 105–6, 145–6. Temple also considered the possibility that God might not give Britain a victory through arms: 'Christ was right; Christ trusted God; and Christ was crucified' (*Go Forward*, p. 14).
72 Paget, pp. 312, 322n.
73 p. 399.
74 Temple, *A Challenge to the Church*, pp. 41–2.
75 pp. 31–2.
76 Furse, pp. 85–8.
77 Matthews, p. 85.
78 Cross, p. 121.
79 p. 276.
80 Prestige, pp. 225–6.
81 Wand, pp. 37–8; cf. Archbishop Fisher's warm but critical estimate in Purcell, *Fisher*, pp. 80–1; Fisher succeeded him as Bishop of London.
82 *The Church in Time of War*, pp. 7, 11–13, 24.
83 ibid., p. 21.
84 ibid., p. 240; *Guardian*, 24 June 1915.
85 *The Potter and the Clay*, p. 229.
86 *The Soul of a Nation* (1915), pp. 5, 7, 11.
87 *The Spirit of Peace*, p. 195.
88 He 'welcomed' in Convocation the proposal to omit the Imprecatory Psalms from the Church's liturgy (*Guardian*, 5 July 1917).
89 *The Church in Time of War*, pp. 33–4.
90 Rosen, p. 200.
91 *Sermons for the Times, No. 4: Sermons on the Holy War* (1914).
92 Cf. *Commonwealth*, April 1916, for further criticisms of 'Holy War' talk, and of Winnington- Ingram.
93 pp. 9, 13–14.
94 *For All We Have and Are*, p. xxiv.
95 pp. 2–4.
96 pp. 76–7.
97 pp. 101–2.
98 Keeling, pp. 259–60.
99 (1914 edn), p. ix.
100 p. 150.
101 p. 152; this was also the theme of *The Passing of War* (1913), by Canon W. L. Grane, of the Church of England Peace League.
102 pp. 183–4.
103 p. 3.
104 p. 175; cf. Gore, *War and the Church*, Chap. II.
105 p. 57.
106 p. 60; he frequently pointed out in the *Manchester Guardian* (e.g. 18 February 1915) that the war had created a new interest in the nature of Christian ethics. The revival of Anglican moral theology in the post-war period under the influence of Kenneth Kirk was a not wholly satisfying response to this new interest in ethics. Kirk's *Some Principles of Moral Theology* (1920), which grew out of his lectures given to chaplains in 1918, was mainly a guide to spiritual direction along the lines

he had adumbrated in his essay in *The Church in the Furnace*. His *Conscience and Its Problems* (1927) was a rather wooden attempt to apply the methods of casuistry to moral dilemmas, personal and social. If Kirk represented the ethical thinking of Anglo-Catholicism, Hastings Rashdall's *Conscience and Christ* (1916) may be taken as an index to the ethical thinking of liberal theologians of the period.

107 pp. 85–6.
108 p. 117.
109 p. 127.
110 p. 130.
111 p. 137.
112 p. 140.
113 p. 145.
114 p. 157.
115 pp. 164–5.
116 p. xii.
117 p. 21.
118 p. 57.
119 p. 111.
120 p. 113.
121 pp. 115–16.
122 p. 239.
123 p. 248.
124 pp. 251, 255; cf. Henson, *War-Time Sermons*, p. 221: 'Undenominational Christianity, purged at last of its political connexions, will be finally vindicated, and will build religious toleration on a sure foundation.' But the war, Henson believed, had done nothing to vindicate the claims of episcopacy!

CHAPTER 11 PREPARING FOR PEACE

1 C. S. Peel, *How We Lived Then 1914–18* (1929), p. 173.
2 MacDonagh, pp. 327–8.
3 Fox, p. 138.
4 *Retrospect*, i, 311–12; cf. ii, 100.
5 *Retrospect*, ii, 57.
6 David M. Thompson, *Nonconformity in the Nineteenth Century* (1972), p. 273.
7 Robert Currie, *Methodism Divided* (1968), pp. 180, 182.
8 Bell, pp. 949–50.
9 *More Letters*, p. 13.
10 Harford, p. 281.
11 *Manchester Guardian*, 13 November 1918.
12 *Commonwealth*, however, in January 1919 expressed disgust at the meanness and hatred which the election had revealed.
13 Bell, pp. 934–9, 942, 947–9.
14 *Retrospect*, ii, 56.
15 Brabant, pp. 73–4.
16 Lockhart, ii, 246; *Church Quarterly*, January 1919, p. 339; *Guardian*, 5, 12 December 1918.
17 June 1919.

18 *Guardian*, 5, 12 December 1918; *Church Times*, 6 December 1918.
19 *Guardian*, 5 December 1918.
20 Iremonger, p. 376.
21 Stephenson, p. 252.
22 Oliver, p. 34.
23 Tatlow, pp. 313, 613, 622–8.
24 When, early in the war, liberal Christians voiced their dislike of the traditional second and third verses of the National Anthem, Percy Dearmer drew attention to the internationalism of the final verse of the form given in the *English Hymnal*, which he had edited, as well as to the value of other hymns in that collection (*Challenge*, 21 August 1914). *The National Mission Hymn Book* (1916) contained several hymns which expressed Christian social concern, some new to congregations. But Peter Green, dismissing it as a 'thoroughly unsatisfactory production, ill-selected and ill-arranged', complained that it reproduced several hymns easily available elsewhere, and provided none specifically for the Eucharist (*Manchester Guardian*, 6 July 1916). Dearmer first realized the lack of hymns on social questions in 1894, when as Secretary of the London branch of the Christian Social Union he arranged C.S.U. midday services at a city church: *Songs of Praise Discussed* (1933), p. 172; this hymn-by-hymn commentary reveals the theological principles behind the selection of hymns for *Songs of Praise*.
25 Grane, p. 85.
26 On Lord Robert Cecil's work for the League, see Rose, Chap. 6.
27 Bell, pp. 891, 910–14.
28 ibid., pp. 1207–9.
29 *More Letters*, p. 139.
30 *The Spirit of Peace*, pp. 44, 247.
31 June 1919, p. 143.
32 Prestige, pp. 404–6, 409, 434.
33 Thomas Jones, p. 160.
34 See Reinhold Niebuhr, *Moral Man and Immoral Society* (published in 1932; 1963 edn), pp. xx–xxiii, 79.
35 pp. 128, 200.
36 Brabant, p. 71.
37 Bell, p. 961.
38 Iremonger, p. 220.
39 Bell, p. 968.
40 Gore, *The Holy Spirit and the Church* (1924), pp. 352–7.
41 Bell, pp. 969–73.
42 *Retrospect*, i, 208, 305, 308.
43 Nan Dearmer, *Percy Dearmer* (1941), pp. 213–14.
44 Kenneth A. Thompson, *Bureaucracy and Church Reform* (1970), p. 152.
45 Bell, p. 975.
46 Ellis Roberts, pp. 118–19.
47 *National Mission: Chaplains' Replies*, pp. 19–20.
48 Thompson, p. 158.
49 For Temple's theology in wartime, see his *Mens Creatrix* (1917); the Preface declared his 'master-influences' to be St John, Plato, and Browning.
50 *Letters*, pp. 202–3.

51 p. 214.

52 pp. 218–19.

53 *Retrospect*, ii, 68–74.

54 Maurice Headlam, *Bishop and Friend: Nugent Hicks* (1944), pp. 69, 71.

55 R. V. H. Burne, *Knutsford* (1960), p. 25.

56 Barry, *Period*, pp. 66–7.

57 Lever, p. 78.

58 Barry, *Haigh*, p. 53.

59 ibid., pp. 54, 66–7.

60 ibid., pp. 54–5.

61 Moorman, pp. 43, 104–5.

62 *Period*, p. 72; *Haigh*, p. 57.

63 pp. 111–12, 280–2.

64 Bell, p. 908; Cross, pp. 159–60.

65 *Crockford Prefaces* (1947), p. 33.

66 p. 129.

67 pp. 35–6.

68 Jackson, p. 160.

69 Dora Pym, *Tom Pym* (1952), p. 73.

70 Cf. *Notes on Venereal Disease and 'The Moral Question', From a Chaplain's Point of View* (n.d.).

71 *Church Council on War Problems: Report of Proceedings* (1918).

72 Tatlow, pp. 349, 575–6, 592–611.

73 Mulliner, pp. 51–4, 92–3.

74 Groves, pp. 160, 180–1, 187, 212.

75 *Autobiography*, p. 114.

76 Purcell, pp. 156, 159, 217; Oliver, pp. 60–5.

77 *Victory and After*, p. 116.

78 H. Maynard Smith, *Frank, Bishop of Zanzibar* (1926), p. 302.

79 Ellis Roberts, p. 105.

80 Norman, pp. 286–90.

81 *The Proceedings of COPEC* (1924), pp. 287–9.

82 G. K. A. Bell (ed.), *The Stockholm Conference on Life and Work 1925* (1926), pp. 710–11.

83 ibid., p. 452.

84 ibid., p. 681.

85 *Proceedings*, p. 162.

86 *Stockholm*, p. 530.

87 ibid., p. 498; cf. pp. 447–8.

88 An American delegate said at Stockholm: 'Aside from the insane outbreak of 1914, I doubt not that the world is improving in nearly every way' (*Stockholm*, p. 662).

89 Cf. Temple, in *Doctrine in the Church of England* (1938), pp. 16–17.

90 Woods and Macnutt, pp. 76–8, 90–1, 109–12, 118.

91 Oliver, pp. 45, 47.

92 See Oliver, Chap. 7; Roger Lloyd, *The Church of England 1900–1965* (1966), Chap. 15.

93 See Oliver, Chaps. 3, 4; Norman, pp. 258–60, 326–36; Bell, Chap. LXXX; Stuart Mews, 'The Churches', in M. Morris (ed.), *The General Strike* (Penguin 1976).

94 Bell, p. 1154.

95 Nan Dearmer, pp. 269–70.

96 ibid., pp. 245–7.

97 Prestige, p. 435.

98 Dillistone, pp. 143–7.

99 *Selected Essays* (1951 edn), pp. 16–17.

100 The Society of SS. Peter and Paul was founded in 1911 to oppose the 'English Use' and to promote a continental baroque style in vestments, architecture, and worship; on both movements, see P. F. Anson, *Fashions in Church Furnishings 1840–1940* (1960).

101 p. 125.

102 *The Religious and the Secular* (1969), p. 66.

103 See, for example, David Martin, *A Sociology of English Religion* (1967); Robin Gill, *The Social Context of Theology* (1975); Robert Bocock, *Ritual in Industrial Society* (1974).

104 *Religion and Change* (1969), p. 271.

105 *Life and Letters*, ii, 384.

106 Hansard XVIII, col. 1200; cf. Valerie Pitt, in *Church and State* (1970).

107 Kenneth Thompson, 'Church of England bishops as an elite', in Philip Stanworth and Anthony Giddens (eds), *Elites and Power in British Society* (1974), p. 200.

108 To describe this decline of institutional religion as clear evidence of 'secularization' *tout court* is to overlook the widespread credence given in our contemporary society to the non-Christian supernaturalism of astrology, of the occult, and of science fiction. It may be that the decline of institutional religion is not only a sign of secularization but also part of a general scepticism in England towards institutionalized life – hence the small number of members attending trade union branch meetings, the financial and membership problems of the major political parties, and the striking failure of the British Humanist Association, formed in 1963, to create a popularly based movement – its membership at present is a mere 2,000!

109 *Facts and Figures about the Church of England* (1962); *Church of England Year Book* (1976). *Churches and Churchgoers: Patterns of Church Growth in the British Isles since 1700* (1977), by R. Currie, A. Gilbert, and L. Horsley, appeared too late for its findings to be included in the text of this chapter. The authors argue that 'church policy is on the whole of less significance than external influences such as secularization, industrialization, urbanization, trade fluctuations, political changes, and war' when assessing the reasons for growth or decline of church membership (p. v); that since about 1700 British (especially English) society has been both 'secular and tolerant' by European standards (p. 2); that during both world wars church membership fell; that after each war membership figures at first recovered, only to decline again during the political and economic crises of the late 1920s and 1930s, and of the 1960s and early 1970s (pp. 30, 113–15).

110 Bell, p. xii.

111 Norman, p. 10.

CHAPTER 12   REMEMBRANCE

1 Foakes-Jackson, p. 248.
2 *More Letters*, p. 16.
3 Harford, p. 283.
4 p. 68.
5 *The Times*, 7 November 1919.
6 Owen Chadwick, 'Armistice Day', in *Theology*, November 1976.
7 *The Times*, 12 November 1919.
8 Nicolson, p. 343.
9 *The Times*, 12 November 1920; British Legion: *The Unknown Warrior* (n.d.). The articles on the subject give slightly differing details: *British Legion Journal*, November 1929, November 1939, August 1955; *Legionary*, August 1955; *Fidac*, June 1933.
10 Lucy Masterman, p. 318.
11 Cf. the self-conscious use of legend and liturgy in David Jones, *In Parenthesis* (1937).
12 M. H. Fitzgerald, *A Memoir of Herbert Edward Ryle* (1928), pp. 312–15.
13 *Our Empire*, November 1931.
14 Keeling, p. 303.
15 Bell, p. 1037.
16 Von Hügel, *Letters*, p. 282.
17 24 October, 14 November 1919. The proposal in an early sketch by Lutyens that an urn with a perpetual flame should crown the Cenotaph was never carried out.
18 p. 27.
19 Blythe, pp. 62, 68–9, 74.
20 Fussell, pp. 246–50.
21 Information from the Imperial War Museum.
22 Gavin Stamp, *Silent Cities* (1977), p. 19.
23 Philip Longworth, *The Unending Vigil* (1967).
24 Charles Carrington, *Rudyard Kipling* (Penguin edn 1970), pp. 513–14, 529–31.
25 Graves, p. 260.
26 *Soldier from the Wars Returning*, p. 257.
27 *Short Journey* (1942), pp. 116–17.
28 (1974 edn), pp. 255–6.
29 *Soldier from the Wars Returning*, pp. 243, 252–3.
30 Duff Cooper, ii, 421, 424.
31 Rogers, p. 130; *Challenge*, 26 June, 11 October 1918.
32 Clayton, p. 163.
33 Ellis Roberts, p. 118; there are some striking tributes to Creighton in Martin Andrews, *Canon's Folly* (1975).
34 Much of the foregoing account of Toc H is derived from Lever, Chaps. 8–11, 14.
35 ibid., pp. 128–9.
36 ibid., p. 151.
37 *Haigh*, p. 53.
38 Neville Ward, *Friday Afternoon* (1976), p. 60.
39 T. S. Eliot, 'Little Gidding'.

Biographical Notes on Principal Figures

BARNES, Ernest William (1874–1953): Fellow of Trinity College, Cambridge, 1898–1916; Master of the Temple 1915–19; Canon of Westminster 1918–24; Bp of Birmingham 1924–53.

BARRY, Frank Russell (1890–1976): Fellow of Oriel College, Oxford, 1913–15; Army Chaplain 1915–19; Principal of Knutsford Ordination Test School 1919–23; Professor at King's College, London, 1923–7; Vicar of St Mary's, Oxford, 1927–33; Canon of Westminster 1933–41; Bp of Southwell 1941–63.

BELL, George Kennedy Allen (1883–1958): Chaplain to Abp of Canterbury 1914–24; Dean of Canterbury 1924–9; Bp of Chichester 1929–57.

BLACKBURNE, Harry William (1878–1963): Trooper in Boer War 1900; Army Chaplain 1903–24; Vicar of Ashford 1924–31; Canon of Windsor 1931–4; Dean of Bristol 1934–51.

BOURCHIER, Basil Graham (1881–1934): Vicar of St Jude's, Hampstead, 1908–1930; Army Chaplain 1915–16; Rector of St Anne's, Soho, 1930–3.

BURROUGHS, Edward Arthur (1882–1934): Fellow of Hertford 1905–20; Fellow of Trinity College, Oxford, 1920–1; Dean of Bristol 1921–6; Bp of Ripon 1926–34.

CAMPBELL, Reginald John (1867–1956): Congregationalist Minister at Brighton 1895–1902; Minister at City Temple 1903–15; ordained in Church of England 1916; Curate of Birmingham Cathedral 1916–17; Vicar of Christ Church, Westminster, 1917–21; Vicar of Holy Trinity, Brighton, 1924–9; Chancellor of Chichester Cathedral 1930–46.

CHAVASSE, Francis James (1846–1928): Principal of Wycliffe Hall, Oxford, 1889–1900; Bp of Liverpool 1900–23.

CLAYTON, Philip Thomas Byard ('Tubby') (1885–1972): Curate, Portsea, 1910–15; Army Chaplain 1915–19; Founded Talbot House ('Toc H') Poperinghe 1915; Tutor at Knutsford Ordination Test School 1919; Founded Toc H movement 1920; Vicar of All Hallows, London, 1922–62.

CREIGHTON, Oswin (1883–1918): Son of Mandell Creighton (Bp of London 1897–1901); Mission work in Canada 1910–14; Army Chaplain 1915–18.

CUNNINGHAM, Bertram Keir (1871–1944): Warden of Farnham Hostel 1900–17; Warden of Chaplains' School in France 1917–19; Principal of Westcott House, Cambridge, 1919–44.

DAVIDSON, Randall Thomas (1848–1930): Chaplain to Abp Tait 1877–83; Dean of Windsor 1883–91; Bp of Rochester 1891–5; Bp of Winchester 1895–1903; Abp of Canterbury 1903–28.

DEARMER, Percy (1867–1936): Vicar of St Mary's, Primrose Hill, 1901–15; Chaplain in Serbia, France, India, 1915–17; Professor of Ecclesiastical Art, King's College, London, 1919–36; Ministered at Guildhouse, Eccleston Square, London, 1920–4; Canon of Westminster 1931–6.

FIGGIS, John Neville CR (1866–1919): Lecturer at St Catharine's College, Cambridge, 1897–1902; Rector of Marnhull, Dorset, 1902–7; Member of Community of the Resurrection from 1907.

FRERE, Walter Howard CR (1863–1938): Member of Community of the Resurrection from 1892; Superior 1902–13, 1916–22; Bp of Truro 1923–35.

GARBETT, Cyril Forster (1875–1955): Vicar of Portsea 1909–19; Bp of Southwark 1919–32; Bp of Winchester 1932–42; Abp of York 1942–55.

GORE, Charles (1853–1932): Principal of Pusey House, Oxford, 1884–93; Founded Community of the Resurrection 1892; Vicar of Radley 1893–4; Canon of Westminster 1894–1902; Bp of Worcester 1902–5; Bp of Birmingham 1905–11; Bp of Oxford 1911–19; President, Christian Social Union, 1902–11.

GREEN, Peter (1871–1961): Rector of Sacred Trinity, Salford, 1901–11; wrote as 'Artifex' in *Manchester Guardian* from 1910; Residentiary Canon of Manchester 1911–56; Rector of St Philip's, Salford, 1911–51.

GWYNNE, Llewellyn Henry (1863–1957): Archdeacon of Sudan 1905–8; Bp of Khartoum 1908–14; Army Chaplain 1914–15; Deputy Chaplain-General 1915–19; Bp of Egypt and the Sudan 1920–45.

HAIGH, Mervyn (1887–1962): Army Chaplain 1916–19; Tutor at Knutsford Ordination Test School 1919–24; Senior Chaplain at Lambeth 1924–31; Bp of Coventry 1931–42; Bp of Winchester 1942–52.

HALIFAX, Lord (Wood, Charles Lindley, 2nd Viscount Halifax) (1839–1934): President, English Church Union, 1868–1919, 1927–34.

HEADLAM, Arthur Cayley (1862–1947): edited *Church Quarterly Review* 1901–21; King's College, London: Professor of Dogmatic Theology 1903–18, Principal 1903–12; Regius Professor of Divinity, Oxford, 1918–23; Bp of Gloucester 1923–45.

HENSON, Herbert Hensley (1863–1947): Dean of Durham 1912–18; Bp of Hereford 1918–20; Bp of Durham 1920–39.

HICKS, Edward Lee (1843–1919): Rector of St Philip's, Salford, and Canon Residentiary of Manchester 1892–1910; Bp of Lincoln 1910–19; President, Church of England Peace League, 1910–19.

HOLLAND, Henry Scott (1847–1918): Canon of St Paul's 1884–1910; Regius Professor of Divinity, Oxford, 1910–18; Founded *Commonwealth* 1895, organ of Christian Social Union.

INGE, William Ralph (1860–1954): Lady Margaret Professor of Divinity, Cambridge, 1907–11; Dean of St Paul's 1911–34.

KEMPTHORNE, John Augustine (1864–1946): Bp of Hull 1910–13; Bp of Lichfield 1913–37; Chairman of Industrial Christian Fellowship 1924–37.

KIRK, Kenneth Escott (1886–1954): Army Chaplain 1914–19; Chaplain of Trinity College, Oxford, 1922–33; Regius Professor of Moral and Pastoral Theology, Oxford, 1933–7; Bp of Oxford 1937–54.

KNOX, Edmund Arbuthnott (1847–1937): Bp of Coventry 1894–1903; Bp of Manchester 1903–21.

KNOX, Ronald Arbuthnott (1888–1957): son of Bp E. A. Knox; Chaplain of Trinity College, Oxford, 1912–17; received into Roman Catholic Church 1917.

LANG, Cosmo Gordon (1864–1945): Vicar of St Mary's, Oxford, 1894–6; Vicar of Portsea 1896–1901; Bp of Stepney 1901–8; Abp of York 1908–28; Abp of Canterbury 1928–42.

LANSBURY, George (1859–1940): Anglican layman; Labour MP 1910–12, 1922–40; Leader of Labour Party 1931–5; Editor of *Daily Herald* 1913–14, 1919–22.

LYTTELTON, Edward, Hon. (1855–1942): Headmaster of Haileybury 1890–1905, of Eton 1905–16; Rector of Sidestrand, Norfolk, 1918–20; Dean of Whitelands College 1920–9.

MATTHEWS, Walter Robert (1881–1973): Vicar of Christ Church, Crouch End, 1916–18; Professor of Philosophy of Religion, Dean and Fellow, King's College, London, 1918–31; Dean of Exeter 1931–4; Dean of St Paul's 1934–67.

MILNER-WHITE, Eric (1884–1963): Army Chaplain 1914–17; Dean of King's College, Cambridge, 1918–41; Dean of York 1941–63.

MOULE, Handley Carr Glyn (1841–1920): Principal of Ridley Hall,

Cambridge, 1881–99; Norrisian Professor of Divinity, Cambridge, 1899–1901; Bp of Durham 1901–20.

MOZLEY, James Bowling (1813–78): Regius Professor of Divinity, Oxford, 1871–8.

NOEL, Conrad le Despenser Roden (1869–1942): Vicar of Thaxted, Essex, 1910–42.

PAGET, Henry Luke (1853–1937): Bp of Stepney 1909–19; Bp of Chester 1919–32.

PERCIVAL, John (1834–1918): Bp of Hereford 1895–1917.

PYM, Thomas Wentworth (1885–1945): Chaplain of Trinity College, Cambridge, 1911–14; Army Chaplain 1914–19; Head of Cambridge House, Camberwell, 1919–1925; Canon of Bristol Cathedral 1929–32; Chaplain of Balliol 1932–8.

RAVEN, Charles Earle (1885–1964): Dean of Emmanuel College, Cambridge, 1910–14; Assistant Master at Tonbridge 1915–17; Army Chaplain 1917–18; Dean of Emmanuel 1918–20; Rector of Bletchingley 1920–4; Canon of Liverpool 1924–32; Regius Professor of Divinity, Cambridge, 1932–50; Master of Christ's College 1939–50.

ROGERS, (Travers) Guy (1876–1967): Vicar of St John's, Reading, 1909–15; Army Chaplain 1915–16; Vicar of West Ham 1916–25; Rector of Birmingham 1925–48.

ROYDEN, Agnes Maude (1876–1956): Anglican laywoman; feminist; pacifist; lay preacher; assistant preacher at City Temple 1917–19; ministered at Guildhouse, Eccleston Square, London, 1920–36.

RYLE, Herbert Edward (1856–1925): Bp of Winchester 1903–10; Dean of Westminster 1911–25.

SHEPPARD, Hugh Richard Lawrie ('Dick') (1880–1937): Chaplain in France 1914; Vicar of St Martin-in-the-Fields 1914–26; Dean of Canterbury 1929–31; Canon of St Paul's 1934–7.

SMITH, John Taylor (1860–1938): Canon of St George's, Freetown, 1891–7; Bp of Sierra Leone 1897–1901; Chaplain-General to the Forces 1901–25.

STONE, Darwell (1859–1941): Principal of Pusey House, Oxford, 1909–34.

STUDDERT KENNEDY, Geoffrey Anketell (1883–1929): Vicar of St Paul's, Worcester, 1914–21; Army Chaplain 1915–19; Messenger of the Industrial Christian Fellowship 1921–9.

TALBOT, Edward Keble CR (1877–1949): Son of Bp E. S. Talbot; Member of

Community of the Resurrection from 1910, Superior 1922–40; Army Chaplain 1914–19.

TALBOT, Edward Stuart (1844–1934): Bp of Rochester 1895–1905; Bp of Southwark 1905–11; Bp of Winchester 1911–23.

TALBOT, Gilbert (1891–1915): Son of Bp E. S. Talbot; killed in action 1915; Talbot House ('Toc H') named after him.

TALBOT, Neville Stuart (1879–1943): Son of Bp E. S. Talbot; army service in Boer War 1899–1903; Chaplain of Balliol 1909–14; Army Chaplain 1914–19; Bp of Pretoria 1920–33.

TAWNEY, Richard Henry (1880–1962): Anglican layman; economic and social historian; served in army in First War; Fellow of Balliol 1918–21; Lecturer in Economic History, London University, 1921–31; Professor 1931–49; President of WEA 1928–44.

TEMPLE, William (1881–1944): Son of Abp Frederick Temple; Headmaster of Repton 1910–14; Rector of St James's, Piccadilly, 1914–18; Editor of *Challenge* 1915–18; organized Life and Liberty movement 1917–20; Canon of Westminster 1919–21; Bp of Manchester 1921–9; Abp of York 1929–42; Abp of Canterbury 1942–4.

WAKEFIELD, Henry Russell (1854–1933): Dean of Norwich 1909–11; Bp of Birmingham 1911–24.

WILBERFORCE, Albert Basil Orme (1841–1916): Son of Samuel Wilberforce, Bp of Oxford (1845–69); Rector of St John's Westminster, Chaplain of the House of Commons 1896–1916; Archdeacon of Westminster 1900–16.

WINNINGTON-INGRAM, Arthur Foley (1858–1946): Head of Oxford House, Bethnal Green, 1888–95; Rector of Bethnal Green 1895–7; Bp of Stepney, 1897–1901; Bp of London 1901–39.

WOODS, Edward Sydney (1877–1953): Brother of F. T. Woods; Chaplain at Lausanne 1912–14; Army Chaplain 1914–18; Vicar of Holy Trinity, Cambridge, 1918–27; Vicar of Croydon 1927–37; Bp of Croydon 1930–7; Bp of Lichfield 1937–53.

WOODS, Frank Theodore (1874–1932): Brother of E. S. Woods; Vicar of Bradford 1912–16; Bp of Peterborough 1916–24; Bp of Winchester 1924–32.

Bibliography

Except where otherwise stated, all books listed were published in London.

1. BIOGRAPHY AND MEMOIRS

Andrews, Martin, *Canon's Folly*. 1975

Barnes, R. L. CR, *A War-Time Chaplaincy*. 1939

Barry, F. R., *Mervyn Haigh*. 1964

— *Period of My Life*. 1970

Bedoyere, Michael de la, *The Life of Baron von Hügel*. 1951

Bell, G. K. A., *Randall Davidson*. 1952 edn.

Blackburne, Haidee, *Trooper to Dean*. Bristol, 1955

Blackburne, Harry W., *This Also Happened on the Western Front*. 1932

Blunden, Edmund, *Undertones of War*. 1928; 1930 edn.

Brabant, F. H., *Neville Stuart Talbot*. 1949

Braley, E. F. (ed.), *Letters of Herbert Hensley Henson*. 1950

— *More Letters of Herbert Hensley Henson*. 1954

Brill, Kenneth (ed.), *John Groser*. 1971

Carey, Walter, *Goodbye to My Generation*. 1951

Carpenter, S. C., *Winnington-Ingram*. 1949

Carpenter, William Boyd, *Further Pages of My Life*. 1916

Carrington, Charles, *Rudyard Kipling*. 1955, Penguin 1970

— *Soldier from the Wars Returning*. 1965

Chapman, Guy, *A Kind of Survivor*. 1975

— *A Passionate Prodigality*. 1933, 1965 edn.

Clayton, P. B., *Tales of Talbot House*. 1919

Cohen, Joseph, *Journey to the Trenches: The Life of Isaac Rosenberg 1890–1918*. 1975

Cooper, Duff, *Haig*. 2 vols. 1935

Coppard, George, *With a machine gun to Cambrai*. 1969

Creighton, Louise (ed.), *Letters of Oswin Creighton*. 1919

— *Life and Letters of Mandell Creighton*. 2 vols. 1904

Cross, F. L., *Darwell Stone.* 1943

Dearmer, Nan, *The Life of Percy Dearmer.* 1941

Dillistone, F. W., *Charles Raven.* 1975

Fitzgerald, M. H., *A Memoir of Herbert Edward Ryle.* 1928

Fowler, J. H., *The Life and Letters of Edward Lee Hicks.* 1922

Fox, Adam, *Dean Inge.* 1960

Furse, Michael, *Stand Therefore!* 1953

Garvie, A. E., *Memoirs and Meanings of My Life.* 1938

Gollancz, Victor, *More for Timothy.* 1953

Gordon, Huntly, *The Unreturning Army.* 1967

Gowing, E. N., *John Edwin Watts-Ditchfield.* 1926

Graves, Robert, *Goodbye to All That.* 1929; Penguin 1960

Grisewood, Frederick, *The World Goes By.* 1952

Groves, Reg, *Conrad Noel and the Thaxted Movement.* 1967

Hardy, G. H., *Bertrand Russell and Trinity.* 1970

Hardy, M., *Hardy, V.C.* 1920

Harford, John B. and MacDonald, Frederick C., *Handley Carr Glyn Moule.* 1922

Hastings, Michael, *Rupert Brooke.* 1967

Headlam, Maurice, *Bishop and Friend: Nugent Hicks.* 1944

Henson, Herbert Hensley, *Retrospect of an Unimportant Life.* 3 vols. 1942, 1943, 1950

Hobhouse, Stephen, *Forty Years and An Epilogue.* 1951

Holland, Bernard (ed.), *Baron von Hügel: Selected Letters.* 1933 edn.

Hopkinson, A. W., *Pastor's Progress.* 1942

Hyman, Alan, *The Rise and Fall of Horatio Bottomley.* 1972

Inge, W. R., *The Diary of a Dean.* 1949

Iremonger, F. A., *William Temple.* 1948

Jackson, H. C., *Pastor on the Nile.* 1960

Jasper, R. C. D., *George Bell.* 1967

— *Arthur Cayley Headlam.* 1960

Jones, Thomas, *Lloyd George.* 1951

Keeling, F. H., *Letters and Recollections.* 1918

Kemp, Eric W., *Kenneth Escott Kirk.* 1959

Knox, E. A., *Reminiscences of an Octogenarian.* 1935

Lancelot, J. B., *Frederick James Chavasse.* 1929

Langston, E. L., *Bishop Taylor Smith.* 1939

Lever, Tresham, *Clayton of Toc H.* 1971

Lockhart, J. G., *Charles Lindley, Viscount Halifax.* 2 vols. 1936

— *Cosmo Gordon Lang.* 1949

Lodge, Oliver, *Raymond.* 1916
Lyttelton, Edward, *Memories and Hopes.* 1925
MacDonagh, Michael, *In London during the Great War.* 1935
Major, H. D. A., *The Life and Letters of William Boyd Carpenter.* 1925
Martin, Kingsley, *Father Figures.* Penguin 1969
Masterman, Lucy, *C. F. G. Masterman.* 1939
Matheson, P. E., *Hastings Rashdall.* 1928
Matthews, W. R., *Memories and Meanings.* 1969
Maynard Smith, H., *Frank, Bishop of Zanzibar.* 1926
Montague, C. E., *Disenchantment.* 1922
Moorman, John R. H., *B. K. Cunningham.* 1947
Morgan, Kenneth O., *Keir Hardie.* 1975
Mosley, Nicholas, *Julian Grenfell.* 1976
Moynihan, Michael (ed.), *People at War 1914–18.* Newton Abbot, 1973
Mozley, J. K. (ed.), *G. A. Studdert Kennedy by his Friends.* 1929
Mulliner, H. G., *Arthur Burroughs.* 1936
Newton, Lord, *Lord Lansdowne.* 1929
Nias, John, *Flame from an Oxford Cloister: The Life and Writings of Philip Napier Waggett SSJE.* 1961
Nicolson, Harold, *King George the Fifth.* 1952
Noel, Conrad, *An Autobiography.* 1945
Oldmeadow, Ernest, *Francis, Cardinal Bourne.* 2 vols. 1944
Owen, Frank, *Tempestuous Journey: Lloyd George.* 1954
Padwick, Constance, *Temple Gairdner of Cairo.* 1929
Paget, Elma K., *Henry Luke Paget.* 1939
Paget, Stephen, *Henry Scott Holland.* 1921
Pare, Philip, and Harris, Donald, *Eric Milner-White.* 1965
Postgate, Raymond, *The Life of George Lansbury.* 1951
Prestige, G. L., *Charles Gore.* 1935
Purcell, William, *Fisher of Lambeth.* 1969
— *Woodbine Willie (G. A. Studdert Kennedy).* 1962
Pym, Dora, *Tom Pym.* 1952
Raven, Charles, *Musings and Memories.* 1931
— *A Wanderer's Way.* 1928
Reckitt, Maurice B., *P. E. T. Widdrington.* 1961
Richards, Frank, *Old Soldiers Never Die.* 1933, 1964 edn.
Roberts, R. Ellis, *H. R. L. Sheppard.* 1942
Rogers, Guy, *A Rebel at Heart.* 1956

Rose, Kenneth, *The Later Cecils*. 1975

Rowse, A. L., *A Cornish Childhood*. 1974 edn.

Russell, G. W. E., *Basil Wilberforce*. 1917

Ryder, Rowland, *Edith Cavell*. 1975

Sassoon, Siegfried, *Complete Memoirs of George Sherston*. 1937; 1940 edn.

Scott, Carolyn, *Dick Sheppard*. 1977

Sheen, H. E., *Canon Peter Green*. 1965

Smith, G. Vernon, *The Bishop of London's Visit to the Front*. 1915

Smyth, Charles, *Cyril Forster Garbett*. 1959

Stallworthy, Jon, *Wilfred Owen*. 1974

Stephenson, Gwendolen, *Edward Stuart Talbot*. 1936

Sundkler, Bengt, *Nathan Söderblom*. 1965

Swayne, W. S., *Parson's Pleasure*. 1934

Symons, Julian, *Horatio Bottomley*. 1955

Talbot, Mrs E. S., *Gilbert Walter Lyttelton Talbot: A Memoir*. 1916

Taylor, A. J. P. (ed.), *Lloyd George, A Diary by Frances Stevenson*. 1971

Temple, William, *The Life of Bishop Percival*. 1921

Terraine, John (ed.), *General Jack's Diary*. 1964

Thomas, Helen, *As It Was and World Without End*. 1972 edn.

Tomkins, Oliver, *Edward Woods*. 1957

Tucker, Maurice G., *John Neville Figgis*. 1950

Vaughan Williams, Ursula, *R. V. W.: A Biography of Ralph Vaughan Williams*. 1964

Wakefield, Henry Russell, *A Fortnight at the Front*. 1915

Wand, J. W. C., *Changeful Page*. 1965

Waugh, Evelyn, *Ronald Knox*. 1959

Whitlow, Maurice, *J. Taylor Smith*. 1938

Wilkinson, J. T., *Arthur Samuel Peake*. 1971

Wilkinson, Patrick, *Eric Milner-White*. 1963

Winnington-Ingram, A. F., *Fifty Years' Work in London*. 1940

Woods, Edward S. and Macnutt, Frederick B., *Theodore, Bishop of Winchester*. 1933

Woodward, E. L., *Short Journey*. 1942

Woolf, Leonard, *Downhill All the Way*. 1967

2. LITERATURE OF THE PERIOD

Adams, J. Esslemont, *The Chaplain and the War*. 1915

Anon., *Notes on Venereal Disease and 'The Moral Question' from a Chaplain's Point of View* (n.d.)

The Army and Religion. 1919

Barbusse, Henri, *Under Fire.* 1917, Everyman edn 1969

Barry, F. R., *Religion and the War.* 1915

— *The War and Christian Ethics.* 1914

Baverstock, A. H., *The Unscathed Crucifix.* 1916

Beeching, H. C., *Armageddon, A Sermon preached in Norwich Cathedral.* 1914

Bell, G. K. A. (ed.), *The Stockholm Conference on Life and Work, 1925.* 1926

— *The War and the Kingdom of God.* 1915

Bevan, H. E. J., Speech in *Church Congress Report.* 1900

Boddy, A. A., *The Real Angels of Mons.* 1915

Bourchier, Basil, *For All We Have and Are.* 1915

— *Safety Last.* 1927

— (ed.), *What is Wrong: Nine Addresses for the National Mission.* 1916

Bridges, Robert (ed.), *The Spirit of Man.* 1916

Bull, Paul CR, *God and our Soldiers.* 1904

— *Peace and War.* 1917

Burroughs, E. A., *The Valley of Decision.* 1916

Campbell, R. J., *The New Theology.* 1907

— *The War and the Soul.* 1916

Cathcart-Wason, J., *The Beast.* 1915

Chapman, Guy (ed.), *Vain Glory.* 1968

Church Congress Reports: 1896, 1900, 1902, 1906

Church Council on War Problems: Proceedings. 1918

Collegium, The, *International Relationships in the light of Christianity.* 1915

Davidson, Randall T., *'Quit You like Men'.* 1915

— *The Testing of a Nation.* 1919

Dearmer, Percy, *The Legend of Hell.* 1929

— *Patriotism.* 1915

— *The Sin Obsession.* 1927

— *Songs of Praise Discussed.* 1933

— *The Truth about Fasting.* 1929

Duddon, F. H., *The Problem of Human Suffering and the War.* 1916

English Church Union, *Religious Ministrations in the Army.* 1916

Evans, Charles S. (compiler), *Our Glorious Heritage: A Book of Patriotic Verse for Boys and Girls.* Introduction by H. C. Beeching, 1914

Figgis, J. Neville CR, *Anti Christ, and other sermons.* 1913

Figgis, J. Neville, *Civilisation at the Cross Roads*. 1912

— *Hopes for English Religion*. 1919

Foakes-Jackson, P. J. (ed.), *The Faith and the War*. 1916

Ford, Hugh E., *Pope Benedict's Note to the Belligerents*. 1917

Forms of Prayer for Private and Public Use in Time of War. 1915

Forms of Prayer for Public Use on 4th and 5th August 1917. 1917

A Form of Thanksgiving and Prayer for 6th July 1919. 1919

Forsyth, P. T., *The Justification of God*. 1916

Friendly Relations between Great Britain and Germany: Souvenir Volume of the Visit to Germany of Representatives of the British Christian Churches. Berlin, 1910

Gore, Charles, *Belief in God*. 1921

— *The Holy Spirit and the Church*. 1924

— *The Incarnation of the Son of God*. 1891

— (ed.), *Lux Mundi*. 1889

— Sermon in *Church Congress Report*. 1906

— *The War and the Church*. 1914

Grane, William L., *The Passing of War*. 1912; rev. edn 1913

Gray, A. Herbert, *As Tommy Sees Us*. 1918

Green, Peter ('Artifex'), Weekly articles in *Manchester Guardian*

Gwynne, L. H., (Introd.), *Religion and Morale: The Story of the National Mission on the Western Front*. 1917

Halifax, Lord, *'Raymond' – Some Criticisms*. 1917

Hankey, Donald, *A Student in Arms*. 1916

Henson, Herbert Hensley (ed.), *Church Problems*, 1900

— *A Kingdom That Cannot be Shaken*. 1919

— *War-Time Sermons*. 1915

Hicks, E. L., *The Church and the War*. 1915

Hobhouse, Mrs Henry (Margaret), *I Appeal unto Caesar*. 1917

Housman, Laurence, *War Letters of Fallen Englishmen*. 1930

Kipling, Rudyard, *Debits and Credits* ('On the Gate: a Tale of '16'; 'The Gardener'), 1949 edn

Kirk, Kenneth, *A Study of Silent Minds*. 1918

Laffin, John (ed.), *Letters from the Front 1914–18*. 1973

Lang, C. G., *The Church and the Clergy in this Time of War*. 1916

Lyttelton, Edward, *Britain's Duty To-day*. 1914

— *What Are We Fighting For?* 1914

Macnutt, F. B., (ed.), *The Church in the Furnace*. 1917

Masterman, C. F. G., *The Condition of England*, 1909; 1960 edn, ed. J. T. Boulton

Masterman, C. F. G., *Tennyson as a Religious Teacher*. 1900

Masterman, J. H. B. *et al*., *Three Sermons* (Church of England Peace League 1914)

Matthews, Basil (ed.), *Christ: and the World at War*. 1917

Maud, John, *Our Comradeship with the Blessed Dead*. 1915

Mercier, Cardinal J. D., *An Appeal to Truth*. 1915

Mitchell, P. Chalmers, *Evolution and the War*. 1915

Moberly, W. H., *Christian Conduct in War Time*. 1914

Mozley, J. B., 'War', in *Sermons Preached before the University of Oxford*. 1876

National Mission, *The National Mission Hymn Book*. 1916

— *Reports of the Archbishops' Committees of Inquiry*. 1919

— *A Report of the Chaplains' Replies to the Bishop of Kensington*. 1916

Northampton, Bishop of, *The Neutrality of the Holy See*. 1915

Owen, Wilfred, *Collected Letters*, ed. Harold Owen and John Bell. 1967

— *Collected Poems*, ed. C. Day Lewis, 1967 edn.

Oxford Pamphlets. 1914–15

Paget, Elma K., *The Woman's Part*. 1914

Paget, Henry Luke, *In the day of Battle*. 1915

Papers for War-Time. 1914–15

Peace and the Churches: Souvenir Volume of the Visit to England of Representatives of the German Christian Churches. 1909

Peake, A. S., *Prisoners of Hope*. 1918

Pym, Tom, and Gordon, Geoffrey, *Papers from Picardy*. 1917

Raven, Charles, *What Think Ye of Christ?* 1916

Rawnsley, H. D., *Against a Premature and Inconclusive Peace*. 1917

— *What the War is all about*. 1915

Reason, Will (ed.), *The Proceedings of COPEC*. 1924

Rogers, Guy *et al*., *Liberal Evangelicalism*. 1923

Royden, A. Maude, *The Great Adventure*. 1915

Ryle, H. E., *The Attitude of the Church towards War*. 1915

Sassoon, Siegfried, *Selected Poems*. 1968

Scott Holland, Henry, *So As by Fire*. 1915

Selbie, W. B., *The War and Theology*. 1915

Selwyn, E. G. (ed.), *Essays Catholic and Critical*. 1926

Shaw, George Bernard, *Common sense about the War*. 1914

— Postscript to *Androcles and the Lion*. 1915

— Preface to *St. Joan*. 1924

Sherriff, R. C., *Journey's End*. 1928

S.P.C.K., *War Time Tracts for the Workers*. 1915–16

Streeter, B. H. (ed.), *Foundations*. 1913

Streeter, B. H., *War, This War and the Sermon on the Mount*. 1915

Studdert Kennedy, G. K. A., *The Hardest Part*. 1919

— *Lies*. 1919, 1932 edn.

— *Rhymes*. 1929 edn.

— *Rough Talks by a Padre*. 1918

Talbot, Edward S. *Aspects of the Church's Duty*. 1915

— Sermon in *Church Congress Report*. 1902

— 'The Clergy and Military Service', *Contemporary Review*. Feb. 1916

Talbot, Neville S., *Religion behind the Front and after the War*. 1918

Tawney, R. H., *The Attack*. 1953

Teilhard de Chardin, P., *Writings in Time of War*. 1968

Temple, William, *A Challenge to the Church*. 1917

— *Christianity and War*. 1914

— *Church and Nation*. 1916

— *Fellowship with God*. 1920

— *Go Forward. Thoughts on the National Crisis*. 1915

— *Mens Creatrix*. 1917

— *Our Need for a Catholic Church*. 1915

Terry, Charles S., *Treitschke, Bernhardi, and Some Theologians*. Glasgow, 1915

Thomson, J. Arthur, *Biology and War*. 1915

To the Christian Scholars of Europe and America: A Reply from Oxford to the German Address to Evangelical Christians. 1914

Wakefield, Henry Russell, *Charge Delivered by the Bishop of Birmingham*. 1915

— *The Bishop's Visitation Charge*. 1919

Warren, Herbert, *Poetry and War*. 1915

Wells, H. G., *God, The Invisible King*. 1917

— *Mr Britling Sees It Through*. 1916, 1969 edn.

Wilberforce, Basil, *The Battle of the Lord*. 1915

Wilson, William, *Christ and War*. 1913; 1914 edn.

Winnington-Ingram, A. F., *A Call to Arms*. 1914

— *The Church in Time of War*. 1915

— *A Day of God*. 1914

— *Good Friday and Easter Thoughts*. 1915

— *Into the Fighting-Line*. 1910

— *The Potter and The Clay*. 1917

— *Rays of Dawn*. 1918

Winnington-Ingram, A. F. *et al.*, *Sermons for the Times No 4: Sermons on the Holy War*. 1914.
— *The Soul of a Nation*. 1915
— *The Spirit of Peace*. 1921
— *Under the Dome*. 1902
— *Victory and After*. 1920
Woods, H. G., *Christianity and War*. 1916

3. PERIODICALS
Alsager Parish Magazine
Challenge
Church Quarterly Review
Church Times
Commonwealth
CR – Quarterly Review of the Community of the Resurrection
Culham Club Magazine
Graphic
Guardian
Illustrated London News
Manchester Guardian
The Modern Churchman
Sphere
The Times

4. GENERAL
Anderson, Olive, 'The Reactions of Church and Dissent towards the Crimean War', *Journal of Ecclesiastical History*, October 1965
Annan, Noel, 'Remembrance Sunday', *Theology*. November 1961
Bailey, Sydney D., *Prohibitions and Restraints in War*. 1972
Bainton, Roland H., *Christian Attitudes toward War and Peace*. 1961
Balleine, G. R., *A History of the Evangelical Party in the Church of England*. 1951 edn.
Baynes, John, *Morale*. 1967
Baynham, Henry, *Men from the Dreadnoughts*. 1976
Bentley, James, 'The Bishops, 1860–1960: An Elite in Decline', in *A Sociological Yearbook of Religion in Britain* No. 5. (ed. Michael Hill) 1972
Blythe, Ronald, *Akenfield*. 1969
Bocock, Robert, *Ritual in Industrial Society*. 1974
Booth, Alan, *Not Only Peace*. 1967

Bullock, F. W. B., *A History of Training for the Ministry of the Church of England 1875–1974*. 1976

Burne, R. V. H., *Knutsford*. 1960

Butterfield, Herbert, *Christianity and History*. 1949; Fontana 1957

Carpenter, Edward, *Cantuar: The Archbishops in their office*. 1971

Chadwick, Owen, *The Secularization of the European Mind in the Nineteenth Century*. 1975

— *The Victorian Church*. 2 vols. 1966, 1970

Chickering, Roger, *Imperial Germany and a World without War: The Peace Movements and German Society 1892–1914*. Princeton, N. J. 1975

The Church of England Year Book, various dates

Clark, G. Kitson, *Churchmen and the Condition of England 1832–1885*. 1973

Clements, K. W., 'Baptists and the outbreak of the First World War', *Baptist Quarterly*, April 1975

Cockburn, Claud, *Bestseller*. 1972

Coppin, Ronald, 'Remembrance Sunday', *Theology*. November 1965

Cotton, V. E., *The Book of Liverpool Cathedral*. 1964

Crockford Prefaces, 1947

Currie, Robert, *Methodism Divided*. 1968

Davidson, Randall T. (ed.), *The Six Lambeth Conferences*, 1920

Davies, Horton, *Worship and Theology in England: Volume 5 The Ecumenical Century 1900–1965*. 1965

Douglas, Mary, *Natural Symbols*. 1970

Edwards, David L., *Leaders of the Church of England 1828–1944*. 1971

— *Religion and Change*. 1969

Eliot, T. S., 'Tradition and the Individual Talent' (1919), in *Selected Essays*. 1951 edn.

Elliott-Binns, L. E., *English Thought 1860–1900: The Theological Aspect*. 1956

Facts and Figures about the Church of England. 1962

Ferguson, John, and Clark, Francis, *War, Peace and Religion*. Open University, 1973

Fussell, Paul, *The Great War and Modern Memory*. 1975

Gardner, Brian, *Up the Line to Death: The War Poets 1914–1918*. 1976 edn

Gilbert, A. D., *Religion and Society in Industrial England*. 1976

Gill, Robin, *The Social Context of Theology*. 1975

Gooch, John, 'Attitudes to War in late Victorian and Edwardian England', in *War and Society*, ed. Brian Bond and Ian Roy. 1975

Gorer, Geoffrey, *Death, Grief and Mourning*. 1965

Gross, John (ed.), *Rudyard Kipling*. 1975

Haupt, Georges, *Socialism and the Great War*. 1972

Hill, Susan, *Strange Meeting*. 1971

Hudson, Darril, *The Ecumenical Movement in World Affairs*. 1969

Inglis, K. S., *Churches and the Working Classes in Victorian England*. 1963

Jones, Barbara, and Howell, Bill, *Popular Arts of the First World War*. 1972

Jones, David, *In Parenthesis*. 1937

Jones, Peter d'A., *The Christian Socialist Revival 1877–1914*. Princeton, N.J. 1968

Kent, John, 'The Study of Modern Ecclesiastical History since 1930', in *Pelican Guide to Modern Theology*, Vol 2. 1969

Koss, Stephen (ed.), *The Anatomy of an Anti-War Movement: The Pro-Boers*. 1973

— *Nonconformity in British Politics*. 1975

Lloyd, Roger, *The Church of England 1900–1965*. 1966

Longworth, Philip, *The Unending Vigil: A History of the Commonwealth War Graves Commission*, 1967

Malden, R. H., *The English Church and Nation*. 1952

Marrin, Albert, *The Last Crusade: The Church of England in the First World War*. Duke University Press 1974

Martin, Christopher, *English Life in the First World War*. 1974

Martin, David, *Pacifism: An Historical and Sociological Study*. 1965

— *The Religious and the Secular*. 1969

— *A Sociology of English Religion*. 1967

Marwick, Arthur, *The Deluge: British Society and the First World War*. 1965; 1973 edn

McLeod, Hugh, *Class and Religion in the Late Victorian City*. 1974

Mews, Stuart P., 'Religion and English Society in the First World War', unpublished Ph.D. Thesis. Cambridge 1973

— 'Spiritual Mobilization in the First World War' *Theology*. June 1971

Moorman, John R. H., 'Archbishop Davidson and the Church' *Theology*. July 1956

Mozley, J. K., *Some Tendencies in British Theology*. 1951

Newsome, David, *Godliness and Good Learning*. 1961

Nicholls, David (ed.), *Church and State in Britain since 1820*. 1967

Niebuhr, Reinhold, *Moral Man and Immoral Society*. 1932; 1963 edn

Norman, E. R., *Church and Society in England 1770–1970*. 1976

Obelkevich, James, *Religion and Rural Society*. 1976

Oliver, John, *The Church and the Social Order: Social Thought in the Church of England 1918–1939*. 1968

Panichas, George A. (ed.), *Promise of Greatness: The War of 1914–1918*. 1968

Paul, Leslie, *A Church by Daylight*. 1973

— *The Deployment and Payment of the Clergy*. 1964

Playne, Caroline E., *Britain Holds On*. 1933

— *Society at War*. 1931

Ponsonby, Arthur, *Falsehood in War Time*. 1928

Pound, Reginald, *The Lost Generation*. 1964

Preston, Ronald H., 'R. H. Tawney as a Christian Moralist', *Theology*. April, May, June 1966

Rae, John, *Conscience and Politics: The British Government and the Conscientious Objector to Military Service 1916–1919*. 1970

Ramsey, Arthur Michael, *Gore to Temple*. 1960

Read, Donald, *Documents from Edwardian England*. 1973

— *Edwardian England*. 1972

Reckitt, Maurice B., *Maurice to Temple: A Century of the Social Movement in the Church of England*. 1947

Reffold, A. E., *Wilson Carlile and the Church Army*. 1956 edn

Rosen, Andrew, *Rise Up Women!* 1971

Rouse, Ruth, and Neill, Stephen (eds), *A History of the Ecumenical Movement 1517–1948*. 1967 edn

Rowell, Geoffrey, *Hell and the Victorians*. 1974

Smyth, John, *In This Sign Conquer: The Story of the Army Chaplains*. 1968

Spinks, G. S. (ed.), *Religion in Britain since 1900*. 1952

Stamp, Gavin, *Silent Cities: An Exhibition of the Memorial and Cemetery Architecture of the Great War*. 1977

Summerton N. W., 'Dissenting Attitudes to Foreign Relations, Peace and War 1840–1890', *Journal of Ecclesiastical History*, April 1977

Tatlow, Tissington, *The Story of the Student Christian Movement*. 1933

Taylor, A. J. P., *English History 1914–1945*, 1965

— *The First World War*, Penguin 1966

Thompson, Kenneth A., *Bureaucracy and Church Reform*. 1970

Thompson, Kenneth A., 'Church of England bishops as an elite' in *Elites and Power in British Society*. 1974 ed. Philip Stanworthy and Anthony Giddens

Towler, Robert, *Homo Religiosus*. 1974

Turner, John M., 'J. N. Figgis: Anglican Prophet', in *Theology*. October 1975

Vidler, A. R., 'Bishop Barnes': *The Modern Churchman*. Spring 1975
— *20th Century Defenders of the Faith*. 1965

Walsh, Colin (ed.), *Mud, Songs and Blighty: A Scrapbook of the First World War*. 1975

Webb, Clement C. J., *A Study of Religious Thought in England from 1850*. 1933

Webster, Alan, 'The Taylor Cut Church', in *Theology*. September 1966

Wickham E. R., *Church and People in an Industrial City*. 1957

Williams, John, *The Home Fronts, Britain, France and Germany, 1914–1918*. 1972

ADDENDA TO BIBLIOGRAPHY

Budd, K. G., *The Story of Donald Hankey*. 1931

Currie, Robert, *et al.*, *Churches and Churchgoers: Patterns of Church Growth in the British Isles since 1700*. 1977

Haste, C., *Keep the Home Fires Burning: Propaganda in the First World War*. 1977

Marwick, Arthur, *Women at War 1914–1918*. 1977

Mews, Stuart P., 'The Churches', in M. Morris (ed.), *The General Strike*. Penguin 1976

Thompson, D. M., 'The Politics of the Enabling Act (1919)', in *Studies in Church History*, vol. 12, ed. Derek Baker. 1975

Index

An asterisk before a name indicates an entry in 'Biographical Notes on Principal Figures' (pp. 339–43).